The Science Fiction Handbook

The Science Fiction Handbook

M. Keith Booker
and
Anne-Marie Thomas

WILEY-BLACKWELL

A John Wiley & Sons, Ltd., Publication

This edition first published 2009
© 2009 by M. Keith Booker and Anne-Marie Thomas

Wiley-Blackwell is an imprint of John Wiley & Sons, formed by the merger of Wiley's global Scientific, Technical, and Medical business with Blackwell Publishing.

Registered Office
John Wiley & Sons Ltd, The Atrium, Southern Gate, Chichester, West Sussex, PO19 8SQ, UK

Editorial Offices
The Atrium, Southern Gate, Chichester, West Sussex, PO19 8SQ, UK
9600 Garsington Road, Oxford, OX4 2DQ, UK
350 Main Street, Malden, MA 02148–5020, USA

For details of our global editorial offices, for customer services, and for information about how to apply for permission to reuse the copyright material in this book, please see our website at www.wiley.com/wiley-blackwell.

The right of the authors to be identified as the authors of this work has been asserted in accordance with the Copyright, Designs and Patents Act 1988.

Wiley also publishes its books in a variety of electronic formats. Some content that appears in print may not be available in electronic books.

Designations used by companies to distinguish their products are often claimed as trademarks. All brand names and product names used in this book are trade names, service marks, trademarks or registered trademarks of their respective owners. The publisher is not associated with any product or vendor mentioned in this book. This publication is designed to provide accurate and authoritative information in regard to the subject matter covered. It is sold on the understanding that the publisher is not engaged in rendering professional services. If professional advice or other expert assistance is required, the services of a competent professional should be sought.

Library of Congress Cataloging-in-Publication Data

Booker, M. Keith.
The science fiction handbook / M. Keith Booker and Anne-Marie Thomas.
    p. cm.
Includes bibliographical references and index.
    ISBN 978-1-4051-6205-0 (hardcover: alk. paper)
    ISBN 978-1-4051-6206-7 (pbk.: alk. paper)
1. Science fiction, English — History and criticism — Handbooks, manuals, etc.   2. Science fiction, American — History and criticism — Handbooks, manuals, etc.   3. Science fiction — History and criticism — Handbooks, manuals, etc.   I. Thomas, Anne-Marie.   II. Title.
    PR830.S35B66 2009
    823′.087609—dc22

                                                              2008044598

British Library Cataloguing-in-Publication Data

A catalogue record for this book is available from the British Library.

Set in Sabon 10/13 pt
by SPi Publishers Services Ltd, Pondicherry, India
Printed in Singapore by Fabulous Printers Pte Ltd
1   2009

For our students
And for Amy, Adam, Skylor, and Benjamin Booker

Contents

Part 1

Introduction

Science Fiction in Western Culture

Most readers of science fiction spend little time or energy worrying about a definition of the genre or attempting to determine whether any given text is science fiction or not. They tend to know what sorts of stories and books they regard as science fiction and have little trouble locating works in the category to read. Scholars and critics tend, however, to be more cautious (and finicky) about categorization, so that many studies of science fiction as a genre begin with lengthy meditations on the definition of science fiction, often in order to distinguish it from other forms of "speculative" fiction, such as fantasy and horror. Such efforts tend to reveal that science fiction might not be so simple to define as first meets the eye. For example, most of the essays in James Gunn's collection, *Speculations on Speculation*, attempt in one way or another to define the characteristics of the genre and to "address the difficulties in delimiting the field of science fiction," as Gunn puts it in his own introductory remarks (*Speculations*, 1). Indeed, the first essay in this collection is Gunn's own "Toward a Definition of Science Fiction," the very title of which suggests that even Gunn (who has spent decades as a science fiction scholar and novelist) is unable to complete the task of defining science fiction, or "sf" as we will frequently call it in this book.

Gunn begins his essay by avowedly declaring that "the most important, and most divisive, issue in science fiction is definition" (*Speculations*, 5). He then goes on, not really to define science fiction, but to characterize it. Primarily, for Gunn, science fiction is a literature set in worlds different from our own – and different in ways that invite the reader to interrogate these differences, to ask "hard questions" about them in terms of what they can tell us about our own world. Though Gunn oddly fails to mention Darko Suvin in this brief essay, his vision of science fiction is very much congruent with Suvin's now classic argument that science fiction is a literature of "cognitive estrangement," a literature that places readers in a world different from our own in ways that stimulate thought about the nature of those differences, causing us to view our own world from a fresh perspective. Suvin's discussion of cognitive estrangement (which has played a founding role in the history of serious academic criticism of science fiction) is included in his book *Metamorphoses of Science Fiction* (1979). It is also included as the third chapter in Gunn's collection, which includes a second essay by Suvin as well.

In this volume we will work primarily from Suvin's definition of science fiction as the literature of cognitive estrangement, while remaining aware that this definition is a bit incomplete. After all, cognitive estrangement is very similar to the phenomenon of defamiliarization that the Russian formalists saw as the central strategy of all literature. Indeed, it could be argued that all literature produces cognitive estrangement to some extent, an observation that leads Carl Freedman to declare that, in this sense, all fiction could be considered science fiction and that the latter may actually be a broader category than the former (*Critical*, 21). On the other hand, Freedman (citing Suvin) goes on to argue that the designation "science fiction" is best "reserved for those texts in which cognitive estrangement is not only present but dominant" (*Critical*, 22). In other words, while all fiction produces cognitive estrangement, it is only in science fiction that such estrangement is the principle goal and project of the text.

Still, even with this basic notion in place, Freedman spends an introductory chapter of over twenty pages attempting to define science fiction and distinguish it from other genres. Ultimately, he arrives at his final focus on cognitive estrangement via a dialectical negotiation between what he sees as the two basic tendencies in attempts to construct definitions of science fiction: the narrow tendency to view science fiction only as that fiction which derives directly out of the American pulp tradition that began with the founding of *Amazing Stories* by Hugo Gernsback in 1926, and the broad tendency to consider virtually all "arealistic" literature, from Lucian and other early satirists to Pynchon and other postmodernists, as science fiction (*Critical*, 14–15).

For our purposes, science fiction might be defined as fiction set in an imagined world that is different from our own in ways that are rationally explicable (often because of scientific advances) and that tend to produce cognitive estrangement in the reader. But, in employing this definition, we follow Freedman in attempting to negotiate between "narrow" and "broad" conceptions of science fiction as we discuss the genre in this book. It is, for example, important to note that sf has many important predecessors in the Western literary tradition. Thus, in his history of science fiction, Adam

Roberts locates the origins of sf in the ancient Greek novel, devoting separate chapters to "ancient" sf and to sf in the seventeenth, eighteenth, and nineteenth centuries, respectively.[1] The arealistic satire of Jonathan Swift's *Gulliver's Travels* (1726) is quite frequently discussed in relation to science fiction, and it is significant that Swift's book appeared as a sort of countercurrent in British literature just as Daniel Defoe and others were helping to launch the realist novel as a major literary force. The barbs of *Gulliver's Travels* are aimed at what Swift saw as the dehumanizing aspects of scientific modernity and thus in many ways run counter to the celebration of scientific and technological progress that informs so much science fiction, but Swift's satire (designed to reveal the follies of his contemporary society by displacing them onto unfamiliar turf) definitely relies on cognitive estrangement for its effects. In any case, critiques of the possible negative consequences of unrestrained scientific and technological advancement are an important strain within modern science fiction. Mary Shelley's *Franken-stein: Or, the Modern Prometheus* (1818), often identified as the first genuine work of science fiction and at the very least an important literary predecessor of science fiction in its modern form, is similarly concerned with science overstepping its bounds, even as it draws upon earlier models such as the various literary incarnations of the Faust story.

Such predecessors clearly indicate that science fiction has strong historical connections within mainstream literary connections. Indeed, it has affinities with numerous established genres. Among other things, the emphasis in science fiction on change (and the often-noted ability of the genre itself to change dramatically over time in conjunction with technological and other changes in the world at large) would link science fiction to the genre of the novel in general. Mikhail Bakhtin has famously characterized the novel an ever-evolving genre that changes continually over time, largely because of its ability to maintain close contact with developments in the world outside the novel, leading to an intense contemporaneity that is also reflected in the novel's ability to maintain contact with "extraliterary genres, with the genres of everyday life and with ideological genres" (*Dialogic*, 33). Science fiction might, of course, be considered one of these "extraliterary" genres, but it is also the case that most of Bakhtin's descriptions of the novel as a complex, dialogic genre that absorbs the characteristics of all other genres with which it comes into contact also apply to science fiction.

Science fiction bears special similarities to certain specific novelistic sub-genres. For example, the tendency of science fiction to be set in historical periods different from those in which it is written suggests parallels with the subgenre of the historical novel, identified by important critics such as Georg Lukács as perhaps the quintessential form of the realist novel.

In his highly influential *The Historical Novel* (first published in 1937, though not translated into English until 1962), Lukács argues that the great historical novels of the early nineteenth century are the quintessential literary expressions of the ideology of the European bourgeoisie in their period of ascent to power. In particular, Lukács argues that these novels uniquely captured the dynamic energies of this revolutionary historical change, though they declined in power as the bourgeoisie became conservative and decadent after establishing their dominance. This ability to reflect historical change is one that is often associated with science fiction. Indeed, the historical novel and science fiction as a whole have more in common than might first be obvious. As Edward James notes, "Of all the non-sf genres, only historical fiction presents readers, and authors, with problems that resemble those of sf" (*Science*, 112).

In the same vein, Freedman, building upon the work of the important Marxist critic and theorist Fredric Jameson, presents an extensive elaboration of the parallels between science fiction and the historical novel (*Critical*, 50–62). Jameson, in fact, has pointed out on several occasions a connection between science fiction and the historical novel, as when he describes science fiction as "a historically new and original form which offers analogies with the emergence of the historical novel in the early nineteenth century" (*Postmodernism*, 283). Jameson presses this point further in *Archaeologies of the Future*, where he argues that Lukács's historical model of the decline of the historical novel can be completed by extending it one step further, to include the emergence of science fiction, "which now registers some nascent sense of the future, and does so in the space on which a sense of the past had once been inscribed" (*Archaeologies*, 286). Science fiction, in short, inherits the mantle once worn by the historical novel as the utopian literary genre par excellence and as the genre most capable of capturing the energies of the historical process.

From this point of view, it may be significant that science fiction as we know it began to take form as a genre in the nineteenth century, just when, according to Lukács, the historical novel was in a state of decline. In any case, it was with the "scientific romances" of H. G. Wells at the end of the nineteenth century that modern science fiction began to emerge in an identifiable form – though we should also note that sf, as a publishing category, did not then exist and that Wells's romances were not, at the time, easily distinguishable from other contemporary forms (the utopian fictions of Edward Bellamy and William Morris, the imperial romances of H. Rider Haggard and Rudyard Kipling). Wells, who would go on to even greater success in the early years of the twentieth century as an author of realist satires such as *The History of Mr Polly* (1910), in many ways towered over the genre of science fiction for the next several decades, adding a modicum of literary respectability to a form that really became visible as a separate entity only with the success, beginning in the 1920s, of American pulp magazines devoted to science fiction.

Science fiction as a selfconscious publishing category is generally considered to have begun in 1926, when editor Hugo Gernsback published the first issue of *Amazing Stories*, the first magazine devoted exclusively to science fiction. *Amazing Stories* was marked by an extremely optimistic vision of a technology-driven future, foreshadowing such later visions as the future technological utopia of *Star Trek*. However, pulp science fiction quickly began to gain complexity and sophistication, especially with the work of John W. Campbell, who assumed the editorship of the pulp magazine *Astounding Stories* beginning in 1937. Campbell's quest for stories with greater complexity and literary merit led to the discovery of such writers as Isaac Asimov, Lester Del Rey, Robert Heinlein, Theodore Sturgeon, and A. E. Van Vogt. Retitled *Astounding Science-Fiction* in 1938, Campbell's magazine dominated the genre through the World War II years and beyond, helping to make the period from the end of the 1930s to the end of the 1950s what has come to be known as the Golden Age of Science Fiction.

The 1950s saw the proliferation of other important magazines, including *The Magazine of Fantasy and Science Fiction* and *Galaxy Science Fiction*, as the short story continued to be a vital form for the exploration of new sf ideas. Meanwhile, the genre was changed forever with the rise, during that decade, of the science fiction novel as a specific publishing category, in the midst of an explosion in paperback publishing in general, especially in the US. However, the science fiction "novel" was initially dominated by the conversion of previously-published magazine fiction (such as Isaac Asimov's "Robot" and "Foundation" stories) into book form. The rise of the science fiction novel (with Wells still looming as an important precedent) provided room for Golden Age writers such as Heinlein and Asimov to exercise their imaginations in more expansive ways – and in ways that often differed dramatically from the innocent optimism of the Gernsback era. The opportunities offered by the expanding sf publishing industry of the 1950s also helped to launch the careers of younger writers with genuine literary talents, such as Alfred Bester and Philip K. Dick, who began to take science fiction in new and more literary directions.

One could argue, though, that it is a mistake to try to "justify" science fiction by pointing out what it has in common with the more mainstream tradition of Western canonical literature. Indeed, much of what makes science fiction important (and gives it a special ability to produce cognitive estrangement) is the way in which it departs from canonical literary traditions. For example, while the realist novel is a strongly individualist genre focusing on the attempts of strong individual protagonists to surmount personal difficulties, the science fiction novel often deals with the life-or-death fates of entire cultures or planets. As a result, science fiction tends to be weak on characterization in relation to the literary novel, but strong in its exploration of important social and political issues. In addition, pulp sf magazines have remained crucial to a fan culture that has helped sf readers to establish communities of a kind unknown among devotees of "high" literature, including an array of popular sf conventions in which fans can meet each other as well as well-known authors.

The existence of a vibrant fan culture helped to drive the rise of the science fiction film in the 1950s. American films fueled by Cold War anxieties – especially alien invasion films such as *The Day the Earth Stood Still* (1951) and *The Invasion of the Body Snatchers* (1956) – were particularly important here, though the horror movies of Hammer Films in England (as well as apocalyptic Japanese monster movies) were part of the same phenomenon. Such films demonstrated that even the "lowest" of cultural forms could respond to important social and political issues, and perhaps in ways that engaged with contemporary concerns far more directly than loftier cultural forms.

Among other things, the pulp aspects of science fiction at least potentially endow the genre with certain folk energies, while allowing the "lowly" genre to explore certain themes in ways that would never be possible in more "respectable" venues. Alan Wald, for example, has noted how left-leaning American writers during the repressive years of the McCarthyite 1950s often diverted their critique of American capitalism into popular genres such as science fiction in order to avoid censorship. Or, as sf master Frederik Pohl has put it, science fiction writers can "say things in hint and metaphor that the writer dares not say in the clear" (*Politics*, 10). As a result, Pohl notes, 1950s science fiction might well have been able to get away with political statements that other forms could not and may therefore have represented "the only truly free speech left in America" at the time (*Politics*, 12). The diversion of leftist energies into popular genres in the 1950s produced a few interesting works by genuinely leftist writers – such as Ben Barzman's *Twinkle, Twinkle Little Star* (1960) – and there are certainly a number of works of 1950s' sf – such as Pohl and C. M. Kornbluth's classic *The Space Merchants* (1952) – that include strong liberal (if not radical) political commentary.

This tradition of political commentary may explain why science fiction was able to respond to the changing political climate of the 1960s with a so-called New Wave (a term borrowed from the French *nouvelle vague* movement in film) that emphasized social and political relevance as well as greater literary complexity. Thus, if the Golden Age was dominated by "hard" science fiction (in which the emphasis is on particular technologies and on scientific accuracy), the New Wave signaled a turn toward "soft" science fiction, which is more character driven and more concerned with the social and political ramifications of technological developments than with the technologies themselves.

The New Wave was spearheaded by editors such as Britain's Michael Moorcock (*New Worlds* magazine) and America's Judith Merril (in the anthology *England Swings*). Such editors attempted to make sf more sophisticated in terms of literary style as well as content, responding especially to trends of the 1960s to include franker treatment of issues such as sexuality. In addition to Moorcock himself, leading New Wave writers include Brian Aldiss, J. G. Ballard, M. John Harrison, John Brunner, Samuel Delany, Thomas Disch, Harlan Ellison, Ursula K. Le Guin, Robert Silverberg, and Norman Spinrad. The New Wave was dominated to some extent by short stories, but New Wave writers also produced important novels, including Spinrad's *Bug Jack Barron* (1969) and Delany's *Triton* (1976). Television's *Star Trek*, which enjoyed only moderate success in its original broadcast run (1966–1969), also echoed many of the concerns of the New Wave – and would go on to become arguably the most important single phenomenon in the history of science fiction, spurring a particularly enthusiastic fan culture and eventually triggering an extensive sequence of film adaptations and spin-off television series.

The quest for social and political relevance that fueled the New Wave also helped to drive related phenomena, such as an important resurgence in utopian fiction (especially that by women writers such as Le Guin and Joanna Russ) in the 1970s, though Brunner's dystopian fictions of the late 1960s and early 1970s provided an important counter-trend. By the early 1980s, however, the science fiction novel seemed to have reached a certain stagnation, partly because the New Wave had narrowed the gap between science fiction and mainstream fiction, depriving sf of some of what made it special and important in the first place. It was also the case that phenomena such as the end of the space race and increasing concerns about technology-induced environmental decay (the near-disaster at the Three Mile Island nuclear plant in 1979 can be taken as a key marker) had, by the 1980s, seriously muted public excitement about the potential of technology to change the world in positive ways.

On the other hand, written science fiction also suffered in the late 1970s and early 1980s because science fiction film, from the release of *Star Wars* in 1977 to the release of *The Terminator* in 1984, was experiencing an unprecedented period of critical and commercial success, even if the films of the period often showed more nostalgia than optimism, more anxiety over the threat of technology than excitement over its possibilities. This brief period saw the release of such important films as *Close Encounters of the Third Kind* (1977), *Star Trek: The Motion Picture* (1979), *Alien* (1979), *E.T. the Extraterrestrial* (1982), and *Blade Runner* (1982), as well as the first two *Star Wars* sequels: *The Empire Strikes Back* (1980) and *The Return of the Jedi* (1983). In subsequent years, advances in the technology of computer-generated imagery would continue to make science fiction film a hugely popular phenomenon, though the increasing emphasis on displays of dazzling special effects sometimes made sf film more spectacular at the expense of being less thoughtful.

The success of the *Star Wars*, *Star Trek*, *Alien*, and *Terminator* sequences of films brought sf to wider audiences than ever before and helped to fuel a Golden Age in sf television in the 1990s.[2] Meanwhile, written science fiction proved more resilient than it might have first appeared as the skepticism of the early 1980s helped to fuel the rise of "cyberpunk" science fiction, a movement that revitalized science fiction and drove it in important new (postmodern) directions. With writers such as William Gibson and Bruce Sterling leading the way, the cyberpunks combined an individualist punk sensibility with a keen awareness of the implications of the emergent computer technologies of the era. They also employed an array of styles derived from other genres (hardboiled detective fiction provided a particularly important stylistic model), indicating a tendency toward postmodern pastiche that allowed the cyberpunks to produce something genuinely inventive by reassembling bits and pieces of the works of the past, drawing upon important sf predecessors such as Bester and Dick, in addition to more mainstream authors such as Thomas Pynchon. The result was a hipper and edgier form of science fiction that was well in tune with the popular imagination of the cynical 1980s.

This cynicism is often reflected in cyberpunk fiction itself, which tends to be set in near future worlds in which technology (especially computer-based virtual reality technology) has advanced significantly, but in which these advances have done little to solve the sorts of social, political, and economic problems that were already prevalent in the 1980s. Partly because of this inability (or unwillingness) to imagine a better future, the original wave of cyberpunk science fiction was relatively short-lived, and some observers have seen Neal Stephenson's *Snow Crash* (1992), with its lighter satirical tone, as announcing the end of the original movement and the beginnings of what would come to be called "postcyberpunk."

In the years since the publication of *Snow Crash*, postcyberpunk fiction has continued to evolve, often blending with a new tendency toward "posthuman" science fiction, which imagines a future in which technological changes have brought about dramatic physical and intellectual changes in the human species itself – or even rendered that species irrelevant through the rise of superior artificial intelligence (AI) technologies. Meanwhile, the release of *The Matrix* in 1999 signaled the first truly successful cyberpunk film, while cyberpunk has exercised a major influence in the realm of comic books and graphic novels; Japanese comics (*manga*) and animated films (*animé*) have show a strong cyberpunk influence as well. Other trends in science fiction have also remained vital and Kim Stanley Robinson's "Mars" trilogy (1993–1996), which has little in common with cyberpunk, may be the most significant work of both hard and soft science fiction to have been produced in the 1990s, thus illustrating that the "hard" and "soft" designations are not mutually exclusive.

In the realm of posthuman science fiction, the work of the Australian writer Greg Egan is worthy of special mention, though developments in postcyberpunk and posthumanist science fiction have been largely dominated by a group of writers who have collectively constituted a "Boom" in British sf from the mid-1990s to the present. British Boom science fiction is often highly literary and fiercely political; it might be noted that Roger Luckhurst interestingly echoes Wald on the American 1950s when he suggests that the Boom has been made possible partly because the low value accorded science fiction, fantasy, and the Gothic has allowed these genres to "flourish largely below the radar" of the British cultural establishment ("Cultural," 423). Luckhurst further notes that this situation in contemporary British science fiction has parallels with that of American science fiction in the repressive days of the 1950s. He suggests, however, that the situation in Britain is much less repressive than that which prevailed in the United States in the McCarthy era, providing an atmosphere conducive to a genuine Boom in political science fiction, as opposed to the scattered works of politically-engaged sf in the US in the 1950s.

The British Boom writers represent a sort of culmination of the history of science fiction to this point. Their work is marked by high literary merit, yet often draws in important ways on pulp traditions. The British Boom writers also draw on virtually every previous science fiction subgenre, in addition to related genres such as fantasy and horror, particularly re-energizing such genres as the space opera and cyberpunk, previously thought to have seen their best days. The genre-bending fiction of China Miéville, combining a basic fantasy matrix with images from horror and the cognitive power of science fiction, may be the single most important example of British Boom sf. Meanwhile, writers such as Ken MacLeod, Charles Stross, Iain M. Banks,

Justina Robson, and Richard K, Morgan have helped to reinvigorate both the space opera and cyberpunk, partly through multigeneric combinations of the two in single works.

The quality and quantity of the work produced by the British Boom writers – along with the rise of Australian writers such as Egan and the continued productivity of American sf writers such as Robinson – suggests that science fiction as a whole is currently in a particularly rich period that shows no sign of ending soon. The complex, multi-generic nature of British Boom fiction also helps to call attention to the variety of subgenres that has informed the historical development of science fiction. As a result, we attempt no comprehensive overall history of science fiction in this volume.[3] Instead, we present, via the individual chapters in Part 2 of this book, overviews of the development of a number of important subgenres, always taking account that there is considerable crossover among subgenres and that an individual work might participate in several subgenres at once. These overviews also include extensive lists of recommended reading within these subgenres, as well as lists of related works of science fiction film.

Part 3 of this volume includes brief biographies of a number of important science fiction writers, adding a further historical dimension by tracing the careers of these individual writers. Part 4 includes extensive critical analyses of some of the most important works of science fiction, chosen both for their merit and for their ability collectively to represent as many different science fictional phenomena as possible. Part 5 then closes the volume with a brief, selected glossary of terms relevant to the study of science fiction.

Notes

1   Adam Roberts, *The History of Science Fiction*, 2005.
2   See the discussion of this phenomenon in Booker, *Science Fiction Television*, 111–47.
3   Such attempts do, however, abound. Roberts's volume is particularly far-ranging in its historical coverage, while James's *Science Fiction in the 20th Century* (1994) is particularly good on science fiction from Wells forward. Luckhurst's *Science Fiction* (2005) is also especially good for its emphasis on the evolution of science fiction within larger cultural contexts. For an overview of the history of sf film, especially in the US, see Booker, *Alternate Americas*, (1–25).

Part 2

Brief Historical Surveys of Science Fiction Subgenres

The Time-Travel Narrative

Time travel is an extremely rich science fiction motif offering numerous possibilities, not only for inventive plotting, but also for speculation on the fundamental nature of time – and of reality itself. In addition, the cognitive dissonance that occurs via a sudden movement from one time period to another potentially makes the time-travel narrative a paradigmatic science fictional form. The time-travel motif also presents extensive opportunities for humor and satire, giving the genre a particularly wide range. Indeed, the flexibility of the time-travel story has made it a favorite science fiction subgenre on television and in film, as well as in the novel and short story.

Narratives involving travel through time represent one of the oldest subgenres in all of science fiction. Even a story as old as Washington Irving's "Rip Van Winkle" (1819) involves time travel of a sort, in that the protagonist sleeps for twenty years, awaking to a much-changed world and experiencing a shock of cognitive estrangement of the kind that is often central to the time-travel narrative. This motif was later extended in Edward Bellamy's utopian classic *Looking Backward* (1888), whose protagonist goes into a hypnotic trance in 1887 and awakes to a utopian world in the year 2000. H. G. Wells's *When the Sleeper Wakes* (1899) similarly features a protagonist who goes into a long sleep and awakes in a very different (this time dystopian) future. More literal time-travel narratives appeared as early as early as 1881 in Edward Page Mitchell's short story "The Clock that Went Backward." Wells explored the motif in his 1888 story "The Chronic Argonauts," and Mark Twain produced a novel-length time-travel tale in 1889 with the publication of *A Connecticut Yankee in King Arthur's Court*. However, the true founding text of the genre is probably Wells's classic novel *The Time Machine* (1895), the first genuinely science fictional exploration of time travel in book-length form, though this pre-Einstein narrative did not actually explore the physics of time travel. *The Time Machine* has exercised an extensive influence on the time-travel genre, including the production of George Pal's 1960 film adaptation of the novel, one of the classic science fiction films of its era. Perhaps the most notable example of a novel influenced directly by *The Time Machine* is Stephen Baxter's *The Time Ships* (1995), a sequel to Wells's novel that captures the style of the original while expanding Wells's brief narrative into a much more detailed exploration that takes the Time Traveler through a virtual compendium of science fiction motifs.

Einstein's meditations on time provided a scientific basis for future time-travel narratives. Nevertheless, it has remained common for time-travel narratives simply to posit the possibility of time travel without exploring the actual mechanics of the process. Typical here is Peter Delacorte's charming *Time on My Hands* (1997) – in which a time traveler from 1994 travels back to the 1930s to try to change history so that Ronald Reagan can never become president. In this novel, the traveler uses a found time machine from the future; he himself doesn't understand the technology, so he doesn't have to explain it to us, either. In Terry Pratchett's *Night Watch* (2002), part of his massive "Discworld" series, time travel occurs literally by magic. And in one popular motif, the "time slip," a character is simply transported from one time period to another, though neither the character nor the reader has any idea how this movement occurred – as when Billy Pilgrim, the protagonist of Kurt Vonnegut's *Slaughterhouse Five* (1969) famously becomes "unstuck in time," perhaps owing to the intervention of aliens from the planet Tralfamadore. The time slip often appears in fantasy narratives, though texts with a more science fictional feel can employ the motif as well. A classic case is Octavia Butler's *Kindred* (1979), in which a modern black woman repeatedly finds herself transported back into the antebellum South, enabling a complex meditation on racism and slavery. In other cases, a kind of time travel is merely a side effect of other technologies, as in Joe Haldeman's *The Forever War* (1974), in which the time dilation effect associated with space travel at near light speeds introduces an important element of temporal displacement.

Science fiction narratives play with aberrations in the flow of time in other ways as well, as in Robert Wilson's Hugo Award-winning *Spin* (2005), where mysterious aliens seal the Earth inside a barrier that causes time on Earth to pass much more slowly than time in the universe at large, so that billions of years pass in the cosmos during the lives of individual humans on Earth. Meanwhile, Philip K. Dick's decidedly strange *Counter-Clock World* (1967) imagines a late-twentieth-century Earth on which time has begun to move backward, owing to a cosmic phenomenon of unknown origin or cause. While life in many ways proceeds as it always had, anyone who has died before this phenomenon began comes back to life as time retreats to the moment of his or her death. Those who are alive, age backward, becoming younger and younger until they eventually re-enter a womb, then undergo a reverse pregnancy until they finally cease to exist in an act of sexual intercourse that must occur as time reaches their moment of conception.

Brian Aldiss's *Cryptozoic!* (1967) also posits the flow of time in reverse as its central motif, its late twenty-first-century characters eventually discovering that when they "mind travel" by means of a psychoactive drug to what they believe is the distant past, they are in fact witnessing the future. It is only human perception that time moves forward, an illusion that provides protection against the knowledge of humanity's ultimate dissolution. In this scenario, life begins at death, whereas the womb is considered the "grave" of the human race. Similarly, the narrator of Martin Amis's *Time's Arrow* (1991) begins his story from death, but unlike Aldiss's characters, he literally experiences life backwards in time. His mind inhabits the body of a Nazi surgeon, observing the events of the doctor's life, but in reverse chronological order. Thus, the narrator witnesses the events of the Holocaust, but experiences them not as the extermination of the Jews, but as a miraculous act of healing, in which the dead are resuscitated and sent back to their homes.

One of the earliest detailed science fictional explorations of time travel in the more literal sense is Isaac Asimov's *The End of Eternity* (1955), which follows *The Time Machine* in using the time-travel conceit to explore the future course of human evolution – though in this case the evolution turns out to be more social and intellectual than biological. This book also introduces the notion of the "time cop," an operative who is officially assigned to manipulate history via time travel. While we still get very few details about the time travel technology involved (other than the indication that it uses some sort of "temporal field"), Asimov's novel does present us with the most elaborate exploration of the possibilities of time travel that had been produced up to the time of its publication. In particular, it envisions an organization called Eternity, whose agents live outside of time, traveling freely both "downwhen" and "upwhen," both observing the course of history and instituting carefully calculated "reality changes" that modify the course of history to prevent various undesirable developments. *The End of Eternity* addresses a number of aspects of time travel, including time-travel paradoxes. Indeed, we learn that the Eternity organization was enabled by the work of an Eternity agent who traveled back in time to develop the temporal-field technology that made Eternity possible in the first place. It turns out, however, that the attempts of Eternity to prevent catastrophe have moved the course of human history into a comfortable mediocrity, removing the kinds of challenges and crises that drive the most daring technological advances. Ultimately, though, humans from the far future engineer a plot (with the mostly unwitting help of protagonist Andrew Harlan, an agent of Eternity) to prevent the establishment of Eternity in the first place, leading to technological advances that allow the establishment of a galactic empire that could be read as the one described in Asimov's "Foundation" trilogy.

Asimov's novel is the prototype of a large number of time-travel tales that feature powerful, often bureaucratic organizations that attempt to manage the potentially disastrous consequences of time travel. Typical of such organizations is the Time Patrol of Poul Anderson's interlinked short-story collection *The Guardians of Time* (1960), whose task it is to ensure that time travelers do not alter the "true" past. Bureaucrats of a ravaged future attempt to use time travel to correct the events that led to their current dire state in Terry Gilliam's excellent time-travel film *Twelve Monkeys* (1995), while in John Varley's *Millennium* (1983, adapted to film in 1989) a far-future bureaucracy oversees attempts to extract resources (mostly healthy human bodies) from the past in an effort to save a sickly humanity from extinction owing to disastrous environmental devastation.

Millennium is an excellent time-travel novel that contains a number of classic meditations on the nature of time and implications of time travel. It is in many ways reminiscent of the work of science fiction master Robert A. Heinlein, an extremely important figure in the development of the time-travel narrative. Heinlein's early short story "By His Bootstraps" (1941), for example, brought the time-travel narrative into science fiction's Golden Age. This story involves an early example of the time-travel "loop," in which travelers in time find that the principal events of history remain unchanged no matter what interventions are attempted. This story is a forerunner of numerous time-loop narratives, including those in which the passage of time is caught in a recursive loop, so that a given period of time is repeated over and over. This particular motif has been used in numerous television programs, though the best known example is probably the film *Groundhog Day* (1993). Ken Grimwood's novel *Replay* (1987), in which the central character repeatedly relives the period between 1963 and 1988, is a particularly interesting example of the time loop motif. This motif also underlies Heinlein's brief "All You Zombies" (1959). One of the classic works of time-travel fiction, this story involves a temporal manipulation agent whose time travels allow him to become his own father – and mother! At the same time, however, his activities do not change the course of his personal history but simply enable the history to be what it has been all along.

A similar vision of time travel informs Heinlein's novel *The Door into Summer* (1957). Actually, this story involves two kinds of time travel.

Protagonist Daniel Boone Davis is an engineer and entrepreneur who goes into suspended animation in the year 1970 after being cheated out of the ownership of his own robotic inventions by his erstwhile fiancée and his unscrupulous business partner. When he awakes in the year 2000, he has become a time traveler somewhat in the mode of Rip Van Winkle. However, he also learns that the technology for literal time travel has by this time been developed (though it is still in the experimental stage). He then cleverly uses this technology to travel back to 1970 to turn the tables on his would-be nemeses, then returns to a happy life in 2000. Importantly, though, this 2000 is very much the same one he found on his initial awakening, once again suggesting that history is immutable.

David Gerrold's *The Man Who Folded Himself* (1973) takes its cue from "All You Zombies" in presenting a time traveler whose movements in time (via a "timebelt" whose origin and workings are never explained) enable him to become both his own mother and his own father. Here, however, this situation is enabled by a vision of time travel as movement among different parallel universes. Each trip taken by the traveler results in a slight change in history, creating a new timeline in which the traveler has a slightly (or in some cases greatly) changed identity – while the original timeline continues unabated in parallel. Ultimately, a male and female version of the traveler meet and produce a son – who grows into the version of the protagonist we had met in the beginning of the novel.

Jack Womack's *Terraplane* (1988), an early entry in a series of novels in which the author explores a future world increasingly dominated by the sinister Dryco Corporation, is also centrally concerned with time travel and parallel universes. Here, however, there are only two parallel worlds, which are virtually identical but which have recently taken different historical paths (possibly owing to the effects of nuclear explosions), including the fact that the second world now runs several decades in time behind "our" (i.e., Dryco's) world. A machine developed by a Russian scientist (and eventually conscripted by Dryco) allows travel between the worlds, and is used, in *Terraplane*, by the scientist in an attempt to retrieve Joseph Stalin from the parallel world so that he can try to set things right in the chaotic postcommunist Russia of our world. Meanwhile, in *Elvissey* (1993), Dryco operatives travel to the "slow" universe to retrieve a young Elvis Presley whom they hope to use to combat an Elvis cult whose power is beginning to rival their own in the "fast" universe.

In Jack Finney's *Time and Again* (1970), a scientist, Dr. Danziger, develops an unlikely method of time travel that essentially involves transporting travelers to earlier eras simply by placing them in the mindset of that era. However this book is uninterested in presenting a believable method of time travel. Instead, it focuses on a detailed description of 1882 Manhattan, to which protagonist Simon Morley travels. Morley encounters considerable difficulties in this past world, but ultimately concludes that the world of 1882 is more civilized and humane than the world of 1970 – especially after the government-sponsored project for which he is working shows signs of military-inspired interest in manipulating the past for their own ends. He thus decides to stay permanently in 1882. In a classic time-travel plot twist, he also manages to prevent Danziger's parents from meeting in that year, thus averting the eventual birth of the scientist and the founding of the time-travel project that sent Morley to 1882 in the first place.

Gregory Benford's *Timescape* (1980) represents one of the few attempts to present a detailed and believable scientific basis for time travel, while at the same time making an important contribution to environmentalist science fiction. In particular, the book presents a detailed depiction of both the personal and the professional lives of two groups of scientists who are involved in the development of a viable time-travel device. Having discovered a way to use tachyons (subatomic particles that are found to travel backward in time) to send coded messages into the past, Cambridge scientists in 1998 work to send warnings to a second group of scientists back in 1962 in an attempt to prevent ecological disasters that have ravaged the world's oceans in the intervening time and that threaten to wreak havoc on Earth's environment in the world of 1998. Among other things, *Timescape* presents an argument for the value of basic scientific research, which here helps to solve a problem crucial to the future of humanity, even though none of the research involved has any direct connection to the problem involved.

In *Doomsday Book* (1992), Connie Willis places the mechanism for time travel in the hands of twenty-first-century Oxford historians, who use the internet as a research tool, in this case to study the Middle Ages. In Willis's universe, time travel itself appears to have little value outside of academia since it cannot be readily exploited for economic gain, as it is in Michael Crichton's *Timeline* (1999), a novel that converts a number of the plot elements of *Doomsday Book* into Crichton's patented action-thriller format. Willis herself extends the ideas of *Doomsday Book* in *To Say Nothing of the Dog* (1997), describing the temporal continuum as a chaotic system in which tiny perturbations can cause major far-reaching effects. This system, however, also has the ability to correct potentially damaging incongruities introduced by time travelers; it protects itself from continuum paradoxes using "slippage," a shift in time that prevents actions that could alter history. Similar to Willis's story "Fire Watch," in which historians witness the efforts to save St. Paul's Cathedral during the Blitz, *To Say*

Nothing of the Dog centers around the destruction of Coventry Cathedral during World War II, as well as its subsequent twenty-first-century reconstruction. Considerably lighter in mood than *Doomsday Book*, which concerns the devastating effects of both a twenty-first-century pandemic and the fourteenth-century Black Death, Willis's novel also involves a hilarious romp through Victoriana, drawing upon Jerome K. Jerome's 1889 comic classic *Three Men in a Boat (to Say Nothing of the Dog)*, from which Willis's book takes its title.

Orson Scott Card's *Pastwatch: The Redemption of Christopher Columbus* (1996) is an interesting variant on the theme of time travel, this time based on an assumption of the mutability of history. Here, scientists from the twenty-third century (working for the Pastwatch organization) develop a technology that allows them to travel back to the time of Christopher Columbus in an effort to avert the baleful consequences of the European colonization of the Americas. In this novel, Card makes a laudable attempt at acknowledging the horrors wrought upon the inhabitants of the New World as a result of the arrival of European colonizers at the end of the fifteenth century, suggesting that virtually any alternative would be preferable. Thus, the Pastwatch scientists opt to intervene in the past, even though they know that this action will send history off in a radically different (and largely unpredictable) direction, which will mean that their own reality will paradoxically never have existed. Unfortunately, Card is unable to overcome his own religious biases, ultimately constructing a "successful" scenario in which Native Americans are "saved" from colonialism by putting aside their own savage culture and replacing it with a healthy dose of Christianity and by the building of an indigenous American empire of which Columbus himself is a central organizer.

John Kessel's *Corrupting Dr. Nice* (1997) is a relatively lighthearted novel that nevertheless manages to create both political satire and a thoughtful vision of the possible implications of time travel. Here, time travel is again predicated upon the existence of an infinite number of parallel universes. Thus, if time travelers wreak changes in the past, there are no consequences for the original timeline, which continues unchanged while the manipulation of the past leads to the creation of a new alternative timeline that branches off from the original at the point of intervention. As a result, time travel is practiced extensively, mostly under the control of the powerful Saltimbanque Corporation, which uses the infinite pasts as a limitless collection of tourist destinations. These pasts also provide an inexhaustible source of resources, as when oil is imported from various pasts in which the supply of that commodity is still rich. Even people are routinely imported from the past, including various versions of Jesus Christ, still popular in the future even though access to the past has made it clear that he did not rise from the dead or otherwise have supernatural powers. On the other hand, there are those who are uncomfortable with the unrestrained exploitation of the past, organizing protests against the practice on the grounds that it may have consequences that are not yet known and that, in any case, it disrupts the lives of people in the past, even if they live in alternative timelines. Kessel's time-traveling protagonist is aided (or not) by an artificial intelligence implanted in his brain, indicating the influence of recent cyber-technology – as well as cyberpunk science fiction. This same influence can be seen in such works as George Foy's *The Shift* (1996) and Joe Haldeman's *Old Twentieth* (2005), which use virtual reality technology to allow "travel" into computer simulations of the historical past. *Corrupting Dr. Nice* also engages in an extensive dialogue with contemporary popular culture, including both music and film. Indeed, much of the novel's plot is taken from Preston Sturges's screwball comedy *The Lady Eve* (1941).

Kessel's use of images from the history of film points toward the extensive use of time-travel narratives in film itself. All of the *Terminator* films depend centrally on time travel, even if such travel is not absolutely central to the action of the films, while *Twelve Monkeys* was one of the most effective science fiction films of the 1990s. Gilliam's *Time Bandits* (1981) demonstrates the comic effects of the time-travel subgenre, as does the extremely successful sequence of *Back to the Future* films that appeared between 1985 and 1990. On American television, virtually all major science fiction series have employed the time-travel motif at one time or another, including all entries in the *Star Trek* television franchise – culminating in *Star Trek: Enterprise* (2001–2005), in which a "Temporal Cold War" plays a central role. Other series have been devoted specifically to time travel, beginning with Irwin Allen's *The Time Tunnel* (1966–1967) and extending through such series as *Voyagers!* (1982–1983) and *Quantum Leap* (1989–1993), whose protagonist randomly jumps not only into different time periods but into the identities of various different individuals. Time travel is also central to the series *The 4400* (2004–). The long-running British television series *Doctor Who* quite often employs the time-travel motif, and the doctor's TARDIS is able to travel as easily through time as through space. Finally, the American series *Sliders* (1995–2000) involves protagonists who travel among parallel universes, often in a mode that essentially involves travel to different time periods in our own world.

Meanwhile, the use of the parallel universe motif in so many time-travel narratives, while offering numerous time-traveling possibilities, also indicates a kinship between the time-travel subgenre and the alternate history subgenre, which explores different courses that might have been taken by history had certain events turned out differently. Works in this genre thus revisit the past in a mode that is akin to time travel, especially as time-travels are often concerned with the creation (intentional or not) of alternative histories.

The alternative history narrative has typically been considered marginal to the enterprise of science fiction, partly because such narratives typically involve little or no actual science and partly because so many alternative histories (the ever-popular alternative histories of the prolific Harry Turtledove are typical here) seem more interested in using the alternative past as a setting for rollicking adventures than in genuine meditations on the historical process. However, as Karen Hellekson notes in her recent book-length study of the genre, the alternative history has grown more respectable and mainstream.

The alternative history novel typically looks at a single crucial turning point in history (the "point of divergence") and then attempts to explore the different ways history might have proceeded had that turning point played out differently. For example, numerous novels conjecture possible alternative paths that might have been taken by history had the South won the Civil War – as in Ward Moore's *Bring the Jubilee* (1953) – or the Axis powers won World War II – as in Philip K. Dick's *The Man in the High Castle* (1962). In keeping with the central interests of science fiction, some alternative history stories have imagined the impact on history of the availability of different technologies, as in the so-called steampunk narrative, epitomized by *The Difference Engine* (1990) written by cyberpunks William Gibson and Bruce Sterling. At first glance, then, the alternative history novel would appear to be more closely related to the genre of the historical novel than to science fiction. On the other hand, the alternative history novel achieves many of the same effects of cognitive estrangement that are central to the science fiction novel as a whole. In particular, the reader's awareness of the course taken by history in our world (or "our timeline" as it is often put) creates an immediate cognitive gap between that history and the fictionalized history proposed in the novel. The reader is then presumably encouraged to view history in a new light and to understand that the outcome of history depends upon specific human actions and is not foreordained.

The entire course of modern history turns out differently in a work such as Keith Roberts's much respected *Pavane* (1968), which explores a world in which the Catholic Church and medieval aristocracy were able to defend their power successfully and to defeat the emergent bourgeois revolution in Europe (thanks partly to the assassination of Queen Elizabeth I and the victory of the Spanish Armada over the English forces in the famous battle of 1588). In the case of Roberts's novel, the Catholic Church's resistance to scientific advancement (familiar in our own history) turns out to be motivated by a desire to avoid repetition of an earlier cycle of history in which such advancement ultimately led to a nuclear holocaust.

If *Pavane*'s Catholic Church seeks to avert the destructive consequences of the rise of capitalist modernity, other alternative histories have similarly imagined a world in which Western-style modernity fails to achieve global hegemony. For example, in Christopher Evans's *Aztec Century* (1993), America is not subjugated by European colonization, but the reverse is in fact beginning to be true. The novel focuses on an alternative twentieth-century England that, as the novel begins, has just been conquered by the rival Aztec empire, which has been gradually encroaching on the British Empire for some time. In *Lion's Blood* (2002) and *Zulu Heart* (2003), Steven Barnes imagines an America that has been colonized by Africa, rather than Europe. Robert Silverberg's *The Gate of Worlds* (1967) envisions a world in which the fourteenth-century plagues that swept Europe had been far more damaging than they actually were, crippling Europe to the point that its subsequent rise to global dominance would have been made impossible.

While Silverberg's novel fails to flesh out its world in any real detail, Kim Stanley Robinson's *The Years of Rice and Salt* (2002) starts from a similar premise and demonstrates that a science fiction novel can, in fact, do such things. Here, Robinson begins with a history-altering premise quite similar to that of Silverberg's *The Gate of Worlds*, but then provides a convincing panoramic view of the social, political, economic, and intellectual history of the globe for a period of roughly seven hundred years – extending well into what would be the twenty-first century in our timeline.

To make this daunting task more manageable, Robinson does not attempt to construct a continuous narrative but instead provides a series of snapshots of key historical moments via a series of ten novellas that explore gradually advancing periods of history, constructing a consistent and credible narrative of world history, fleshed out by extremely detailed and convincing depictions of life in particular places and times during the course of this history. With Europe and Christianity removed from the historical stage, world history in *The Years of Rice and Salt* is driven largely by the rivalry between China and Islam (which eventually includes a resettled Europe), each of which is itself a complex culture. Chinese culture is itself informed by a rivalry between Buddhism and Confucianism, while Islam contains the same division that it does in our world: the opposed tendencies toward militant expansionism and benevolent egalitarianism. In any case, *The Years of Rice and Salt* gives us a detailed look at both of these rival cultures, providing in the process some of the most compelling descriptions of non-Western cultures in all of science fiction. On the other hand, many aspects of Robinson's sweeping alternative history resemble our own time-line quite closely, suggesting that history is driven by powerful forces that are not easily diverted by specific individual events – and also recalling the way in which the manipulations of the past in time-travel narratives often have surprisingly little effect on the eventual outcome of history.

Together, the time-travel narrative and the alternative history narrative provide opportunities for science fictional explorations of numerous aspects of the history of our world – and of the nature of history itself. The "what if" scenarios generated in these subgenres provide new points of view from which to examine the "what was" and "what is" of our own world, while at the same time often providing reminders that the outcome of history is not foreordained but is contingent upon human action, even if that action is limited by certain fundamental conditions of possibility. As a result, these narratives have great potential for creating the kind of thought-provoking reading experience that is central to all the best science fiction.

Suggested Further Reading

Hellekson, Karen, *The Alternate History: Refiguring Historical Time*, Kent, OH: Kent State University Press, 2001.

Nahin, Paul J., *Time Machines: Time Travel in Physics, Metaphysics, and Science Fiction*, 2nd edition, New York: Springer-Verlag, 1999.

Westfahl, Gary, George Slusser, and David Leiby, eds. *Worlds Enough and Time: Explorations of Time in Science Fiction and Fantasy*, Westport, CT: Greenwood Press, 2002.

Notable Time-Travel Fiction

Brian Aldiss, *Cryptozoic!* (1967).
Martin Amis, *Time's Arrow* (1991).
Poul Anderson, *The Guardians of Time* (1960).
Isaac Asimov, *The End of Eternity* (1955).
Stephen Baxter, *The Time Ships* (1995).
Edward Bellamy, *Looking Backward* (1888).
Gregory Benford, *Timescape* (1980).
Octavia Butler, *Kindred* (1979).
Orson Scott Card, *Pastwatch: The Redemption of Christopher Columbus* (1996).
Michael Crichton, *Timeline* (1999).

Peter Delacorte, *Time on My Hands* (1997).
Philip K. Dick, *Counter-Clock World* (1967).
Jack Finney, *Time and Again* (1970).
George Foy, *The Shift* (1996).
David Gerrold, *The Man Who Folded Himself* (1973).
Ken Grimwood, *Replay* (1987).
Joe Haldeman, *The Forever War* (1974) and *Old Twentieth* (2005).
Robert A. Heinlein, "By His Bootstraps" (1941), *The Door into Summer* (1957), and "All You Zombies" (1959).
Washington Irving, "Rip Van Winkle" (1819).
Jerome K. Jerome, *Three Men in a Boat (to Say Nothing of the Dog)* (1889).
John Kessel, *Corrupting Dr. Nice* (1997).
Richard Matheson, *Bid Time Return* (1975).
Edward Page Mitchell, "The Clock that Went Backward" (1881).
Terry Pratchett, *Night Watch* (2002).
John Varley, *Millennium* (1983).
Kurt Vonnegut, *Slaughterhouse-Five* (1969) and *Timequake* (1996).
H. G. Wells,"The Chronic Argonauts" (1888), *The Time Machine* (1895), and *When the Sleeper Wakes* (1899).
Connie Willis,"Fire Watch" (1983), *Doomsday Book* (1992), and *To Say Nothing of the Dog* (1997).
Jack Womack, *Terraplane* (1988) and *Elvissey* (1993).

Notable Alternative-History Fiction

Kingsley Amis, *The Alteration* (1976).
Steven Barnes, *Lion's Blood* (2002) and *Zulu Heart* (2003).
Terry Bisson, *Fire on the Mountain* (1988).
Orson Scott Card, *Pastwatch* (1996).
Philip K. Dick, *The Man in the High Castle* (1962).
Christopher Evans, *Aztec Century* (1994).
Amitav Ghosh, *The Calcutta Chromosome* (1995).
William Gibson and Bruce Sterling, *The Difference Engine* (1990).
Ward Moore, *Bring the Jubilee* (1953).
Audrey Niffenegger, *The Time Traveler's Wife* (2003).
Christopher Priest, *The Separation* (2002).
Keith Roberts, *Pavane* (1968).
Kim Stanley Robinson, *The Years of Rice and Salt* (2002).
Robert Silverberg, *The Gate of Worlds* (1967).
Brian Stableford, *Empire of Fear* (1991).
Harry Turtledove, *In the Balance* (1994), *Second Contact* (1999), *American Front* (1998), *Blood and Iron* (2001), and *Return Engagement* (2004).

Notable Films

Back to the Future. Dir. Robert Zemeckis, 1985.
Back to the Future II. Dir. Robert Zemeckis, 1989.
Back to the Future III. Dir. Robert Zemeckis, 1990.
Bill and Ted's Excellent Adventure. Dir. Stephen Herek, 1989.
The Butterfly Effect. Dir. Eric Bress and J. Mackie Gruber, 2004.
Déjà Vu. Dir. Tony Scott, 2006.
Donnie Darko. Dir. Richard Kelly, 2001.
Frequency. Dir. Gregory Hoblit, 2000.
Goundhog Day. Dir. Harold Ramis (1993)
Millennium. Dir. Michael Anderson, 1989.
Primer. Dir. Shane Carruth, 2004.
Somewhere in Time. Dir. Jeannot Szwarc, 1980.
Star Trek IV: The Voyage Home. Dir. Leonard Nimoy, 1986.
Star Trek: First Contact. Dir. Jonathan Frakes, 1996.
The Sticky Fingers of Time. Dir. Hilary Brougher, 1997.
The Terminator. Dir. James Cameron, 1984.
Terminator 2: Judgment Day. Dir. James Cameron, 1991.
Terminator 3: Rise of the Machines. Dir. Jonathan Mostow, 2003.
Time after Time. Dir. Nicholas Meyer, 1979.
Time Bandits. Dir. Terry Gilliam, 1981.
The Time Machine. Dir. George Pal, 1960.
Timecop. Dir. Peter Hyams, 1994.
Timeline. Dir. Richard Donner, 2003.
Twelve Monkeys. Dir. Terry Gilliam, 1995.

The Alien Invasion Narrative

Narratives involving the invasion of the Earth by alien forces from outer space are among the oldest forms of science fiction. Such narratives were particularly popular in Great Britain in the late nineteenth century, culminating in the publication of H. G. Wells's *The War of the Worlds* in 1898. Wells's novel established many of the conventions of the alien invasion subgenre and set a standard against which subsequent alien invasion narratives have tended to be compared. Among other things, *The War of the Worlds* demonstrates the potential of alien invasion narratives to serve as commentaries on real-world social and political phenomena, especially colonialism. Narratives of alien invasion experienced a particular flowering in the United States in the 1950s, responding to a paranoid sense of threat that was central to American culture in the peak Cold War years. Since that time, alien invasion narratives have remained popular, branching out in a variety of directions, often demonstrating an extremely sophisticated ability to deal with complex social and political issues.

The War of the Worlds was written as British colonial expansion around the globe proceeded at a rapid pace, often leading to the violent destruction of the peoples and cultures being colonized. It is a powerful critique of British colonialism that works through the reversal of asking British readers to view colonialism from the point of view of the colonized, rather than their accustomed position as colonizer. Most of the texts that immediately followed *The War of the Worlds*, however, were fantasies that again placed Western readers in the position of colonizer, generally with no criticism of colonialism intended. For example, Garrett Serviss's *Edison's Conquest of Mars* (serialized in *The New York Evening Journal* in 1898) is a sort of American sequel to Wells's novel in which the famous inventor Thomas Edison leads the forces of Earth in a retaliatory strike against Mars.

Though few novel-length alien invasion stories followed immediately in the footsteps of *The War of the Worlds*, the subgenre came into its own in the 1950s, when such works as Robert A. Heinlein's *The Puppet Masters* (1951) imagined alien invasions that could often be read fairly transparently as allegories of the threat of communism. In Heinlein's novel, parasitical alien slugs (from Titan, a moon of Saturn) land in Iowa and begin attaching themselves to the backs of human hosts, whose minds they then control. Using these human puppets to do their bidding, the alien masters quickly move forward on a program of global conquest. Much of the book is straightforward Cold War propaganda in which the slugs are depicted as being much like communists. Indeed, Heinlein is careful to ensure that this connection will be made even by the most literal-minded of readers. Heinlein also gets in a few shots at communist sympathizers, noting that the only thing more disgusting than a human mind in the grip of the slugs is the idea of humans who willingly work in complicity with the slugs, even without having a parasite directly attached (*Puppet*, 251).

In the end, the valiant (and resourceful) Americans manage to defeat the slugs through the use of germ warfare, a controversial weapon in the 1950s, and one the use of which Heinlein here wholeheartedly endorses. Indeed, one of the central messages of the book is that we need not only to remain eternally vigilant, but also to be willing to use any resources at our disposal to defeat our enemies. Cavanaugh, who has at one point been taken over by one of the slugs, bears them a particular animosity, but his "kill-all-slugs" expressions of racial hatred can be taken as a pretty clear expression of Heinlein's attitude toward America's communist enemies. It is thus with particular satisfaction that Heinlein (through Cavanaugh) reports the apparently complete destruction of all slugs on Earth, even though he warns that we still need to be alert, lest there be others lurking in some obscure Third World hideout, like the Amazon (*Puppet*, 321). Meanwhile, the Americans prepare to launch an all-out genocidal assault on Titan itself so they can wipe out the slugs once and for all. Cavanaugh goes along on the mission, gleefully ending his narrative with the announcement, "Puppet masters – the free men are coming to kill you! *Death and Destruction!*" (*Puppet*, 340, Heinlein's italics).

One of the best-known alien invasion stories of the 1950s is Jack Finney's *Invasion of the Body Snatchers*, serialized in *Collier's* magazine in 1954 and first published in book form as *The Body Snatchers* in 1955. Here, alien seed pods blow in from outer space, settling in the small California town of Mill Valley. The pods have the ability to grow into exact replicas of any human beings with whom they come into contact, and the citizens of Mill Valley are gradually replaced by the resulting replicants. Ultimately, only physician Miles Bennell is left to resist the alien takeover of the town, which threatens to spread from there to encompass the entire country, or even the world. Luckily, however, he is able to inflict so much damage that the pods decide to leave Earth to look for another planet that will be more easily colonized.

Finney's novel was the basis for the 1956 film *Invasion of the Body Snatchers* (remade in 1978 under the same title). The film follows the book fairly closely, but ends on a less optimistic note. Bennell has finally been able to alert the authorities outside of his town (called Santa Mira in the film), but the pods have already spread beyond the town and it is not at all clear that they can still be stopped. The notion of stealthy invaders who essentially take over the minds of normal Americans, converting them to an alien ideology, resonates in an obvious way with the Cold War fear of communist subversion. Indeed, the film has come to be widely regarded as an iconic cultural representation of its contemporary climate of anticommunist paranoia. It is certainly the case that the replacements, who look the same as everyone else, but feel no emotion and have no individuality, directly echo the era's most prevalent stereotypes about communists. Thus, the assurances given Bennell by the replacements that his life will be far more pleasant if he simply goes along with the crowd and learns to live without emotion can be taken as echoes of the supposed seductions offered by communist utopianism.

On the other hand, the makers of the film (and, for that matter, the author of the original novel) have stated that they intended no such allegorical commentary on the threat of communism. Meanwhile, even if one does choose to see communism as the indirect topic of the film, it is also quite possible to read the paranoid vision of the film as a subtle critique of anticommunist hysteria. By this reading, the film suggests that the notion of communists secretly taking over various aspects of American life is about as likely as tiny seeds blowing in from outer space, then developing into large pods that grow perfect replicas of specific human beings, whom they then do away with and replace. In this view, the film suggests that the communist conspiracy warned against by anticommunist alarmists such as Senator Joseph McCarthy is incredibly farfetched, the stuff of B-grade science fiction.

Invasion of the Body Snatchers is now regarded as one of the signature films of the 1950s. It is, in fact, the principal reason that Finney's novel is still so well known. The alien invasion subgenre was to a large extent dominated by films in the 1950s, including a 1953 film adaptation of *The War of the Worlds*, as well as such interesting films as Christian Nyby's *The Thing from Another World* (1951), William Cameron Menzies's *Invaders from Mars* (1953), and Jack Arnold's *It Came from Outer Space* (1954). Many of these films were overt expressions of anticommunist paranoia, including such tawdry efforts as *Invasion USA* (1952) and *Red Planet Mars* (1952). Others were extremely low-budget attempts to capitalize on the popularity of alien invasion movies in the 1950s, including such works as Ed Wood's *Plan 9 from Outer Space* (1959), now notorious as perhaps the worst film ever made. Such films, now regarded with nostalgia by many, provided much of the inspiration for Tim Burton's *Mars Attacks!* (1995), perhaps the finest – or at least funniest – comic science fiction film ever made, rivaled only by *Men in Black* (1997), another alien invasion film. Meanwhile, the popularity of Roland Emmerich's *Independence Day* (also released in 1996) indicated the ongoing viability of the alien invasion film as the twentieth century drew to a close.

Among the many alien invasion films of the 1950s, one that stands out is Robert Wise's *The Day the Earth Stood Still* (1951). Far from feeding the anticommunist frenzy of the time, Wise's film is a plea for global peace and understanding – and a warning that the Cold War arms race might ultimately lead to disaster for the entire planet. Here, the Christlike alien Klaatu (Michael Renny), accompanied by his imposing robot, Gort, comes in peace, but is greeted with violence. Still, he survives to issue a stern warning: human civilization will be destroyed (by an intergalactic robot peacekeeping force) if it seeks to extend its violent ways beyond Earth. This rejection of the Cold War arms race was a courageous gesture in a film that was produced at the height of American Cold War hysteria and at a time when Hollywood itself was under siege by anticommunist zealots in Washington. The success of the film thus demonstrated the way in which science fiction, because it is perceived by many as divorced from contemporary reality, can serve as a venue for trenchant social and political commentary that might have been judged too controversial in a more "mainstream" form.

Among the novels of the 1950s, Arthur C. Clarke's *Childhood's End* (1953) is notable for its treatment of alien invaders as essentially benevolent. Here, partly through genuinely advanced technology and partly through trickery, a contingent of alien Overlords establishes dominion on Earth, imposing rules that are designed to prevent the human race from destroying itself and the rest of the planet. One rule, for example, forbids cruelty to animals. The most important rule involves the establishment (working through the UN) of a single World State that makes Earth's nations obsolete. The rule of the Overlords, led by Supervisor Karellen, issues in an unprecedented era of peace and prosperity for the Earth, though some find this utopian existence a bit boring, given that humanity now has no real challenges to face. Artistic and other forms of creativity are greatly curtailed as well, introducing some fairly standard meditation on the possible downside of utopia. Some early critique of television is introduced as well: one reason artistic creativity seems to have failed is that human culture comes to be dominated by television. Meanwhile, the Overlords themselves remain mysterious and distant. Indeed, for more than fifty years they stay entirely out of sight, revealing themselves only after decades of their presence have prepared the human race for their appearance – which is exactly like devils, complete with wings, horns, and pointed tails. (It turns out that this vision, so common in world mythology, has come about as a result of a sort of echo memory from the future, a phenomenon that accounts for a variety of "racial" memories.)

In the final analysis, it is revealed that the Overlords have come to Earth at the behest of their own master, a sort of collective "Overmind" that consists of the fusion of a variety of species with vastly advanced psychic abilities. Despite their own advanced material state, the Overlords have no such abilities. As a result, they are at an evolutionary dead end; their function in the galaxy is simply to help races (such as humanity) that do potentially have such abilities survive until evolution brings those abilities to fruition. In the end, this evolutionary leap does occur, eventually leading to a situation in which almost all of the world's children under ten years old have them.

The Overlords continue to oversee the remainder of the human race, though, with no racial future, many humans commit suicide, either alone or en masse. The transformed children, meanwhile, are moved to a separate area of their own. Eventually, the untransformed humans die out, except for Jan Rodricks, an engineering student who had stowed away aboard an Overlord supply ship in order to view the amazing wonders of the Overlord home world. He returns after the eighty-year round trip (during which he ages only four months owing to relativistic time dilation) to find himself the last man on Earth. As the children prepare to join the Overmind, the Overlords finally evacuate Earth for their own safety, leaving Jan behind to broadcast to them what he sees of the final process, which leads to the complete dissolution of the Earth.

As Cold War tensions eased in the 1960s, the alien invasion subgenre receded into the background of contemporary sf. Interesting works did continue to appear, however. Indeed, the very fact that no particular version of the alien invasion narrative was especially popular during the 1960s and 1970s meant that the subgenre was able to branch out in a number of new directions. For example, Thomas Disch's *The Genocides* (1965), once again presents advanced alien invaders bent on the destruction of the human race. However, the tone here is very different from that of the paranoid works of the 1950s, and Disch's novel is more a warning against human arrogance than against the possibility of sinister alien forces lurking just outside our planet (or our country). Here, the aliens identify the Earth as a perfect spot for growing the huge, fast-growing plants that they use for food. So they seed the planet with the crop and then set about eradicating the various pests that might interfere with its growth, including human beings (who are compared in the text to worms burrowing into an apple).

Michael Crichton's *The Andromeda Strain* (1969) can almost be read as a reversal of *The Genocides* in the sense that the alien invaders here are lowly crystalline microbes picked up in orbit by an American spacecraft. When the craft subsequently crashes, the alien plague threatens to run rampant on Earth, to the potential destruction of humankind. Earth is saved at the last moment by the organism's own mutation into a form that is not harmful to humans, but the near-miss serves (in a novel published in the year of the first manned landing on the moon) as a warning of the potential dangers of contamination from outer space. *The Andromeda Strain* was made into a successful film (directed by Robert Wise) in 1971, thus launching Crichton's work as one of the most commercially successful multimedia franchises in science fiction history.

John Varley's *The Ophiuchi Hotline* (1977) deals not with an alien invasion in itself, but also with the aftermath of an alien invasion that has left mysterious invaders (who seem to exist largely in another dimension) in control of Earth, while humanity is essentially in exile in the rest of the solar system. In addition, a second group of aliens has, for the past four hundred years, been broadcasting high-tech data into the solar system (apparently from the star system 70 Ophiuchi). Much of this data is indecipherable, but the part that can be decoded has become the basis for most human techno-logical advances during this period. These advances are considerable, and *The Ophiuchi Hotline* is a veritable catalog of science fictional technologies, including space habitats, cloning, digital uploading of consciousness, and interstellar travel. Ultimately, it is revealed that the hotline information comes not from 70 Ophiuchi but from a starfaring race known as the Traders, who have established a broadcasting station only one-half-light year from the solar system. In return for all the data they have supplied over the centuries, these Traders eventually demand payment in the form of detailed knowledge about human culture so that they can assimilate it into their own civilization. They also reveal to the humans in the solar system, many of whom dream of retaking Earth, that the invaders (who have actually taken Earth not for themselves but to liberate the dolphins and whales there, whom they regard as far more intelligent than humans) are far too sophisticated and powerful ever to be repelled. Humanity's best hope is to strike out into the galaxy in search of life in another star system, and that project begins as the book ends.

In the world of film, Steven Spielberg's *Close Encounters of the Third Kind* (1977) and *E.T. the Extraterrestrial* (1982) provide looks at benevolent alien visitors who differ dramatically from the sinister bug-eyed invaders of most previous alien invasion films. They also provide sharp critiques of certain elements of human society. Still, the treatment of aliens and alien cultures in American culture in the 1980s was not, as a whole, particularly generous. During that decade, the anti-Soviet rhetoric of the Reagan administration often sounded like something from the paranoid 1950s, so perhaps it is no surprise that the alien invasion subgenre sometimes returned to the spirit of the 1950s as well. *Footfall* (1985), by Larry Niven and Jerry Pournelle, was one of the most successful alien invasion novels of the 1980s. It is also a highly representative work of its time in that it seems designed, at least partly, as an expression of support for the development of superweapons programs, including the Reagan administration's "Star Wars" Strategic Defense Initiative. Using a format that is reminiscent of any number of disaster films, *Footfall* presents a detailed account of actual combat between the Earth and an alien spaceship and the impact of this combat on a number of individual characters. In the novel, a huge alien spacecraft approaches Earth, demanding unconditional surrender from the Earthlings. The aliens, known as the fithp, look very much like baby elephants, except that they have two trunks, each of which has finger-like tentacles on the end. In a bit of anticommunist allegory that harkens back to the 1950s, the fithp are a herdlike species who act in groups and are virtually incapable of taking individual action, resulting in considerable miscommunication between them and the individualistic Earthlings they encounter. They also seem less intelligent than humans and less able to deal with unfamiliar situations, while the digits on their "trunks" are far less nimble than human fingers.

Ultimately, the fithp are defeated when the US, employing the advice of a number of science fiction writers conscripted as consultants, conceives a plan to build a huge, nuclear-powered spacecraft that will be able to carry heavy weapons and thus engage the fithp mothership in a battle for superiority in space. This project succeeds, and the new ship successfully battles the fithp until they finally issue an unconditional surrender, even agreeing to work with humans to reconstruct the modified Bussard ramjet that originally allowed them to undertake their interstellar flight to Earth, which means that humans will acquire this technology as well.

Greg Bear's *The Forge of God* (1987), like *Footfall*, employs the disaster-thriller format to explore the motif of alien invasion, though the vaguely liberal politics of Bear's novel can be taken as a sort of riposte to the conservatism of Niven and Pournelle. Here, a mysterious alien force of "planet-eaters" literally dismantles the Earth in order to use it for raw materials, while we observe the activities of a variety of characters as they await the inevitable end. Meanwhile, in a bit of political satire that comments on the religious rhetoric of the contemporary Reagan administration (but even more strikingly looks forward to the religiosity of the administration of George W. Bush), Earth's response to the crisis is given a twist when US President William Crockerman takes no action at all because he interprets the attack as the wrath of God and the destruction of Earth as the Biblical apocalypse. Luckily, a second force of benevolent aliens spirits away a select group of humans (as well as a collection of human cultural artifacts) on a series of space arks – enabling, among other things, Bear's 1992 sequel, *Anvil of Stars*, in which the surviving humans seek revenge against the planet-eaters.

In film, James Cameron's *The Abyss* (1989) combines with *The Day the Earth Stood Still* to bookend the period of the Cold War arms race with cautionary alien invasion tales on film. Here, highly advanced aliens have set up shop deep beneath the ocean. They then use their extremely sophisticated abilities to manipulate water to create vast tidal waves that threaten to wipe out many of the coastal areas of Earth unless the Eastern and Western blocs begin to set aside their differences and seek a negotiated détente rather than continuing the upward ratcheting of the arms race that had continued through the Reagan years of the 1980s. This intervention is successful, and the film ends on a hopeful note that peace can be maintained on Earth.

The alien invasion novels of the 1980s were topped off by Octavia Butler's "Xenogenesis" trilogy, comprising *Dawn* (1987), *Adulthood Rites* (1987), and *Imago* (1989). This highly complex and ambitious sequence, designed largely as a critique of the aggressive policies of the Reagan administration, addresses a number of crucial issues, including racism, gender, militarism, and colonialism. Here, the alien Oankali (who actually have a great deal in common with Varley's Traders) reach Earth in the wake of a devastating nuclear conflict that has virtually destroyed human civilization on the planet. They then use their highly advanced biotechnology to restore humanity to health, but only in the form of human-Oankali hybrids who are meant to leave the planet and become starfaring gene traders like the Oankali themselves.

One of the most prominent science fiction works of the 1980s was neither a novel nor a film, but a four-hour television miniseries, Kenneth Johnson's 1983 alien invasion epic *V*, which was so successful that it was followed in 1984 by a six-hour sequel, *V: The Final Battle*. The original *V* provided some of the most compelling television viewing of the 1980s, and certainly the most compelling alien invasion narrative on television to that point. In *V*, a virtual compendium of previous alien invasion motifs, huge flying saucers suddenly appear over major cities around the globe. The aliens, who appear to look exactly like humans, then make contact, declaring themselves friendly and announce that they have come to Earth because their planet has serious environmental problems that can be solved only with the use of a chemical that they hope to manufacture on Earth, using the refuse of Earth's cities as raw materials. In return, they promise to provide the people of Earth with high-tech solutions to their own problems. This benevolence turns out to be a ruse, however, and the aliens have really come to Earth to harvest the planet's vast water supplies for their own use. What's worse, the aliens (whose real appearance turns out to be reptilian) plan to harvest the planet's human population as well, some to use as soldiers in their various wars of conquest, but most simply to be used as a source of food. Ultimately, however, human resistance forces mobilize to repel the invasion and save the planet.

Of course, alien invasions had figured prominently in such classic television series as *The Twilight Zone*, *The Outer Limits*, and *Doctor Who* and had provided the entire matter of at least one entire reasonably successful series, *The Invaders* (1967–1969), in which alien invaders disguised as humans made life miserable for protagonist David Vincent (Roy Thinnes). The alien invasion motif of the latter involved a paranoia that made it a clear predecessor to *The X-Files*, so much so that the success of the latter series in the early 1990s led to a miniseries sequel to *The Invaders* in 1995, while Thinnes himself became a recurring guest star on *The X-Files*.

The X-Files itself was clearly the most important alien invasion television series of the 1990s, and probably of all time. Running through nine seasons from 1993 to 2002, this paranoid conspiracy thriller introduced a number of new high-tech concepts to the alien invasion television subgenre. It is, however, distinguished more by its air of paranoid suspicion toward shadowy forces within the US government than by its fear of sinister aliens. Audiences were also attracted to the air of sexual tension between the FBI-agent protagonists Mulder and Scully, and by the show's postmodern sense of epistemological uncertainty. Finally, despite the tense drama with which its central alien invasion conspiracy motif is presented, *The X-Files* is also highlighted by the comic quips of Mulder and by a number of playful episodes that spoof the normal seriousness of the program.

Other notable alien invasion television series of the 1990s included *Space: Above and Beyond* (1995–1996), created by two of the producers of *The X-Files*. This series is essentially a gritty combat drama in which forces from Earth battle against the Chigs, an alien race determined to conquer the planet. Also worthy of note were the 1998 BBC miniseries *Invasion Earth: The World War Has Begun* and the highly interesting *Earth: Final Conflict*, created by *Star Trek* creator Gene Roddenberry, which ran for five seasons, beginning in 1997. *Earth: Final Conflict* is a highly inventive series, though in its final seasons it grew more and more reminiscent of *The X-Files*, involving plots to create alien-human hybrids through secret genetic experiments and also suggesting sinister secret forces at work within the US government.

The most notable development within the subgenre of the alien invasion novel in the 1990s was the return to prominence of British writers. Perhaps most notable in this regard is the "Aleutian" trilogy by Gwyneth Jones, comprising *White Queen* (1991), *North Wind* (1996), and *Phoenix Café* (1998). Jones's trilogy draws upon insights from contemporary poststructuralist theory to develop a postmodernist challenge to conventional Enlightenment (and colonialist) notions of Self and Other. It also shows a sophisticated understanding of colonial history, which the trilogy extensively allegorizes. The "Aleutian" trilogy also imagines some genuinely inventive aliens. Apparently lacking the high-powered information sources of many sf aliens, Jones's aliens stumble upon the Earth having had no idea a habitable planet was there. Further, they are not an official expedition, but essentially an independent crew of entrepreneurs. Described by Jones herself in an essay on the trilogy as a "feckless crew of adventurers and dreamers," they have been wandering the galaxy in search of profit, though they eventually become extensively entangled in the global politics of Earth, leading to considerable confusion and unrest when they finally depart in the third volume after a 300-year stay.

Actually, Jones's aliens are quite similar to humans (and some can even pass for humans), but this similarity only serves to make the encounter between the two species even more complex. For example, this similarity causes each species to view the other through its own cultural expectations and conventions, leading to considerable miscommunication and confusion, a situation that is often reflected in the disorientation of the reader, who often finds herself in the same position as the human characters in the book: struggling to learn about and understand the Aleutians by putting together the bits and pieces of information that are available. Conversely, the attempts of the Aleutians to understand humans provide a defamiliarizing perspective on human culture and society. By the end of the trilogy, the human characters and their culture seem as strange and alien as do the Aleutian characters. Indeed, the boundary between human and Aleutian is progressively blurred as Jones's sequence proceeds.

The aliens of Ian McDonald's *Sacrifice of Fools* (1996) are in many ways reminiscent of Jones's Aleutians and encounter many of the same sorts of cultural confusion as they try to co-exist with humans on Earth. In *Evolution's Shore* (1995) and *Kirinya* (1998), McDonald breaks significantly new ground in the alien invasion genre with his vision of strange alien "biological packages" that land on Earth and then proceed to move across the landscape, transforming everything in their path through a sort of nanotechnology. This transformation includes human beings, who appear on the verge of a new evolutionary leap thanks to the effects of the alien technology.

Another recent examples of the British alien invasion novel is Liz Williams's *Empire of Bones* (2002), which proposes that humanity is actually descended from the írRas, a race of interstellar travelers whose principal reason for being is to colonize various worlds around the galaxy, at the same time extending the evolutionary range of their already extremely diverse race. In the novel, the írRas return to Earth after a long period of being out of contact – and find that their evolutionary plans for the planet have gone seriously awry. *Empire of Bones* is set in India, which helps to make its exploration of the intersection of medicine, disease, and colonialism particularly rich.

Also of interest among recent works is *The Mount* (2002), by the American feminist writer Carol Emshwiller, an allegorical fable in which a weak-legged alien race, the Hoots, have colonized the Earth, using enslaved humans as mounts upon which the ride about the countryside. The Hoots proudly proclaim the kindness with which they rule their human subjects and indeed point out how much better off humans are to have Hoots to take care of them. As such, they not only recall the paternalist rhetoric of Western colonialism on Earth, but also in many ways echo the strategies by which the working classes are governed under capitalism. Novels such as *The Mount* and *Empire of Bones* indicate the ongoing vitality of the alien invasion narrative as a mode of social and political critique as we move into the early part of the twenty-first century.

Suggested Further Reading

Booker, M. Keith. *Alternate Americas: Science Fiction Film and American Culture.* Westport, CT: Praeger, 2006.

Booker, M. Keith. *Monsters, Mushroom Clouds, and the Cold War: American Science Fiction and the Roots of Postmodernism, 1946–1964.* Westport, CT: Greenwood, 2001.

Booker, M. Keith. *Science Fiction Television.* Westport, CT: Praeger, 2004.

Slusser, George, and Eric S. Rabkin, eds. *Aliens.* Carbondale: Southern Illinois University Press, 1987.

Notable Fiction

Greg Bear, *The Forge of God* (1987).

Octavia Butler, "Xenogenesis" trilogy: *Dawn* (1987), *Adulthood Rites* (1987), and *Imago* (1989).

Arthur C. Clarke, *Childhood's End* (1953).

Michael Crichton, *The Andromeda Strain* (1969).

Thomas M. Disch, *The Genocides* (1965).

Carol Emshwiller, *The Mount* (2002).

Jack Finney, *The Body Snatchers* (1955).

Robert A. Heinlein, *The Puppet Masters* (1951).

Gwyneth Jones, "Aleutian" trilogy: *White Queen* (1991), *North Wind* (1996), and *Phoenix Café* (1998).

Ian McDonald, *Evolution's Shore* (1995), *Kirinya* (1998), and *Sacrifice of Fools* (1996).

Larry Niven and Jerry Pournelle, *Footfall* (1985).

Garrett Serviss, *Edison's Conquest of Mars* (1898).

John Varley, *The Ophiuchi Hotline* (1977).

H. G. Wells, *The War of the Worlds* (1898).

Liz Williams, *Empire of Bones* (2002).

Notable Films

The Abyss. Dir. James Cameron, 1989.

The Andromeda Strain. Dir. Robert Wise, 1971.

Close Encounters of the Third Kind. Dir. Steven Spielberg, 1977.

The Day the Earth Stood Still. Dir. Robert Wise, 1951.

E.T. the Extraterrestrial. Dir. Steven Spielberg, 1982.

Independence Day. Dir. Roland Emmerich, 1996.

Invasion of the Body Snatchers. Dir. Don Siegle, 1956.

It Came from Outer Space. Dir. Jack Arnold, 1953.

Mars Attacks! Dir. Tim Burton, 1995.

Men in Black. Dir. Barry Sonnenfeld, 1997.

The Thing from Another World. Dir. Christian Nyby, 1951.

The Space Opera

During the years of the 1930s, when written science fiction was dominated by the pulp magazines and the most prominent science fiction works on film were the "Buck Rogers" and "Flash Gordon" serials, stories of adventure in outer space rose to the center of the genre, though the common term for such stories, "space opera," was not suggested (by sf writer Wilson Tucker) until 1941. This term was originally derogatory, suggesting second-rate, formulaic stories written by untalented hacks. Later, while the term continued to have pulpy connotations, it came to be associated with some the best-known and most-loved works of the entire science fiction genre, from novels of the 1950s by writers such as Isaac Asimov and Robert A. Heinlein, to television series such as the various incarnations of *Star Trek*, to films such as the *Star Wars* sequence. In addition, a renaissance in the subgenre of space opera, beginning in the 1980s, has produced some of the most complex and thought-provoking novels in the history of science fiction, though many recent works look back in a selfconsciously nostalgic way to the swashbuckling action and larger-than-life heroes of the early space opera.

Among the writers who defined the terms of the subgenre in the 1920s and 1930s, E. E. "Doc" Smith stands out as perhaps the most important. Smith wrote space operas from the 1920s to the 1960s. His first novel, *The Skylark of Space*, was originally written during the period 1915–1920, then published in *Amazing Stories* in 1928; it appeared in book form in 1946 and again in a revised edition in 1958. It became the first of a sequence of four "Skylark" novels and has some claim to being the first true space opera. Smith's most important works, however, were the stories and novels of the "Lensmen" series, which established many of the conventions of the genre, while envisioning a great deal of interesting future technologies and describing some of the first genuinely interesting aliens in all of science fiction. Here, two vastly advanced races, the good Arisians and the evil Eddorians, have been battling for supremacy for billions of years. Earth is part of a special breeding program through which the Arisians hope to develop a civilization advanced enough to defeat the Eddorians. (The title comes from the "Lens," a bracelet worn by members of the Arisian Galactic Patrol to give them certain telepathic and other powers.)

Most of the "Lensmen" stories originally appeared in John W. Campbell's *Astounding Science-Fiction*, a venue that contributed a great deal to the development of the space opera. Another early writer of space opera who published extensively in *Astounding Science-Fiction* was Jack Williamson, who added a romantic flourish to the subgenre that marked his long career from such early works as *The Legion of Space* (1934), all the way up to such late works as *The Singers of Time* (1991), on which he collaborated with Frederik Pohl. Campbell himself was an important pioneer in the space opera before taking over the editorship at *Astounding Science-Fiction*, producing a number of stories and novelettes in the early 1930s that were eventually collected into such book-length works as *The Mightiest Machine* (1947), *Islands of Space* (1957), and *Invaders from the Infinite* (1961).

"Black Destroyer," the first science fiction short story by A. E. Van Vogt (who went on to become one of the major figures of Golden Age sf), appeared in *Astounding Science-Fiction* in 1939. This story (widely acknowledged to be one of the sources of the highly successful 1979 film *Alien*) was later folded, along with several other Van Vogt stories, into the novel *The Voyage of the Space Beagle* (1950), an important milestone in the development of the novel-length space opera. Another important early writer of space opera stories was C. L. Moore, one of the first women to write science fiction. Moore, often in collaboration with her husband Henry Kuttner, produced a number of stories of outer-space adventure from 1933 to 1958. Perhaps her best-known published volume is *Judgment Night* (1952), which collects five novellas originally printed in *Astounding Science-Fiction*. Perhaps the most prolific author of classic space opera stories in the 1930s was Edmond Hamilton, whose writing sometimes showed an antiromantic and unsentimental bent that now make them appear ahead of their time.

Isaac Asimov's *The Stars Like Dust* (1951) is space opera in a romantic vein not typical of that highly rational author. More typical of Asimov (and one of the major landmarks in the development of the space opera) is Asimov's "Foundation" trilogy, comprising *Foundation* (1951), *Foundation and Empire* (1952), and *Second Foundation* (1953), all of which consist primarily of combinations of stories originally published in *Astounding Science-Fiction* in the 1940s. Set in the distant future, the "Foundation" novels are in a sense post-holocaust works, in that they detail a time after the collapse of the mighty Galactic Empire plunges the galaxy into a new

Middle Ages. But the novels are typical of much of the science fiction of the 1940s in their assurances of the ultimate beneficial effects of science and technology in expanding the possibilities of humankind (and making these new Middle Ages as brief, and as bright, as possible).

Asimov eventually followed this sweeping saga of a far-flung galactic federation with a fourth installment, *Foundation's Edge* (1982), then attempted to merge the Foundation sequence with his 1950s sequence of "Robot" novels and stories in *The Robots of Dawn* (1983), *Robots and Empire* (1985), *Foundation and Earth* (1986), and *Prelude to Foundation* (1988). After Asimov's death in 1992, a subsequent "Foundation" trilogy was produced, building upon his ideas and written by some of the leading American science fiction writers. This second trilogy includes Gregory Benford's *Foundation's Fear* (1998), Greg Bear, *Foundation and Chaos* (1999), and David Brin, *Foundation's Triumph* (2000).

Robert A. Heinlein also got his start in *Astounding Science-Fiction*, publishing numerous stories there in the vein of space opera. Many of Heinlein's juvenile novels of the 1950s were space operas, as were many of his short stories. The 1950s (a particularly rich decade for the subgenre) introduced a number of variations on the space opera, including novels of interstellar conflict, of which Heinlein's *Starship Troopers* (1959) is a leading early example. Heinlein's novel has influenced any number of future entries in this military variation of the space opera, including some – such as Harry Harrison's *Bill, the Galactic Hero* (1965) and Joe Haldeman's *The Forever War* (1974) – that were constructed partly as parodic responses to *Starship Troopers*. Harrison, incidentally, is also the author of a lengthy sequence of tongue-in-cheek space operas featuring the roguish anti-hero James Bolivar diGriz, better known as the "Stainless Steel Rat," beginning with *The Stainless Steel Rat* (1961) and extending through *The Stainless Steel Rat Joins the Circus* (1999).

Heinlein stories such as "Universe" (1941) and "Common Sense" (1941) pioneered the motif of the "generation starship," in which the long times potentially involved in interstellar travel are dealt with simply by populating the ship with families who live and die on the ship for generation after generation. One of the early classics of this version of the space opera, however, is Brian Aldiss's *Non-Stop* (1958, published in the US in 1959 as *Starship*), which is ostensibly set on a generation starship, but which turns out actually to be set on a ship that is in perpetual orbit around the Earth. Generation starships are typically huge, and their passengers often do not realize that they are on a starship. A variation on this "huge ship" theme is James Blish's "Cities in Flight" sequence, the last three volumes of which – comprising *Earthman, Come Home* (1955); *A Clash of Cymbals* (1958, published in the US as *The Triumph of Time*); and *A Life for the Stars* (1962) – involve entire cities traveling about in space. Much of the time, the inhabitants of these cities are simply looking for work, in a motif that is directly compared to the migrant Okies of the 1930s. In this sense, Blish's sequence is clearly intended to recall John Steinbeck's *The Grapes of Wrath* (1939).

Another variant on the space opera is the relativistic time-dilation novel, in which starships travel near the speed of light, causing time to pass much more slowly for those on board than in the universe at large. The classic example of this sort of space opera is Poul Anderson's *Tau Zero* (1970), though time dilation is also crucial to such important works as Joe Haldeman's *The Forever War* and Orson Scott Card's sequence *Ender's Game* (1985), *Speaker for the Dead* (1986), *Xenocide* (1991), and *Children of the Mind* (1996). The subgenre of space opera is also related to the subgenre of planetary romance, in which the cultures and ecologies of entire alien planets are described. Early examples of the planetary romance include Jack Vance's *Big Planet* (1952), Hal Clement's *Mission of Gravity* (1954), and Poul Anderson's *The Man Who Counts* (1958). Frank Herbert's sf classic *Dune* (1965) is essentially a planetary romance, though its numerous sequels expand into the galactic scale more typical of the space opera proper. Among numerous later examples of the planetary romance, Aldiss's sequence *Helliconia Spring* (1982), *Helliconia Summer* (1983), and *Helliconia Winter* (1985) stands out as a particular high point.

The space opera tended to recede in prominence among the science fiction novels and stories of the 1960s and 1970s, which turned in more literary and more socially engaged directions. However, one might note here the work of the Polish science fiction writer Stanisław Lem, who wrote a number of lampoons of Western space opera during this period, while himself taking the form to a new level of intellectual seriousness in his classic *Solaris* (1961). Meanwhile, the space opera reached unprecedented new audiences with the success of Gene Roddenberry's *Star Trek* television series, which originally ran on NBC in the US from 1966 to 1969, but became even more successful beginning in the 1970s when it was widely rerun in syndication. In fact, the syndicated run of *Star Trek* became one of the most important phenomena in television history and made the series one of the most influential television programs of all time.

In addition to its continual syndicated showings, *Star Trek* has inspired a vast fan culture that includes conventions, merchandising, and an extensive sequence of related novels. The *Star Trek* phenomenon made cultural icons of both its featured spaceship, the *USS Enterprise*, and its central characters (including the histrionic Captain James T. Kirk; the hyper-logical half-Vulcan first mate Mr. Spock; and the irascible medical officer, Dr. McCoy). The original series also grew into an extensive television franchise, spawning a succession of sequels, including *Star Trek: The Next Generation* (1987–1994), *Star Trek: Deep Space Nine* (1993–1999), *Star Trek: Voyager* (1995–2001), and *Enterprise* (2001–2005). Meanwhile, the original series spilled over into theatrical film, becoming one of the most lucrative and successful franchises in movie history. At this writing, there have been ten *Star Trek* films, the first six of which are extensions of the original series, with the original cast, though the advancing age of this cast by the time of *Star Trek VI: The Undiscovered Country* in 1991 became an increasing source of comedy as the rickety *Enterprise* crew dragged itself around the galaxy, thinning hair, thickening waistlines, and all. *Star Trek Generations* (1994) then served as a transition film that killed off Captain Kirk and handed the baton of the film franchise over to the cast and crew of *Star Trek: The Next Generation* which was just coming to the end of its television run at that time.

The collective images that make up the universe of *Star Trek* have by now become a crucial part of the popular Western imagination, while the technological trappings of the *Star Trek* universe – with its warp drives, force fields, phasers, tricorders, communicators, transporters, and replicators – have become a central source of the popular notion of what the technology of the future might be like. The seemingly optimistic political vision of the franchise has been similarly powerful; in *Star Trek* the political oppositions of twentieth-century Earth have seemingly been overcome, making the future Earth of the twenty-third and twenty-fourth centuries the capital of a vast, united, and benevolent "United Federation of Planets" that encompasses much of the galaxy, reaching out to new worlds with its message of tolerance, peace, and interplanetary cooperation.

The long-running British television sf series *Doctor Who* (1963–1989, resurrected in 2005) contained strong elements of space opera, while later television space operas such as *Babylon 5* (1993–1998) and *Farscape* (1999–2003) brought the televised form of the subgenre to a new level of sophistication. In the meantime, films from *Forbidden Planet* (1956), to *2001: A Space Odyssey* (1968), to *Star Wars* (1977) and *Alien* (1979) made space opera a major cinematic form as well. The *Star Wars* films, like the *Star Trek* and *Alien* films, turned out to be the beginning of extensive film sequences. *Star Wars* is a particularly classic example of the space opera, with its intentionally nostalgic look back to the pulps and serials of the 1930s.

While the space opera was a relatively secondary form of written sf from the 1960s to the mid-1980s, occasional important works related to the subgenre continued to appear. Among these, one might single such works as Larry Niven's *Ringworld* (1970), which involves a gigantic ring-shaped artificial world that circles a star. In addition, C. J. Cherryh's *Downbelow Station* (1981) brought a new complexity and sophistication to the treatment of spacefaring adventure, taking such tales far beyond the days of the simplistic early space operas. Frederik Pohl's *Gateway* (1977) is also notable. It employs the standard space-opera device of faster-than-light travel to facilitate interstellar adventure, but adds an extra wrinkle in that this travel is accomplished via ships left behind by the mysterious Heechee alien civilization. The humans who "pilot" these Heechee craft must basically go wherever the ships are programmed to take them – only hoping that the destination will be safe and profitable. Ursula K. Le Guin's entire sequence of "Hainish" novels also centrally rely on the remnants of an ancient, now-lost civilization. This sequence features a far-flung galactic federation, enabled by the fact that ancient explorers from the planet Hain spread human civilization (and DNA) across the galaxy perhaps a million years earlier. The administration of this federation, meanwhile, is facilitated by the development of communication devices known as "ansibles," which allow essentially instantaneous communication across interstellar distances. Many of the Hainish novels are actually detailed explorations of specific planetary cultures, as in *The Left Hand of Darkness* (1969), *The Word for World Is Forest* (1972), and *The Dispossessed* (1974).

Bruce Sterling's *Schismatrix* (1985) was a key text in what turned out to mark the beginning of a resurgence in the space opera in American science fiction. Combining motifs from cyberpunk, posthuman, and alien invasion science fiction with the basic space opera conceit of humans living in manmade outer-space habitats, Sterling's novel demonstrated the ongoing relevance of space opera as a subgenre of written science fiction. It was accompanied by numerous other important works in the subgenre by American writers. Another early entry in the space opera resurgence was Greg Bear's *Eon* (1985), featuring a vast alien space habitat constructed from an asteroid using advanced technologies that make it possible for the inside to be bigger than the outside, apparently even approaching the infinite. Dan Simmons's *Hyperion* (1989, followed the next year by a sequel, *The Fall of Hyperion*) maintains a basic space opera scenario, but adds an exploration of complex metaphysical ideas, while employing a narrative structure of storytelling derived from Chaucer's *Canterbury Tales*. Also important are Vonda McIntyre, who wrote several novels in the *Star Trek* sequence, as well as independent space operas such as *Superluminal* (1977), and Lois McMaster Bujold, much of whose somewhat humorous work (including the early entries in the "Vorkosigan" saga, named for the severely disabled interstellar spy and mercenary Miles Vorkosigan) involves space operas featuring a future universe of space colonies connected by faster-than-light travel via wormholes.

A particularly inventive addition to the space opera is David Brin's "Uplift" sequence, a series of six novels (published between 1980 and 1998) in which Brin imagines a vast and ancient galactic civilization of numerous oxygen-breathing intelligent species (there are also other kinds of intelligent species that are not part of this system), each of which was "uplifted" to sentience through the intervention of another, older sentient species, in a sequence going all the way back to the Progenitors, the first intelligent species in the galaxy. In a sort of echo of the "white man's burden," sentient species generally see it as their duty to uplift any promising pre-sentient species they may encounter, thus enriching galactic culture by expanding the pool of intelligent life. However, newly uplifted species must serve an extended period of apprenticeship in which they serve their patron species essentially as indentured labor – and are sometimes brutally exploited by their patrons.

Brin thus presents as fundamental to intelligent life in the galaxy a paternalistic and hierarchical relation between species that is highly reminiscent of the legacy of colonialism and racism on Earth. On the other hand, his books are often critical of this system (especially as it is abused by certain species), while at the same time presenting the human race as a potential sport that might have evolved intelligence independently without the intervention of a patron. (In turn, humans have uplifted chimpanzees and dolphins even before they encounter the wider galactic civilization, and they seem to treat these "client" species with much more equanimity than is typical in the galaxy.)

Especially noteworthy (but only vaguely space operatic) among the American science fiction novels of the 1990s are the entries in Kim Stanley Robinson's "Mars" trilogy, including *Red Mars* (1993), *Green Mars* (1994), and *Blue Mars* (1996). Here, Robinson elaborates in great technological and sociological detail an effort to terraform Mars to make it suitable for colonization by humans, thus relieving some of the pressures caused by overpopulation and other pressures on Earth. In the meantime, he very deftly explores the various political debates involved in this project to build a new world system that hopefully avoids the previous mistakes made on Earth – while fighting off the attempts of Earth-based corporations to seize control of the project.

Mathematician Vernor Vinge, perhaps best known for his popularization of the idea of the technological singularity, made major contributions to the space opera in the 1990s with his Hugo Award-winning far-future epics

A Fire upon the Deep (1992) and *A Deepness in the Sky* (1999), which take place in a universe mostly divided into two regions, The Slow Zone and The Beyond. Because of the basic physical properties of the universe in each zone, much more advanced thought (including the computational abilities required to develop faster-than-light travel) is possible there. Earth, however, resides in The Slow Zone, limiting the kind of technology that can be developed there. (There is also an additional region, The Transcend, in which almost limitless technological advances are possible, thanks to the existence of vastly superhuman post-singularity artificial intelligences known as The Powers.)

Vinge's notion of such posthuman intelligences makes his work an important forerunner of the numerous space operas that have appeared in the early twenty-first century. For example, the Australian Greg Egan envisions a vastly advanced human race that has largely mastered the stars, sometimes shedding their corporeal bodies to facilitate interstellar travel. Vinge is also an important predecessor of much of the recent resurgence in British science fiction, sometime referred to as the British Boom. Indeed, while some of the best-known British space operas before the 1990s were actually lampoons of the form – including M. John Harrison's *The Centauri Device* (1974) and Douglas Adams's *The Hitchhiker's Guide to the Galaxy* and its variants and sequels – the writers of the British Boom have brought British space opera to the very forefront of the subgenre. These writers have often added a new level of literary sophistication to the space opera, while frequently combining it with themes and technologies more typical of other subgenres, especially cyberpunk.

Both Charles Stross and Ken MacLeod, for example, have envisioned post-singularity universes in which advanced artificial intelligences evolve at spectacular speeds, then develop a variety of high-tech capabilities (including interstellar travel), after which they seemingly wink out of existence, perhaps moving into a different dimension of reality. The remaining humans are able, to some extent, to take advantage of the technologies left behind by the artificial intelligences, though they are sometimes limited by their inability to understand these posthuman technologies. In addition, in the future galaxy of Stross, certain technological advances (especially time travel) are limited by the intervention of a far-future posthuman entity known as the Eschaton, which seeks to prevent any changes in the historical time line that led to its own evolution. Stross's *Singularity Sky* (2003), *Iron Sunrise* (2004), and *Accelerando* (2005) and MacLeod's *The Stone Canal* (1996), *The Cassini Division* (1997), *Cosmonaut Keep* (2001), *Dark Light* (2002), and *Newton's Wake* (2004) – are particularly interested in the social, political, and economic dimensions of their future post-singularity galaxies, producing serious and intelligent explorations of these issues that are a far cry from the pulp origins of the space opera. Meanwhile, MacLeod's recent *Learning the World* (2005) is space opera in a more classic vein, involving an expedition to colonize another star system that turns out already to have intelligent inhabitants.

Peter Hamilton has produced a number of space operas on a grand scale and in a fairly classic vein, updated with the latest in science fiction technology. His space operas include the entries in the "Night's Dawn" trilogy (1996–1999), so massive (more than 1,000 pages each) that they were published in the US in six volumes. *Fallen Dragon* (2001) is a standalone novel that in many ways reads as a condensation of many of the central ideas of "Night's Dawn," while its dark depiction of an ultra-capitalist future world complicates Hamilton's reputation (gained partly from a series of early anticommunist dystopian novels) as a promoter of capitalism. *Pandora's Star* (2004) and *Judas Unchained* (2005) are also large-scale space operas. Also worthy of note are the recent space operas of Alastair Reynolds, including *Revelation Space* (2000), *Redemption Ark* (2002), and *Absolution Gap* (2004). Writing somewhat more in a classic space opera vein than Stross and MacLeod, Reynolds nevertheless resembles them in his combination of motifs (and technologies) from a variety of different science fictional subgenres.

Other important recent British space operas include John Clute's *Appleseed* (2001) and the volumes of Colin Greenland's "Plenty" trilogy, notable for their use of a female protagonist. Harrison, having seemingly dismissed the space opera in *The Centauri Device*, himself returned to the form with *Light* (2002), a rousing entry that enthusiastically employs the space opera form that Harrison had seemingly rejected in *The Centauri Device*. Justina Robson introduces a number of interesting elements to the space opera in *Natural History* (2003), including the notion of "forged," or genetically engineered humans who are designed to performed a variety of specialized tasks, including serving as intelligent starships. Meanwhile, Richard K. Morgan's "Takeshi Kovacs" novels resemble the works of Stross and MacLeod in their use of cyberpunk conceits within the space opera form. In fact, the first novel in this sequence, *Altered Carbon* (2002) is almost pure cyberpunk, but the series evolves in the sequels, *Broken Angels* (2004) and *Woken Furies* (2005), more into the vein of space opera, including an especially interesting treatment of the motif of salvaging leftover alien technologies.

Worthy of special note among the space operas produced in the British Boom are the "Culture" novels of Iain M. Banks, a multinovel sequence that both builds upon a number of classic precedents in science fiction and explores genuinely new territory. These novels elaborate the political, social, and cultural practices of the Culture, a vast (and vastly advanced) intergalactic federation governed by hyper-intelligent artificial intelligences known as Minds. However, Banks gives a refreshing twist to this potentially dystopian motif by instead making it utopian, at least on the surface: the Minds are efficient and benevolent rulers who manage the affairs of humans far better than humans could ever hope to. Further, humans in this highly affluent machine-ruled society live rich, healthy, and active lives (with potentially limitless lifespans), somewhat in the tradition of the technology-enabled utopian future Earth envisioned in the *Star Trek* franchise. Their principal problem is the potential for boredom, given that all of their major problems are solved in advance by the Minds. They do, however, find a variety of exciting and fulfilling ways to spend their time and explore their personal creativity. Perhaps the most problematic aspect of the Culture is its tendency to meddle in the affairs of other civilizations that they encounter in space (one of the ways the humans in the Culture try to add meaning and purpose to their lives), trying to nudge those other civilizations toward the kind of egalitarian society that they themselves have. Among other things, this motif creates sources of conflict that add plot interest, but Banks clearly presents the interventionism of the Culture as a far different phenomenon than the imperialism of Earth's past. While Europeans felt justified in colonizing most of the globe because of their confidence in the superiority of their way of life, the Culture is not interested in colonization. Moreover, the intellects of the Minds are so vast (and so objective) that cultural relativism might not apply here: the Culture may really *be* the best possible society, an achievement it is only attempting to share with others. However, this motif is far from simple in Banks's novels. Even the Minds can make mistakes, and their attempts to intervene in the evolution of other cultures can sometimes lead to unforeseen bad results. Further, Banks maintains a certain tension in his depiction of life within the Culture, leaving open the possibility that life there is not as utopian as it might first appear, possibly because human beings themselves are too limited to exploit fully the opportunities offered them by the Minds.

Suggested Further Reading

Aldiss, Brian W. *Billion Year Spree: The True History of Science Fiction*. Garden City, NY: Doubleday, 1973.

Jameson, Fredric. *Archaeologies of the Future: The Desire Called Utopia and Other Science Fictions*. London: Verso, 2005.

Westfahl, Gary, ed. *Space and Beyond*. Westport, CT: Greenwood Press, 2000.

Westfahl, Gary. "Space Opera." *The Cambridge Companion to Science Fiction*. Eds. Edward James and Farah Mendelsohn. Cambridge: Cambridge University Press, 2003. 197–208.

Notable Fiction

Douglas Adams, *The Hitchhiker's Guide to the Galaxy* (1979).

Brian Aldiss, *Non-Stop* (1958, published in the US as *Starship*), *Helliconia Spring* (1982), *Helliconia Summer* (1983), and *Helliconia Winter* (1985).

Poul Anderson, *The Man Who Counts* (1958), *The High Crusade* (1960), and *Tau Zero* (1970).

Eleanor Arnason, *Ring of Swords* (1993).

Isaac Asimov, *The Stars Like Dust* (1951), *Foundation* (1951), *Foundation and Empire* (1952), *Second Foundation* (1953), *Foundation's Edge* (1982), *The Robots of Dawn* (1983), *Robots and Empire* (1985), *Foundation and Earth* (1986), and *Prelude to Foundation* (1988).

Iain M. Banks, *Consider Phlebas* (1987), *The Player of Games* (1988), *The State of the Art* (1989), *Use of Weapons* (1990), *Excession* (1996), *Inversions* (1998), and *Look to Windward* (2000).

Greg Bear, *Eon* (1985) and *Foundation and Chaos* (1999).

Gregory Benford, *Foundation's Fear* (1998).

James Blish, *Earthman, Come Home* (1955), *A Clash of Cymbals* (1958, published in the US as *The Triumph of Time*), and *A Life for the Stars* (1962).

David Brin, *Sundiver* (1980), *Startide Rising* (1983), *The Uplift War* (1987), and *Foundation's Triumph* (2000).

Lois McMaster Bujold, *The Warrior's Apprentice* (1986) and *The Vor Game* (1990).

Orson Scott Card, *Ender's Game* (1985), *Speaker for the Dead* (1986), *Xenocide* (1991), *Children of the Mind* (1996).

C. J. Cherryh, *Downbelow Station* (1981).

Hal Clement, *Mission of Gravity* (1954).

John Clute, *Appleseed* (2001).

Samuel R. Delany, *Nova* (1968).

Gordon Dickson, *Naked to the Stars* (1961).

Greg Egan, *Quarantine* (1992), *Distress* (1995), *Diaspora* (1997), and *Schild's Ladder* (2002).

Colin Greenland, *Take Back Plenty* (1990), *Seasons of Plenty* (1995), and *Mother of Plenty* (1998).

Joe Haldeman, *The Forever War* (1974).

Peter F. Hamilton, *The Reality Dysfunction* (1996, published in the US in two parts: *Emergence* and *Expansion*), *The Neutronium Alchemist* (1997, published in the US in two parts: *Consolidation* and *Conflict*), *The Naked God* (1999, published in the US in two parts: *Flight* and *Faith*), *Fallen Dragon* (2001), *Pandora's Star* (2004), and *Judas Unchained* (2005).

Harry Harrison, *The Stainless Steel Rat* (1961), *Bill the Galactic Hero* (1965), *The Stainless Steel Rat's Revenge* (1970), *The Stainless Steel Rat Wants You!* (1978), and *The Stainless Steel Rat Joins the Circus* (1999).

John M. Harrison, *The Centauri Device* (1974) and *Light* (2002).

Robert A. Heinlein, "Universe" (1941), "Common Sense" (1941), and *Starship Troopers* (1959).

Frank Herbert, *Dune* (1965).

Ursula K. Le Guin, *The Left Hand of Darkness* (1969), *The Word for World Is Forest* (1972), and *The Dispossessed* (1974).

Stanisław Lem, *Solaris* (1961).

Ken MacLeod, *The Stone Canal* (1996), *The Cassini Division* (1997), *Cosmonaut Keep* (2001), *Dark Light* (2002), and *Newton's Wake* (2004).

Vonda McIntyre, *Superluminal* (1977).

C. L. Moore, *Judgment Night* (1952).

Richard K. Morgan, *Broken Angels* (2004) and *Woken Furies* (2005).

Larry Niven, *Ringworld* (1970).

Frederik Pohl, *Gateway* (1977).

Alastair Reynolds, *Revelation Space* (2000), *Redemption Ark* (2002), and *Absolution Gap* (2004).

Kim Stanley Robinson, *Red Mars* (1993), *Green Mars* (1994), and *Blue Mars* (1996).

Justina Robson, *Natural History* (2003).

Dan Simmons, *Hyperion* (1989) and *The Fall of Hyperion* (1990).

E. E. "Doc" Smith, *The Skylark of Space* (1928).

Bruce Sterling, *Schismatrix* (1985).

Charles Stross, *Singularity Sky* (2003), *Iron Sunrise* (2004), and *Accelerando* (2005).

Jack Vance, *Big Planet* (1952).

A. E. Van Vogt, *The Voyage of the Space Beagle* (1950).

Vernor Vinge, *A Fire upon the Deep* (1992) and *A Deepness in the Sky* (1999).

Jack Williamson, *The Legion of Space* (1934).

Notable Films

2001: A Space Odyssey. Dir. Stanley Kubrick, 1968.
Alien. Dir. Ridley Scott, 1979.
Alien: Resurrection. Dir. Jean-Pierre Jeunet, 1997.
Alien 3. Dir. David Fincher, 1992.
Aliens. Dir. James Cameron, 1986.
Dune. Dir. David Lynch, 1984.
The Fifth Element. Dir. Luc Besson, 1997.
Forbidden Planet. Dir. Fred Wilcox, 1956.

Serenity. Dir. Joss Whedon, 2005.
Silent Running. Dir. Douglas Trumbull, 1972.
Solaris. Dir. Andrei Tarkovsky, 1972.
Space Truckers. Dir. Stuart Gordon, 1996.
Starship Troopers. Dir. Paul Verhoeven, 1997.
Star Trek film series. Various directors, 1979–2002.
Star Wars film series. Various directors, 1977–2005.

Apocalyptic and Post-Apocalyptic Fiction

Ancient literature, produced by a low-technology human culture that was very much at the mercy of natural phenomena, is filled with tales of natural (or supernatural) disaster and its aftermath. However, Mary Shelley's *The Last Man* (1826) – in which a deadly plague gradually wipes out humanity while the immune protagonist looks on – is quite often identified as the first postapocalyptic science fiction tale. Other tales of apocalypse and post-apocalypse appeared over the next 120 years, with Richard Jefferies's *After London* (1885) providing an important milestone in the development of the subgenre into its modern form. However, it was not until the atomic bombing of Hiroshima in August, 1945, followed by Cold War nuclear tensions, that post-apocalyptic stories – especially those dealing with nuclear holocaust and its aftermath – were propelled to the forefront of science fiction.

Writing about the science fiction films of the 1950s, Susan Sontag argues that these films reflect what she calls "the imagination of disaster" (*Imagination*). These films, she notes, are typically about disasters wrought by the irresponsible use of science, though science, used responsibly, can also be the key to dealing with the disasters. The same can be said for many of the novels and short stories of the 1950s. Given the Cold War political climate of the twenty or so years after World War II, it is not surprising that many of the most important science fiction works of the period dealt in one way or another with the possibility of nuclear holocaust and its aftermath. However, one of the first important postwar disaster narratives was George R. Stewart's *Earth Abides* (1949), which deals, not with the impact of nuclear war, but with a mysterious plague that sweeps across America, killing virtually everyone within a matter of days.

In Stewart's plague-decimated US, there are scattered survivors, who are immune to the plague. Some of these survivors ultimately join together to form the Tribe, a group that ultimately moves toward a return to a simpler life as hunter-gatherers, clearly based on the lifestyle of the Native Americans whose culture was virtually destroyed by the advance of modern American civilization. In this sense, Stewart's book anticipates many later post-apocalypse fictions, such as Leigh Brackett's *The Long Tomorrow* (1955), which describes an agrarian, deeply technophobic society that develops after a nuclear war.

Judith Merril's *Shadow on the Earth* (1950) builds directly upon the tensions of the Cold War, presenting an apocalypse that arises precisely from a surprise nuclear attack on the United States, though it does not specifically identify the attackers as Soviets. But Merril's book is highly unusual among post-apocalypse works of the 1950s in its focus on a female protagonist, housewife Gladys Mitchell, who attempts to cope with the aftermath of the nuclear assault, not by exploring the surrounding area or attempting to rebuild society, but simply by keeping her household running and taking care of her two daughters.

In so doing, Gladys must overcome a variety of obstacles, including the American security forces, who take charge in the wake of the attack, allowing them to act out their right-wing male fantasies of domination and control. Far from heroizing the flag-waving patriots who defend us from the Soviet nuclear attack (which arose from conditions in which the Americans were equally culpable), *Shadow on the HEarth* eerily anticipates the Patriot Act era by suggesting that there are opportunists among us who are anxious to use such an attack (or, by extension, even the threat of such an attack) as an excuse for establishing their own repressive measures.

John Wyndham's *The Day of the Triffids* (1951) gives the post-apocalyptic tale a twist that draws upon the horror genre in its vision of deadly, ambulatory, meat-eating plants that spread across the globe, threatening human hegemony over the planet. This threat is made especially serious because humanity has been weakened by widespread blindness as the result of a mysterious meteor shower. Though it does not feature a nuclear war, *The Day of the Triffids* (adapted to film in 1962), shows the impact of Cold War tensions by hinting that the deadly plants may have originally been engineered in the Soviet Union, which hovers in the text as a inscrutable and indefinite menace.

Bernard Wolfe's *Limbo* (1952) is a more clearly political novel, though the exact nature of its politics is difficult to determine. In fact, *Limbo* is ambiguous in a number of ways, and Wolfe's description of the book, in his postscript, as a "grab bag of ideas that were more or less around at the mid-century mark" is accurate (*Limbo*, 435). Nevertheless, the very scope of this grab bag makes *Limbo* a valuable social document, while at the same time serving as a demonstration of the intellectual ambitiousness of the book. The book is also ambitious in a literary sense, making extensive use of allusions, puns, and other wordplay in the midst of an exploration of the baleful aftermath of an all-out nuclear war, as survivors on both the American and Soviet sides strive to rebuild civilization, while ostensibly taking steps to ensure that such a nuclear holocaust can never again occur.

Limbo focuses on the experiences of Martine, a talented brain surgeon, who has been living for eighteen years on a remote Indian Ocean island to which he fled in the midst of World War III. When he returns to civilization, he learns that the United States has now been reduced to the Inland Strip, an area with a population of about 38 million that is the only habitable part of the former US. Both coasts have been devastated in the nuclear war, orchestrated on each side by giant computers. Martine discovers to his horror that both the Inland Strip and the Eastern Union (the remnants of the Soviet Union) are now dominated by a culture of "Immob," or immobilization. Central to this culture is "vol-amp," or voluntary amputeeism, a sort of literalization of the notion of disarmament. It is widely believed in this culture that amputation of the limbs reduces natural human aggression, thus helping to keep the peace and prevent further nuclear wars. Extreme though this measure might be, it is also hypocritical. As it turns out, both sides have been stockpiling nuclear weapons for years, mouthing détente, while secretly preparing for war, which in fact breaks out late in the book.

Limbo is not a serious attempt to envision what life and society might be like in the aftermath of a nuclear holocaust. Rather, it is a Menippean satire that comments on Wolfe's own contemporary world, employing both its future setting and its outrageous images as techniques of cognitive estrangement. Much of Wolfe's critique is aimed at the regimented society of his fictional future, clearly meant as a commentary on the societies of both the United States and the Soviet Union in the 1950s. This critique provides many points of contact between his book and the tradition of dystopian fiction, which clearly has much in common with post-apocalyptic fiction. Even more reminiscent of dystopian fiction is Mordecai Roshwald's *Level 7* (1959), set in a huge underground bomb shelter the inhabitants of which are attempting to survive the effects of a massive nuclear war. In a clear satirical commentary on the regimentation of American life in the 1950s, life in the facility is highly regulated: every activity (including conjugal meetings) must be performed according to a strict schedule. Eventually, even this facility is unable to protect its inhabitants from death, as the devastating effects of the nuclear holocaust gradually seep downward to Level 7, the lowest and presumably most secure level in the facility. Among other things, *Level 7* thus warns Americans not to develop a false sense of security that thorough preparations can save them from the effects of nuclear war.

Richard Matheson's *I Am Legend* (1954) combines Stewart's bio-catastrophe with the fictions of nuclear holocaust that are conventionally associated with the fears of the 1950s. Here, nuclear war somehow spurs the growth of bacteria that turn everyone on Earth (except protagonist Robert Neville) into vampires. Neville spends his life alone, barricaded in his house at night, then carrying out guerrilla raids in the daytime, when the vampires sleep. In response, the vampires lay nightly siege to Neville's house in an attempt to wipe out their last remaining enemy. However, Matheson's treatment of the Us versus Them opposition between Neville and the vampires turns out to be far more interesting than any quick summary of the scenario might lead one to suspect. At the very beginning of the book, Neville recognizes the conformism of the vampires, realizing that they cannot tolerate his difference. He also realizes the irony that the vampires are now on top, having been, throughout history, an outcast minority against whom the majority has shown extreme prejudice. Yet, despite his own embattled predicament, Neville concludes that the historical hatred of vampires might have been unfair. He wonders, for example, if the vampire is "worse than the manufacturer who set up belated foundations with the money he made by handing bombs and guns to suicidal nationalists?" (*Legend*, 32).

In the end, Neville is finally overwhelmed by the vampires as they seek to set up a new vampire society. The book then takes a startling turn when he realizes that the poles of normality and abnormality have now been reversed. As the majority, the vampires are now normal; as a one-of-a-kind freak (who has, among other things, been going about committing mass murder by driving stakes through the hearts of sleeping vampires), he is the abnormal one, the one who is a danger to organized society. Thus, in a final passage that gives the book its title, Neville realizes that he will go down in the history of the new vampire society as a legendary terror, playing the role that Dracula had played in the former human society (*Legend*, 170).

Matheson's basic scenario is so compelling that his novel has been adapted to film three times, though all three adaptations – *The Last Man on Earth* (1964, starring Vincent Price), *The Omega Man* (1971, starring Charlton Heston), and *I Am Legend* (2007, starring Will Smith) have tended to romanticize the protagonist more than does the book. Such romanticization of apocalypse survivors has appeared in numerous novels as well, particularly in works such as Pat Frank's *Alas, Babylon* (1959). Frank's book deals overtly with war between the United States and the Soviet Union, though it provides relatively few details of the war itself, concentrating instead on the struggles of the inhabitants of a small Florida community, Fort Repose, to survive in the wake of the cataclysmic conflict. *Alas, Babylon* (like much of Frank's work) is extremely representative of a certain style of conservative thought in the 1950s in that it treats nuclear war as inevitable, while warning (echoing a central theme of Frank's best-selling nonfictional writings) that the US is sorely prepared for such a war.

Worse, Frank seems almost to revel in the destruction of the modern American system, depicting post-holocaust Fort Repose as a kind of laissez-faire utopia, where strong individuals can work out the solutions to their problems without the interference of government regulations and bean-counting bureaucrats. Indeed, Frank seems relatively unconcerned about the massive destruction and loss of life associated with the nuclear attack. Perhaps there is even a sort of I-told-you-so satisfaction in Frank's fantasy of what will happen to the US as a result of not heeding his warnings. There is also a sense that the destruction of the country returns it to the "good old days" of the American frontier, when men were men and women were women, and the bureaucracy of the modern welfare state did not interfere with the ability of strong individuals to carry out their plans and fulfill their desires.

Perhaps the most critically respected post-holocaust novel of the 1950s is Walter Miller's *A Canticle for Leibowitz* (1959). Actually a series of three novellas, Miller's book employs a vision of cyclic history to trace the course of civilization from the year 2570 (six hundred years after a nuclear holocaust has plunged humanity into a second Dark Ages), to the year 3174 (when a second Renaissance announces a rebirth of science and culture), to the year 3781 (when civilization has recovered its former heights, only again to destroy itself via nuclear war). The book, though informed by considerable ironic humor, suggests an extremely dark and pessimistic vision of human civilization, arguing that humans need to use science and technology in order to fulfill their potential, but that they will inevitably misuse these tools, leading to their own destruction.

Pierre Boulle's *Planet of the Apes* (1963) envisions a postnuclear holocaust world in which human civilization has collapsed, to be replaced by a civilization ruled by intelligent apes. This novel inspired the 1968 film of the same title, which became one of the best-known works in all of American popular culture. Both the novel and the film also contain numerous satirical commentaries on contemporary human society, gaining cognitive dissonance through displacement into the far-future ape-ruled society. The film was remade in 2001, but (reflecting the changed nature of popular anxieties) dropped the nuclear theme and instead viewed the fall of humanity (and rise of the apes) as the result of genetic engineering gone awry.

The true poet of post-apocalypse during the postwar period is probably Philip K. Dick, who wrote a whole series of such fictions, including *The World Jones Made* (1956), *The Man Who Japed* (1956), *Vulcan's Hammer* (1960), *The Penultimate Truth* (1964), and *Dr. Bloodmoney* (1965). Of these, only the last makes any serious attempt realistically to depict conditions that might prevail after a nuclear war, and all are satirical fictions that use their post-holocaust settings merely to provide a fresh perspective from which to critique the already dystopian character of contemporary American capitalist society. However, *Dr. Bloodmoney* is unique among Dick's post-holocaust novels in a number of ways. Most importantly, it is the only one of Dick's post-holocaust novels of the long 1950s that includes important utopian elements, as numerous critics have noted. Ultimately, *Dr. Bloodmoney* is powerful as social commentary because the negative aspects of its post-holocaust world are the ones that most resemble the characteristics of Dick's contemporary America, while the positive aspects of his post-holocaust world are those that differ most dramatically from conditions in America at the end of the long 1950s.

The post-holocaust films that appeared during the 1950s often seemed designed to calm the nuclear fears of the decade, frequently displacing their vision of nuclear holocaust into the far future and often providing happy endings to assure audiences that everything would be fine, nuclear holocaust or no. The post-holocaust films of the decade generally present far less troubling images than do the novels, both in their representation of nuclear devastation and in their commentary on contemporary American society. Still, these films do attempt to make certain political points, ranging from the vaguely left-wing antiracist perspective of Arch Oboler's early effort, *Five* (1951), to the almost deranged anticommunism of William Asher's *The 27th Day* (1957).

Stanley Kramer's *On the Beach* (1959) is one of the most sanitized of all the post-apocalypse films of the 1950s. In this film, set in 1964 and based on Nevil Shute's bestselling 1957 Australian novel of the same title, a global nuclear war has apparently destroyed all human life everywhere on Earth, except Australia, which has been spared because of its remote location. Unfortunately, the clouds of deadly radiation that cover the rest of the globe are headed for Australia as well, so the Australians themselves have only a few months before what seems to be inevitable death.

To an extent, *On the Beach* is more human drama than science fiction, as it details the poignant attempts of the various characters to cope with their impending dooms. Indeed, while the how-could-we-be-so-stupid senselessness of the nuclear war looms in the margin as a message throughout, Kramer also seems to have wanted to make the film a sort of universal commentary on how human beings come to grips with the realization of their own certain mortality. There are no corpses, no radiation burns, not even property damage. While we do see shots of post-holocaust San Francisco and San Diego, the cities are entirely undamaged. The only change is that all the people seem to have disappeared. As such, the film's anti-arms race message is muted, though still clear.

Other post-holocaust films of the long 1950s were even more indirect in their representation of nuclear war and its aftermath: graphic on-screen depictions of the actual effects of nuclear war were rare until the mid-1980s, when a spate of such films appeared, including *The Day After* (1983), *Testament* (1983), and *Threads* (1985). For example, in Edward Bernds's *World Without End* (1956), the nuclear holocaust is projected hundreds of years into the future, and the film itself is set hundreds of years after that, when radiation levels have essentially returned to normal. Many aspects of *World Without End* seem derived from H. G. Wells's classic 1895 novel, *The Time Machine*, the original far-future post-apocalypse tale, which would be adapted more directly to film a few years later in George Pal's *The Time Machine* (1960).

Ray Milland's *Panic in Year Zero* (1962) resembles *On the Beach* in its focus on the human drama of the survivors of the disaster, not the human tragedy of the victims. There are again no actual signs of nuclear destruction, though the film does depict certain negative consequences, such as the looting, rape, and murder that occur in the wake of a nuclear attack. Ultimately, the film becomes a sort of adventure tale, in which the protagonists heroically deal with the adversities they encounter as a result of the nuclear holocaust. A British film, Val Guest's *The Day the Earth Caught Fire*, also released in 1962, is less romantic in its dramatization of nuclear-related destruction, but it displaces this destruction from nuclear war to nuclear testing, which inadvertently sends the Earth careening off course and hurtling toward the sun. Meanwhile, it ends as the Russians and Americans work together to try to save the Earth, but eschews the easy solution of a happy ending, closing with the outcome of these efforts still in doubt.

The nuclear-holocaust films of the 1950s led directly to a series of what might be called pre-holocaust films. No doubt influenced by the perceived close call of the 1962 Cuban missile crisis, each of these films in its own way deals, not with the aftermath of a nuclear holocaust, but with a proposed scenario that might be envisioned as leading to such a holocaust. Such films include John Frankenheimer's *Seven Days in May* (1964) and Sidney Lumet's tense thriller, *Fail-Safe* (1964). The best of these films, however, was Stanley Kubrick's brilliant *Dr. Strangelove, or, How I Learned to Stop*

Worrying and Love the Bomb (1964), which, more than any other single film, captured the lunacy of the Cold War mentality, while at the same time suggesting that certain American attitudes in the Cold War might have been inherited from the Nazis. *Dr. Strangelove* is highlighted by the triple-threat performance of Peter Sellers as its ex-Nazi title character, as well as British air force officer Lionel Mandrake and US President Merkin Muffley. With its parodic focus on the comic absurdity of the arms race, it became a cult favorite of the 1960s' youth movement and was one of the classics of American culture of the 1960s, even though, strictly speaking, it is a British film, produced at London's Hawk Studios.

From the 1960s forward, post-disaster fiction began to focus less on nuclear holocaust and more on the possible disastrous consequences of phenomena such as pollution and overpopulation. For example, Anthony Burgess's *The Wanting Seed* (1962), Harry Harrison's *Make Room! Make Room!* (1966, adapted to film as *Soylent Green* in 1973), and John Brunner's *Stand on Zanzibar* (1968) all deal with the consequences of overpopulation. Ecological catastrophe is at the heart of such works as Brunner's *The Sheep Look Up* (1972), which explores ecological concerns in its projection of future environmental pollution and its social and political consequences, helping to establish an important new strand of apocalyptic fiction, though it might be noted that J. G. Ballard, in a sequence that includes *The Drowned World* (1962), *The Burning World* (1964), and *The Crystal World* (1966) had already envisioned various forms of ecological calamity. Kate Wilhelm's *Where Late the Sweet Bird Sang* (1976) also deals with the aftermath of environmental collapse on Earth. In film, Douglas Trumbull's *Silent Running* (1972) posits a future environmental collapse on Earth, leading to attempts to preserve nature in outer space.

David Brin's *Earth* (1990) provides an effective panoramic look at global environmental degradation, nearly leading to the death of the planet (though featuring a *deus ex machine* rescue in the end). Kim Stanley Robinson has written a number of works warning of the possible disastrous consequences of environmental irresponsibility, beginning with *The Gold Coast* (1988), the middle volume of his "Three Californias" trilogy, in which environmental decay is only one of numerous dire consequences of runaway capitalist development. Robinson's environmentalist concerns are also front and center in his masterwork, the "Mars" trilogy, which produces cognitive dissonance by removing those concerns to another planet. However, Robinson's *Forty Signs of Rain* (2004), *Fifty Degrees Below* (2005), and *Sixty Days and Counting* (2007) constitute a near-future trilogy that gains urgency from its relatively realistic depiction of the potentially disastrous effects of global warming – and the need for more effective official responses to this looming disaster. Global warming and environmental decay also play a role in the social collapse that is central to the dystopian visions in works such as Octavia Butler's "Parable" sequence and Jack Womack's "Dryco" series.

A particularly interesting take on the post-nuclear holocaust narrative is Russell Hoban's *Riddley Walker* (1980), which is especially important for its innovative use of language, as Hoban attempts to portray a post-apocalypse England in which language itself (along with other elements of civilizations) has dramatically decayed. Hoban's credible vision of post-apocalyptic language overcomes a shortcoming of most works of the sub-genre, which typically portray language as relatively unchanged, whatever apocalyptic events might have occurred. *Riddley Walker* has influenced a number of subsequent works, one of the most notable of which is Will Self's *The Book of Dave* (2006), which similarly attempts to imagine the devolved language of a post-apocalyptic England – now largely ruled by a "sacred" text that is actually the ramblings of a deranged twentieth-century London cabbie.

Other recent fictions have posited a variety of possible future disasters. For example, in Brin's *The Postman* (1985, adapted to film in 1997), a series of catastrophes occurs, but the real collapse of civilization is brought about not by the catastrophes themselves, but by the response of right-wing survivalist groups to these catastrophes. Robert Charles Wilson's *Darwinia* (1998) features the sudden and seemingly miraculous disappearance of Europe and parts of Asia and Africa, to be replaced by alien lands inhabited by strange extraterrestrial flora and fauna. In Margaret Atwood's highly literary *Oryx and Crake* (2003), experiments with genetic engineering lead to the spread of a deadly plague that wipes out most of humanity, leaving the protagonist, Snowman, to live as the last man on Earth among a variety of strange genetically engineered hybrid creatures.

Post-apocalyptic narratives potentially contain a strong element of heroic adventure, which probably explains why they have maintained a consistent popularity as a subgenre of film from the 1950s forward. Indeed, some of the best-known science fiction films of all time involve post-apocalyptic elements of one kind or another. For example, the three *Mad Max* films, especially *Mad Max 2: The Road Warrior* (1981), have included some of the most compelling and influential images in recent world cinema. In addition to such classics as *Planet of the Apes* (2001) and *Blade Runner* (1982), the three *Terminator* films are set largely in a pre-apocalypse world, but centrally involve time travelers from a post-apocalyptic future. Terry Gilliam's *Twelve Monkeys* (1995) also involves post-apocalypse time travelers, this time seeking to return to the past to prevent the apocalyptic plague that virtually destroyed their world. The three *Matrix* films take place in a post-apocalyptic world brought about, like that in the *Terminator* films, by a war between humans and intelligent machines. Big-budget films such as *Waterworld* (1995) and *The Day after Tomorrow* (2004) grow out concerns about global warming, while George Romero's various "living dead" zombie films represent another kind of post-apocalyptic tale, as do the graphic zombie horror film *28 Days Later* (2002) and its sequel *28 Weeks Later* (2007).

Post-apocalyptic tales have also been prominent in other forms of popular culture, including television and comics. Television series such as *Jericho* (2006–2008) and *Dark Angel* (2000–2002) have had post-apocalyptic themes, which have also been prominently featured in individual episodes of anthology series such as *The Twilight Zone* and *The Outer Limits*. Meanwhile, one of the most popular comics of recent years has been Brian K. Vaughan's *Y: The Last Man*, which deals with the aftermath of a mysterious plague that suddenly strikes down virtually all males on Earth, except, of course, for the "last man" of the title. Such efforts indicate the ongoing popularity of the subgenre, even more than a decade after the Cold War that originally propelled it into prominence.

Suggested Further Reading

Booker, M. Keith. *Monsters, Mushroom Clouds, and the Cold War: American Science Fiction and the Roots of Postmodernism, 1946–1964*. Westport, CT: Greenwood, 2001.

Biskind, Peter. *Seeing Is Believing: How Hollywood Taught Us to Stop Worrying and Love the Fifties*. New York: Pantheon, 1983.

Brians, Paul. *Nuclear Holocausts: Atomic War in Fiction, 1895–1984*. Kent, OH: Kent State University Press, 1987.

Evans, Joyce A. *Celluloid Mushroom Clouds: Hollywood and the Atomic Bomb*. Boulder, CO: Westview Press, 1998.

Hendershot, Cyndy. *Paranoia, the Bomb, and 1950s Science Fiction Films*. Bowling Green, OH: Bowling Green University Popular Press, 1999.

Seed, David. *American Science Fiction and the Cold War: Literature and Film*. Edinburgh: Edinburgh University Press, 1999.

Sontag, Susan. "The Imagination of Disaster." *Against Interpretation and Other Essays*. New York: Farrar, Straus, and Giroux, 1966. 209–225.

Weart, Spencer R. *Nuclear Fear: A History of Images*. Cambridge, MA: Harvard University Press, 1988.

Notable Fiction

Margaret Atwood, *Oryx and Crake* (2003).
Paul Auster, *In the Country of Last Things* (1987).
J. G. Ballard, *The Drowned World* (1962), *The Burning World* (1964), and *The Crystal World* (1966).
Pierre Boulle, *Planet of the Apes* (1963).
Leigh Brackett, *The Long Tomorrow* (1955).
David Brin, *The Postman* (1985) and *Earth* (1990).
John Brunner, *Stand on Zanzibar* (1968) and *The Sheep Look Up* (1972).
Anthony Burgess, *The Wanting Seed* (1962).
Angela Carter, *Heroes and Villains* (1969) and *The Passion of New Eve* (1977).
Philip K. Dick, *The World Jones Made* (1956), *The Man Who Japed* (1956), *Vulcan's Hammer* (1960), *The Penultimate Truth* (1964), *Dr. Bloodmoney* (1965), and *Do Androids Dream of Electric Sheep?* (1968).
Pat Frank, *Alas, Babylon* (1959).
Harry Harrison, *Make Room! Make Room!* (1966).
Robert A. Heinlein, *Farnham's Freehold* (1964).
Russell Hoban, *Riddley Walker* (1980).
Richard Jefferies, *After London* (1885).
Richard Matheson, *I Am Legend* (1954).
Vonda McIntyre, *Dreamsnake* (1978).
Judith Merril, *Shadow on the HEarth* (1950).
Walter Miller, *A Canticle for Leibowitz* (1959).
Kim Stanley Robinson, *The Gold Coast* (1988), *Forty Signs of Rain* (2004), and *Fifty Degrees Below* (2005), and *Sixty Days and Counting* (2007).
Mordecai Roshwald, *Level 7* (1959).
Will Self, *The Book of Dave* (2006).
Mary Shelley, *The Last Man* (1826).
George R. Stewart, *Earth Abides* (1949).
Kate Wilhelm, *Where Late the Sweet Birds Sang* (1976).
Robert Charles Wilson, *Darwinia* (1998).
Bernard Wolfe, *Limbo* (1952).
John Wyndham, *The Day of the Triffids* (1951).

Notable Films

The 27th Day. Dir. William Asher, 1957.
28 Days Later. Dir. Danny Boyle, 2002.
28 Weeks Later. Dir. Juan Carlos Fresnadillo, 2007.
The Andromeda Strain. Dir. Robert Wise, 1971.
Blade Runner. Dir. Ridley Scott, 1982.

A Boy and His Dog. Dir. L. Q. Jones, 1975.

Dawn of the Dead. Dir. George Romero, 1978.

The Day After. Dir. Nicholas Meyer, 1983.

The Day after Tomorrow. Dir. Roland Emmerich, 2004.

The Day the Earth Caught Fire. Dir. Val Guest, 1962.

The Day of the Triffids. Dir. Steve Sekely, 1962.

The Day the World Ended. Dir. Roger Corman, 1955.

Dr. Strangelove, or, How I Learned to Stop Worrying and Love the Bomb. Dir. Stanley Kubrick, 1964.

Fail-Safe. Dir. Sidney Lumet, 1964.

Five. Dir. Arch Obeler, 1951.

I Am Legend. Dir. Francis Lawrence, 2007.

Land *of the Dead*. Dir. George Romero, 2005.

The Last Man on Earth. Dir. Ubaldo Ragona, 1964.

Mad Max 2: The Road Warrior. Dir. George Miller, 1981.

The Matrix (1999), *The Matrix Reloaded* (2003), and *The Matrix Revolutions* (2003). Dirs. Andy Wachowski and Larry Wachowski, 1999.

Night of the Living Dead. Dir. George Romero, 1968.

The Omega Man. Dir. Boris Sagal, 1971.

On the Beach. Dir. Stanley Kramer, 1959.

Panic in Year Zero. Dir. Ray Milland, 1962.

Planet of the Apes. Dir. Franklin J. Schaffner, 1968.

Planet of the Apes. Dir. Tim Burton, 2001.

The Postman. Dir. Kevin Costner, 1997.

Seven Days in May. Dir. John Frankenheimer, 1964.

Silent Running. Dir. Douglas Trumbull, 1972.

Soylent Green. Dir. Richard Fleischer, 1973.

Tank Girl. Dir. Rachel Talalay, 1995.

The Terminator. Dir. James Cameron, 1984.

Terminator 2: Judgment Day. Dir. James Cameron, 1991.

Terminator 2: Judgment Day. Dir. James Cameron, 1991.

Terminator 3: Rise of the Machines. Dir. Jonathan Mostow, 2003.

Testament. *Dir. Lynne Littman, 1983.*

The Time Machine. Dir. George Pal, 1960.

Threads. Dir. Mick Jackson, 1985.

Twelve Monkeys. Dir. Terry Gilliam, 1995.

Waterworld. Dir. Kevin Reynolds, 1995.

World Without End. Dir. Edward Bernds, 1956.

Dystopian Science Fiction

If a utopia is an imaginary ideal society that dreams of a world in which the social, political, and economic problems of the real present have been solved (or at least in which effective mechanisms for the solutions to these problems are in place), then a dystopia is an imagined world in which the dream has become a nightmare. Also known as anti-utopias, dystopias are often designed to critique the potential negative implications of certain forms of utopian thought. However, dystopian fiction tends to have a strong satirical dimension that is designed to warn against the possible consequences of certain tendencies in the real world of the present. After a flurry of utopian fictions at the end of the nineteenth century, dystopian fiction became particularly prominent in the twentieth century, when suspicions of utopian solutions to political and social problems became increasingly strong as those problems grew more and more complicated and as events such as the rise of fascism in Europe seemed to cast doubt on the whole Western Enlightenment project.

If utopian societies are typically designed to enable the maximum fulfillment of individual human potential, dystopian societies impose oppressive conditions that interfere with that fulfillment. These oppressive conditions are usually extensions or exaggerations of conditions that already exist in the real world, allowing the dystopian text to critique real-world situations by placing them within the defamiliarizing context of an extreme fictional society. Dystopian fiction tends to focus on certain key motifs and ideas that in one way or another involve an opposition between social control and individual desire. In the dystopian state, however, social control generally has the upper hand. Official institutions such as churches, schools, and the police are used to regulate thought, imagination, and behavior, providing individuals with a very limited range for the expression of alternative viewpoints or exploration of alternative lifestyles. Modes of activity that Western societies have traditionally seen as crucial sites for the development of individual identity and fulfillment of individual desire (such as art and sexuality) tend to be monitored and controlled with a special intensity by dystopian regimes, often through the use of high technology devices for surveillance, mind control, and punishment.

The three crucial founding texts of modern dystopian science fiction are Yevgeny Zamyatin's *We* (1924), Aldous Huxley's *Brave New World* (1932), and George Orwell's *Nineteen Eighty-Four* (1949). These three texts directly address (and critique) the two major political systems of twentieth-century modernity. *We* warns against potential abuses of the postrevolutionary system in the Soviet Union; *Brave New World* looks in the other direction, projecting nightmarish extensions of the current system of Western capitalism; *Nineteen Eighty-Four* is suspicious of both capitalism and socialism, suggesting that either, as it exists in Orwell's 1940s world, has the potential to develop into an oppressive totalitarian system devoted primarily to its own preservation rather than to enriching the lives of its citizens. The plots of all three of these novels center around the (failed) attempts of individual heroes (Zamyatin's D-503, Huxley's Bernard Marx, and Orwell's Winston Smith) to overcome the suppression of individualism by their dystopian states. In this and other ways, they set the tone for many of the dystopian texts that followed them.

Written in the early years following the Bolshevik Revolution of 1917, *We* is an openly satirical text that makes no pretense toward realism. However, it establishes numerous motifs that would be central to later works of dystopian fiction, including later Soviet works such as Andrei Sinyavsky's *The Makepeace Experiment* (1963), Alexander Zinoviev's *The Yawning Heights* (1976), and Vladimir Voinovich's *Moscow 2042* (1987). It also exercised an especially obvious influence on Ayn Rand's *Anthem* (1938), an intensely individualistic American work of anti-Soviet dystopian fiction.

We addresses a number of issues and concerns of broad relevance to modern society, though it is most specifically aimed at Zamyatin's own Soviet context. For example, in stark contrast to the faith shown in science, technology, and rationality by Lenin and the other early Soviet leaders, *We* is centrally informed by a fear of the dehumanizing potential of technology and of an excessive insistence on rational solutions to all human problems. Importantly, however, *We* does not reject science and rationalism, per se, nor does it oppose the Bolshevik Revolution in itself. Nevertheless, it is powerful in its depiction of a sterile and stagnant One State of the distant future ruled so thoroughly by scientific and rational principles that its citizens have been stripped of any real humanity. The inhabitants of Zamyatin's dystopian society live in a sterile manmade environment from which nature has been excluded; they have numerical labels instead of names, and they are even referred to as numbers rather than people. These numbers have lost all true individuality; they are merely interchangeable parts in the giant machine of the State.

The rulers of the One State are particularly concerned with exerting control over those aspects of human life that might lead to strong emotions and thus disrupt the rational tranquility of life. For example, "free" sex is openly approved in the One State, though strictly regulated by the official bureaucracy. Poetry and music are similarly administered by the state. However, despite such official attempts to regulate the emotional lives of its citizens, the One State is unable to achieve the level of conformity and strict rationalism that it seeks. Thus, if *We* is extremely pessimistic in its depiction of the oppressive potential inherent in the ideology of the Bolshevik Revolution, it is optimistic in its suggestion that emotional forces like poetry and sexuality are ultimately beyond the complete control of the state. Indeed, as the text ends, an all-out rebellion against the state is underway; though the state responds with strong oppressive measures, the outcome of the rebellion remains in doubt.

If *We* was written at a time of great crisis in Soviet history, then Huxley's *Brave New World*, produced during the early years of the Great Depression of the 1930s, responded to a similar sense of crisis in Western capitalism. However, Huxley's text does not envision the downfall of capitalism, but its ultimate dehumanizing triumph. *Brave New World* portrays a hedonistic future society in which individuals spend most of their time in the pursuit of instant happiness through sex, drugs, and mind-numbing multisensory entertainments like the popular "feelies" that are continually broadcast to keep the minds and senses of the citizenry occupied at all times. At first glance, then, this society is far different from the more somber dystopias produced by writers like Zamyatin and Orwell. However, the emphasis on pleasure in Huxley's future society masks a deep-seated lack of individual liberty. The sex, drugs, and popular culture prevalent in this society are intended primarily to divert attention from social problems and to prevent individuals from developing any sort of strong feelings that might lead them to challenge official authority. This world state is populated by individuals who have been genetically engineered to fill specific roles, leaving little room for individual choice – and the state is willing to take extreme measures to keep it that way. In general, however, Huxley's dystopia works, not through the overt exercise of power that characterizes Zamyatin's One State, but through the more subtle manipulations that are typical of modern bourgeois society in the West.

The Party that rules the dystopian Oceania of Orwell's *Nineteen Eighty-Four* takes dystopian power a step further. Unlike many dystopian regimes, it makes no claims to attempt to save humanity or to improve the quality of human life. Instead, it seeks only to perpetuate its own power, which the Party functionary O'Brien images (echoing Jack London's 1907 dystopian novel *The Iron Heel*) as "a boot stamping on a human face." In short, the Party is consciously seeking to create the ultimate dystopia, a world that "is the exact opposite of the stupid hedonistic Utopias that the old reformers imagined." In describing this project, Orwell's book deals in important ways with almost all of the central motifs associated with dystopian fiction. For example, in the Oceania of Orwell's book certain mechanical applications of technology lend themselves directly to political oppression, even while science itself remains a potentially liberating realm of free thought. Religion has been conscripted by the state in the service of its own ideology, sexuality is strictly controlled to prevent strong emotional attachments between partners, and art and culture are used as tools for direct propagation of the official ideology. Perhaps the two most striking motifs in *Nineteen Eighty-Four*, however, are the revisionist manipulation of history in order to provide support for the programs of the ruling Party and the attempt to institute a new language, "Newspeak," that will allow expression only of ideas that are consistent with the Party's policies.

Orwell's text is a sort of summation of the dystopian tradition through the end of the 1940s. It has exercised a powerful influence on that tradition since its publication, with numerous direct successors, such as Anthony Burgess's *A Clockwork Orange* (1962), perhaps most notable for its depiction of psychological conditioning as a tool of official power. *Nineteen Eighty-Four* also has numerous predecessors, building in a particularly direct way upon a British tradition of dystopian fiction that developed in the 1930s, beginning with *Brave New World*. In *To Tell the Truth ...* (1933), for example, Amabel Williams-Ellis follows Huxley in warning of the dystopian potential of capitalism. She imagines a Britain in which the worst tendencies of the early 1930s have continued to develop, producing a grim, authoritarian, and impoverished (though in many ways technologically advanced) society. Meanwhile, in a motif that echoes *Brave New World*, the cultural apparatus in Britain has been almost entirely successful in suppressing any sense that concerted working-class action might bring about a change in the grim conditions that dominate this society.

Other British dystopian fictions of the 1930s were constructed specifically as warnings against the looming dangers of fascism – itself a sort of dystopian version of capitalism. Works in this vein include Storm Jameson's *In the Second Year* (1936), Katharine Burdekin's *Swastika Night* (1937), and Ruthven Todd's *Over the Mountain* (1939). Of these, Burdekin's book is probably the most important. Set 700 years after a Nazi conquest of

Britain, it imagines a future world dominated by competing German and Japanese empires, with Europe (including Britain) and Africa ruled by the Germans. The dissemination of information in this future world is strictly controlled. Books, in fact, have been entirely banned (except for one sacred "Hitler book"), and virtually all citizens are illiterate. History has been almost entirely forgotten, the only records of the past being highly mythologized versions in which Hitler has been promoted to the status of a god and all memories of any civilizations before German Nazism forgotten.

Sinclair Lewis's *It Can't Happen Here* (1935) provides an American example of the antifascist dystopia, warning that excessive fear of communism might push the United States toward fascism. Meanwhile, the banning of books in Burdekin's fascist dystopia is also a common theme in American dystopian fiction, which often depicts books and literature as powerful threats to the power of dystopian regimes. In the United States, probably the most vivid exploration of this theme appears in Ray Bradbury's *Fahrenheit 451* (1951), where an oppressive state employs teams of "firemen," whose job it is to seek out and burn books, which are strictly forbidden in this society. In lieu of books, the culture of Bradbury's future America (a direct extension of his own early 1950s context) consists of an incessant electronic barrage of popular culture that seems designed partly to purvey the official ideology of the society, but mostly to stupefy the populace by saturating their minds with useless information, much in the mode of the popular culture of *Brave New World*. Meanwhile, Bradbury depicts a thoroughly commercialized consumer culture stripped of all spirituality. The Bible itself is banned, along with all other books, and Jesus Christ now appears on television as a sort of celebrity endorser of commercial products.

Kurt Vonnegut's *Player Piano* (1952) also responds to certain specific American anxieties of the early 1950s, this time focusing on the fear that automation was beginning to make human labor obsolete, while at the same time turning people into machine-like automatons living thoroughly scripted, regulated lives. In the dystopian United States of *Player Piano*, citizens are carefully screened, tested, and categorized during their schooldays so that they can be slotted for their proper place in society. Computerized systems then keep up with these test results to ensure that their recommendations are followed. Meanwhile, even the most minor deviations from accepted behavioral patterns are recorded and stored in a massive police information system, so that potential "saboteurs" can be closely watched.

Player Piano is a typical work of dystopian sf in its concern with technological advances that are clearly intended to bring about a utopian existence but lead instead to the opposite. Then again, there is often a fine line between utopia and dystopia, and one person's dream society might be another person's nightmare. Indeed, many sf novels include both utopian and dystopian characteristics, as in the case of Samuel R. Delany's *Trouble on Triton* (1976). Meanwhile, a work such as B. F. Skinner's *Walden Two* (1948), clearly designed by the author as an exploration of the utopian potential of psychological conditioning and scientific social design, has struck many readers as a dystopian text. Skinner refuses even to give lip service to the notion of individual liberty, arguing that freedom is in fact an illusion and that all human beings are determined rather strictly by their environment. Moreover, he suggests that democracy is an illusion as well, being tantamount to tyranny by a majority that is ill-qualified to make intelligent decisions.

New concerns with environmentalism and overpopulation in the 1960s brought these themes to dystopian fiction as well. Burgess's *The Wanting Seed* (1962) is centrally concerned with the dangers of overpopulation, projecting a future England in which overpopulation has led to a serious decline in the quality of life and to the institution of severe measures to try to limit population growth. In an American context, a similar concern with overpopulation informs Harry Harrison's *Make Room! Make Room!* (1966), which grimly depicts social and political problems arising from overcrowding – though the novel actually lacks the Swiftian theme of using human beings for food that made *Soylent Green*, the 1973 film adaptation of Harrison's novel, so memorable. Meanwhile, this film was typical of the dystopian turn taken by American sf film in the early 1970s. In 1971 alone, several films projected a dark future, with Stanley Kubrick's adaptation of *A Clockwork Orange* and George Lucas's *THX-1138* providing central examples of dystopian film. Other dark visions of the future followed, including Douglas Trumbull's *Silent Running* (1972), Norman Jewison's *Rollerball* (1975), and Michael Anderson's *Logan's Run* (1976). These dystopian visions of the future set a precedent for important films such as Michael Radford's 1984 adaptation of Orwell's *Nineteen Eighty-Four* (1949), perhaps the most important of all dystopian novels. By contrast, Woody Allen's *Sleeper* (1973) is a farcical parody of the dystopian genre, while former Monty Python member Terry Gilliam followed in 1985 with *Brazil*, which also presents a parodic dystopia, but makes many of the same serious satirical points for which the subgenre is well known. Films such as John Carpenter's *They Live* (1988), Andrew Niccol's *Gattaca* (1997), and Alex Proyas's *Dark City* (1998) continue this tradition.

Perhaps the finest dystopian novel about overpopulation is John Brunner's *Stand on Zanzibar* (1968), a massive and highly ambitious work that employs a number of complex literary strategies to explore numerous issues in its fictional world of the early twenty-first-century. *Stand on Zanzibar*, meanwhile, ushered in a remarkable sequence of dystopian novels by Brunner that also included *The Jagged Orbit* (1969), *The Sheep Look Up* (1972), and *The Shockwave Rider* (1975). Of these, *The Jagged Orbit* focuses on racism and the criminalistic tendencies of the military-industrial complex, while *The Shockwave Rider* focuses on the impact of a worldwide communications explosion, in many ways anticipating the later phenomenon of cyberpunk science fiction, a movement that has itself shown considerable dystopian leanings.

If the 1970s saw a resurgence of utopian energy in science fiction, especially in sf written by women, patriarchy and gender discrimination also became central concerns of a number of dystopian novels by women, beginning with works such as Suzy McKee Charnas's *Walk to the End of the World* (1974) and Marge Piercy's *Woman at the Edge of Time* (1976), though the latter is a complex text that projects two alternative futures, one dystopian and one utopian. Joanna Russ's *The Female Man* (1975) also includes both utopian and dystopian elements from a feminist perspective. Probably the leading example of the subgenre of women's dystopian fiction is Margaret Atwood's *The Handmaid's Tale* (1985), which responds to the Reaganite 1980s with a horrifying account of a near future dystopian regime ruled by right-wing religious fundamentalists, much to the detriment of women, who often find themselves employed essentially as sexual slaves for breeding purposes.

An interesting spin on the gender dystopia is *The Children of Men* (1992), by the noted British mystery writer P. D. James. Here, turning the overpopulation theme on its head, all of the world's sperm (including supplies frozen in sperm banks) are suddenly and inexplicably rendered inert in the year 1995, leaving humanity with no prospects of continuing the species beyond the generation born that year. Left without hope for a longterm future, humanity sinks into despair. British society, on which the book focuses, becomes decidedly dysfunctional, until a dictatorial "Warden" manages to reestablish order at the expense of dystopian repression. By the year 2021, in which the book is set, the general population, having grimly acknowledged that humanity is doomed anyway, accepts this repression without complaint.

Grim dystopian futures remain current in American sf as well. Octavia Butler's *The Parable of the Sower* (1993) and Jack Womack's *Random Acts of Senseless Violence* (1993) depict an American society declining into violence and chaos. Womack, meanwhile, has projected a dystopian future dominated by the huge Dryco Corporation in a sequence of novels that includes the highly interesting *Elvissey* (1993), in which a cult based on

Elvis Presley-worship provides the only rival to Dryco's considerable power. Indeed, with the Cold War over and global socialism routed, at least for the time being, many dystopian visions from the 1990s forward focus on the possible abuses of growing corporate power. Examples of this phenomenon range from the rampant privatization depicted in such texts as Neal Stephenson's *Snow Crash* (1992) and Max Barry's *Jennifer Government* (2003), to the sinister manipulation of Third World politics by violence-prone Western corporations in Richard Morgan's *Market Forces* (2005), to a more conventional (if comic) dystopian vision of the dehumanizing consequences of corporate culture in Barry's *Company* (2006). Bruce Sterling's *Distraction* (1998) is also worthy of mention as a dystopian projection of social problems already in evidence in the United States in the late 1990s.

Such films as Ridley Scott's *Blade Runner* (1982), Paul Verhoeven's *Total Recall* (1990), and Steven Spielberg's *Minority Report* (2002) – all based on stories by Philip K. Dick – have presented visions of a dark (often corporate-dominated) future. Indeed, many of Dick's novels and stories include strong dystopian elements, even if they are not pure examples of dystopian fiction. A particularly successful recent dystopian film is *The Matrix* (1999), which is not based on Dick's work, but echoes many of his themes. It depicts a nightmare future in which humanity has been enslaved by machines but is kept unaware of its enslavement though mental entrapment in a virtual alternative reality. Kurt Wimmer's *Equilibrium* (2002), which shows a strong *Matrix* influence, is dystopian in a more classic vein in its depiction of an oppressive future government that insists on the drug-induced repression of all emotion in the general population.

All in all, dystopian fiction remains one of the most important subgenres of science fiction in the early twenty-first century. Dystopian narratives, especially if read as cautionary satires that critique the current order (rather than lurid fantasies that make the current order appear preferable in comparison), also remain one of the most potentially useful forms of sf. This potential is best fulfilled, however, when the dystopian critique of the possible negative consequences of current technological, social, and political trends is accompanied by suggestions of the possibility of viable preferable alternatives. In this sense, it is clear that dystopian fiction is not the opposite of utopian fiction but a kind of supplement to it.

Suggested Further Reading

Baccolini, Raffaella, and Tom Moylan, eds. *Dark Horizons: Science Fiction and the Dystopian Imagination*. New York: Routledge, 2003.

Booker, M. Keith. *The Dystopian Impulse in Modern Literature: Fiction as Social Criticism*. Westport, CT: Greenwood Press, 1994.

Booker, M. Keith. *Dystopian Literature: A Theory and Research Guide*. Westport, CT: Greenwood Press, 1994.

Hillegas, Mark R. *The Future as Nightmare*. New York: Oxford University Press, 1967.

Kumar, Krishan. *Utopia and Anti-Utopia in Modern Times*. Oxford: Blackwell, 1987.

Moylan, Tom. *Scraps of Untainted Sky: Science Fiction, Utopia, Dystopia*. Boulder, CO: Westview Press, 2000.

Notable Fiction

Margaret Atwood, *The Handmaid's Tale* (1985).

Max Barry, *Jennifer Government* (2003) and *Company* (2006).

Katharine Burdekin, *Swastika Night* (1937).

Karin Boye, *Kallocain* (1940).

Ray Bradbury, *Fahrenheit 451* (1951).

John Brunner, *Stand on Zanzibar* (1968), *The Jagged Orbit* (1969), *The Sheep Look Up* (1972), and *The Shockwave Rider* (1975).

Katharine Burdekin, *Swastika Night* (1937).

Anthony Burgess, *A Clockwork Orange* (1962) and *The Wanting Seed* (1962).

Octavia Butler, *The Parable of the Sower* (1993).

Suzy McKee Charnas, *Walk to the End of the World* (1974).

Samuel R. Delany, *Trouble on Triton* (1976).

Philip K. Dick, *Do Androids Dream of Electric Sheep?* (1968).

Thomas M. Disch, *Camp Concentration* (1968).

Harry Harrison, *Make Room! Make Room!* (1966).

Aldous Huxley, *Brave New World* (1932).

P. D. James, *The Children of Men* (1992).

Storm Jameson, *The Second Year* (1936).

Jonathan Lethem, *Amnesia Moon* (1995).

Sinclair Lewis, *It Can't Happen Here* (1935).

Jack London, *The Iron Heel* (1907).

Barry Malzberg, *Guernica Night* (1974).

Richard K. Morgan, *Market Forces* (2005).

Walter Mosley, *Futureland* (2001).

George Orwell, *Nineteen Eighty-Four* (1949).

Marge Piercy, *Woman at the Edge of Time* (1976).

Ayn Rand, *Anthem* (1938).

Joanna Russ, *The Female Man* (1975).

B. F. Skinner, *Walden Two* (1948).

Neal Stephenson, *Snow Crash* (1992).

Bruce Sterling, *Distraction* (1998).
Ruthven Todd, *Over the Mountain* (1939).
Kurt Vonnegut Jr., *Player Piano* (1952).
Annabel Williams-Ellis, *To Tell the Truth* ... (1933).
Jack Womack, *Ambient* (1987), *Heathern* (1990), *Elvissey* (1993), and *Random Acts of Senseless Violence* (1993).
Evgeny Zamyatin, *We* (1924).

Notable Films

Alphaville. Dir. Jean-Luc Godard, 1965.
Blade Runner. Dir. Ridley Scott, 1982.
Brazil. Dir. Terry Gilliam, 1985.
A Clockwork Orange. Dir. Stanley Kubrick, 1971.
Dark City. Dir. Alex Proyas, 1998.
Equilibrium. Dir. Kurt Wimmer, 2002.
Gattaca. Dir. Andrew Niccol, 1997.
Logan's Run. Dir. Michael Anderson, 1976.
The Matrix (1999), *The Matrix Reloaded* (2003), and *The Matrix Revolutions* (2003). Dirs. Andy Wachowski and Larry Wachowski, 1999.
Metropolis. Dir. Fritz Lang, 1927.
Minority Report. Dir. Steven Spielberg, 2002.
Nineteen Eighty-Four. Dir. Michael Radford, 1984.
Rollerball. Dir. Norman Jewison, 1975.
Silent Running. Dir. Douglas Trumbull, 1972.
Sleeper. Dir. Woody Allen, 1973.
Soylent Green. Dir. Richard Fleischer, 1973.
They Live. Dir. John Carpenter, 1988.
THX 1138. Dir. George Lucas, 1971.
Total Recall. Dir. Paul Verhoeven, 1990.
V for Vendetta. Dir. James McTeigue, 2005.

Utopian Fiction

Utopian thought attempts to envision a society in which the various social, political, and economic ills of the real world have been solved, leaving an ideal realm of justice and tranquility. All fiction, by projecting a world that is different from the real, physical one, has a potential utopian component. Indeed, the attempt to imagine a world better than our own has long been recognized as one of the crucial functions of all literature. Nevertheless, some works of literature are more specifically dedicated to the projection of utopian visions than are others. There is, in fact, an entire tradition of utopian fiction, often with a strong science fiction component, that attempts to envision ideal societies, generally far removed from the author's world either temporally or geographically.

The tradition of utopian fiction dates back at least as far as the ancient Greeks, who produced a number of utopian works, the most important of which is Plato's *Republic* (380–370 BC), especially in terms of its influence on later utopian writers. The most fundamental political principle of Plato's ideal republic is rule by an enlightened elite of specially trained, philosophically minded thinkers, known as the Guardians. This elitism, of course, would be abhorrent to many in the modern world, as is Plato's tendency to argue that individual freedom should be sacrificed in the interest of greater happiness for all. This early work thus already indicates the potentially problematic nature of all programmatic utopian visions.

The next major contribution to the tradition of utopian fiction was Sir Thomas More's *Utopia* (1516), the book that gave the tradition its name. More's utopia is more concrete than Plato's in that his ideal society is located in an actual physical setting (an island off the coast of South America), even though the Greek word utopia literally means "no place." More, by describing the visit of a European (Raphael Hythloday) to the island, also gives his work a more narrative bent than Plato's, helping to establish a generic model for future writers of utopian fiction. More's book makes clear the important satirical component that resides in almost all utopian fiction in that his ideal society is quite specifically set against his own present-day England as a way of criticizing the ills of that real-world society.

Other utopian works, such as Tommaso Campanella's *The City of the Sun* (1602–1623) and Francis Bacon's *New Atlantis* (1627) followed soon after More's, but the tradition of utopian fiction received a special boost from the eighteenth century onward, when humanist faith in the potential of science and of human beings in general led to a widespread growth in notions that an ideal society, based on the principles of the Enlightenment, could literally be established. These more modern utopian visions culminated in the late nineteenth and early twentieth centuries, when a spate of utopian fictions, often inspired by socialist ideals, appeared. These centrally included Edward Bellamy's *Looking Backward* (1888), William Morris's *News From Nowhere* (1890), and H. G. Wells's *A Modern Utopia* (1905).

The utopia of *Looking Backward* centrally depends on technological and industrial efficiency and can in some ways be seen as the culmination of the Enlightenment faith in the ability of reason and rationality to build a better world. However, some, even at the time, saw this emphasis on efficiency as potentially dehumanizing, and Morris's more agrarian utopia is in large part a critical response to Bellamy's work. Wells's book, as the title suggests, represents a particular step forward in the genre, away from philosophical and sociological speculation and toward science fiction. Meanwhile, science fiction itself grew into a well-defined genre in the pulp magazines of the 1920s and 1930s, and the stories in these magazines (spurred by the technological optimism of editors such as Hugo Gernsback) typically contained strong utopian elements in their vision of a future world made better thanks to the availability of advanced technologies.

In the meantime, occasional non-technological utopian visions had made their way into modern literature. One of the most influential of these was Charlotte Perkins Gilman's *Herland* (1915), a feminist utopia that provided considerable inspiration for the wave of such utopias that began to appear in the 1970s, drawing upon the momentum of the women's movement of the 1960s. *Herland*, the most important of three utopian novels written by Gilman, describes an all-woman society from which men have been excluded for two thousand years. This highly literary work is openly fictional, employing a number of devices to enhance its central project, which is not so much the projection of a literal feminist society as a satirical critique of Gilman's own early-twentieth-century America through the defamiliarizing lens of the feminist society of the book.

Perhaps the most important book-length fictions informed by utopian themes to appear in the 1930s were those produced by the British socialist writer Olaf Stapledon, including *Last and First Men* (1930) and *Star Maker* (1937). Here Stapledon envisions the development of highly advanced far future societies in which humanity has evolved to the point of over-coming the negative inclinations (such as individualism) of our own world. Stapledon's interests are largely philosophical and he deals relatively little with advanced technology or with politics, though his work is informed by a consistent antipathy toward capitalism and fascism and often nods toward commentary on his contemporary world.

One of the most interesting and unusual utopian fictions to appear in the 1940s also did not depend on technological optimism, but instead envi-sioned an idyllic South Pacific island paradise in which technology was virtually non-existent. *Islandia* (1942) is the result of the extensive attempts of legal philosopher Austin Tappan Wright to imagine a realistic island utopia over a period that began in his childhood in the late nineteenth century and extended to his death in 1931. As a result of Wright's exhaus-tive work on the project, *Islandia* (edited after his death into the form of a publishable novel by his widow and daughter) presents one of the most detailed descriptions of a utopian society in all of literature. The book is especially forward-looking in its treatment of women, and its anticolonial-ism (which emerges as a result of a conflict between the culture of the community of Islandia and that of the United States, clearly resolved in favor of the former) is ahead of its time as well. On the other hand, Wright was more interested in constructing a model society than in storytelling, so the narrative elements of the book are unusually weak, even for a subgenre that has often been criticized for the weakness of its narratives. This weak-ness might help to explain the relative absence of genuine utopias in science fiction film, though it should be pointed out that the future Earth that serves as a background to the various *Star Trek* television series (which inspired a string of feature films as well) is a utopian society in which all social, economic, and political problems appear to have been solved, largely because advanced technologies have ushered in a post-scarcity era.

The best-known utopian work of the 1940s is B. F. Skinner's *Walden Two*, in which the author, himself a well-known behavioral psychologist, envisions a presumably ideal community centrally informed by the careful behavioral conditioning of the entire population. Skinner's book focuses on the "Walden Two" of the title, a utopian community set in the American countryside. Walden Two works, Skinner insists, because it is based on a plan that produces citizens who are specifically conditioned to live happily and well within the structure of this particular community. Most of the action concerns a tour of the community by a group of outside visitors who have come to see how it functions. The founder and principal planner of

Walden Two conducts the tour and explains (to the visitors and thus to readers) the principles upon which the community is based. Central to these principles is a respect for science and scientific principles of efficiency. This efficiency includes many elements within the purview of traditional utopian thought, including the usual social factors like education and economics, with a particular emphasis on undoing the negative effects of the traditional family structure. Skinner acknowledges his place in the tradition of utopian literature with frequent allusions to predecessors like More, Bellamy, Wells, and Morris, clearly drawing upon many of the conventions of the subgenre as established by these predecessors. On the other hand, though intended by its author as a serious exploration of the possibility of a *utopian* society, *Walden Two* nicely demonstrates the fine line between utopia and dystopia in the way that its ideal society strikes so many readers as *dystopian*. For example, in their massive 1952 anthology of utopian thought, Negley and Patrick declare Skinner's book an outrage to the utopian spirit and describe his vision as a "shocking horror" (*Quest*, 590). Indeed, many readers have found in the psychological determinism of *Walden Two* a nightmare dystopian vision in which human beings are reduced to unthinking automatons.

By the time the science fiction novel came into its own amid the post-World War II boom in paperback publishing, science fiction (largely owing to the development of nuclear weapons) was growing more and more skeptical that technology was necessarily a boon to humanity. However, at least one key sf novelist of the 1950s, Theodore Sturgeon, stands out for the strong utopian dimension that informs his work, perhaps as a reaction against the anti-utopianism of most of the culture around him. Sturgeon's *Venus Plus X* (1960) tops off his work of the 1950s with a novel that explicitly describes a potentially utopian society. Actually, *Venus Plus X* has a dual plot structure. In one plot line, protagonist Charlie Johns awakes, bewildered, in Ledom (read "Model"), apparently a utopian society of the far future. In the alternating chapters, Herb Raile and family live a typically 1950s suburban existence. Raile works for an advertising agency and is thus ideally placed to observe the emerging consumer culture of the 1950s, which is starkly contrasted with the nonconsumerist society of Ledom.

Life in Ledom heavily depends on advanced technology, though all of the inhabitants value agrarian existence and spend considerable time in the countryside. Ledom differs most dramatically from 1950s America, however, in its attitudes toward sex and gender. As opposed to the repressive attitudes of the 1950s (which are foregrounded in the alternating chapters), sex in Ledom is considered a normal and healthy activity that is undertaken only as an expression of mutual affection. Further, this attitude is supported because all citizens of Ledom undergo surgical procedures that efface biological gender difference by making all Ledomians hermaphrodites, leaving gender entirely as a social construction. This motif, however, suggests that, in order to achieve utopian conditions, it is necessary to alter human nature, in this case by surgery. Moreover, that this surgery involves an eradication of gender difference suggests that utopia cannot be achieved without the suppression of difference. On the other hand, the book ends with the revelation that Johns is actually Quesbu, a Ledomian who has not undergone the procedure – and he is allowed to remain unaltered, along with his mate, Soutin, in a move toward restoration of the original human race.

Venus Plus X anticipates many of the concerns about sex and sexuality of the 1960s, though it is clearly rooted in the 1950s, including the fact that its version of the 1950s ends in an apparent nuclear holocaust – though the Ledomians live on in their domed city, which turns out (in one of several late plot twists) not to exist in the far future at all. Among other things, the novel thus reminds us that the resurgent utopianism of the 1960s had roots in the 1950s and should not be read merely as a reaction against the earlier decade. In fact, while the utopian dimension of Western culture in general became particularly weak in the postwar period, thinkers such as the Marxist utopian Ernst Bloch both kept the utopian spirit alive and developed more sophisticated and open-ended visions of what utopian might be. In particular, for Bloch utopia is not an achieved goal but a future potential to be continually sought after, even after oppression and exploitation have been eliminated from human society.

Bloch's work exerted an important influence on the oppositional political movements of the 1960s, which themselves inspired something of a renaissance in the subgenre of utopian fiction in the 1970s, heralded by the appearance of such precursor works as R. A. Lafferty's *Past Master* (1968) and Monique Wittig's *Les Guérillères* (1969). Of these, the latter is informed by strong feminist impulses that foreshadow the centrality of feminist themes – or at least themes related to gender – to the utopian renaissance of the 1970s. Among the works of this renaissance (many of which also include dystopian elements) are Christiane Rochefort's *Archaos, or the Sparkling Garden* (1972), Suzy McKee Charnas's *Walk to the End of the World* (1974) and *Motherlines* (1978), Joanna Russ's *The Female Man* (1975), Marge Piercy's *Woman on the Edge of Time* (1976), E. M. Broner's *A Weave of Women* (1978), Louky Bersianil's *The Eugélionne* (1978), Sally Miller Gearheart's *The Wanderground: Stories of the Hill Women* (1978), and Suzette Haden Elgin's *Native Tongue* (1984). Gender was also central to the utopian visions of two of the most important science fiction novels of the 1970s, Ursula K. Le Guin's *The Dispossessed* (1974) and

Samuel R. Delany's *Trouble on Triton* (1976), both of which illustrate particularly well the attempts of the utopian science fiction novels of the 1970s to overcome conventional concerns that utopian societies inevitably drift into stagnation and repression. They thus contributed to the growth of the so-called "open" or "critical" utopias that were typical of this period.

Le Guin is worthy of special mention among the utopian writers of the 1970s. Not only is *The Dispossessed* possibly the centerpiece of the decade's utopian renaissance, but several of Le Guin's works include utopian elements, as when *The Lathe of Heaven* (1971) explores a variety of both utopian and dystopian scenarios. Also worthy of special mention in this context is Mack Reynolds, a former socialist labor party activist who produced a large volume of science fiction in the 1960s to the 1980s, most of it clearly informed by his leftist political vision. Much of his work is set in future utopian societies based on socialist principles, including the novels *Looking Backward, from the Year 2000* (1973) and *Equality in the Year 2000* (1977), both of which revisit and update the late-nineteenth-century socialist vision of Bellamy's utopian novels.

Though Reynolds's utopian vision grows out of older socialist traditions, most of the utopias of the 1970s were more specifically keyed to the political concerns of the moment, as with the utopias that grew out of the women's movement. Ernest Callenbach's *Ecotopia* (1975) is a central literary expression of the utopian hopes of several of the oppositional political movements of the 1960s. Informed especially by the insights of the emergent environmentalist movement, *Ecotopia* describes a secessionist utopian state on the west coast of the United States, organized according to largely socialist principles and dedicated to respect for and preservation of the Earth's natural environment. In a classic utopian motif, reporter William Weston travels to Ecotopia to do a story for his newspaper, and his observations reveal the society to readers as well. Perhaps the most striking aspect of Ecotopia is the disavowal of growth. It is a zero sum "stable state" society that maintains stability – but not stagnation. That is, zero sum means no net growth but it in no way implies the absence of change. This stable state is furthered through a variety of environmentally friendly policies, such as an extensive recycling program. Liberal education and penal policies help to maintain human conditions for all citizens, while sexual attitudes generally reflect the sexual revolution of the 1960s. Anticapitalist economic measures have driven most US corporations out of Ecotopia. The remaining economic system, though it retains some elements of free-market capitalism, has numerous socialist characteristics, including relative economic equality for all citizens, worker-owned companies, reformed working conditions, and universally guaranteed social services.

Ecotopia was followed by a less successful prequel, *Ecotopia Emerging* (1981), while *Ecotopia* itself has shown surprising staying power as a text that is still read and studied more than thirty years after its initial publication. It also exerted a clear influence on the "green" utopia of Kim Stanley Robinson's *Pacific Edge* (1990), the third volume of Robinson's remarkable "Three Californias" trilogy. Both utopian and environmental concerns remained central to Robinson's subsequent career, which has included, among other things, the editing of *Future Primitive: The New Ecotopias* (1994), a collection of stories describing ecological utopias.

Distinctive among the utopias of the 1970s for the way it looks back to the technological optimism of earlier decades is George Zebrowski's *Macrolife* (1979). Building upon the speculative vision of scientist Dandridge Cole (who coined the term "macrolife") Zebrowski imagines the development of high-tech space habitats (the first of which is merely a hollowed-out asteroid) that travel about the galaxy while their inhabitants (human, alien, artificial, or hybrid) gradually develop their individual potentials thanks to a post-scarcity economy that has solved all social ills and a high-tech environment that has, among other things, made it possible for individuals to live practically forever. On the other hand, individualism as we know it eventually ceases to exist as the individuals in these habitats become increasingly networked into one huge system. In fact, each of these traveling habitats, or "macroworlds," is envisioned essentially as a giant organism of which each individual (whether organic beings or artificial intelligences) is a component part. The smooth functioning of the macroworld thus requires particularly close cooperation and agreement among the individuals that compose it, but this is no real problem, even in the early stages of the evolution of macrolife, when distinct individuals still exist: as disagreements naturally arise, additional worlds are simply manufactured and subsequently inhabited by members of subgroups who have similar opinions and outlooks.

Eventually, macrolife spreads across the universe, advancing for billions of years into a highly evolved state. Virtually all obstacles have been surmounted, except one: the eventual collapse and death of the universe itself. Macrolife is by this time so advanced, however, that it manages to concoct a successful scheme to survive even this cataclysm, moving forward into the birth of a subsequent universe – followed, as it turns out, by another, older, form of macrolife that had surreptitiously survived the collapse of a still earlier universe, living on into our own. In its vision of radical far future evolution, *Macrolife* has often been compared to the work of Stapledon, though its vision of social evolution relies much more on specific advanced technologies than does Stapledon's.

The Reagan–Thatcher neo-conservative retrenchment of the 1980s was also accompanied by a waning in the production of utopian fictions, especially as science fiction came, for a brief period, to be dominated by the cyberpunk subgenre, the utopian dimensions of which were notoriously weak, or at least difficult to discern. However, with the sudden fall of the Soviet Union in 1991, the political climate in the United States and Britain, where utopianism had come to be vaguely associated with the presumed evils of the Soviet menace, became much more hospitable to the production of utopian fictions. Indeed, the most important science fiction work of the 1990s, Kim Stanley Robinson's "Mars" trilogy, is particularly rich in utopian energies. In *Red Mars* (1993), *Green Mars* (1994), and *Blue Mars* (1996) Robinson relates the colonization and terraforming of the red planet, including detailed debates among its colonists of the directions in which they should move to take maximum advantage of the utopian potential of an entire new planet.

The 1990s were also remarkable in the history of science fiction for the emergence into prominence of a talented group of British science fiction and fantasy writers (collectively constituting what came to be known as the British Boom) who added new utopian energies to a variety of older genres of speculative fiction. For example, China Miéville, perhaps the central figure in the British Boom, has injected new utopian energies into the genre of fantasy (once dominated by Tolkienesque escapism) by establishing clear connections between his imaginary worlds and the real contemporary world in which we all live. Among more properly science fictional subgenres, space opera and cyberpunk (now morphed into postcyberpunk) have been particularly re-energized by British Boomers such as the politically aware Scottish authors Charles Stross and Ken MacLeod, both of whom have imagined socialist-anarchist utopian futures made possible by vast advances in computer technology and artificial intelligence, though both (in good Blochian fashion) are more interested in the movement toward utopia (beginning with a sudden, explosive advance in the capabilities of artificial intelligence via a technological singularity) than in the description of actual existing ideal societies.

Within the context of overt utopianism, the leading figure of the British Boom is probably still another Scottish writer, Iain M. Banks. A writer with a substantial reputation as an author of both literary fiction and science fiction, Banks also envisions a post-singularity world inhabited by vastly advanced artificial intelligences. However, Banks goes well beyond Stross and MacLeod in providing a detailed description of an interstellar socialist utopia, known as the Culture. The product of thousands of years of biological, social, and cultural evolution, the Culture employs ultra-advanced technology (managed by sophisticated artificial intelligences known as Minds) to produce post-scarcity conditions in which the human (or, more accurately, posthuman) inhabitants live rich and virtually endless lives devoted to leisure, recreation, culture, education, and exploration of their individual potentials.

Banks takes a science fiction scenario (rule by machines) that has often been treated as dystopian and makes it unapologetically utopian, informed by both socialist and anarchist principles. The Minds are far superior to humans in intelligence, but they are also deeply devoted to caring for humans and to making it possible for humans to live the richest lives possible. There are no actual laws, and behavior is regulated largely by social convention in an almost aesthetic way as individuals seek to live their lives in good style. Because there is plenty of wealth for everyone, the society functions smoothly with a minimum of interference from the Minds, who intercede in human affairs only when necessary, preferring simply to provide a framework within which humans can live. This framework includes extensive interstellar travel, though most humans live primarily on huge Orbitals, artificial ring-like structures (with populations of many billions) that rotate in space near stars, something like the Ringworld envisioned by Larry Niven in his 1970 novel of the same title, except that an Orbital is much smaller and does not extend around its star, as does Niven's Ring-world.

Though the problems of ordinary existence within the Culture have largely been solved, the Culture must also coexist with other civilizations that are not necessarily so advanced. This situation sometimes leads to all-out war, as in the conflict between the Culture and the religious, warlike Idirans in Banks's first Culture novel, *Consider Phlebas* (1987). Such conflicts help Banks to create interesting narratives, while also providing a dialectical vision of the Culture through descriptions of it by outsiders and even enemies. The most problematic aspect of the Culture is its tendency toward interventionism, in which it surreptitiously attempts to steer less-advanced civilizations in more positive and humane directions. In this, the Culture would seem to echo all too closely the imperialist tendencies of advanced nations on Earth, except that here one must consider that the Minds are so advanced that they really *are* qualified to guide other societies, whereas the wealthier and more powerful nations on Earth are not.

The works of writers such as Robinson, Stross, MacLeod, and (especially) Banks show a refreshing resurgence of hope in the ability of technology to bring about better societies. In this, they look back to the science fiction of the 1930s, except that their technological projections are much more believable, while the novels are also informed by much more sophisticated social and political ideas. The fictions of such writers thus suggest a potential renaissance in utopian thinking, a phenomenon that itself suggests bold new possibilities for the evolution of real-world human societies as we move into a new millennium.

Suggested Further Reading

Bartkowski, Frances. *Feminist Utopias*. Lincoln, NE: University of Nebraska Press, 1989.

Bloch, Ernst. *The Principle of Hope*. 3 vols. Trans. Neville Plaice, Stephen Plaice, and Paul Knight. Cambridge, MA: MIT Press, 1995.

Firchow, Peter Edgerly. *Modern Utopian Fictions from H. G. Wells to Iris Murdoch*. Washington, DC: Catholic University of America Press, 2007.

Jameson, Fredric. *Archaeologies of the Future: The Desire Called Utopia and Other Science Fictions*. London: Verso, 2005.

Kumar, Krishan. *Utopia and Anti-Utopia in Modern Times*. Oxford: Basil Blackwell, 1987.

Manuel, Frank and Fritzie P. Manuel, eds. *Utopian Thought in the Western World*. Cambridge, MA: Harvard University Press, 1979.

Negley, Glenn, and J. Max Patrick, eds. *The Quest for Utopia: An Anthology of Imaginary Societies*. New York: Henry Schuman, 1952.

Sargent, Lyman Tower. "The Three Faces of Utopianism Revisited." *Utopian Studies* 5.1 (1994): 1–37.

Schaer, Roland, Gregory Claeys, and Lyman Tower Sargent, eds. *Utopia: The Search for the Ideal Society in the Western World*. New York: Oxford University Press, 2000.

Wegner, Phillip E. *Imaginary Communities: Utopia, the Nation, and the Spatial Histories of Modernity*. Berkeley: University of California Press, 2002.

Notable Fiction

Iain M. Banks, *Consider Phlebas* (1987), *The Player of Games* (1988), *Use of Weapons* (1990), *Excession* (1996), *Inversions* (1998), and *Look to Windward* (2000).

Edward Bellamy, *Looking Backward* (1888).

Louky Bersianil, *The Eugélionne* (1978).

E. M. Broner, *A Weave of Women* (1978).

Ernest Callenbach, *Ecotopia* (1975) and *Ecotopia Emerging* (1981).

Suzy McKee Charnas, *Walk to the End of the World* (1974) and *Motherlines* (1978).

Samuel R. Delany, *Trouble on Trion* (1976).

Suzette Haden Elgin, *Native Tongue* (1984).

Sally Miller Gearheart, *The Wanderground: Stories of the Hill Women* (1978).

Charlotte Perkins Gilman, *Herland* (1915).

R. A. Lafferty, *Past Master* (1968).

Ursula K. Le Guin, *The Lathe of Heaven* (1971), *The Dispossessed* (1974).

William Morris, *News from Nowhere* (1890).

Sir Thomas More, *Utopia* (1516).

Larry Niven and Jerry E. Pournelle, *Oath of Fealty* (1981).

Marge Piercy, *Woman on the Edge of Time* (1976).

Plato, *Republic* (380–370 BC).

Kim Stanley Robinson, "Three Californias" trilogy: *The Wild Shore* (1984), *The Gold Coast* (1988), *Pacific Edge* (1990);*Future Primitive: The New Ecotopias* (editor, 1994); "Mars" trilogy: *Red Mars* (1993), *Green Mars* (1994), and *Blue Mars* (1996); and *Antarctica* (1997).

Mack Reynolds, *Looking Backward, From the Year 2000* (1973), *Equality in the Year 2000* (1977).

Christiane Rochefort, *Archaos, or the Sparkling Garden* (1972).

Joanna Russ, *The Female Man* (1975).

B. F. Skinner, *Walden Two* (1949).

Olaf Stapledon, *Last and First Men* (1930) and *Star Maker* (1937).

Theodore Sturgeon, *Venus Plus X* (1960).

H. G. Wells, *A Modern Utopia* (1905).

Monique Wittig, *Les Guérillères* (1969).

Austin Tappan Wright, *Islandia* (1942).

George Zebrowski, *Macrolife* (1979).

Notable Films

Demolition Man. Dir. Marco Brambilla, 1993.

Just Imagine. Dir. David Butler, 1926.

Lost Horizon. Dir. Frank Capra, 1937.

Things to Come. Dir. William Cameron Menzies, 1936.

Feminism, Science Fiction, and Gender

Although Mary Shelley's *Frankenstein* (1818) is often credited as the progenitor of modern science fiction, the genre has been popularly conceived as a primarily masculine domain. Certainly male writers catering to a largely male readership were predominant in science fiction throughout the early and mid-twentieth century, but women were hardly absent, either as writers or readers. As characters, however, the women in the majority of these early science fiction texts (when present at all) are often peripheral, or else represented as threatening alien Others. Traditional gender roles are unchallenged; heterosexuality is compulsory. Much of the literature is frankly misogynistic. And yet it is the figure of the feminine alien Other, who threatens male dominance and is routinely vanquished in order to restore patriarchal order, that women writers have claimed as their own. Imbued with the ominous power that many male writers bestowed upon her, she became a literary tool designed to disrupt the sexual hierarchy and challenge the construction of "woman." For writers from the pulp era to those of the present day, then, science fiction has offered women a medium through which to explore their own sense of alienation within the genre itself and society at large. The genre has also enabled both men and women writers to fruitfully explore issues of gender and sexuality, including those relating to gay, lesbian, and bisexual identities. Informed by the feminist politics of the 1960s and 1970s, these texts are some of the most exciting and richly rewarding works in all of science fiction.

Women writers such as Leigh Brackett, Katherine MacLean, Marion Zimmer Bradley, and Judith Merril established a presence in science fiction from 1930s through the 1950s. However, many of these early women writers, such as C. L. Moore and Andre Norton, adopted masculine or non-gender specific pseudonyms in order to avoid prejudice by a predominantly male audience. Nevertheless, these writers often explored gender-related issues in interesting and provocative ways. C. L. Moore, for example, frequently employed male protagonists in stories that also featured versions of the female Other remarkable for their strength and independence. In Moore's story "No Woman Born" (1944), Deirdre is a famous entertainer who, terribly burned in a theater fire, finds a new incarnation in a golden body in which her brain is housed. Determined to act again, Deirdre creates the illusion of femininity within her featureless cyborg frame, demonstrating through her grace and projection of feminine sexuality that gender is a kind of performance. Like Frankenstein's Creature, Deirdre welcomes her superhuman strength and speed, though she recognizes her alienation from the rest of humanity. By calling traditional definitions of "woman" into question, Moore's early feminist work is an example of science fiction's potential for challenging the notion that gender is an essential feature of human nature. In addition, Deirdre herself embodies Haraway's construction of the cyborg as a liberatory metaphor that transcends the essentialism of the gendered body.

Even well into the 1970s, a writer such as Alice Sheldon was still employing a masculine pseudonym, using the name James Tiptree Jr., until her true identity was revealed (to the consternation of many) in 1977. By this time, however, women writers were beginning to make a more significant impact in the world of science fiction, spurred by the feminist movements gaining power in America, Canada, Britain, and Europe in the 1960s, now referred to as Second Wave feminism. Having achieved suffrage in the first wave, feminists of the second wave pushed for greater equality in all aspects of society, including the home. Because of its speculative nature and freedom from the constraints of realism, science fiction offers a uniquely appropriate form for feminist concerns. Using cognitive estrangement and extrapolation, feminist science fiction writers render transparent the types of patriarchal structures that are so prevalent as to be almost invisible. Such a strategy serves as an effective critique of existing patriarchal conditions, destabilizing traditional assumptions about gender and highlighting its socially constructed nature. In addition, feminists carve out imaginative spaces in which they examine alternatives to patriarchal structures, perhaps the most notable of these being the feminist utopias of the 1970s.

Ursula K. Le Guin's *The Left Hand of Darkness* (1969) depicts the planet Gethen, a world populated exclusively by hermaphrodites, or androgynes. Gethenians are neither male nor female, except during "kemmer," a phase during a monthly cycle in which, triggered by the hormonal secretions of their partners, they can take the role of either sex and thus can bear or father children. In effect, sexism does not exist in this world, since sex itself is not a fixed category. For Terran narrator Genly Ai, however, such a disruption of the gender binary is difficult to grasp. Sent as an ambassador to the planet in order to persuade the inhabitants to join the Ekumen, a vast association of planets and cultures, Genly is forced to examine his assumptions about gender as he interacts with the Gethenians. Initially, he simply categorizes them as men, which allows him to operate according to his own two-sexed notions of sexual difference. Binary thinking, however, becomes less and less effective for Genly; the fluidity of Gethenian sexual identity confounds such rigid categorization, and he is continually uneasy with what he identifies as feminine manifestations.

It is through Genly's close relationship with Lord Estraven, a politician who befriends him and who enters into kemmer as a female as they travel together, that he begins to accept the Gethenian identity as at totality rather than a contradiction. As Genly's assumptions about gender are challenged, so are the readers', and the constructed nature of gender is revealed. However, despite the utopian possibilities implicit in the depiction of a genderless and warless civilization, the novel has been criticized as portraying the Gethenians as largely male, thereby eliminating women from the text. Homosexuality is also effectively ruled out, since kemmer partners of the same sex are extremely rare. Nevertheless, *The Left Hand of Darkness* is a groundbreaking exploration of gender in science fiction. Its publication spurred numerous writers to challenge the conventions of gender relations, many within the context of utopian fiction and a number of whom explore gay and lesbian themes.

Joanna Russ's "When It Changed" (1972) is a representative feminist utopia that uses separatism to prioritize women over men in an attempt to reverse the dominant ideology of gender that pervades much of traditional science fiction. Separation from men enables Russ's characters a measure of empowerment and the opportunity to develop a society without the built-in structures of the patriarchy. The emphasis on communal values, expulsion of males from the dominant culture, and rejection of patriarchal values are all hallmarks of the feminist utopia. In the story, a plague wipes out the male population of the planet Whileaway, and over the next six hundred years, the survivors develop a non-hierarchical, cooperative, and stable society, one in which women merge ova in order to reproduce. The utopianism of this separatist lesbian society rests on the assumption that women are in some ways superior to men; this is emphasized by the nature of the encounter between the Whileawayans and the men from Earth who come to the planet to renew relations with them. The egalitarianism of Whileaway is thrown into relief by the men's calm sense of superiority and their refusal to accept an all-female society as self-sufficient, or even human.

Whileawayans also make an appearance in *The Female Man* (1975), Russ's most critically acclaimed novel. Here Whileaway functions in contrast to three other settings, one of which is a dystopia in which men and women form separate societies and engage in a literal war between the sexes. Formally experimental, the novel is narrated by four women from parallel worlds with different time probabilities, all of whom eventually interact and who are also versions of the same woman. More so than "When It Changed," *The Female Man* provides a challenge to compulsory heterosexuality in its depiction of explicit lesbian eroticism. In their use of queer content, Russ's works differ markedly from precursors of the modern feminist utopia, such as Charlotte Perkins Gilman's *Herland* (1915), which also posits a society in which women exist and prosper without men but which is entirely without sex.

Like *The Female Man*, the novels of Suzy McKee Charnas's *Holdfast Chronicles* juxtapose a separatist lesbian utopia alongside a nightmarish dystopia, in this case a post-apocalyptic Earth civilization in which women are enslaved by men and are considered subhuman. The first of four novels in the series, *Walk to the End of the World* (1974) focuses primarily on the patriarchal oppression in the city of Holdfast, while its sequel *Motherlines* (1978) portrays the lives of women who escape into the Wild outside the city. Alldera, the pregnant slave who escapes from Holdfast at the end of the first novel, lives among two communities of women known as the Riding Women and the Free Fems, whose difficult lives in the wilderness nevertheless represent a utopian alternative. Like the Whileawayans, the Riding Women reproduce without any input from men; they use their horses to aid in a parthenogenic process that results in clones of the mothers. Mothering duties are shared among all the women, whose cooperative, democratic culture serves as a stark contrast to that of the Holdfast men. The suggestion here, as in Russ and in other works such as Sally Miller Gearhart's *The Wanderground* (1979) and Sheldon/Tiptree's "Houston Houston, Do You Read?" (1976), is that women can realize utopian possibilities only in the absence of men. Since these communities form in opposition to patriarchal structures, and therefore their inhabitants define themselves in relation to these structures, the question arises as to whether separatist feminist utopias are themselves constrained by the very gender assumptions they seek to challenge. While the strategy of separatism liberates and empowers women, it has also been criticized for simply reproducing fixed categories of gender, and thus reinforcing essential notions of masculinity and femininity. The more recent separatist feminist utopia *Ammonite* (1994), by Nicola Griffith, interrogates the lesbian separatist strategy while maintaining a continuity with the tradition of its 1970s predecessors.

Another significant contribution to the feminist utopia of the 1970s is Marge Piercy's *Woman on the Edge of Time* (1976), in which protagonist Connie Ramos uses telepathic powers to travel to a utopian future where men and women peacefully coexist. In Mattapoisett, sexual differences based on gender roles are effaced, and therefore sex discrimination does not exist. Culturally, the people are androgynous. Women do not give birth; babies gestate in artificial wombs à la *Brave New World*, and both men and women breastfeed. While Piercy's vision is not separatist, it does share with other feminist utopias an emphasis on communality, nurturing, tolerance, and partnership with nature. In addition, the inhabitants of Mattapoisett enjoy sexual freedom from an early age, and routinely form attachments with members of both sexes. Like Piercy, Samuel R. Delany explores freedom from sexual taboos and from heterosexual norms in a setting that, while it is not strictly a utopia, has numerous utopian features. In *Trouble on Triton* (1976), the citizens of the heterotopia Tethys are free to enjoy all manner of sexual activities (as long they are deemed consensual), and sexual identity is fluid – anyone can undergo surgical alteration and psychological therapy in order to change gender, sex, and orientation. In Tethys, a society that recognizes multiple genders, the term gender *binary* loses its meaning. Like the lesbian communities depicted by Russ and Charnas, Delany's Tethys and Piercy's Mattapoisett provide a positive representation of alternative sexualities, as well as a radical critique of compulsory heterosexuality.

Critical responses to the separatist lesbian utopias of the 1970s include Joan Slonczewski's *A Door into Ocean* (1986) and Sheri S. Tepper's *The Gate to Women's Country* (1988). *A Door into Ocean* contrasts the utopian lesbian civilization of the moon Shora with that of the planet it orbits, a patriarchal imperialist dictatorship called Valedon. Slonczewski's depiction of the two societies bears some similarities to the civilizations of the planet Urras and its moon Anarres in Le Guin's novel *The Dispossessed* (1974), which contrasts a dystopian, patriarchal culture with a utopia in which men and women enjoy equality. In *A Door into Ocean*, however, there are no males in the utopia of Shora. Although the Valans share an identical genetic heritage with the Shorans, they view them as alien, marked as Other by the genetically engineered adaptations that enable them to live comfortably on an ocean planet. In addition, Shorans are no longer capable of interbreeding with Valans, instead merging ova in order to reproduce. Envious and fearful of the Shorans' advanced science, the Valans attempt to annex the moon, only to meet with successful forms of nonviolent resistance. Unlike previous lesbian utopias, however, Shora is open to the possibility of including men, provided they are willing to adapt to the community. This possibility is embodied in Spinel, a young male Valan who joins the Shorans in their resistance against Valedon. Falling in love with a Shoran, Spinel decides to become a fully fledged member of Shoran society. Tepper's *A Gate to Women's Country* also suggests that genuine equality and harmony between men and women is possible, but only though a process of selective breeding, so that what are believed to be problematic aspects of masculine behavior – aggression, dominance, violence – are bred out by matriarchal societies. The assumption by the women who orchestrate the breeding is that warlike behavior is genetic rather than learned, and they justify the manipulation and murder of the men who exhibit this behavior with the essentialist argument that they are creating an ideal society by filtering out undesirable characteristics that tend to be innate in men. Apparently, the ideal society does not include homosexuality, as it is intentionally eradicated through reproductive technology. In eliminating both separatism and homosexuality, Tepper levels a disconcerting critique at the feminist lesbian utopia's tendency to exclude men.

A key element of feminist utopias, the control of reproductive technology by women shifts back to the patriarchy in Margaret Atwood's *The Handmaid's Tale* (1985), a dystopian novel that draws upon anxieties about reproductive rights in the midst of the conservative backlash of the 1980s. In Atwood's Republic of Gilead, a near future repressive state governed by right-wing religious fundamentalists, women are primarily valued for their ability to breed. Those who are unable to do so fulfill other social roles in line with patriarchal notions of gender, such as those of wife, domestic servant, and prostitute. Considered little more than vessels, the handmaids of the novel's title are conscripted by the state for breeding purposes. Octavia Butler treats a similar subject in "Bloodchild" (1984), with a twist: men are used as vessels to incubate the eggs of the insect-like alien species known as Tlic. When the eggs hatch, the Tlic cut the men's abdomens open and remove the alien grubs – provided the grubs have not already devoured their hosts, a possibility that recalls the gruesome image of alien offspring bursting from the (male) character Kane's torso in the film *Alien* (1979). Although men may be impregnated against their will, the female Tlic attempt to obtain their voluntary participation by creating a loving environment and incorporating themselves into the structure of human families. Gan, the story's protagonist, is motivated by his love for the Tlic T'Gatoi who has designated him as her host, but he also feels powerless to deny her; he and the other humans on the Tlic world have escaped from slavery on Earth and are kept by the Tlic on a Preserve for their own protection. Not only does the story suggest that oppression and exploitation are not unique to the patriarchy – Tlic civilization is matriarchal – but by forcing men to experience sex and reproduction from the position of women in a patriarchal culture, it also responds to controversies about reproductive rights prevalent in the 1980s. In addition, the story recalls the subjugated position of black women slaves in the United States, who like Gan were forced to carry the offspring of their alien masters.

The humans of the postapocalyptic Earth of Butler's "Xenogenesis" trilogy also submit to a reproductive partnership with an alien race, but one that involves genetic exchange (as opposed to parasitism) between the alien Oankali and humans, resulting in human–alien hybrids. The aliens, however, are very much in charge, seeking to eradicate by genetic exchange what they believe is humanity's natural (and highly destructive) tendency toward hierarchical behavior. Butler's human-Oankali hybrids transgress imposed boundaries and culturally constructed categories, which metaphorically aligns them with Donna Haraway's boundary-crossing cyborg identities and their utopian possibilities.

The interface between human and machine in cyberpunk fiction also points toward the potent fusion and dangerous possibilities suggestive of the cyborg metaphor. However, this interface has been described in largely masculinist terms, and cyberpunk has been widely criticized for reinforcing gender binaries in its privileging of the mind, coded masculine, over the feminized body. Despite claims in the cyberpunk manifestos of the 1980s of a science fiction lineage that rarely included women, the subgenre in fact has precursors in feminist science fiction, including Joanna Russ's *The Female Man* and Marge Piercy's *Woman on the Edge of Time*. One early work that can claim predecessor status is Sheldon/Tiptree's "The Girl Who Was Plugged In" (1973). Like the console cowboys in William Gibson's *Neuromancer* (1984) who "jack in" to the feminized matrix of cyberspace, the female protagonist P. Burke spends the majority of her time "plugged in" to a computer system – in this case, a computer system designed by a powerful corporation. P. Burke, in other words, is plugged into masculine structures of *power*. And while Gibson's cowboys experience a sense of bodiless exultation in cyberspace, P. Burke experiences a different kind of embodiment by remotely animating the cyborg body of Delphi. Beautiful but empty, Delphi is an organic human body grown specifically for the purpose of serving as a living advertisement to sell products in a future where ads have been legally banned. P. Burke, deformed and therefore considered defective in a world that values the cultural ideal of feminine beauty embodied by Delphi's form, performs femininity in a manner to similar to that of Deirdre in Moore's "No Woman Born." P. Burke does not experience cyborgian transcendence, however; she can only perform Delphi, not fuse with her. In the end she is rejected – and accidentally killed – by the object of Delphi's affections, who is horrified when he catches a glimpse of the woman behind the beautiful shell he loves. The romance is no more "natural" than the gendered ideal that P. Burke presents to the world through Delphi, and the commodification of this ideal by the technologies of consumerism is at the heart of the story's unsettling satire.

If the male-dominated cyberpunk of the 1980s was influenced by feminist science fiction, the opposite is also true. While Pat Cadigan is the only woman associated with the original movement, other writers such as Candas Jane Dorsey, Lisa Mason, Kathy Acker, Melissa Scott, Maureen F. McHugh, Emma Bull, Laura Mixon, Nalo Hopkinson, Nicola Griffith, and Justina Robson have incorporated cyberpunk motifs while challenging the politics of gender and sexuality fundamental to many of these texts. In addition, male writers such as Jeff Noon and Don Sakers employ feminist sensibilities in their cyberpunk-inflected novels. Feminist reinterpretations of cyberpunk envision the human–machine interface as a site for the exploration of gender and identity, but they also explore the social consequences of the interface. Cadigan's *Synners* (1991), for example, presents an alternative vision to the masculinist cyberpunk texts that often uncritically celebrate technology and privilege electronic transcendence over the mundane experience of the body, or "meat prison." Cadigan taps into the concerns that women, who have long struggled to establish a bodily presence in a patriarchal system that renders them invisible or absent, may have about embracing complete bodily transcendence.

Marge Piercy, who consciously draws upon motifs and images from Gibson's cyberpunk, sets her novel *He, She, and It* (1991) in a familiar dystopian near future characterized by environmental degradation and dominated by multinational corporations. Shira, the novel's heroine and an expert in cybernetics, returns from the artificial environment of a corporate dome to the independent free town of Tivka where she is asked to help socialize Yod, a cyborg programmed to defend the town from threats posed by the Multis and a criminal underworld. Cyborgs are banned by corporations, and thus Yod's ability to pass as human is crucial to the town's survival. Much of the novel centers around the relationship that develops between Shira and Yod, and the questions that arise about what it means to be human. Disembodied in Gibson, artificial intelligence in Piercy is entirely rooted in the technologically constructed body, unsettling the boundaries between human and machine. Further, Yod is constructed in a way that problematizes conventional notions of gender: although his form is male, his programming lends him an androgynous personality. Yod may be read as a literal though not entirely successful embodiment of Haraway's cyborg metaphor, since despite his androgyny, he is depicted as the ideal man – i.e. a biologically male and empathic lover who is sensitive to Shira's needs and desires.

Melissa's Scott's characters in *Trouble and Her Friends* (1994) take pleasure in the freedom from a fixed identity available on the Net. This freedom from race, gender, and all identifiable bodily markers, serves as a marked contrast to the marginalization Trouble and her fellow hackers experience in the corporeal world, due in part to their queer status. The fluidity of identity can be unsettling, too, however, as when Trouble's ex-lover Cerise has virtual sex on the Net with someone she believes to be a woman, but who is in actuality the avatar of a teenaged boy. Scott emphasizes the vulnerability and embodiedness of the virtual subject, imagining possibilities both liberating and dangerous. She also challenges the compulsory heterosexuality of much of cyberpunk fiction, with *Trouble and Her Friends* joining Laura Mixon's *Glass Houses* (1992) and Mary Rosenblum's *Chimera* (1993) in feminist cyberpunk explorations of gay and lesbian identity.

An increasing number of gay, lesbian, and bisexual characters populate science fiction texts, demonstrating the field's potential to engage with issues of sexuality and providing intersections with gay and lesbian studies and queer theory. Samuel Delany and John Varley, both of whom radically deconstruct both gender and sexuality in their works, have a long history of exploring alternative sexualities in science fiction; recent works that posit multiple versions of homosexuality include Delany's *Stars in My Pocket Like Grains of Sand* (1984) and Varley's *Steel Beach* (1992). Among works that focus on the marginalization of gay/lesbian identities is Geoff Ryman's *The Child Garden* (1989), which features a world where genetically engineered viruses educate the populace, eradicating homosexuality as "bad grammar." The lesbian protagonist Milena, however, turns out to be immune to the viruses, but her potential love affair with the genetically engineered polar bear/woman Rolfa is doomed by the viruses that eradicate Rolfa's own lesbianism. Eleanor Arnason's *The Ring of Swords* (1993) also features interspecies homosexual love. For the militaristic, fur-covered *hwarhath*, however, homosexuality is the norm, and heterosexuality is considered grossly deviant. Thus the *hwarhath* consider it completely normal that their military leader Gwarha could love another male – what is odd is that his lover is Nicholas Sanders, a human whose own people view him as a traitor. Unlike Sanders, the gay protagonist in Maureen McHugh's *China Mountain Zhang* (1992) keeps his orientation under wraps, as he lives in a near future America in which the People's Republic of China is in control and intolerant of difference.

In Gwyneth Jones's *Life* (2004), human sexuality is set to be transformed by the agency of a virus, but the implications for that change are not necessarily revolutionary. Anna Senoz, a genetics research scientist, discovers that the Transferred Y viroid is a genetic trigger housed in human DNA that will ultimately lead to the disappearance of the Y chromosome. That does not mean, however, that biological males will disappear, but it does suggest that the gender binary as we know it will no longer exist. Such a fundamental transformation on the horizon suggests utopian possibilities, but Anna, who struggles with sexual harassment, the glass ceiling, and juggling career and a family, is pessimistic about whether or not fundamental changes in the material reality of women's everyday lives will actually occur. The cultural construction of gender, the novel suggests, might prove to be far more intractable than the Y chromosome. By extrapolating discoveries in contemporary genetics, Jones, who also explores the malleability of gender in her critically acclaimed "Aleutian" trilogy, both interrogates our assumptions about sex and gender and speculates about the future of humanity. How that future is to be determined, however, rests upon our shoulders.

Science fiction film and television have done far less than novels and short stories to provide thoughtful explorations of questions related to gender. However, they have led the way in the development of a major strain in contemporary popular culture: the female action hero. Film protagonists such as Ellen Ripley of *Alien* (1979) and its sequels and extending through Sarah Connor of *Terminator 2* (1991), and Trinity of *The Matrix* (1999) and its sequels have been crucial to this phenomenon, which has also included the protagonists of such television series as *Dark Angel* (2000–2002), *Battlestar Galactica* (2004–), and *Bionic Woman* (2007–). Such protagonists suggest an expansion in the roles that are available to women in popular culture, even if they are problematic in their potential glorification of the violence once associated with men. More measured depictions of women who assume traditionally masculine roles include Captain Janeway of *Star Trek: Voyager* (1995–2001) and special agent Dana Scully, the scientist and skeptic of *The X-Files* (1993–2002).

All in all, science fiction has been important in demonstrating that challenges to conventional gender roles constitute an urgent and ongoing political project. The genre's ability to engage with this project by providing sophisticated commentary on the gender issues that shape and inform our contemporary existence is what makes it so attractive as a medium for feminist concerns, as well as for explorations that serve to reveal the constructed nature of gender. Science fiction allows us to redefine gender and sexuality in ways that expand rather than limit, and it has proven to be fertile ground for examinations of alternative sexualities. Perhaps the most tangible evidence that explorations of gender now constitute a primary concern in science fiction is the establishment of Tiptree Award, which recognizes science fiction or fantasy that explores or expands our understanding of gender. Instituted in 1991, the award is named after James Tiptree Jr., the authorial persona of Alice Sheldon and the woman whose work and public revelation of her true identity helped to break down the false boundaries between men's writing and women's writing in science fiction.

Suggested Further Reading

Attebery, Brian. *Decoding Gender in Science Fiction*. NY: Routledge, 2002.

Barr, Marleen. *Lost in Space: Probing Feminist Science Fiction and Beyond*. Chapel Hill: University of North Carolina Press, 1993.

Barr, Marleen. ed. *Future Females, The Next Generation: New Voices and Velocities in Feminist Science Fiction Criticism*. Lanham, Maryland: Rowman & Littlefield Publishers, 2000.

Bartkowski, Frances. *Feminist Utopias*. Lincoln: University of Nebraska Press, 1989.

Donawerth, Jane L. *Frankenstein's Daughters: Women Writing Science Fiction*. Syracuse, NY: Syracuse University Press, 1997.

Hollinger, Veronica. "Feminist Theory and Science Fiction." *The Cambridge Companion to Science Fiction*. Eds. Edward James and Farah Mendelsohn. Cambridge: Cambridge University Press, 2003, 125–136.

Larbalestier, Justine. *The Battle of the Sexes in Science Fiction*. Middletown, CT: Wesleyan University Press, 2002.

Lefanu, Sarah. *In the Chinks of the World Machine: Feminism and Science Fiction*. London: Women's Press, 1988.

Merrick, Helen. "Gender in Science Fiction." *The Cambridge Companion to Science Fiction*. Eds. Edward James and Farah Mendelsohn. Cambridge: Cambridge University Press, 2003. 241–252.

Pearson, Wendy. "Science Fiction and Queer Theory." *The Cambridge Companion to Science Fiction*. Eds. Edward James and Farah Mendelsohn. Cambridge: Cambridge University Press, 2003. 149–160.

Roberts, Robin. *A New Species: Gender and Science in Science Fiction*. Urbana: University of Illinois Press, 1993.

Wolmark, Jenny. *Aliens and Others*. Iowa City: University of Iowa Press, 1994.

Notable Fiction

Eleanor Arnason, *A Woman of the Iron People* (1991), and *Ring of Swords* (1993).
Margaret Atwood, *The Handmaid's Tale* (1985).

Octavia Butler, "Bloodchild" (1984), "Xenogenesis" trilogy: *Dawn* (1987), *Adulthood Rites* (1987), and *Imago* (1989).

Pat Cadigan, *Synners* (1991).

Suzy McKee Charnas, *Holdfast Chronicles: Walk to the End of the World* (1974), *Motherlines* (1978), *The Furies*, (1994), and *The Conquerer's Child* (1999).

Samuel R. Delany, *Trouble on Triton* (1976) and *Stars in My Pocket Like Grains of Sand* (1984).

Suzette Haden Elgin, *Native Tongue* (1984).

Sally Miller Gearheart, *The Wanderground: Stories of the Hill Women* (1978).

Charlotte Perkins Gilman, *Herland* (1915).

Nicola Griffith, *Ammonite* (1994).

Gwyneth Jones, *Life* (2004), "Aleutian" trilogy: *White Queen* (1991), *North Wind* (1996), and *Phoenix Café* (1998).

Ursula K. Le Guin, *The Left Hand of Darkness* (1969) and *The Dispossessed* (1974).

Maureen McHugh, *China Mountain Zhang* (1992).

Laura Mixon, *Glass House* (1992).

C. L. Moore, "No Woman Born" (1944).

Mary Rosenblum, *Chimera* (1993).

Marge Piercy, *Woman on the Edge of Time* (1976) and *He, She, and It* (1991).

Joanna Russ, "When It Changed," (1972), *The Female Man* (1975), and *The Two of Them* (1978).

Geoff Ryman, *The Child Garden* (1989).

Mary Shelley, *Frankenstein, or, The Modern Prometheus* (1818).

Melissa Scott, *Trouble and Her Friends* (1994).

Joan Slonczewski, *A Door into Ocean* (1986).

Sheri S. Tepper, *The Gate to Women's Country* (1988).

James Tiptree Jr. (Alice Sheldon), "The Girl Who Was Plugged In" (1973) and "Houston, Houston, Do You Read?" (1976).

John Varley, *Steel Beach* (1992).

Joan Vinge, *The Snow Queen* (1980), *World's End* (1984), and *The Summer Queen* (1991).

Notable Films

Alien. Dir. Ridley Scott, 1979.

Alien: Resurrection. Dir. Jean-Pierre Jeunet, 1997.

Alien3. Dir. David Fincher, 1992.

Aliens. Dir. James Cameron, 1986.

Born in Flames. Dir. Lizzie Borden, 1983.

Contact. Dir. Robert Zemeckis, 1997.

The Handmaid's Tale. Dir. Volker Schlöndorff, 1990.

The Matrix (1999), *The Matrix Reloaded* (2003), and *The Matrix Revolutions* (2003). Dirs. Andy Wachowski and Larry Wachowski, 1999.

Terminator 2: Judgment Day. Dir. James Cameron, 1991.

Science Fiction and Satire

Satire is an ancient and distinguished literary mode that typically employs humor to expose and critique the follies of various social or political practices or certain habitual modes of human behavior. Despite its use of humor, satire often makes serious and important points about weighty issues. By its nature, satire usually exaggerates the phenomena that are being criticized in order to produce fresh perspectives on them and to reveal aspects of these phenomena that might otherwise not be as clear. In short, satire depends on the phenomenon of cognitive estrangement in order to achieve its effects. In that, it has much in common with science fiction, so it is not surprising that some of the most important science fiction novels ever written have been openly satirical in their orientation.

There is a long tradition of satirical works that posit worlds that differ from our own in fundamental ways and that therefore belong to the realm of "speculative fiction." Perhaps the most obvious case here would be Jonathan Swift's *Gulliver's Travels* (1726), which among other things lampoons what Swift saw as the follies of the newly emergent science of the eighteenth century. *Gulliver's Travels* is sometimes actually considered an early work of science fiction, though it is probably best considered an example of Menippean satire, a subgenre that dates back to the work of the second-century AD satirist Lucian, who was supposedly inspired by Menippus (for whom the subgenre is named) and whose work included science fiction motifs such as voyages to the moon and Venus. Even earlier works of satire, such as Aristophanes's *The Clouds* (423 BC) contain elements that align them with science fiction.

Many works of science fiction proper contain strongly satirical components, including virtually all of the science fiction of H. G. Wells. The important Czech writer Karel Čapek (perhaps best known for coining the term "robot" in his 1921 play *R.U.R.*) often wrote in a satirical vein, including the dystopian novels *The Absolute at Large* (1922) and *War with the Newts* (1936). Indeed, dystopian fiction is generally satirical by its very nature. Thus, major works of that subgenre – such as Evgeny Zamyatin's *We* (1924), Aldous Huxley's *Brave New World* (1932), and George Orwell's *Nineteen Eighty-Four* (1949) – are among the leading works of twentieth-century satire. In addition, authors of utopian fiction – from Thomas More's *Utopia* (1516) forward – also often construct their alternative societies largely in order to satirize their own societies.

Science fiction that is almost exclusively satirical rose to prominence in the 1950s with the work of authors such as Frederik Pohl, who satirized the emerging tendencies of post-World War II consumer capitalism in a series of short stories and novels, often in collaboration with Cyril M. Kormbluth. For example, the Pohl and Kormbluth satire *The Space Merchants* (1952), which projected a future dystopian Earth thoroughly dominated by soulless corporations (especially advertising firms), is a classic of its kind. Pohl's stories "The Tunnel under the World" (1954) and "The Waging of the Peace" (1959) also comment on the dehumanizing effects of capitalism, with important treatment of Cold War tensions included as well. The latter of these also comments on the dehumanizing potential of increasing automation.

Automation is also a central concern of *Player Piano* (1952), an early satirical novel by Kurt Vonnegut Jr. *Player Piano* responds to a number of anxieties in American life in the early 1950s with its depiction of an administered society in which human labor has been made superfluous by advanced technology, resulting in a populace that itself feels superfluous and without purpose. *Player Piano* addresses a growing fear of American workers in the early 1950s that they were in danger of being replaced by automation. In Vonnegut's future America, machines have replaced almost all human workers, except a small elite of engineer-managers who are still required to make the system operate smoothly. But the real political power of Vonnegut's engineer-managers is rather limited. Ultimate planning decisions in this machine-like society are made by a giant computer, EPICAC XIV, making *Player Piano* one of the surprisingly few 1950s science fiction novels to deal in a central way with advances in computer technology.

Vonnegut would go on to become one of the most important American satirists of his generation, often returning to science fiction themes. *The Sirens of Titan* (1959) is, among other things, a spoof of a variety of science fiction motifs, though it also effectively satirizes religion as a sham and as a mind-numbing force that renders individuals susceptible to manipulation by the unscrupulous. *Cat's Cradle* (1963), a narrative of global apocalypse, also satirizes religion, as well as the Cold War arms race. *Mother Night* (1961) features an American named Howard W. Campbell Jr. (apparently based on legendary science fiction editor John W. Campbell Jr.), who becomes a supposed Nazi propagandist during World War II, though he is actually working as a spy for the US *Slaughterhouse-Five* (1969) is an antiwar satire that also deals with World War II (focusing on the bombing of Dresden), but includes science fiction motifs such as time travel and alien intervention. Many of Vonnegut's novels comment on science fiction through the appearances of the fictional science fiction author Kilgore Trout, possibly based on the real science fiction writer Theodore Sturgeon – though partly an alter ego of Vonnegut himself.

One of the most striking science fiction satires of the 1950s is Bernard Wolfe's *Limbo* (1952), an outrageous commentary on the Cold War arms race set in a postapocalyptic world in which citizens, not wishing to repeat the mistakes of the past, express their support for disarmament by literally having their own arms (or other limbs) removed. Described by Clute and Nicholls in *The Encyclopedia of Science Fiction* as "perhaps the finest sf novel of ideas to have been published during the 1950s," *Limbo* addresses a variety of serious issues, despite its outrageous premise (*Encyclopedia*, 1337). In particular, it satirizes the conformist corporate culture of 1950s America as a dehumanizing force that contributes to the insanity of the arms race.

Robert Sheckley was another major sf satirist of the 1950s. His story "The Prize of Peril" (1958) portrays a game-show contestant who must avoid assassins for a week in order to win, satirizing the game-show craze of the 1950s, but also foreshadowing the later reality television craze, as well as sf media satires such as the film *The Running Man* (1987). Sheckley's satirical novels include *Immortality, Inc.* (1958), which later became the basis for the film *Freejack* (1992). A somewhat darker satire, *The Status Civilization* (1960), portrays the nightmarish society of a strictly hierarchical prison planet that suspiciously mirrors modern American society.

In Robert Silverberg's *Invaders from Earth* (1958), an unscrupulous Earth corporation seeks to manipulate governmental authorities to aid it in its colonization and exploitation of Ganymede (the largest moon of Jupiter), which has been discovered to be inhabited by intelligent (but apparently primitive) life. Silverberg's novel is thus prototypical of sf narratives in which the colonization of other planets parallels the phenomenon of colonialism on Earth. Following in the footsteps of *The Space Merchants*, Silverberg's novel focuses on an advertising firm that has been hired to do public relations work to popularize the colonization process. *Invaders from Earth* stands out among sf novels of the 1950s for its sympathetic (if a bit stereotypical) treatment of the gentle inhabitants of Ganymede in the face of their exploitation (and possible extermination) in the interest of corporate gain.

Invaders from Earth is an early product of Silverberg's prolific career and not one of his more polished novels, especially in its somewhat contrived ending. It shows a strong influence of the early work of Philip K. Dick, virtually all of whose work contains strong satirical components. In one way or another, the work of Dick, with its distinctive mixture of zaniness and poignancy, satirizes virtually every aspect of American society (and of "reality" itself) from the 1950s to the 1970s. For example, in *The Man in the High Castle* (1962), his alternative history based on an Axis victory in World War II, Dick subtly but inexorably outlines parallels between the triumphant German Nazis and the militarist-imperialist tendencies of his own modern America, which was at that very time laying the groundwork for the debacle in Vietnam. Particularly prescient is Dick's concern with the growing power of the media in American life, which shows up at numerous points in his work, perhaps most effectively in *Do Androids Dream of Electric Sheep?* (1968), in which television is empowered by the spiritual emptiness of life in the real world.

Dick is a one-of-a-kind writer, though his satirical treatment of various aspects of American society in the 1960s loosely aligns him with the concerns of the so-called New Wave of science fiction writers in that decade. One might say much the same thing for the British author J. G. Ballard, whose unique career fits only loosely within the bounds of science fiction, but whose satirical short stories provided a key contribution to the success of Michael Moorcock's *New Worlds* magazine, the flagship publication of the New Wave. Ballard's satirical novels, such as *Crash* (1973), are important as well, especially for their dark take on the psychic consequences of the directions being taken by corporate capitalism. These novels are also important forerunners of cyberpunk science fiction.

New Wave writers (who also include Sheckley and Silverberg) were often sharply satirical of the British and American societies of the time. Harlan Ellison's short story "Repent, Harlequin!" Said the Ticktockman," a dystopian satire of the growing regimentation of modern life, is a typical New Wave satire. Among novel-length works, John Sladek's *The Müller-Fokker Effect* (1970) foreshadows cyberpunk science fiction in its portrayal of an attempt to record human personalities on tape, an attempt that goes sadly awry (as technology often does in Sladek's work). In the process, Sladek lampoons various central phenomena in modern American life, including anticommunist paranoia, corporations, and religion.

One of the most effective and best known New Wave satires is Norman Spinrad's *Bug Jack Barron* (1969), whose open treatment of themes related to drugs and sex was paradigmatic of the New Wave – but also caused it to be declared obscene by many early reviewers. Its title character is a former

1960s Berkeley student radical who went on to help found a major national political party and then to become the host of the eponymous television talk show in which viewers call in live by videophone to air their various grievances. Set roughly twenty years into the future relative to the writing of the book, *Bug Jack Barron* seems prescient in its vision of the increasing mediatization of American society, while the television program at its center in many ways anticipates such phenomena as the growth of talk radio and reality television.

Bug Jack Barron can be taken as an endorsement of the counterculture of the 1960s. Meanwhile, the mainstream power structure of American society is satirized as thoroughly corrupt, dominated, and driven by financial interests with no regard for human beings. The principal villain of the novel is magnate Benedict Howards, the wealthiest and most powerful man in America. Much of the plot involves Barron's discovery and revelation of a project through which Howards and his Foundation for Human Immortality have developed a longevity treatment that is affordable only by the rich and that requires the gruesome sacrifice of young children.

Spinrad's *The Iron Dream* (1972) is based on an alternative history premise in which Adolf Hitler emigrated to New York in 1919 and thus never rose to power in Germany. Except for a brief "About the Author" segment at the beginning and a mock critical commentary in the Afterword, the entire novel consists of the text of *Lord of the Swastika*, an outrageous fantasy novel that obviously enacts Hitler's personal fantasies. In this post-apocalyptic novel, most of the human race has been polluted by radiation-induced mutations as a result of an earlier nuclear war. But Hitler's alter ego, the magnificent Feric Jaggar, a genetically pure human, rises to power and manages to re-establish the dominion of pure humans on Earth, defeating the evil forces of the mutant stronghold of Zind, an obvious stand-in for the Soviet Union. In the end, Jaggar even begins a project to colonize the stars with clones of his pure human storm troopers. *Lord of the Swastika* (which, in this alternative universe, wins a Hugo Award) lampoons certain right-wing tendencies in both science fiction and fantasy novels, but does so in a way that satirizes phenomena (such as militarism) in our own world that facilitate such novels (and that made Hitler's real-world rise to power possible).

There is, of course, a rich tradition of militaristic science fiction, of which Robert A. Heinlein's *Starship Troopers* (1959) is perhaps the best known example. There are also numerous science fiction satires that critique militarism. Harry Harrison's *Bill the Galactic Hero* (1965), generally read as a direct response to *Starship Troopers*, is a leading example of such satire with its hilarious portrayal of the insane zealotry that drives an interstellar war.

Joe Haldeman's later *The Forever War* (1974) is also partly a response to Heinlein, but functions primarily as a satirical critique of the Vietnam war. That war was the object of other satires as well, one of the best of which is Ursula K. Le Guin's *The Word for World Is Forest* (1972), though this highly serious novel lacks the humor of most conventional satire. While Le Guin's book has been widely considered to be an allegory of the American experience in Vietnam, it also addresses the colonial situation in a much more general way, at the same time dealing with issues related to gender and environmentalism. Here, human colonists are engaged in an effort to "tame" (which largely means devastate) the forest planet Athshe (also known as New Tahiti), which is highly valuable as a source of lumber to be sent back to a deforested Earth, where wood is now a rare and precious commodity. There are no humans living on Athshe when the colonists arrive, though the planet does have some sentient inhabitants, whom the human colonizers refer by the derogatory term "creechies," regarding them as decidedly subhuman. In an especially clear repetition of the history of the European encounter with Africa, the Athsheans are rounded up and used as slave labor. At the same time, the forests so dear to their culture are systematically destroyed in logging operations. However, the Athsheans turn out to be more intelligent (and formidable) than the humans realize. In fact, they have a highly sophisticated culture, though the colonizers from Earth are unable to recognize it as such because it is so different from their own. The abusive treatment of the Athsheans by the humans leads to a violent uprising, while the racist and sexist attitudes of some of the human colonists provide Le Guin with the opportunity to comment on the contribution of these attitudes in our own world to colonialism in general and the American invasion of Vietnam in particular.

Le Guin's suggestion of the patriarchal foundations of colonialism points toward the satirical aspects of the numerous feminist utopias that appeared in the 1970s and 1980s, including such works as Suzy McKee Charnas's *Walk to the End of the World* (1974) and *Motherlines* (1978), Joanna Russ's *The Female Man* (1975), and Marge Piercy's *Woman at the Edge of Time* (1976). Margaret Atwood's *The Handmaid's Tale* (1985), like most dystopian texts, is highly satirical as well. These texts tend toward darkness in their satires of patriarchy, though they can at times be quite lively.

More humorous satires of the 1970s and 1980s include Barry Malzberg's *Herovit's World* (1973), which satirizes the market pressures that drive the business aspects of science fiction writing, though in a way that comments on the sad status of the individual in modern consumer society as a whole. Meanwhile, Somtow Sucharitkul's *Mallworld* (1981) skewers consumerism in its depiction of a shopping mall the size of a planet, patronized by a variety of alien races. The most prominent satires of this period, however, are Douglas Adams Pythonesque *The Hitchhiker's Guide to the Galaxy* (1979) and its various sequels, which together lampoon life, the universe, and everything (and which may have been influenced by Sheckley's 1968 novel *The Dimension of Miracles*). Adams's sequence began as a BBC radio serial in 1978, became a BBC television miniseries in 1981 and a feature-length theatrical-release motion picture in 2005. In all media, it is a work of high silliness, featuring a heavy dose of toilet humor. However, it also contains a great deal of social satire, though the completely unserious way in which it lampoons various human foibles make it almost a parody of social satire rather than social satire proper. It is also more a parody of science fiction than science fiction proper, various staples of the genre (space travel, time travel, galactic empires, dangers of arrant technological development, planetary catastrophes, and so on) being treated with anything but respect and seriousness.

The various versions of the *Hitchhiker's Guide* sequence illustrate the multimedia potential of science fiction satire. Indeed, while science fiction television series devoted exclusively to satire have been relatively rare, numerous important series have included strong satirical components, from *The Twilight Zone* (1959–1964) to *The X-Files* (1993–2002). The long-running British classic *Doctor Who* (1963–1989, resurrected in 2005) has often been highly satirical, while the campy German-Canadian production *Lexx* (1997–2001) brought television sf satire to a new level of outrageousness. *Lexx*, like the British sf sitcom *Red Dwarf* (which ran off and on from 1988 to 1999), aims much of its satire at the sometime self-seriousness of science fiction itself, while addressing a number of other social and political issues as well.

In the realm of film, Stanley Kubrick's *Dr. Strangelove, or How I Learned to Stop Worrying and Love the Bomb* (1964) remains perhaps the most effective science fiction satire of all time. This film, featuring Peter Sellers in the title and several other roles, captured, more than any other single work, the lunacy of the Cold War mentality, while at the same time suggesting that certain American attitudes in the Cold War might have been inherited from the German Nazis. Indeed, the film's crisis is triggered by literal insanity, that of General Jack D. Ripper (played with appropriately grim lunacy by Sterling Hayden), commander of Burpelson Air Force Base and of a wing of the Strategic Air Command's fleet of B-52 nuclear bombers. Unhinged by his extreme anticommunist paranoia, Ripper orders his bombers to attack the Soviet Union, thereby triggering the labyrinthine security procedures that make it almost impossible to recall such an order, leading to global nuclear apocalypse.

Based (loosely) on the novel *Red Alert* (1958) by Peter George, *Dr. Strangelove* goes well beyond the novel in its absurdist satire of the ideology of the Cold War arms race. *Dr. Strangelove* became a cult favorite of the 1960s youth movement and was one of the classics of American culture of the 1960s, even though, strictly speaking, it is a British film, produced at London's Hawk Studios. The film is so representative, in fact, that historian Margot Henriksen entitled her own study of the ideology of Cold War America *Dr. Strangelove's America.*

Any number of other science fiction films have strong satirical components, as when Franklin Schaffner's *Planet of the Apes* (1968) comments on racism or when Paul Verhoeven's *Total Recall* (1990, based on Dick's 1966 short story "We Can Remember It for You Wholesale") satirizes the exploitative practices of capitalism. Some of the most purely satirical sf films include Woody Allen's *Sleeper* (1973), Brian Forbes's *The Stepford Wives* (1975), Terry Gilliam's *Brazil* (1985), Paul Verhoeven's *Robocop* (1987), John Carpenter's *They Live* (1988), Stuart Gordon's *Space Truckers* (1996), Tim Burton's *Mars Attacks!* (1995), and Luc Besson's *The Fifth Element* (1997).

Among more recent writers of sf satire, Terry Bisson established himself as a major new voice with *Voyage to the Red Planet* (1990), a wacky satirical romp that features the first manned trip to Mars – not for colonization or scientific research, but essentially as a publicity stunt to aid in the marketing of a film to be made during the expedition. (The novel makes it clear that the film could easily have been made via computer-generated imagery without actually going to Mars.) This motif allows for a considerable amount of satire about the entertainment industry, while Bisson actually describes a substantial amount of fairly convincing science fiction hardware, though some of his technology is satirically farfetched, as in his description of a device that allows energy (such as sunlight) to be digitized and stored on CDs for later playback. The most memorable aspects of *Voyage to the Red Planet* are its satirical presentation of a near-future corporate-dominated Earth. In Bisson's near-future America, privatization has reached new heights, and former government organizations (such as the US Navy, the National Park Service, and the UN) are under corporate ownership, a vision of sweeping privatization that would become a virtual cliché of near-future science fiction in the 1990s. By the time the voyage and the film (which has the same title as Bisson's novel) are completed, corporate takeovers have left the entire project under the ownership of the giant Disney-Gerber corporation, which heavily promotes the film with an eye toward winning as many profit-generating Oscars as possible. Indeed, it is clear that the actual trip to Mars is necessary only for marketing purposes: The resultant commentary on the commercialization of the film industry (one award given in the Academy Award ceremony that ends the book is for "Best Tie-in Merchandising") is quite effective. The projection of the eventual impact of computer-generated imagery on filmmaking now seems more and more prescient as well.

Bisson's *Pirates of the Universe* (1996) is a postapocalyptic novel that satirizes the bureaucratic tendencies of both business and government, while *The Pickup Artist* (2001) satirizes the contemporary American loss of historical sense. A riff on Ray Bradbury's *Fahrenheit 451* (1951), this novel portrays the adventures of a "pickup artist," an agent of the government assigned to collect copies of "deleted" books, films, recordings, and other artworks so that they can be destroyed to make room for new works in a world overcrowded with people, things, culture, and information. Much of Bisson's most important satirical writing has appeared in his short stories, the best known of which is the weird but poignant Hugo and Nebula Award-winning "Bears Discover Fire" (first published in 1990 and republished in 1993 in the collection *"Bears Discover Fire" and Other Stories*).

Recent science fiction satires have typically concentrated on various aspects of contemporary consumer capitalism. For example, the portrayal of the franchising of traditional government services in Neal Stephenson's postcyberpunk classic *Snow Crash* (1992) indicates the growing intrusion of private corporations into every aspect of American life. Cyberpunk, in fact, is often highly satirical, though in *Distraction* (1998), former cyberpunk guru Bruce Sterling departs from the cyberpunk mode entirely in his presentation of a darkly comic vision of a 2044 America coming apart at the seams, largely owing to environmental decay. Meanwhile, in the lively *Down and Out in the Magic Kingdom* (2003), Canadian Cory Doctorow satirizes the Disneyfication of America and the emptiness of life in what otherwise seems to be a consumerist paradise.

The novels of Connie Willis often contain a strong satirical element, as when *Remake* (1995) satirizes the Hollywood film industry in its vision of a politically correct attempt to retroactively sanitize films of the past. Meanwhile, the banal films of the present are made (as in *Voyage to the Red Planet*) strictly via computer-generated imagery, no actors needed. In *Bellwether* (1996) Willis pokes relatively lighthearted fun at how capricious and haphazard scientific discoveries can be (or how they are just completely random, as much as we would like to pretend there's an order to these things). She also satirizes the corporate control of scientific research and the bureaucratic conformism of corporate culture.

Bellwether is typical of much recent satire in its satire of corporatism. For example, Jack Womack's dystopian novels featuring the machinations of the evil Dryco Corporation contain strongly satirical components. *Elvissey* (1993) is one of the most satirical of these novels. Here, the corporation retrieves an alternative Elvis from a parallel universe in order to attempt to use him in their attempt to counter the growing power of the Church of Elvis (their only major rival for power in this future world). Some of the most effective satires of corporate capitalism reside in the recent novels of the Australian Max Barry, as in his vision of a near-future world dominated by American corporations in *Jennifer Government* (2003). Barry's elaboration of the goings-on of Zephyr Holdings Corporation in *Company* (2006) is not openly science fictional, but its combination of Dilbert with Kafka creates a vision of the company as a dystopian microcosm of modern America.

As with *Company*, many of the best recent satires of capitalism contain science fictional components, even if the works are not themselves science fiction proper. One might also mention the marginally science fictional novels of Chuck Palahniuk (sometimes compared with Ballard), beginning with *Fight Club* (1996). The short stories of Paul Di Filippo are particularly important as satires of capitalism, though they are more purely science fictional. Some of the best recent satires of capitalist globalization have come from the writers of the British Boom. For example, Richard K. Morgan's *Market Forces* (2005), an exemplary case of speculative, satirical science fiction that shows us, in its imaginative (and exaggerated) vision of a future capitalist nightmare, many of the central tendencies that are already present in the capitalism of our own day. Set in the year 2049, Morgan's novel presents us with a picture of a London in which class difference has been solidified by physical separation. The poor and disenfranchised of Morgan's London live in the cordoned zones, in which chaos and mayhem reign, with little police interference. The borders of these zones, however, are patrolled by heavily armed guards, who are there to prevent this mayhem from spreading into the more affluent parts of the city, where middle-class professionals can live out their domestic lives in relative order and security. Their professional lives, though, are another matter entirely. Morgan presents us with a vision of capitalism run amok in which individuals can advance within corporations by killing their rivals in ritual conflict, while rival corporations compete for contracts through violent road battles in armored cars. Many of these contracts, meanwhile, involve investments in the numerous local wars and revolutions that are endemic in the book's future Third World and that Western corporations engineer for their own profit.

Market Forces is in the best tradition of satirical science fiction – or of satire as a whole – in that it presents a seemingly outrageous exaggeration of existing circumstances that, on reflection, turns out to be much closer to reality than first appears. It also joins works from *The Space Merchants* forward in demonstrating the special satirical potential of the cognitive estrangement that is produced by all of the best science fiction. Collectively, the many important works of science fiction satire provide one of the best illustrations of the power of science fiction to produce compelling social and political commentary.

Suggested Further Reading

Booker, M. Keith. *Monsters, Mushroom Clouds, and the Cold War: American Science Fiction and the Roots of Postmodernism, 1946–1964*. Westport, CT: Greenwood, 2001.

Clute, John and Peter Nicholls, eds. *The Encyclopedia of Science Fiction*. New York: St. Martin's, 1995.

Freedman, Carl. *Critical Theory and Science Fiction*. Hanover, NH: Wesleyan University Press, 2000.

Seed, David. *American Science Fiction and the Cold War: Literature and Film*. Edinburgh: Edinburgh University Press, 1999.

Notable Fiction

Douglas Adams, *The Hitchhiker's Guide to the Galaxy* (1979).

Margaret Atwood, *The Handmaid's Tale* (1985).

J. G. Ballard, *Crash* (1973).

Max Barry, *Jennifer Government* (2003) and *Company* (2006).

Terry Bisson, "Bears Discover Fire" (1990), *Voyage to the Red Planet* (1990), *Pirates of the Universe* (1996), and *The Pickup Artist* (2001).

Suzy McKee Charnas, *Walk to the End of the World* (1974) and *Motherlines* (1978).

Philip K. Dick, *Time Out of Joint* (1959), *The Man in the High Castle* (1962), *Martian Time-Slip* (1964), *The Three Stigmata of Palmer Eldritch* (1965); *The Zap Gun* (1967), *Do Androids Dream of Electricc Sheep?* (1968), *Ubik* (1969), and *A Scanner Darkly* (1977).

Cory Doctorow, *Down and Out in the Magic Kingdom* (2003).

Harlan Ellison, "'Repent, Harlequin!' Said the Ticktockman" (1965).

Joe Haldeman, *The Forever War* (1974).

Harry Harrison, *Bill the Galactic Hero* (1965).

Robert A. Heinlein, *Starship Troopers* (1959) and *Stranger in a Strange Land* (1961).

Ursula K. Le Guin, *The Word for World is Forest* (1972).

Barry Malzberg, *Herovit's World* (1973).

Edson McCann (Pohl and Lester Del Rey), *Preferred Risk* (1955).

Ward Moore, *Greener Than You Think* (1947).

Richard K. Morgan, *Market Forces* (2005).

Lance Olsen, *Time Famine* (1996).

Chuck Palahniuk, *Fight Club* (1996).

Marge Piercy, *Woman at the Edge of Time* (1976).

Frederik Pohl and C. M. Kormbluth, *The Space Merchants* (1952) and *Gladiator-at-Law* (1955).

Joanna Russ, *The Female Man* (1975).

Robert Sheckley, *Immortality, Inc.* (1958), "The Prize of Peril" (1958), and *The Dimension of Miracles* (1968).

Robert Silverberg, *Invaders from Earth* (1958).

John Sladek, *The Müller-Fokker Effect* (1970).

Norman Spinrad, *Bug Jack Barron* (1969) and *The Iron Dream* (1972).

Neal Stephenson, *Snow Crash* (1992).

Bruce Sterling, *Distraction* (1998).

Somtow Sucharitkul (S. P. Somtow), *Mallworld* (1981).

Kurt Vonnegut Jr., *Player Piano* (1952), *The Sirens of Titan* (1959), *Mother Night* (1961), and *Cat's Cradle* (1963).

Connie Willis, *Remake* (1995) and *Bellwether* (1996).

Bernard Wolfe, *Limbo* (1952).

Jack Womack, *Elvissey* (1993).

Notable Films

Brazil. Dir. Terry Gilliam, 1985.

Dr. Strangelove, or How I Learned to Stop Worrying and Love the Bomb. Dir. Stanley Kubrick, 1964.

The Fifth Element. Dir. Luc Besson, 1997.

The Hitchhiker's Guide to the Galaxy. Dir. Garth Jennings, 2005.

Mars Attacks! Tim Burton, 1995.

Planet of the Apes. Dir. Franklin Schaffner, 1968.

Robocop. Dir. Paul Verhoeven, 1987.

The Running Man. Dir. Paul Michael Glaser, 1987.

Sleeper. Dir. Woody Allen, 1973.

Space Truckers. Dir. Stuart Gordon, 1996.

The Stepford Wives. Dir. Brian Forbes, 1975.

They Live. Dir. John Carpenter, 1988.

Total Recall. Dir. Paul Verhoeven, 1990.

Cyberpunk and Posthuman Science Fiction

Emerging in the 1980s as a literary movement significant for its rejection of the technological utopianism of much traditional sf, cyberpunk fiction explores the often uncomfortably close relationship between humans and technology. In its near-future depiction of biomedical and electronic body modifications, direct interfaces between human brains and computers, artificial intelligences equipped with "human" qualities, and the electronic transcendence provided by new technological spaces, cyberpunk not only calls into question what it means to be human, but also suggests that the posthuman is an inevitable consequence of the dissolution of boundaries between human and machine. A challenge to the traditional model of the human subject is mirrored in the typical cyberpunk landscape, a dystopian post-industrial world governed largely by multinational corporations (in place of nation-states), dominated by urban sprawl and rife with subcultures from which its outlaw and misfit heroes are drawn. In short, cyberpunk is a fictional attempt to grapple with the realities of our postmodern condition. Initially a response to the technological explosion and postmodern culture of the 1980s, and arguably the most important sf trend of that era, its influence has spread far beyond the boundaries of science fiction, essentially outliving the cyberpunk movement itself.

The term "cyberpunk," introduced in 1983 by Bruce Bethke in a short story bearing that title and published in *Amazing Science Fiction Stories*, was first employed by editor and critic Gardner Dozois in a 1984 *Washington Post* article to describe the fiction of such up-and-coming authors as William Gibson, Bruce Sterling, Pat Cadigan, and Greg Bear. Emblematic of the juxtaposition of punk or countercultural attitudes with high technology (usually involving computers), the term quickly caught on, both as a useful descriptor and as a marketing device. However, as demonstrated in

Mirrorshades: The Cyberpunk Anthology (1986) – which includes short stories by the previously mentioned cyberpunks in addition to those by such authors as Rudy Rucker, John Shirley, Tom Maddox, and Lewis Shiner – works that fell under the blanket term of cyberpunk did not necessarily share the coherent vision representative of the subgenre as described by editor and self-proclaimed cyberpunk spokesperson Bruce Sterling. In the introduction to *Mirrorshades*, Sterling lays out the tenets of the movement, positing cyberpunk's innovative integration of technology with 1980s counterculture as a revolution in sf while claiming kinship with both the genre's hard science tradition and New Wave writers such as Samuel Delany and J. G. Ballard. Sterling also identifies postmodernist authors Thomas Pynchon and William S. Burroughs as forerunners of cyberpunk.

The writer most clearly identified with the cyberpunk literary movement is William Gibson. Gibson's early works, which include the "Sprawl" trilogy: *Neuromancer* (1984), *Count Zero* (1986), and *Mona Lisa Overdrive* (1988), as well as a collection of short stories entitled *Burning Chrome* (1986), exemplify cyberpunk fiction, with *Neuromancer* largely agreed upon as the premier cyberpunk novel. With its publication, Gibson's concept of the computer-generated alternative reality of cyberspace gained a wide currency, eventually becoming part of mainstream culture. In the novel, antihero "console cowboy" Case accesses cyberspace via a neural interface with a computer, and such is his preference for the euphoric experiences in this virtual realm that he disdains the body as a "meat prison." The "meat" in Gibson's near-future universe can easily be reshaped and augmented, as evidenced by the cyborg assassin Molly Millions, Case's partner in a high-tech heist orchestrated by the AI Wintermute; such casual modifications of bodies blur the boundaries between organic and artificial in a way that suggests posthumanity is an inevitability, but it is not clear that the hybrid posthuman represents an improvement over the outmoded human. Certainly the technological saturation of Gibson's world does not lead to a resolution of the kinds of social, political, and economic problems that were prevalent in the 1980s, and in fact they are magnified in a dystopian future where the majority of power lies with ruthless multinational corporations and the physical landscape is marked by environmental degradation and cluttered with *gomi* (junk). In *Mona Lisa Overdrive*, central characters Bobby Newmark and Angie Mitchell simply replace existence in the real world with electronic immortality in cyberspace, choosing to die "on the outside" in the ultimate example of the privileging of mind over body that is prevalent in cyberpunk.

For some critics, cyberpunk's primary contribution is its distinctive style, a surface texture that is evocative of the information overload characteristic of contemporary postmodern culture. The kind of dense prose employed by a masterful stylist like Gibson – who crowds his sentences with street slang, brand names, high art and pop culture references, and high-tech jargon – often creates a sense of disequilibrium in the reader, who may find its intensity by turns exhilarating and confusing. Echoing other postmodern writers who create pastiche through their stylistic borrowings, Gibson borrows extensively from other genres, for example, fusing science fiction with the hard-boiled detective narrative perfected by Raymond Chandler and Dashiell Hammett. Like his own fictional junk artists, who create powerful works of art using the *gomi* that surrounds them, Gibson generates literary collage by reassembling bits and pieces of the literary past, playfully subverting these genres in the process. Additionally, Gibson and other cyberpunks pay homage to their sf predecessors. For example, the forerunner of cyberpunk antiheroes can be discerned in the work of Alfred Bester, whose troubled and cybernetically enhanced protagonist Gully Foyle in *The Stars My Destination* (1957) serves as a foil to the corruption that surrounds him in the form of family-owned corporate clans; Bester's kinetic prose in this novel and in the earlier *The Demolished Man* (1953) also anticipates the textured rendering of surface reality in cyberpunk.

Philip K. Dick's *Do Androids Dream of Electric Sheep?* (1968) is often considered a proto-cyberpunk work, featuring a bleak near future in which bounty hunter Rick Deckard is assigned to retire six androids that escape from the Mars colony and attempt to blend in on post-apocalyptic Earth. The line between androids and humans is a thin one, with androids exhibiting human qualities and desires and humans ritually "programming" themselves with a mood organ that allows them to set their mood for the day. Technology permeates all aspects of the characters' lives, and Dick's decaying urban landscapes are distinctive for their profusion of kipple (the refuse of post-industrial society) – a precursor of the *gomi* that clutters the cities of Gibson's texts, which is the outcome of unrestrained consumer desires. This sense of decay is translated as the dark, polluted, and trash-lined streets of 2019 Los Angeles in the classic proto-cyberpunk film *Blade Runner* (1982), an adaptation of Dick's novel directed by Ridley Scott. *Blade Runner* melds *film noir* conventions with dystopian sf, and its futuristic cityscape, dominated by massive skyscrapers and neon, has a distinctly Asian influence. As in cyberpunk fiction, the setting not only conveys the sense that contemporary cities like Hong Kong and Tokyo are already futuristic, but also reflects the widespread anxiety prevalent in the 1980s that Asia, and specifically Japan, would usurp the dominance of the American economy.

A literary forebear who anticipates the cyberpunk treatment of humans and their relationship with computers is John Brunner's *Shockwave Rider*

(1975), in which fugitive Nick Haflinger uses expert computer skills to evade governmental authorities in a dystopian near future America. Eventually, he propagates what Brunner coins a "worm" (a self-replicating program akin to the contemporary computer virus) that is designed to reveal all of the government's nefarious secrets to users of the global computer network and essentially nullifies the surveillance of its citizenry. A prototype of the cyberpunk hacker, Haflinger's facility with computers is unmatched, but he is subject to crippling bouts of information overload, a side effect of living in a society where the frenetic pace of technological change is often too much for humans to handle. Another recognizable antecedent of the console cowboy is P. Burke in "The Girl Who Was Plugged In" (1973), a story by Alice Sheldon, writing as James Tiptree Jr. Rather than being "jacked in" to cyberspace, where Gibson's (almost exclusively male) hackers experience an exhilarating disembodiment, deformed P. Burke is "plugged in" to a corporate-owned computer network that enables her to experience a different kind of embodiment by animating the beautiful (and thus universally desired) cyborg body of Delphi, an empty shell that serves as a living advertisement for the GTX corporation.

Sterling's *The Artificial Kid* (1980) also features a technologically mediated body – the Kid – that is inhabited by a separate personality, in this case a politician whose personality and memories are inserted prior to his death. Like Delphi, the Kid, a combat artist, is filmed by cameras everywhere he goes, and his street fights are commodified and sold to an adoring public. Although not generally considered cyberpunk, Sterling's second novel encapsulates a number of its themes, which he develops in later works. His most significant contribution to cyberpunk is *Schismatrix* (1985), which differs from Gibson's version in a few key respects: it takes place in the far-flung future, Earth does not figure prominently in the action, and computers are relegated to the background. The novel's emphasis on posthumanism as a result of genetic and technological modification, however, combined with its breakneck pace, information-dense prose, and punk sensibility, mark it as characteristically cyberpunk. Hopelessly outmoded in Sterling's future, the human has largely been supplanted by two parallel strands of posthuman development, known as the Shapers and the Mechanists. The Shapers are genetically reshaped, equipped with enhanced intelligence, immunity, and muscle control, in addition to extended life spans. The rival Mechanists are cyborgs, augmenting their bodies with electronic and mechanical prosthetics. The pure human does still exist – unmodified – on Earth, and protagonist and Shaper Lindsay Abelard serves in his youth as a Preservationist dedicated to defending the purity of human culture. By the end of the novel, however, Abelard, who earlier offends Shaper sensibilities with the addition of a prosthetic arm (symbolic of the crossbreeding that eventually takes place between Shapers and Mechanists), fuses with an alien entity and abandons his body altogether. Ever evolving, Abelard's transformations suggest that the human is not a stable, fixed category, nor is there such a thing as an essential human nature. Abelard's optimism and openness to new experiences and forms of embodiment also indicate that Sterling does not share Gibson's ambivalence about the posthumanist future.

A famously short-lived literary movement, with even Gibson shrugging off the label, cyberpunk was declared dead as early as the publication of the *Mirrorshades* anthology, a suggestion that once the general public is introduced to a cultural production considered hip and cutting-edge, it no longer is. As the number of imitators of the original cyberpunks – especially Gibson – grew, writers who had been associated with the movement often distanced themselves, fearing a ghettoizing effect upon their work. It is also the case, however, that the works of those who had been originally hailed as cyberpunks are sometimes only marginally related to the elements considered representative of the subgenre. Greg Bear's *Blood Music* (1985), for example, poses a radical transformation of the human through genetic engineering, featuring a posthumanism that – like Sterling's – goes far beyond our current notions of what it means to be human, but the novel lacks the trademark punk sensibility and stylistic innovation of cyberpunk. Scientist Vergil Ulam injects biochips, a form of nanotechnology, into his bloodstream, setting off a chain reaction that ends with the evolved microorganisms infecting most of North America and literally dissolving the boundaries of the human body, while incorporating the essence of individual humans into a greater whole.

Mirrorshades contributor Rudy Rucker, whose "bopper" novels include *Software* (1982), *Wetware* (1988), *Freeware* (1997) and *Realware* (2000), also interrogates the traditional boundaries of the human subject in his near future saga of self-replicating robots and artificial life forms that have succeeded humanity's control of the Earth and the moon. As has often been noted, these novels are closer to the work of Dick, stylistically and philosophically, than to to the cyberpunk of Gibson or Sterling. However, Rucker's treatment of cyborgs, genetic engineering, artificial intelligence, drug use, and electronic transcendence are very much in line with typical cyberpunk concerns.

The permeability of boundaries in cyberpunk not only serves to de-emphasize the integrity of the human body, but also destabilizes traditionally held notions of the self. In a universe where personality and memories can be digitally encoded and copied, concepts like subjectivity and identity are radically undermined. K. W. Jeter, whose *Dr. Adder* (1984) has sometimes been called the first cyberpunk novel (it was written in 1972 but failed to find a publisher for over a decade), explores the fragmentation of subjectivity in *The Glass Hammer* (1985), a novel that largely consists of protagonist Ross Schuyler watching the novelized form of his life on video. He becomes a popular media figure as a result of his success delivering black market computer chips to European buyers, racing across the Arizona desert and evading the missiles from government satellites that have killed so many of his fellow drivers; his races are filmed and broadcast all over the world. The self in the video biography, packaged and scripted, is ironically more real to Schuyler than his "real" self, which he seems to view as almost irrelevant.

Along these lines, the irreverent computer-generated personality of Max Headroom, star of the British television film *20 Minutes into the Future* (1985) and various (American) spin-offs, is an electronic copy of the real newscaster Edison Carter, while Carter himself seems like a pale imitation of his alter ego. Identity, in cyberpunk, can be cheaply acquired. In George Alec Effinger's trilogy *When Gravity Fails* (1987), *A Fire in the Sun* (1990), and *The Exile Kiss* (1991), unique among cyberpunk for its futuristic Middle Eastern setting, characters can simply plug a software personality module ("moddy") into their modified brains and acquire real and fictional personalities.

In "Pretty Boy Crossover" (1986), Pat Cadigan's story about video celebrity via digital translation, the two main characters are offered the opportunity to cross over and live an ageless, immortal existence as Self-Aware Data, shown as living video for the consumption of others in the dance clubs they frequent. While Bobby chooses digital existence, Cadigan's nameless protagonist turns it down, preferring his own embodied subjectivity. Cadigan, the only woman associated with the original cyberpunk movement, as well as the only one included in the *Mirrorshades* anthology, questions the tendency of cyberpunk to privilege electronic transcendence over embodiment, reflecting the discomfort that many women have about the erasure of the body. Treated as invisible by patriarchal systems, women have long struggled to overturn the traditional notion of "human" as being the default for "male." In Cadigan's *Synners* (1991), embodied subjectivity is viewed as a valid choice for Gina Aiesi, the novel's protagonist; she recognizes her body's limits but does not see it as confining, nor does she think of technology as a means of escape, but rather as a means of connection. As in much of cyberpunk, implants are common in *Synners*, and the closeness of the human–computer interface is facilitated by a technology that allows the user – through the implantation of brain socket implants made of living tissue – to plug directly into the global communications network called the System. Synners – video artists who synthesize rock music and images to make virtual reality music videos – use the brain sockets to transmit their vision directly to the consumer, who must also be outfitted with the sockets. Pawns of a large corporation that acquires both their music production company and the company that invents the sockets, Gina and her lover Visual Mark are among the very first to undergo socket implantation. What they eventually discover is that although the brain sockets facilitate undreamed of heights of creativity, they are also unstable, and can cause cerebral strokes in its users. When Mark suffers a stroke while hooked into the System, the stroke takes the form of a computer virus and a contagion, destroying both the System and the brains of those plugged into it. Eventually the virus is defeated by hackers, and the novel ends with Visual Mark going on-line permanently and abandoning his body. That Mark sloughs off his body and Gina preserves hers suggests that Cadigan does not challenge gender stereotypes that associate men with mind and women with body; however, the novel critiques earlier cyberpunk texts by emphasizing the importance of the materiality of bodies and the necessity of making technology accountable.

Cadigan has consistently explored cyberpunk themes in her works, beginning with *Mindplayers* (1987), which features the memorable Deadpan Allie, a specialist in brain-to-brain interface. Later novels include *Fools* (1992), *Tea from an Empty Cup* (1998), and *Dervish Is Digital* (2000). Although Cadigan was for a time the lone woman in the midst of a movement that rarely claimed women writers as part of its science fiction lineage, she was quickly joined by a number of women writers – including Candas Jane Dorsey, Kathy Acker, and Lisa Mason – who applied feminist sensibilities to the subgenre, often critiquing, for example, the failure of cyberpunk to explore the implications of its cyborg metaphors in terms of gender, as in the work of Donna Haraway. Such writers explore notions of gender and identity in the human–machine interface and challenge the underlying politics of gender and sexuality in much of cyberpunk fiction. Interestingly, despite the movement's disavowal of the 1970s as the "doldrums" of sf, cyberpunk has predecessors in the feminist science fiction of that decade. As already mentioned, Tiptree's "The Girl Who Was Plugged In" is a proto-cyberpunk story, and Jael, the feminist assassin with prosthetic claws and steel teeth used to maim and kill men in Joanna Russ's *The Female Man* (1975) is a forerunner of Gibson's cyborg razor girl Molly Millions. Marge Piercy's *Woman on The Edge of Time* (1976) prefigures the dystopian cityscape, bodily modification, and dominance of multinational corporations in cyberpunk. With the publication of *He, She, and It* (1991), however, the influence is Gibson's, as Piercy consciously critiques his work in her feminist revision of cyberpunk involving the cyborg Yod and his relationship with the protagonist Shira.

Emma Bull's *Bone Dance* (1991) is also indebted to Gibson's noir-inflected cyberpunk, featuring small-time hustlers who do "biz" in a post-apocalyptic near future. Sparrow, Bull's androgynous protagonist, makes a living from finding and selling technological artifacts, and over the course of the novel it becomes clear that she is a genetically engineered cyborg, designed to be gender neutral and "ridden" by another group of powerful cyborgs. Thus Bull uses the cyberpunk tropes of genetic engineering, body invasion, and mind control to deconstruct gender binaries and create new forms of identity. Cyberpunk themes also provide rich ground for the exploration of gay and lesbian identities, as demonstrated by Laura Mixon's *Glass Houses* (1992), Maureen McHugh's *China Mountain Zhang* (1992), Mary Rosenblum's *Chimera* (1993), and Melissa Scott's *Trouble and Her Friends* (1994).

Although short-lived, the cyberpunk movement has proven highly influential on sf as a whole, and numerous contemporary texts routinely employ cyberpunk motifs and themes. During the 1980s, cyborgs became popular figures in sf film, as in *The Terminator* (1984) and *Robocop* (1987), while the television miniseries *Wild Palms* (1993) openly alludes to cyberpunk and even features a cameo appearance by Gibson. The film *Johnny Mnemonic* (1995) was adapted from a Gibson short story with a screenplay by Gibson himself, but fails to bring the dynamic energies of cyberpunk to the screen. Attempts to bring a true cyberpunk sensibility to film or TV would not be successful until 1999, with the release of the virtual reality thriller *The Matrix* (1999).

One popular literary offshoot of cyberpunk is steampunk, developed in the early 1980s by K. W. Jeter, James Blaylock, and Tim Powers, and attaining a higher profile with the publication of William Gibson and Bruce Sterling's joint effort, *The Difference Engine* (1990). Set in a Victorian England, the premise of the novel is that Charles Babbage's proposed steam-driven analytical engine was actually built, thus setting off the computer revolution over a century early. The early 1990s also saw the growth of what some have labeled "postcyberpunk," works that feature a somewhat less angst-ridden and alienated sensibility than their precursors, and which often employ a humorous tone and display a sense of optimism about the future. The writer most often associated with the designation is Neal Stephenson, whose third novel *Snow Crash* (1992) is a satirical take on the cyberpunk tradition, featuring the adventures of Hiro Protagonist, one of the original designers of the Metaverse, Stephenson's update of Gibsonian cyberspace. Stephenson's *The Diamond Age: Or, a Young Lady's Illustrated*

Primer (1995) moves further away from cyberpunk, revolving around a neo-Victorian enclave near a futuristic Shanghai where nanotech is the dominant technology. Nell is the Dickensian hero, a working-class girl outside of the enclave who is educated to become a revolutionary figure by an interactive primer intended for an aristocrat's child.

Postcyberpunk encompasses a wide range of sf, including later works by original cyberpunks Gibson and Sterling, with Sterling's *Islands in the Net* (1988) as probably the earliest example. And while much of postcyberpunk appears hopeful about the future, dystopian and noir elements may still be discerned in works such as K. W. Jeter's *Noir* (1998), a grimly satirical tale of a blasted cityscape where the rich can legally murder the homeless, and the dead can be brought back to life as laborers in order to pay off their debts.

Richard K. Morgan's *Altered Carbon* (2002) also draws heavily from the hard-boiled detective narrative, deriving its style and content more directly from that tradition than Gibson ever did, while depending crucially on cyberpunk conceits such as the downloaded personality. Indeed, Morgan's central novum is the cortical stack, a small device implanted at the base of the brain that contains this downloaded personality. In the course of a lifetime, a given personality might be implanted in a number of different bodies, so much so that these bodies are referred to as "sleeves," indicating that they are regarded merely as disposable containers for the true self, which is contained in the stacks in digital form. Indeed, different sleeves can be chosen to help individuals (such as protagonist Takeshi Kovacs) undertake different missions with different physical requirements. Morgan's work is also indicative of the way in which the writers of the British Boom have frequently drawn upon cyberpunk in their work, sometimes taking it in distinctively new directions or combining it with other subgenres. For example, *Altered Carbon* has two sequels – *Broken Angels* (2004) and *Woken Furies* (2005) – which continue the engagement with cyberpunk, but also move into the realm of space opera. This particular generic combination is also crucial to the work of Charles Stross and Ken MacLeod, whose fiction typically revolves around technological singularities that produce runaway advances in artificial intelligence. The Minds of the "Culture" novels of Iain M. Banks (which can be seen as an update of the Machines of *I, Robot*) are also examples of post-singularity artificial intelligences that go well beyond the intellectual capabilities of humans.

The work of writers such as Stross, MacLeod, and Banks thus adds a new dimension to posthuman science fiction by focusing on artificially created entities that move beyond human intelligence but do not evolve through modification of humans. When British Boom writers have focused on modifications of human beings, they have typically taken the Shaper route, rather than the "Mechanist" one, taking a particular interest in the possibilities offered by genetic engineering. MacLeod's *Learning the World* (2005), for example, features explorers who roam the galaxy seeding posthuman colonies, but who in this case encounter a civilization of intelligent aliens who are, we come to realize, more like us humans of Earth's early twenty-first century than are our own descendants, who have evolved so far into the posthuman as to be more alien than the aliens.

One of the more interesting examples of genetic manipulation into the posthuman is Justina Robson's *Natural History* (2003), which envisions a future world in which genetic engineering has advanced to the point where human beings can be custom designed to perform virtually any task, including serving functions formerly reserved for machines. They can, for example, be starships, a fact that is crucial to the basic space opera plot of the novel. The availability of this advanced technology leads to the development of such fanciful creatures that the book almost takes on the feel of fantasy, though it retains a virtual catalog of science fiction motifs, meanwhile also providing a serious explanation of the tensions between these modified (or Forged) posthumans and Unevolved humans who maintain their natural genetic structures.

Of course, this motif of imagining the ramped-up evolution of human beings into what is effectively a new species goes back in British science fiction at least to Arthur C. Clarke's *Childhood's End* (1953), in which alien intervention facilitates the process. Such intervention, meanwhile, is explored in much more detail (and with a much better understanding of the possibilities of genetic engineering) in the "Xenogenesis" trilogy (1987–1989) of the American sf writer Octavia Butler. Meanwhile, what is effectively a form of genetic engineering goes all the way back to H. G. Wells's *The Island of Dr. Moreau* (1896), in which genetic modifications lead not to advances, but to horror, in a mode that anticipates the sometime gruesome Remaking of humans in the Bas-Lag novels of key British Boomer China Miéville.

One of the most important forerunners of the more recent British Boom explorations of the possibilities of genetic engineering can be found in *The Child Garden* (1989), by Geoff Ryman, who was born in Canada and reared partly in the US, but who has lived his adult life in the UK and is usually associated with the British Boom. Ryman's stylish rendition of a future London is set in a post-Revolution future world in which vaguely socialist principles reign supreme and in which Chinese culture is central to a world society. Mechanical technology has become almost non-existent, replaced by a variety of biotechnologies. Perhaps most striking of these is the extensive use of viruses with which individuals are treated, endowing them with specific knowledge or capabilities. Buildings, even spacecraft, are grown rather than built, and the world is ruled by a giant biocomputer collective consciousness known as the Consensus, into which the complete mental pattern of each individual is added after being "Read" at the age of ten.

Finally, no discussion of posthuman sf would be complete without a mention of the work of the Australian sf writer Greg Egan, whose striking vision of a future human race vastly changed by technological advances looks back both to cyberpunk and to such farflung philosophical visions as the novels of Olaf Stapledon in the 1930s. Thus, Egan's *Permutation City* (1994) deals primarily with the cyberpunk trope of the computer simulation of human consciousness, while *Diaspora* (1997) presents a more adventurous exploration of the multiple possibilities of posthuman evolution. Here, some humans maintain their biological bodies, though generally with substantial enhancements, while others inhabit advanced robot bodies or even exist as disembodied intelligences with no bodies whatsoever.

Egan's work is particularly noted for its sophisticated use of hard sf concepts derived from quantum physics and mathematics, but what is perhaps more important is its willingness to imagine a future world in which technological advances have made fundamental changes not only to the nature of humanity but to the nature of reality itself. In this, his work is indicative of the way in which contemporary science fictional explorations of the posthuman move beyond the limited near-future imagination of cyberpunk to explore future possibilities rendered all the more startling because they are made plausible by contemporary real-world advances in computer technology and genetic engineering. There are, indeed, good reasons to believe that we are on the verge of staggering technological advances that will lead to unprecedented changes in the basic texture of our lives, changes for which posthuman science fiction, perhaps more than any other cultural form, might help us to prepare.

Suggested Further Reading

Bukatman, Scott. *Terminal Identity: The Virtual Subject in Postmodern Science, Fiction*. Durham: Duke University Press, 1993.

Cavallaro, Dani. *Cyberpunk and Cyberculture: Science Fiction and the Work of William Gibson*. New Brunswick, NJ: Athlone, 2000.

Foster, Thomas. *The Souls of Cyberfolk: Posthumanism as Vernacular Theory*. Minneapolis: University of Minnesota Press, 2005.

Hayles, N. Katherine. "How We Became Posthuman: Virtual Bodies in Cybernetics, Literature, and Informatics." Chicago: University of Chicago Press, 1999.

Heuser, Sabine. *Virtual Geographies: Cyberpunk at the Intersection of the Postmodern and Science Fiction.* Amsterdam: Rodopi, 2003.

McCaffery, Larry, ed. *Storming the Reality Studio.* Durham: Duke University Press, 1991.

Vint, Sheryl. *Bodies of Tomorrow: Technology, Subjectivity, Science Fiction.* Toronto: University of Toronto Press, 2007.

Notable Cyberpunk and Postcyberpunk Fiction

John Brunner, *Shockwave Rider* (1975).

Emma Bull, *Bone Dance* (1991).

Pad Cadigan,"Pretty Boy Crossover" (1986), *Mindplayers* (1987), *Synners* (1991), *Fools* (1992), *Tea from an Empty Cup* (1998), and *Dervish Is Digital* (2000).

Cory Doctorow, *Down and Out in the Magic Kingdom* (2003).

George Alec Effinger, *When Gravity Fails* (1987), *A Fire in the Sun* (1990), and *The Exile Kiss* (1991).

William Gibson, *Neuromancer* (1984),*Burning Chrome* (1986), *Count Zero* (1986), *Mona Lisa Overdrive* (1988), *Virtual Light* (1993), *Idoru* (1996), and *All Tomorrow's Parties* (1999).

William Gibson and Bruce Sterling, *The Difference Engine* (1990).

K. W. Jeter, *Dr. Adder* (1984), *The Glass Hammer* (1985) and *Noir* (1998).

Ken MacLeod, *The Star Fraction* (1995), *The Stone Canal* (1996), *The Cassini Division* (1998), and *The Sky Road* (1999), and *Learning the World* (2005).

Ian McDonald, *River of Gods* (2005) and *Brasyl* (2007).

Laura J. Mixon, *Glass Houses* (1992).

Richard K. Morgan, *Altered Carbon* (2002), *Broken Angels* (2004), and *Woken Furies* (2005).

Marge Piercy, *He, She, and It* (1991).

Justina Robson, *Silver Screen* (1999).

Mary Rosenblum, *Chimera* (1993).

Rudy Rucker, *Software* (1982), *Wetware* (1988), *Freeware* (1997), *Realware* (2000).

Don Sakers *Dance for the Ivory Madonna* (2002).

Melissa Scott, *Trouble and Her Friends* (1994).

Alice Sheldon (as James Tiptree, Jr.), "The Girl Who Was Plugged In" (1973).

Neal Stephenson, *Snow Crash* (1992) and *The Diamond Age* (1995).

Bruce Sterling, *The Artificial Kid* (1980), *The Schismatrix* (1985), *Mirrorshades: The Cyberpunk Anthology* (editor, 1986), *Islands in the Net* (1988), *Holy Fire* (1994), and *Distraction* (1998).

Notable Posthuman Fiction

Poul Anderson, *Genesis* (1999).
Isaac Asimov, *I, Robot* (1950), *The Caves of Steel* (1954), and *The Naked Sun* (1957).
Greg Bear, *Blood Music* (1985) and *Darwin's Radio* (1999).
Alfred Bester, *The Demolished Man* (1953) and *The Stars My Destination* (1957).
Octavia Butler, *Wild Seed* (1985); "Xenogenesis" series: *Dawn* (1987), *Adulthood Rites* (1987), and *Imago* (1989).
Arthur C. Clarke, *Childhood's End* (1953).
Philip K. Dick, *The Simulacra* (1964), *We Can Build You* (1972), and *Do Androids Dream of Electric Sheep?* (1968).
Greg Egan, *Permutation City* (1994), *Diaspora* (1997), and *Schild's Ladder* (2002).
Joe Haldeman, *Forever Peace* (1997).
Nancy Kress, *Beggars in Spain* (1993).
Ken MacLeod, *Learning the World* (2005).
China Miéville, *Perdido Street Station* (2000), *The Scar* (2002), and *Iron Council* (2004).
Linda Nagata, *The Bohr Maker* (1995), *Tech Heaven* (1995), *Deception Well* (1997), and *Vast* (1998).
Jeff Noon, *Vurt* (1993) and *Pollen* (1995).
Justina Robson, *Natural History* (2004).
Geoff Ryman, *The Child Garden* (1989).
Mary Shelley, *Frankenstein* (1818).
Robert Silverberg, *Dying Inside* (1972).
John Sladek, *The Reproductive System* (1968), and *Roderick* (1980).
Joan Slonczewski, *Brain Plague* (2000).
Cordwainer Smith, *Norstrilia* (1975).
Olaf Stapledon, *First and Last Men* (1930), *Odd John* (1935), and *Star Maker* (1937).
Charles Stross, *Accelerando* (2005).
Theodore Sturgeon, *More Than Human* (1953).
A. E. Van Vogt, *Slan* (1940).
Joan Vinge, *Psion* (1982), *Catspaw* (1988), *Dreamfall* (1996).
H. G. Wells, *The Island of Dr. Moreau* (1896).

Notable Films

Artificial Intelligence: AI. Dir. Steven Spielberg, 2001.
Blade Runner. Dir. Ridley Scott, 1982.
eXistenZ. Dir. David Cronenberg, 1999.

Gattaca. Dir. Andrew Niccol, 1997.

Ghost in the Shell. Dir. Mamoru Oshii, 1995.

Hardware. Dir. Richard Stanley, 1990.

I, Robot. Dir. Alex Proyas, 2004.

Johnny Mnemonic. Dir. Robert Longo, 1995.

The Matrix (1999), *The Matrix Reloaded* (2003), and *The Matrix Revolutions* (2003). Dirs. Andy Wachowski and Larry Wachowski.

Robocop. Dir. Paul Verhoeven, 1987.

Strange Days. Dir. Kathryn Bigelow, 1995.

The Terminator (1984) and Terminator 2: Judgment Day (1991). Dir. James Cameron.

Tron. Dir. Steven Lisberger, 1982.

Virtuosity. Dir. Brett Leonard, 1995.

Videodrome. Dir. David Cronenberg, 1983.

Multicultural Science Fiction

In its potential for imagining both "Otherness" and alternatives to the status quo, science fiction has proven to be as effective a literary form for deconstructing the category of race as it has been for gender. Traditionally, however, the field has been dominated by white writers, with people of color frequently excluded from the ranks of writers as well as from the fiction itself. The technological expansionism characteristic of much early sf – often accompanied by the conquest and colonization of alien peoples and planets – served to alienate many readers of color, who rarely saw representations of themselves as major human characters in these texts. They could, however, often detect a reflection of themselves in the (typically negative) depiction of alien Others, ranging from the conquered to threatening invaders. And while a number of works attempted to deal with contemporary racial tensions by positing futures or worlds in which racism does not exist and multiple races coexist peacefully, these utopian scenarios frequently sacrificed difference in order to promote a vision of racial harmony. In response, avid minority readers of early sf who recognized its shortcomings in addressing race drew upon the flexibility of the genre to accommodate difference, becoming writers who – writing from the position of metaphorical Other – interrogated the trope of colonization and explored their own sense of alienation within sf and society at large. Additionally, in recent years postcolonial writers have begun to turn to sf to express the strangeness of their societies' historical encounters with Western modernity. At least for Western readers, the perspectives of these writers produce a double sort of cognitive estrangement growing out because they write from non-Western cultural positions, while at the same time employing the usual cognitive resources of science fiction as a genre.

Western science fiction has at least made the attempt to help Western readers think beyond their own experience, often in ways that are directly and specifically relevant to the relationship of those readers and their cultures with the people and cultures of the rest of the world. Indeed, a substantial number of science fiction novels are specifically set in the colonial or postcolonial world or derive their material directly from colonial and postcolonial cultures. Although many of these, like Frank Herbert's classic *Dune* (1965), with its ostensibly positive inflection of Arab Bedouin culture, inadvertently repeat certain stereotypes of colonialist discourse, most at least attempt to be sensitive to the cultures they portray rather than simply using these locales as exotic settings for lurid adventures.

One of the writers best known for these kinds of works is the American Mike Resnick, whose recreations of Kenya and Kenyan culture in such works as *Paradise* (1989) and *Kirinyaga* (1998) are among the most straightforward of science fictional attempts to create new perspectives on the colonization of Africa by transposing that historical event (and African culture itself) into the future colonization of outer space. In *Evolution's Shore* (1995, originally published in the UK as *Chaga*) and *Kirinya* (1998), British writer Ian McDonald depicts an Africa in the throes of globalization and coping with an alien invasion – in the form of an enigmatic life form dubbed the Chaga – that seems designed to spur human evolution in dramatic new directions. McDonald explores the effects of globalization in other postcolonial settings with recent novels *River of Gods* (2005), which takes place in the India of 2047, and *Brasyl* (2007), set in past, present, and near future Brazil. Canadian-British writer Geoff Ryman also explores globalization and the impact of Western technologies on the rest of the cultures of the world with the novel *Air* (2004), which depicts a technology that allows a vast information network to connect directly to the brains of individual people. This technology allows all the world's cultures exactly the same access to information and services – though of course users are better equipped to cope with the new technologies in some parts of the world than in others. Ryman's novel focuses on the small village of Kizuldah – described as the last village in the world to go online – in the fictional central Asian republic of Karzistan. In particular, it focuses on village denizen Chung Mae, as she learns to take advantage of the utopian possibilities of the new technology while mourning its negative effects upon her culture.

While paranoid visions of the Other are rampant in Western science fiction television and film, particularly in the 1950s, the liberalism of the 1960s fueled more positive representations and a sensitivity to multicultural perspectives. The iconic *Star Trek* (1966–1969), for example, sought mightily to avoid xenophobia and to insist on the fundamental humanity of all intelligent species, meanwhile featuring a multi-ethnic central cast. Later *Star Trek* series – especially *Deep Space Nine* (1993–1999) – go even further in the attempt to break the dominance of American white male characters in central roles, as well as to avoid colonialist stereotyping. Partly as a result of the enormous influence of *Star Trek*, virtually every major science fiction series since the mid-1990s – *Firefly* (2002–2003) and *Battlestar Galactica* (2004–) are notable examples – has featured a multi-ethnic cast. Meanwhile, racism and xenophobia have been critiqued in a number of sf films, from *Alien Nation* (1988) to *Children of Men* (2006). *The Matrix* (1999) and its sequels feature a multi-ethic underclass that opposes the tyrannical machines that control them, with the mixed race Neo (Eurasian Keanu Reeves) as its hero. And African American Will Smith, who has had lead roles in films such as *Independence Day* (1996); *Men in Black* (1997); *I, Robot* (2004); and *I Am Legend* (2007), is surely the single biggest sf film star.

Such attempts to represent the points of view of other cultures accurately and sympathetically are a step in the right direction, but the true promise of sf in this sense lies in the representation of other cultural perspectives by those who occupy them. While such writers have been rare in sf to this point, the great success achieved by African American sf writers such as Samuel R. Delany and Octavia Butler demonstrates the promise of sf as a vehicle for the representation of cultural perspectives that differ from the white, male, middle-class mainstream of Western culture. Though doubly marginalized by virtue of being both African American and openly gay, Delany is one of the foremost figures in the history of science fiction, a highly influential author and critic whose many works have helped to redefine the genre. Beginning in the 1960s, Delany introduced a perspective that was entirely lacking in sf, and his sophisticated exploration of issues related to race and gender set his work apart from many of his contemporaries. Delany's work is also formally complex and sophisticated, informed by the latest developments in poststructuralist and postmodernist theory. From his earliest works, Delany has been concerned with sign systems and social structures, key elements explored in *Babel-17* (1966), the first novel to garner the author major recognition within the field. A space opera that features galactic warfare between the Alliance (which includes Earth among its forces) and the Invaders, the novel follows the adventures of Alliance poet, telepath, and starship captain Rydra Wong, who discovers that an effective weapon used by the Invaders is actually a new language called Babel-17. Formulated to turn anyone against the Alliance who learns it, the language alters even Wong's sense of reality as she begins to learn it, demonstrating the extent to which language has the ability to structure experience. Wong, whose diverse and hastily assembled crew eventually succeeds in communicating with one another despite speaking a variety of languages, is with their help able to avoid being completely trapped by Babel-17 and manages in the end to turn the weapon against its creators.

Delany's *The Einstein Intersection* (1967), a post-apocalyptic tale in which difference – whether figured in terms of race, gender, genetics, or extraordinary abilities – is revealed to be the primary strength of the mutated posthumans or aliens who inhabit an Earth long abandoned by humanity. Attempting to live out the myths of their human predecessors, the mutants only begin to realize their potential as separate beings when they embrace rather than denigrate their own diversity and hybridity, leaving the ill-fitting human ways behind. Lo Lobey, a dark-skinned musician who hears music in others' minds, which he then replicates on his musical machete, is the embodiment of a difference that opens up possibilities for the future – his music has the potential to help usher in a new world order. "Difference," while it signifies much more than race in the novel, is also handled in a way that clearly resonates with debates about race in the 1960s, and Lobey's self-described appearance – brown, physically imposing, and gorilla-like – is a play on negative racial stereotypes about African Americans. That Lobey triumphs over the villain Kid Death, whose skin has a pure white cast, is symbolic of the destruction of constraints upon his people's potential to make the world new.

Dhalgren (1975), Delany's best-known novel, is remarkable for its literary experimentation and complexity, as well as for producing a radical cognitive estrangement that seems designed to make readers question everything they think they know about the world. The novel may also be seen as a commentary on the social unrest in African American urban communities in the 1960s and 1970s. Set in the fictional midwestern city of Bellona at a time roughly contemporaneous with the novel's publication, *Dhalgren* explores the social dynamics of the city in the aftermath of some unnamed catastrophe that has left it cut off from the outside world. When the Kid – an unnamed bisexual poet of apparently Native American heritage – enters the smoking ruins of Bellona, he finds most of the population gone, no governmental organizations in existence, and "normal" social structures rapidly deteriorating. The Kid thrives in this seemingly chaotic environment, producing poems and entering into meaningful and experimental sexual arrangements with women and men that pose a clear challenge to compulsory heterosexuality. In addition, Delany's treatment of an ostensible rape between a black man and a white teenage girl – the circumstances of which become murkier and less certain as the novel progresses and different points of view are introduced – challenges mythologies associated with black male sexuality. Some semblance of order in Bellona is achieved by the presence of gangs, most of whose members are black, and Kid eventually joins one known as the scorpions and becomes its *de facto* leader. Despite the scorpions' condemnation by the local newspaper (run by what remains of the white establishment in Bellona) as destructive and lawless – echoing descriptions in the 1960s mainstream media of urban African Americans who rioted as a result of the injustices of institutionalized racism – the gang is a locus of potentially revolutionary energy that turns the traditional notion of law and order on its head. With its emphasis on an oppositional underclass that makes its own rules in a wasted urban landscape, *Dhalgren* is a forerunner of cyberpunk, though issues concerning racial conflict are frequently absent in the latter.

With *Trouble on Triton* (1976), the potentially revolutionary space for alternative sexualities suggested in *Dhalgren*'s Bellona finds its ultimate fulfillment in the heterotopia of Tethys, where citizens are free to change gender, sex, and orientation at will (through surgical and therapeutic means) and enjoy a stunning variety of sexual activities. Sexual taboos are absent, genders are multiple, and the society is defined by openness and plurality. However, for protagonist Bron Helstrom, an immigrant from the far less tolerant Mars, the lack of traditional and restrictive structures in Tethys is repellant and confusing, and despite his attempts to adapt (he even undergoes a procedure to become a woman), he never feels at home there.

Stars in My Pockets Like Grains of Sand (1984) takes another displaced subject – the former slave Rat Korga – and plunges him in a bewildering new world after his own is destroyed. His coming together with the Industrial Diplomat Marq Dyeth, a respected liaison between different cultures and species in a Federation comprised of over six thousand planets, serves as the primary plot of the novel. Theirs is a union in which each is the other's erotic ideal, and in which the difference each represents is a major part of the mutual attraction. Their brief relationship is a kind of microcosm of the staggering cultural diversity to be found among the Federation planets, and Delany's attempt to capture the difference suggested by this almost unimaginably complex universe is perhaps his most ambitious undertaking to date.

The African American Butler is widely recognized as one of the finest writers in the field. A woman and a feminist, Butler writes from a position of opposition to the ways race and gender have been traditionally represented in sf, and her fiction consistently uses the figure of the alien (whether extraterrestrial or not) to challenge these culturally constructed categories. With the "Patternist" novels, a series that includes *Patternmaster* (1976), *Mind of My Mind* (1977), *Survivor* (1978), *Wild Seed* (1980), and *Clay's Ark* (1984), Butler's examination of power relations involving race and gender are explored through psionic powers, mind transfer, viral infection, genetic engineering, and a representation of the alien that disrupts the binary of self and other, thereby calling into question what it means to be human. Spanning hundreds of centuries in an alternative history of the Earth, the series details the origin and ascendance of a selectively bred group of telepaths, who are eventually linked together in a psychic pattern. The founder of this elite community is the genetic mutant and psychic parasite Doro, a four-thousand-year-old Nubian who oversees the breeding of his descendants in a bid to create a race of superhumans, and who ensures his own survival by killing and then transferring his essence to suitable host bodies. *Wild Seed* recounts the history of Doro's breeding program, and the novel begins in seventeenth-century Africa in the midst of the slave trade. Butler draws parallels between Doro's proprietary feelings for his descendants and those of white slave masters, as well as his callously matter-of-fact attitude toward breeding people (often without their consent). When he meets the "wild seed" Anyanwu, a three-hundred-year-old Igbo healer and shapeshifter who has heretofore existed without his knowledge, he threatens to harm her family if she does not participate in his breeding plans. Although she initially submits, Anyanwu escapes by taking the form of different animals, in addition to changing both sex and race. While her identity remains stable, the fluidity of her changes dissolves boundaries between black and white, male and female – effectively destabilizing power structures based on race and gender. Doro, for his part, also inhabits bodies of different races and sexes, but he cannot track Anyanwu when she takes animal form.

Eventually Doro and Anyanwu establish an uneasy truce in the United States, and Anyanwu becomes Emma of *Mind of My Mind*, a matriarch who oversees the vast twentieth-century family that she and Doro have created. She chooses to die when Doro is killed by his young African American daughter Mary, a powerful telepath who establishes the first pattern and thus becomes a rival to her father's power. Though something of a symbiont rather than a parasite, Mary shares her father's proprietary feelings for her people and feeds upon the network of telepaths, garnering mental and emotional strength. She also manipulates non-telepaths (mutes) to aid her family in raising telepath children, while the subjugated position of the mutes allegorizes race relations in the US. By the time of *Pattern-master*, which takes place long after the events in *Mind of My Mind*, the mutes are little more than slaves to their telepath masters.

Disease in *Clay's Ark* enables a posthumanism of a more radical sort than that orchestrated by Doro; an extraterrestrial virus carried by explorers returning to a dystopian, near-future Earth so completely transforms human cells that the hosts produce beast-like quadruped children with increased sensory perception and maturation levels. The hybrid children create anxiety in the humans who come into contact with them, including their own parents, who find it difficult to come to terms with the difference their offspring represents. Known simply as Clayarks in *Pattern-master* and *Survivor*, the descendants of these hybrids wage war with the telepaths, who consider them to be non-human and kill them in vast numbers.

Although many of Butler's novels carry allusions to the slave narrative, it is *Kindred* (1979) that most clearly incorporates the form, combining it with a time travel story. Dana Franklin, a young African American writer, finds herself periodically transported from her 1976 California home to an ante-bellum Maryland plantation. The mechanism of her transport is never explained, and her involuntary trips leave her disoriented – an echo, per-haps, of the transport her slave ancestors endured in the middle passage from Africa to America. Drawn into the past whenever her ancestor Rufus Weylin, the white son of a plantation owner, is endangered, Dana rescues him several times. At first, she saves him unthinkingly, but as he grows from an abused child to a cruel patriarch, Dana begins to suppress her own instincts in order to help him survive (and thus ensure her own survival). She makes a place for herself in the slave community as she awaits her return to the present, but in adopting the role of slave, she allows herself to be treated like one. Her complicated, interdependent relationship with Rufus – who both fears and loves her – ends when he attempts to seduce and dominate her as he had other slaves. Refusing to give up the autonomy left to her, Dana kills Rufus, and in the process loses an arm to his grip. She returns home to the present mutilated, a grim reminder of the legacy of slavery that still haunts Americans, both black and white.

The "Xenogenesis" trilogy, which includes *Dawn* (1987), *Adulthood Rites* (1987), and *Imago* (1989), is generally regarded as Butler's master-piece. Faced with the radical difference represented by the alien Oankali, who attempt to rescue what remains of humanity in the wake of a nuclear holocaust, humans struggle with accepting the terms the aliens offer: humanity will become obsolete, replaced by human-alien hybrids produced as a result of genetic exchange between Oankali and human. Only by embracing difference will humans survive, a strategy that requires them to overcome the visceral horror they feel in relation to the truly alien Oankali. The novels follow the trajectory of their resistance and the radical transfor-mations that result from their reluctant cooperation with the aliens. Although the Oankali are more benevolent than Doro, their enforced breed-ing program carries the same echoes of slavery – and the Oankali simply sterilize humans who refuse to participate.

Survival – at whatever cost – is also a major theme of Butler's "Earthseed" novels, which include *The Parable of the Sower* (1993) and its sequel *The Parable of the Talents* (1998). Set in a dystopian, anarchic 2024 California where the gaps between the haves and have-nots have widened considerably, *The Parable of the Sower* is the story of Lauren Olamina, an African American teenager who is an empath, sharing others' pain and pleasure. When the walled suburban enclave in which she lives is destroyed, Lauren and the few survivors travel up the coast, seeking affordable water and jobs. Eventually they accumulate other travelers and attempt to form a utopian community away from the chaos that surrounds them. Lauren, meanwhile, develops a religion that she calls "Earthseed," which is based on the notion that "God is change" and holds that adaptation is the key to survival and to humanity's eventual progress to the stars. In order to survive, however, it is sometimes necessary to use violence, a strategy that is at odds with the utopian imagination but unavoidable in the face of threats posed by the social and economic collapse in the US. In *The Parable of the Talents*, the Earthseed community comes under attack by religious fundamentalists in the service of a new conservative president, whose brutal methods include separating parents from their children. Earthseed, however, lives on, and the book ends with Lauren watching the first starship leaving the Earth, a symbol of utopian ambitions fulfilled.

While Butler and Delany are the superstars among African American sf writers, a number of black writers have come into their own in recent years. For example, in *Lion's Blood* (2002) and *Zulu Heart* (2003) Steven Barnes produces a powerful form of cognitive estrangement in his alternative history of an America colonized by Africans who employ European slaves, deconstructing racial oppositions and demonstrating that people are fundamentally the same, though they may find themselves in very different circumstances. Walter Mosley, better known for his work in other genres, has ventured into sf with his novels *Blue Light* (1998) and *The Wave* (2005), as well as the cyberpunk-inflected short story collection *Futureland* (2001), which features a variety of black protagonists struggling to survive in a brutal dystopian near future. Seeking to demonstrate that there is, in fact, a long and rich tradition of speculative fiction by black writers, Sheree R. Thomas's two groundbreaking *Dark Matter* anthologies (published in 2000 and 2004) include selections from a wide variety of prominent and lesser known writers, among them Delany, Butler, Barnes, Charles Saunders, Tananarive Due, Nalo Hopkinson, and black sf pioneer George Schuyler.

Another important anthology is *So Long Been Dreaming: Postcolonial Science Fiction and Fantasy* (2004), edited by Nalo Hopkinson and Uppinder Mehan, which can be taken as an announcement that science fiction and fantasy written by writers from the postcolonial world now exist as recognizable literary phenomena. Many of the stories in the volume address issues that are crucial to the phenomenon of colonialism and its aftermath. Hopkinson, a Jamaican-born Canadian novelist, argues in the introduction that science fiction, however Western its origins, offers potentially powerful tools to postcolonial writers. It is an argument that she has set out to prove in her own fiction, works that have garnered her major recognition in the field. Her first novel *Brown Girl in the Ring* (1998) features characters of Caribbean descent in the decaying urban dystopia of Toronto, in which the deterioration of the inner city has caused it to be abandoned by both the government and corporate capital, leaving an impoverished and anarchic environment dominated by the gangleader Rudy (who practices *obeah*, a sort of Caribbean black magic) and his minions. The "Burn," as the inner city is called, is in many ways a nightmarish landscape, yet the remaining inhabitants (a disproportionate number of whom are black) work together to help each other survive, establishing localized senses of community that are often lacking in the alienated urban environments of our own contemporary cities. Many of the characters are aided in their cooperative efforts by Caribbean traditions, reflecting both the author's background and because the real-world Toronto hosts a large and vibrant Caribbean community. Hopkinson's prominent use of images and motifs from Caribbean folklore give the book a specifically anticolonial slant, identifying indigenous cultures as a source of strength and as a rallying point for the collective action she celebrates. Indeed, young single mother and protagonist Ti-Jeanne draws upon Caribbean spiritual practices she once rejected, enabling her in the end to defeat Rudy with the help of others in the community.

Midnight Robber (2000), Hopkinson's second novel, also contains numerous instances of the downtrodden working to help each other. The text suggests that shared cultural traditions can help hold people together as a community even in new and very different surroundings, such as the prison planet of New Half-Way Tree. It is on this planet that Tan-Tan, a young girl descended from Caribbean colonists, finds herself permanently exiled from her home planet of Touissant after her father kidnaps her. Eventually, with the help of an indigenous alien race and sympathetic humans, Tan-Tan manages to create a place for herself and heal her psychological wounds.

Another up-and-coming Caribbean writer is Tobias Buckell, born in Grenada and raised in various Caribbean locales. Buckell's debut novel *Crystal Rain* (2006) is set on the planet Nanagada, settled by culturally and ethnically diverse human colonists who have developed a culture reminiscent of Caribbean cultures. Like Hopkinson, Buckell incorporates Caribbean dialect into the novel, and his characters are also far removed – in terms of time and space – from their origins. Cut off from the rest of the universe for centuries as the result of an alien war, the technology the humans employ on Nanagada is somewhat primitive, which gives their civilization a steampunk flavor. In the opening of the novel, the Nanagadans who occupy the peninsula are under attack from an enemy known as the Azteca, humans living on the other side of a mountain range who worship their alien rulers (known as the Toetl) as gods – and who perform blood sacrifice identical to that practiced by ancient Aztecs. What ensues is an adventure story revolving around the characters John de Brun and Pepper, two ragamuffins, or technologically enhanced spacefaring freedom fighters, who have been trapped on the planet for three hundred years and who help the peninsula-dwelling Nanagadans defend themselves from the Azteca. Following *Crystal Rain* are the space operas *Ragamuffin* (2007) and *Sly Mongoose* (2008), which take place in the same universe but whose heroes are no longer planet-bound.

Although science fiction of the African diaspora continues to grow, Africa itself has produced relatively little of it by comparison. However, Africa does have a strong dystopian tradition, with South Africa as the source for many of these works, both in print and on radio programs. Other countries are not quite as fertile, though interest in the genre appears to be growing. Well-known Nigerian author Buchi Emecheta ventures into sf territory in her seemingly postapocalyptic novel *The Rape of Shavi* (1985), in which a group of Westerners attempting to escape what they believe to be an impending nuclear holocaust flee England in an experimental aircraft and crash in the Sahara Desert; however, the novel employs a vaguely science fictional framework to create a sort of parable of cross-cultural exchange that relies rather little on the usual technological trappings of science fiction.

There are signs that science fiction in a more conventional sense may be on the verge of a boom among postcolonial writers, however, as the rise of authors such as Hopkinson and Buckell attest. Another sign of this potential boom is the increased critical attention that has recently been shown to science fiction traditions (especially in Latin America) that have existed outside the Western mainstream for some time now. In the recent anthology *Cosmos Latinos* (2003), for example, editors Andrea L. Bell and Yolanda Molina-Gavilan collect more than two dozen sf stories (written in either Spanish or Portuguese) from Spain and Latin America, published in the range from 1862 to 2001. The Portuguese-language stories are from Brazil, which has a particularly rich tradition of science fiction writing. Although Mexico is more generally known for its incorporation of sf conventions in its cinema than in its fiction, its literary output is growing. A book such as In *The Law of Love* (1996; translated from *Ley del Amor*), a blend of science fiction with romance in twenty-third-century Mexico City written by popular novelist Laura Esquivel, suggests that the genre's profile is rising.

As with Brazil and other parts of Latin America, in India there is a fairly long and diverse tradition of science fiction, but the works belonging to this tradition are little known in the West because few of them were written in or have been translated into English. In terms of English language works, Salman Rushdie is perhaps the best-known novelist who employs science fiction conventions in his works. He began his career, in fact, with the sf novel *Grimus* (1975), which features the adventures of a Native American protagonist in a parallel universe. The novel mixes its numerous echoes of Western literary and mythological sources with a rich hodgepodge of materials from non-Western culture. The parallel-universe motif is also central to Rushdie's *The Ground Beneath Her Feet* (1999), a rock-music retelling of the Orpheus myth.

Amitav Ghosh's novel *The Calcutta Chromosome* (1995) is, like *Grimus*, another potent combination of East and West that suggests there are more kinds of knowledge and more kinds of power than can be encompassed by Western Enlightenment models. Ghosh combines a science fiction framework with a sort of historical detective story, the solution to which suggests that the Nobel Prize-winning discovery by British scientist Ronald Ross that malaria is transmitted through the bite of the anopheles mosquito was achieved not merely through Western-style scientific inquiry but through the intervention of Eastern-style mysticism. The novel's intricate interweaving of Western science and Eastern mysticism undermines the privileging of the former in colonialist discourse, but also retain a strong connection between the two.

The work of novelists such as Delany, Butler, Hopkinson, Buckell, Ghosh, and Rushdie suggests a potentially bright future for multicultural science fiction. Shored by the cognitive estrangement provided by the science fictional frameworks within which they write, these authors remind us of the plurality of and richness of different cultures teeming across the globe. At the same time, the novels of these writers, especially when they are produced within the typically Western genre of science fiction, are suggestive of our commonalities – especially in juxtaposition to the potentially radical differences we may eventually encounter elsewhere in the universe.

Suggested Further Reading

Booker, M. Keith. "African Literature and the World System: Dystopian Fiction, Collective Experience, and the Postcolonial Condition." *Research in African Literatures* 26.4 (1995): 58–75.

DeGraw, Sharon. *The Subject of Race in American Science Fiction*. New York: Routledge, 2007.

Grayson, Sandra M. *Visions of the Third Millennium: Black Science Fiction Novelists Write the Future*. Trenton, NJ: Africa World Press, 2003.

Leonard, Elisabeth Anne, ed. *Into Darkness Peering: Race and Color in the Fantastic*. Westport, CT: Greenwood, 1997.

Leonard, Elisabeth Anne, "Race and Ethnicity in Science Fiction." *The Cambridge Companion to Science Fiction*. Eds. Edward James and Farah Mendelsohn. Cambridge: Cambridge University Press, 2003. 253–263.

Pordzik, Ralph. *The Quest For Postcolonial Utopia: A Comparative Introduction to the Utopian Novel in New English Literatures*. New York: Peter Lang, 2001.

Tucker, Jeffrey Allen. *A Sense of Wonder: Samuel R. Delany, Race, Identity, and Difference*. Middletown, CT: Wesleyan University Press, 2004.

Notable Fiction

Steven Barnes, *Lion's Blood* (2002), *Zulu Heart* (2003).

Andrea L. Bell and Yolanda Molina-Gavilan (eds.), *Cosmos Latinos* (2003).

Michael Bishop, *Transfigurations* (1979).

David Brin, *Sundiver* (1980), *Startide Rising* (1983), and *The Uplift War* (1987).

Tobias Buckell, *Crystal Rain* (2006), *Ragamuffin* (2007), and *Sly Mongoose* (2008).

Octavia Butler, "Patternist" series: *Patternmaster* (1976), *Mind of My Mind* (1977), *Survivor* (1978), *Wild Seed* (1980), and *Clay's Ark* (1984); *Kindred* (1979); "Xenogenesis" series: *Dawn* (1987), *Adulthood Rites* (1987), and *Imago* (1989); *The Parable of the Sower* (1993); and *The Parable of the Talents* (1998).

Orson Scott Card, *Speaker for the Dead* (1986, revised 1994).

Samuel R. Delany, *Babel-17* (1966), *The Einstein Intersection* (1967), *Dhalgren* (1975), *Trouble on Triton* (1976), and *Stars in My Pocket Like Grains of Sand* (1984).

Buchi Emecheta, *The Rape of Shavi* (1985).

Laura Esquivel, *The Law of Love* (1996).

Minister Faust, *The Coyote Kings of the Space-Age Bachelor Pad* (2004).

Amitav Ghosh (India), *The Calcutta Chromosome* (1995).

Kathleen Ann Goonan, *The Bones of Time* (1996).

Frank Herbert, *Dune* (1965).

Nalo Hopkinson, *Brown Girl in the Ring* (1998), *Midnight Robber* (2000), *The Salt Roads* (2003), and *So Long Been Dreaming: Postcolonial Science Fiction and Fantasy* (2004, edited with Uppinder Mehan).

Ursula K. Le Guin, *The Word for World Is Forest* (1972).

Ian McDonald, *Evolution's Shore* (1995), *Kirinya* (1998), *Sacrifice of Fools* (1996), *River of Gods* (2005), and *Brasyl* (2007).

Maureen F. McHugh, *Nekropolis* (2001).

Walter Mosley, *Blue Light* (1998), *Futureland* (2001), and *The Wave* (2005).
Larry Niven and Jerry Pournelle, *The Mote in God's Eye* (1974).
Mike Resnick, *Paradise* (1989) and *Kirinyaga* (1998).
Salman Rushdie, *Grimus* (1975) and *The Ground Beneath Her Feet* (1999).
Geoff Ryman, *Air* (2004).
Don Sakers, *Dance for the Ivory Madonna* (2002).
Robert Silverberg, *Invaders from Earth* (1958) and *Downward to the Earth* (1969).
Sheree R. Thomas (ed.), *Dark Matter* anthologies (2000, 2004).
Liz Williams, *Empire of the Bones* (2002).

Notable Films

Alien Nation. Dir. Graham Baker, 1988.
Children of Men. Dir. Alfonso Cuaron, 2006.
Enemy Mine. Dir. Wolgang Peterson, 1985.
I Am Legend. Dir. Francis Lawrence, 2007.
Independence Day. Dir. Roland Emmerich, 1996.
I, Robot. Dir. Alex Proyas, 2004.
The Matrix (1999). *The Matrix Reloaded* (2003), and *The Matrix Revolutions* (2003). Dirs. Andy Wachowski and Larry Wachowski, 1999.
Men in Black. Dir. Barry Sonnefeld, 1997.
Serenity. Dir. Joss Whedon, 2005.

Part 3

Representative Science Fiction Authors

Isaac Asimov (1920–1992)

Born to Jewish parents in Petrovichi, Russia, Asimov grew up in Brooklyn, New York, eventually graduating from Columbia University in 1939; he received his doctorate in biochemistry from the same school in 1948. He then joined the faculty of the Boston University School of Medicine, though by this time he was already an established writer of science fiction short stories, having published frequently in John W. Campbell's *Astounding Science-Fiction*. Asimov's early stories include the classic "Nightfall" (1941), as well as the stories that would later be compiled into *I, Robot* (1950) and the "Foundation" trilogy: *Foundation* (1951), *Foundation and Empire* (1952), and *Second Foundation* (1953). A central figure in the rise of the science fiction novel in the 1950s, Asimov extended his groundbreaking "Robot" series with the novels *The Caves of Steel* (1954) and *The Naked Sun* (1957). The concepts in this series, especially the Three Laws of Robotics, are among the most important and influential in the history of science fiction. The "Foundation" trilogy has been extremely influential as well, extending Asimov's importance to science fiction well beyond his own writing in the field.

A sort of science fiction reinscription of Gibbon's *Decline and Fall of the Roman Empire* (set in the distant future), the "Foundation" novels detail a time after the collapse of the mighty Galactic Empire plunges the galaxy into a new Middle Ages. But the novels ultimately show faith in the beneficial effects of science and technology in expanding the possibilities of humankind. A similar pro-technology theme is central to Asimov's robot stories and novels, which explore the potential benefits of intelligent robots to humankind. Asimov virtually ceased writing fiction in 1958, concentrating instead on the prolific production of nonfiction works on a wide variety of subjects, including popular science, literature, religion, and autobiography. These nonfiction works, like his fiction, reflect his commitment to liberal humanism and to rationality as the key to solving humanity's problems. They remain the bulk of the more than five hundred volumes that he wrote or edited during his lifetime. Asimov did, however, return to fiction in 1982 with the publication of *Foundation's Edge* (1982). He further extended the "Foundation" saga with *Foundation and Earth* (1986), *Prelude to Foundation* (1988), and the posthumous *Forward the Foundation* (1993). He also extended the "Robot" series during this last period of his career with the publication of *The Robots of Dawn* (1983), *Robots and Empire* (1985), and *The Positronic Man* (1993, written with Robert Silverberg and based on Asimov's earlier story "The Bicentennial Man").

As testimony to the enduring legacy of the "Foundation" series, a subsequent "Foundation" trilogy was produced after Asimov's death, building upon his ideas and written by some of the leading American sf writers. These volumes include Gregory Benford's *Foundation's Fear* (1998), Greg Bear's *Foundation and Chaos* (1999), and David Brin's *Foundation's Triumph* (2000). Asimov's work has also been the subject of a substantial body of criticism, including the book-length studies by Gunn (1996), Palumbo (2002), and Patrouch (1974).

Margaret Atwood (1939–)

Born in Ottawa and educated at the University of Toronto and Harvard University, Margaret Atwood is probably the best-known Canadian writer to have worked since the 1960s, when she first rose to prominence. Especially important as a poet and novelist, she is also an essayist, television scriptwriter, and political activist. She has written children's fiction and short stories as well as novels, and has also edited anthologies of fiction and poetry. Atwood's most important work of criticism is the 1972 volume *Survival: A Thematic Guide to Canadian Literature*, which, influenced by the myth criticism of Northrop Frye, describes a national typology of patterns of plot and character through which Canadian literature expresses victimization and survival rather than heroism and triumph. Her poems, as in the volumes *Power Politics* (1971) and *You Are Happy* (1974), address many of the same issues as do her novels, including a critique of traditional patterns of relationships between men and women in patriarchal societies. This focus has led Atwood to be described as a feminist writer, though her work explores a wide range of themes and issues, including Canadian national identity and Canada's relations with the United States.

From the beginning, Atwood's novels have been marked by an unusual diversity in subject matter and genre, though they have often veered into the fantastic, the Gothic, and the speculative. Atwood's 1985 novel *The Handmaid's Tale*, which portrays a near-future dystopian society dominated by misogynist religious fundamentalism, is her best-known novel, as well as her most important foray into science fiction. *The Handmaid's Tale* won the 1987 Arthur C. Clarke Award for the best annual sf novel by a writer from the British Commonwealth; it remains one of the most successful examples of science fiction by a writer not typically associated with the genre. Atwood returned to science fiction in 2003 with the publication of *Oryx and Crake*, a postapocalyptic novel that takes place in the wake of a catastrophic genetic engineering accident that has wiped out most of humanity. Atwood's other novels include such examples of "Southern Ontario Gothic" as *Cat's Eye* (1989), *Alias Grace* (1996, winner of the Giller Prize), and *The Blind Assassin* (2000, winner of the Booker Prize).

Octavia E. Butler (1947–2006)

Born in Pasadena, California, the daughter of a shoeshiner and a maid, Octavia Butler was a shy child who began writing at age ten to combat loneliness and boredom. She began publishing short stories in 1971 and remained an important writer of short stories throughout her career. She published her first novel, *Patternmaster*, in 1976. This novel went on to become the first of five volumes in the far-ranging "Patternist" series, while Butler herself went on to become the twentieth-century's leading African American woman writer of science fiction and one of the most important science fiction writers of all time.

The "Patternist" series traces an alternative history of Earth from the seventeenth century to the far future, addressing fundamental questions about what it means to be human and involving issues such as race, gender, power, genetic engineering, plagues, and psychic powers. As such, it established early on many of the characteristic concerns of Butler's fiction. It also established Butler as a major figure in American science fiction. In addition to *Patternmaster*, this series includes the novels *Mind of My Mind* (1977), *Survivor* (1978), *Wild Seed* (1980), and *Clay's Ark* (1984).

In 1979, Butler published *Kindred*, which remains her most widely read (and taught) novel. Here, an African American woman living in 1976 finds herself periodically drawn (by means that are never explained) back into the antebellum South, a time-travel scenario that allows Butler to produce detailed descriptions of the experience of slavery, especially for women, somewhat in the mode of Toni Morrison's later *Beloved* (1987). *Kindred* represents some of Butler's most graphic explorations of race and gender within the context of power relationships.

Butler's most important sequence of novels is probably the "Xenogenesis" trilogy, an alien invasion narrative that includes the novels *Dawn* (1987), *Adulthood Rites* (1987), and *Imago* (1989). This trilogy, republished in a single volume as *Lilith's Brood* in 2000, is a virtual compendium of science fictional motifs. In addition to its basic alien invasion scenario, it touches on the themes of nuclear apocalypse, biotechnology, terraforming, and the evolution of the human race into a new race of human–alien hybrids, while maintaining Butler's characteristic focus on race, gender, and power.

Butler followed "Xenogenesis" with *The Parable of the Sower* (1993), a vivid and compelling evocation of an anarchic 2024 America in a state of economic and social collapse, seen through the eyes of narrator/protagonist Lauren Olamina, an African American teenager. Seeking meaning in the midst of chaos, Lauren invents a new religion, which she calls "Earthseed," based on the fundamental premise that "God is change" and the belief that it is the ultimate destiny of humanity to expand into the stars. In a sequel, *The Parable of the Talents* (1998), Lauren struggles to establish a utopian community amid the dystopian conditions that prevail in the world at large, which now include a particularly ominous threat from religious fundamentalism, in addition to anarchy and environmental collapse.

Butler apparently intended to produce other "Earthseed" novels, perhaps detailing the movement into space, but none were to appear. She produced no further novels until the vampire tale *Fledgling* (2006), which appeared shortly before her accidental death from a fall.

Samuel R. Delany (1942–)

Born in New York City and raised in Harlem, Samuel R. Delany began publishing science fiction at the age of twenty and quickly drew considerable attention for the sophistication and literariness of his writing. Early novels such as *Babel-17* (1966) and *The Einstein Intersection* (1967) won Nebula Awards, though Delany's last three (to date) sf novels are the most important, including *Dhalgren* (1975), *Triton* (1976, later republished as *Trouble on Triton*), and *Stars in My Pocket Like Grains of Sand* (1984). Delany is also important as the writer of a series of fantasy stories and novels with potential political implications that set them apart from the escapism of most traditional fantasy works. Published volumes in this series include *Tales of Nevèrÿon* (1979), *Nevèrÿona* (1983), *Flight from Nevèrÿon* (1985), *The Bridge of Lost Desire* (1987, revised as *Return to Nevèrÿon*, 1994).

At the time of writing a professor in the English Department at Temple University after having held similar positions at the University of Massachusetts at Amherst and The University at Buffalo, Delany has long shown a sophisticated awareness of contemporary phenomena such as poststructuralism and postmodernism. This awareness is especially reflected in the self-conscious postmodernism of his later novels. It is also important to his substantial body of published criticism – including volumes such as *The Jewel-Hinged Jaw* (1977) – which makes him one of the most important sf critics and theorists of his generation. An openly gay African American, Delany also shows a strong concern with social and political issues in his work; his novels from *Dhalgren* onward are especially strong in their exploration of issues related to race and gender. These later novels are also unusual in science fiction for their open and explicit depiction of sex and sexuality, a characteristic that is foregrounded even more in his later, non-sf fictions – including *The Mad Man* (1994), *Hogg* (1995),

Atlantis: Three Tales (1995), and *Phallos* (2004) – which Delany himself has categorized as works of pornography.

In addition to these late fictional works, Delany's writing since 1984 has been devoted primarily to criticism, social commentary, and autobiography. His memoir *The Motion of Light in Water* (1988), focusing on his experiences as a young gay science fiction writer, won a Hugo Award. Further demonstrating Delany's versatility, one of his autobiographical writings, *Bread and Wine: An Erotic Tale of New York* (1999), is in the format of a comic, illustrated by Mia Wolff with an introduction by legendary comics author Alan Moore (Delany also authored two issues of the *Wonder Woman* comic in 1972). Also particularly interesting is *Times Square Red, Times Square Blue* (1999), an autobiographical socio-sexual history of New York's Times Square. *Aye, and Gomorrah, and Other Stories* (2002) is a collection of Delany's short stories. His work has generated a substantial body of criticism, including several book-length studies, such as those by Sallis (1996) and Tucker (2004).

Philip K. Dick (1928–1982)

Born in Chicago, Philip K. Dick spent most of his life in California, where much of his fiction is set. He achieved limited recognition during his lifetime, though he was prolific, producing over forty novels and many dozens of stories, most of which is science fiction. Since his death, Dick's critical reputation has grown dramatically, and he is now considered to be in the very first rank of science fiction authors. Many of his books have been reprinted in a uniform quality paperback edition, and a number of his novels and stories have inspired films. He has been the subject of many books and articles, including book-length studies by Robinson (1984), Sutin (1989), and Williams (1986). The eminent Marxist critic Fredric Jameson, in an obituary, hailed Dick as "the Shakespeare of science fiction." Beyond science fiction, an increasing number of critics rank Dick as one of the most important and original American novelists during the second half of the twentieth century.

Dick's works often question the nature (or even existence) of objective reality. However, his serious philosophical concerns are typically combined with a darkly humorous and satirical critique of American society. Unlike much science fiction, Dick's work is normally set on Earth and in the near future, making his work of clear relevance to his own contemporary world. His visions of the growing commercialization of life and the increasing power of government have often proven chillingly prescient. His many works were often written hastily and are not necessarily well crafted, though they tend to show piercing insights and brilliant creativity.

Dick's work is also somewhat uneven, though there is some critical consensus about which of his many novels are the most important. The earliest among these is *The Man in the High Castle* (1962), which won a Hugo Award. This alternative-history novel envisions a world in which the Axis has won World War II and divided the United States into German and Japanese sectors, though it ultimately questions the nature of reality in more profound ways. In *Martian Time-Slip* (1964), a colonized Mars provides the occasion for considerable commentary on trends in the US in the 1960s. *Dr. Bloodmoney* (1965) is the best of Dick's numerous post-holocaust novels written from the late 1950s to the mid-1950s. *Do Androids Dream of Electric Sheep?* (1968) interrogates the nature of humanity by exploring the uncertain boundary between humans and androids (and, more generally, between the real and the unreal). It is probably best known through Ridley Scott's film adaptation *Blade Runner* (1982). *Ubik* (1969) explores the theme of multiple realities in a particularly profound, terrifying, and hilarious way, while *A Scanner Darkly* (1977), Dick's personal favorite among his novels, offers a science fictionalized version of the drug culture of which Dick himself had considerable experience. It was the basis of Richard Linklater's 2006 film of the same title, the most faithful film adaptation of any of Dick's works.

William Gibson (1948–)

Though born in Conway, South Carolina, and still a US citizen, William Gibson has spent most of his life as a resident of Canada (he now lives in Vancouver), where he fled in 1967 to avoid the Vietnam-era draft. Gibson began publishing short stories, largely about the near-future effects of cybernetic technologies on human beings, in 1972. Many of these stories are printed in the collection *Burning Chrome* (1986). These early stories built toward the publication, in 1984, of *Neuromancer*, Gibson's first novel and the book that is generally taken to have announced the arrival of cyberpunk as a full-blown literary phenomenon. That book's combination of sf futurism and hard-boiled style and action became virtually synonymous with cyberpunk, as did its vision of a troubled near future in which high-crime urban squalor mixes uneasily with high-tech virtual reality and human enhancement. *Neuromancer* became the first volume of the "Sprawl" trilogy, which was completed by *Count Zero* (1986) and *Mona Lisa Overdrive* (1988).

Gibson is generally taken to be, along with Bruce Sterling, one of the iconic figures of the cyberpunk movement. In addition, his collaboration with Sterling, *The Difference Engine* (1990), is typically seen as a founding text in the "steampunk" movement, with its vision of an alternative Victorian England in which mechanical computer technology is a crucial factor. Gibson continued his work in sf with a second group of novels, the "Bridge" trilogy, that includes *Virtual Light* (1993), *Idoru* (1996), and *All Tomorrow's Parties* (1999). This trilogy continues the interests of the "Sprawl" trilogy, though it drifts even closer to contemporary reality in its depiction of a dystopian near-future driven by cybernetic technologies and pop culture. By the time of *Pattern Recognition* (2003), Gibson shifted his setting entirely from the future to the present. A thriller whose protagonist is hypersensitive to brands and corporate logos, this novel eschews the projection of future technologies in favor of an exploration of the image-based texture of postmodern reality. It has sometimes been described as the first major literary work to have been impacted by the September 11, 2001, bombings of the World Trade Center, to which it alludes several times. Gibson's latest novel, *Spook Country* (2007), is an espionage thriller heavily concerned with the effects of contemporary media culture.

Gibson's work has proved notoriously resistant to film and television adaptation, though the film *Johnny Mnemonic* (1995), scripted by Gibson himself, is loosely based on one of Gibson's short stories. The 1993 television mini-series *Wild Palms* was also heavily influenced by Gibson's fiction. However, the most prominent example of such influence is probably in *The Matrix* (1999) and its sequels, though Gibson himself (suggesting that *The Matrix* might be the ultimate work of cyberpunk) has argued that the film resembles the work of Philip K. Dick more than his own. Gibson is also the author of numerous articles (especially for *Wired* magazine) and reviews. His work has been the subject of a substantial body of criticism, remaining central to all critical discussions of cyberpunk. Book-length studies devoted specifically to the work of Gibson include those by Cavallaro (2000) and by Olsen (1992).

Nicola Griffith [1960–]

Born in Leeds, England, Nicola Griffith moved to the United States in 1988, where she attended the Clarion Workshop for Science Fiction and Fantasy Writers held at Michigan State University. At the time of writing a resident of Seattle, Griffith resists labels to describe her work, arguing that genre is a marketing convenience and that critics tend to fixate on the lesbian perspectives in her fiction to the exclusion of all else. Nevertheless, her fiction does fall into the recognizable categories of science fiction, fantasy, and detective fiction. Griffith's first novel, *Ammonite* (1994), established her as an important new voice in science fiction and revealed a sophisticated treatment of gender in its update of the feminist utopian tradition of the 1970s. Winner of the James Tiptree Jr. Award, *Ammonite* follows the adventures of anthropologist Marghe Taishan, who visits a planet populated entirely by women who are survivors of a virus that has killed all the men. The novel is significant for its suggestion that the elimination of men does not necessarily guarantee the elimination of structures traditionally associated with the patriarchy.

Slow River (1995), Griffith's Nebula Award-winning second novel, incorporates cyberpunk elements, featuring a near-future setting in which the wealthy daughter of a powerful family (which controls the market for bioengineered organisms used for water purification) is kidnapped; following her escape, she forms a professional and romantic alliance with a computer hacker and hustler who teaches her how to survive in the criminal underworld. As with *Ammonite*, lesbianism is the norm for the major characters, but Griffith's matter-of-fact presentation suggests that sexual orientation is only one aspect of her characters' personalities – these are not "coming out" narratives. With *The Blue Place* (1998), Griffith moved into the realm of detective fiction, introducing Aud Torvingen, a Norwegian former undercover cop, who is also the protagonist in *Stay: A Novel* (2002) and *Always* (2007). In addition to numerous short stories and essays (appearing in such periodicals as *SF Eye* and *Interzone*), Griffith has written the Nebula-Award winning novella "Yaguara" (1994), an erotic tale about two women trying to survive in the Belize jungle amid shapeshifting jaguars. She is also co-editor (with Stephen Pagel) of a three-volume series of anthologies entitled *Bending the Landscape: Fantasy* (1997), *Science Fiction* (1998), and *Horror* (2001). These anthologies explore gay and lesbian issues and have won several awards.

Joe Haldeman (1943–)

Born in Oklahoma City, Joe Haldeman grew up in a variety of locales, ranging from Puerto Rico to Alaska. In 1967, he graduated with a BSc in astronomy from the University of Maryland, but his further education was interrupted when he was drafted into the military in that year. His first novel, *War Year* (1972) is based on his subsequent experiences as a combat engineer in Vietnam (1967–1969), during which time he was wounded in action. His first major work of science fiction was *The Forever War* (1974, revised and preferred edition 1997), an antiwar satire that also draws upon his experience in Vietnam and that won both the Hugo and Nebula Awards. In 1975 Haldeman received a master of fine arts in creative writing from the University of Iowa Writer's Workshop. At the time of writing he splits his time between Gainesville, Florida, and Cambridge, Massachusetts, where he teaches writing at the Massachusetts Institute of Technology.

In addition to *The Forever War* (1974), early highlights of Haldeman's career include *All My Sins Remembered* (1977), which features the typical Haldeman protagonist, a competent man trying to make sense of future chaos on Earth, and *Mindbridge* (1976), a rich work that combines such motifs as space exploration, alien encounters, and psychic powers. It employs modernist narrative techniques influenced by John Dos Passos and John Brunner (the book is dedicated to both). Other early works include two *Star Trek* novels – *Planet of Judgment* (1977) and *World Without End* (1979).

Haldeman has remained consistently productive for more than thirty years, becoming one of the Central American science fiction writers of his era. *The Forever War* eventually grew into a series that included a followup novel, *Forever Peace* (1997), that again won both the Hugo and Nebula Awards. There is also a more direct sequel to *The Forever War,* entitled *Forever Free* (1999). In the midst of the "Forever" sequence, Haldeman published the "Worlds" sequence, which includes *Worlds* (1981), *Worlds*

Apart (1983), and *Worlds Enough and Time* (1992); this sequence features a female protagonist in a near-future Earth threatened by nuclear holocaust, which is soon realized. Humanity survives in space habitats and eventually heads for the stars.

Among Haldeman's most recent work to date is the Nebula Award-winning *Camouflage* (2004), an alien-encounter narrative in which the discovery of an alien artifact leads humanity to the discovery that immortal, shape-shifting aliens have lived on Earth for millions of years. Also interesting is *Old Twentieth* (2005), in which virtual reality adventures provide a means of fighting boredom in a future world where mortality is a thing of the past, until a twist in the plot threatens to undo human immortality. This text gains particular richness because the virtual reality adventures are often set in the past, making the novel a sort of time-travel tale that evokes various key moments from history.

Robert A. Heinlein (1907–1988)

Sometimes called the "dean of science fiction writers," Robert A. Heinlein was one of the leading figures of science fiction's Golden Age and one of the writers most responsible for establishing the science fiction novel as a publishing category. Born in Butler, Missouri, Heinlein graduated from the US Naval Academy in 1929 and subsequently served as an officer in the US Navy until 1934, when he received a medical discharge owing to tuberculosis. Much of his time during the next several years was spent in political activity, including support for Upton Sinclair's unsuccessful bid to become governor of California in 1934 on what was essentially a socialist platform. Heinlein himself unsuccessfully ran for the California Assembly in 1938 on a similar platform, with Sinclair's support. After that campaign he turned to writing; his first story, "Life-Line," was published in John W. Campbell Jr.'s *Astounding Science-Fiction* in 1939. Heinlein quickly became a master of the short story form, contributing greatly to the success of Campbell's magazine, but also moving beyond that forum into the publishing mainstream, beginning in 1947, when "The Green Hills of Earth" appeared in *The Saturday Evening Post*.

Heinlein's elaboration of a complex and consistent "future history" in his early short stories is among his most important contributions to science fiction. However, he is best remembered for his many important science fiction novels, a number of them written for juvenile audiences, beginning with *Rocketship Galileo* (1947), the basis for the 1950 film *Destination Moon*, for which Heinlein wrote the script. Heinlein's first major adult novel was *The Puppet Masters* (1951), an alien invasion narrative that serves as a thinly-veiled warning about the dangers of a communist invasion of the US. This novel indicates the turn to the political right taken by Heinlein beginning in the late 1940s, a crucial element of which was his staunch anticommunism during the peak years of the Cold War. Other key novels of the 1950s include the Hugo Award-winning political satire

Double Star (1956), the time-travel narrative *The Door into Summer* (1957), and *Starship Troopers* (1959, basis for the 1997 Paul Verhoeven film of the same title).

Starship Troopers, though also a Hugo Award-winner, was seen by many as a celebration of militarism that was virtually fascist in its politics. However, Heinlein's right-wing political vision was of a libertarian, rather than fascist variety. This libertarianism is also evident in the Hugo Award-winning novel *Stranger in a Strange Land* (1961), which made Heinlein something of a hero among the 1960s counterculture, many of whose members interpreted that book's seeming endorsement of mind-expanding drugs and free sex as congruent with their own worldview. Heinlein won still another Hugo Award for best novel for *The Moon Is a Harsh Mistress* (1966), which provides perhaps the clearest picture of Heinlein's political vision with its depiction of a lunar libertarian society that rebels against the rule of Earth. Heinlein continued to write and publish into the 1980s, but produced no other fiction that rivaled the importance of his work through the mid-1960s. His work has received considerable critical attention, though Bruce Franklin's 1980 study *Robert A. Heinlein: America as Science Fiction* remains the best discussion of Heinlein's writing, especially from a political perspective.

Nalo Hopkinson (1960–)

Born in Kingston, Jamaica, Nalo Hopkinson spent her formative years in Trinidad, Guyana, and – briefly – the United States before settling with her family in Toronto, Canada. Her father, a Guyanese poet, playwright, and actor, was a member of the influential Trinidad Theatre Workshop, and he and Hopkinson's mother fostered her early interest in the arts. Hopkinson received a BA degree from Toronto's York University in 1982 and a Master of Arts degree in Writing Popular Fiction from Seton Hill University in 1995. She began publishing science fiction short stories shortly after her tenure at the Clarion Science Fiction and Fantasy Writers Workshop at Michigan State University in 1995. Her work is distinctive for its innovative fusion of Afro-Caribbean folklore and culture with the conventions of science fiction and fantasy, as well as its sophisticated exploration of themes related to race and gender. Primarily a fiction writer, Hopkinson is also an editor and critic, and has recently moved to the very forefront of postcolonial science fiction writers.

Brown Girl in the Ring (1998), Hopkinson's debut novel, blends Caribbean dialects and folklore with the dystopian science fiction setting of a near-future Toronto, in which the inner core of the city (the "Burn") has been barricaded and abandoned by the government after an economic collapse. In the absence of any governmental authority, gangs have become the *de facto* rulers. A single mother with a newborn living in the Burn, the protagonist Ti-Jeanne learns from her grandmother to embrace the traditional spirituality that she had previously rejected, which becomes for her an empowering practice in her goal to defeat a powerful gang leader. The novel won the Warner Aspect First Novel Contest and the Locus Award for Best First Novel and was short-listed for the Philip K. Dick Award. Hopkinson's second novel, *Midnight Robber* (2000), also draws on Caribbean cultural traditions in important ways, but it is more solidly science fictional than the first, involving such familiar motifs as artificial intelligence, interplanetary colonization, parallel universes, and alien contact. The novel was nominated for the Philip K. Dick Award, the James Tiptree Jr. Award, the Hugo Award, and the Nebula Award.

Much of Hopkinson's other prolific output has focused even more on traditions of Afro-Caribbean fabulism, as in her story collection *Skin Folk* (2001), her novels *The Salt Roads* (2003) and *The New Moon's Arms* (2007), and her edited anthologies *Whispers from the Cotton Tree Root: Caribbean Fabulist Fiction* (2000) and *Mojo: Conjure Stories* (2003). Other anthologies edited by Hopkinson include *So Long Been Dreaming: Postcolonial Science Fiction and Fantasy* (2004, with Uppinder Mehan), and *Tesseracts 9* (2005, with Geoff Ryman), a compilation of Canadian-authored science fiction and fantasy.

Ursula K. Le Guin (1929–)

Born Ursula Kroeber in Berkeley, California, Ursula K. Le Guin is one of the most important women writers in the history of science fiction. After an extended period of experimenting with short stories, Le Guin published her first novel, *Rocannon's World*, in 1966. Two other sf novels quickly followed, but it was with the publication of *The Left Hand of Darkness* in 1969 that Le Guin burst into sf stardom, winning both the Hugo and Nebula Awards. This novel, like its three predecessors, deals with the Ekumen, a far-flung galactic empire, the creation of which is probably Le Guin's most lasting contribution to science fiction. *The Left Hand of Darkness* is still considered one of the finest uses of science fiction to effect a re-examination of assumptions and stereotypes about gender. It thus indicates Le Guin's importance as a woman writer, though feminism and gender issues are not typically as important to her work as that of many of the women writers who followed her. As well as numerous short stories, other well-known novels in the Ekumen sequence include *The Word for World Is Forest* (1972, expanded version 1976), and *The Dispossessed* (1974), both of which won Hugo awards. Le Guin returned to the Ekumen universe with *The Telling* in 2000, the first Ekumen novel since *The Dispossessed*.

Le Guin is also a leading writer of fantasy, of which her "Earthsea" sequence constitutes a leading example. This sequence, which began with *The Wizard of Earthsea* in 1968, also includes *The Farthest Shore* (1972, winner of the National Book Award) and *Tehanu: The Last Book of Earthsea* (1990, winner of the Nebula Award). Despite the latter title, Le Guin returned to the "Earthsea" sequence in 2002 with the publication of *The Other Wind*, which won a World Fantasy Award for Best Novel. Le Guin has also written a number of other books and short stories for both adults and children. Her short stories are among the most often anthologized in all of sf, with stories such as "The Ones Who Walk Away from Omelas" appearing particularly often in sf story collections. Known both for the elegance of her style and the richness of her use of materials from disciplines such as political science, sociology, anthropology, and Eastern and Western philosophies, Le Guin has a substantial critical reputation. Book-length studies include those by Bucknall (1981), Cummins (1990), and Spivak (1984).

Ian McDonald (1960–)

Son of an Irish mother and Scottish father, Ian McDonald was born in Manchester, England, emigrating as a child to Belfast, Ireland, where he still resides. Having grown up during the sectarian violence between Catholics and Protestants in Northern Ireland known as the "Troubles," McDonald became sensitized from a young age to the plight of his adoptive home as a postcolonial society struggling with the legacy of its colonial past. This sensitivity informs his science fiction, much of which takes place in postcolonial settings. McDonald's numerous works are distinctive for their exploration of the transformation of postcolonial cultures through technology and encounters with alien cultures, as well as for their fine characterization.

Desolation Road (1988), McDonald's first novel, is a hybrid of science fiction and magical realism that combines the texture of Gabriel García Márquez's *One Hundred Years of Solitude* with the Martian colonization narrative to produce a story with a Third World feel that reinforces the notion of a symbolic link between the formerly colonized world on Earth and the potentially colonized worlds of outer space. It was eventually followed by a sequel, *Ares Express* (2001) in somewhat the same vein. McDonald's "Irish" trilogy – comprising *King of Morning, Queen of Day* (1991); *The Broken Land* (1992); and *Sacrifice of Fools* (1996) – contains much material relevant to the colonial history of Ireland, and explores its current condition. *Sacrifice of Fools*, which is set in Northern Ireland and features an alien invasion of the Earth by the Shian, a species who agree to share their advanced technology with humans in exchange for permission to settle in certain prescribed areas, is an excellent example of the use of science fiction as a sort of laboratory experiment in the appreciation of Otherness, as readers learn the pitfalls of making easy assumptions and jumping to quick conclusions about the nature and culture of those who are different from themselves.

Set in Africa, McDonald's "Chaga" saga, which includes *Chaga* (1995, US title *Evolution's Shore*) and *Kirinya* (1998), features a distinctively original conception of an alien life form in the Chaga, an extraterrestrial ecosystem that seeds the southern hemisphere. Possibly through the use of a form of nanotechnology, the Chaga spreads across the landscape, transforming it in almost unrecognizable – though seemingly benevolent – ways. This phe-nomenon prompts a United Nations intervention in Africa that essentially serves as a neocolonial exertion of power. Irish journalist Gaby McAslin, the central character in both novels, exposes the corruption of the UN (as well as that of the United States) and struggles with the fallout of her own transformation by the Chaga.

In *River of Gods* (2005, shortlisted for both the Hugo and Clarke Awards in 2005 and the winner of best novel of 2004 from the British Science Fiction Association), McDonald turns his attention to India in 2047, the centennial of India's independence from British colonial rule. Featuring a wide array of characters and technologies, the novel illustrates the ways in which Indian culture is transformed by technology at the same time that it retains many of its customs. McDonald's most recent novel, *Brasyl* (2007, short-listed for the Hugo Award in 2008 and winner of best novel of 2007 from the British Science Fiction Association), weaves together three differ-ent tales of varying timelines, all of which take place in Brazil. With his talent for constructing challenging, provocative narratives in unusual or postcolonial settings, Ian McDonald is a key figure of the British Boom and a genuinely original voice in science fiction.

China Miéville (1972–)

China Miéville was born in Norwich and grew up mainly in London, though at age eighteen he moved to Egypt, where he taught English for a year. Subsequently, he returned to England and received his BA in social anthropology from Cambridge and an MA and PhD in international relations from the London School of Economics. His doctoral dissertation, published in book form as *Between Equal Rights: A Marxist Theory of International Law* (Haymarket Books, 2006), illustrates his commitment to Marxist ideas, as does his membership in the British Socialist Workers Party and activism in British leftist politics.

As Andrew Butler notes, Miéville comes as close as anyone to being the signature figure of the British Boom in science fiction ("Thirteen Ways," 376). However, Miéville's complex, genre-bending work, a melding of science fiction, fantasy, and horror, is extremely difficult to classify. He himself prefers the term "weird fiction" and has been seen as the leading figure in a movement of mostly British writers described as the "new weird," a movement dedicated, among other things, to moving beyond the clichés and superficiality of many works in the fantasy genre, especially those written or inspired by J. R. R. Tolkien.

Miéville burst upon the scene in 1998 with his highly inventive first novel, *King Rat*, which drew considerable attention and was nominated for several awards within the realm of horror writing. However, the book's strange evocation of an alternative, multicultural London in which a humanoid half-rat protagonist leads a political revolution of London's rats against both the King Rat of the title and the Pied Piper of Hamelin demonstrates a concern with political issues and an imaginative range seldom seen in the horror genre.

With the publication of *Perdido Street Station* (2000, winner of the 2001 Arthur C. Clarke Award), Miéville became a truly major figure in contemporary British literature. In his stunningly detailed creation of the city of

New Crobuzon (and the world that surrounds it), Miéville succeeds as well as anyone ever has in creating political commentary through imaginative fiction. *Perdido Street Station* was followed in 2002 by a sequel, *The Scar* (shortlisted for the 2003 Clarke Award), another work with strong political implications. It is, however, in still another sequel, *Iron Council* (2004, winner of the 2005 Clarke Award), that the political inclinations become most clear. Most obviously, the two central events of that novel are rebellions against repressive authority, one in the city of New Crobuzon and one among the workers on a railway that is being built in an attempt to connect New Crobuzon with distant lands. Miéville's first collection of short fiction, *Looking for Jake* (2005), includes *The Tain*, a novella (originally published in 2002) that is both a truly original vampire tale and an allegorical tale of revolutionary liberation from political oppression. Finally, in *Un Lun Dun* (2007), Miéville entered the realm of children's fantasy fiction, of which there is a particularly rich vein in the British literary tradition. Given the quality and quantity of Miéville's output as a writer thus far, his future as a major producer of innovative "weird fiction" seems assured.

George Orwell (1903–1950)

"George Orwell" was the pen name of British journalist, essayist, and novelist Eric Arthur Blair, born in British colonial India, where his father was a civil servant. However, Blair was taken by his mother to England at the age of one; he grew up and was educated there, where he proved to be a talented enough student to win a scholarship to the prestigious Eton College, where he studied from 1917 to 1921 and where one of his teachers was Aldous Huxley. Unable to afford university study, Blair returned to southern Asia, where he joined the Imperial Police in Burma in 1922. Disillusioned by his experiences as a colonial policeman, Blair returned to England in 1927 a bitter opponent of imperialism. He was also determined to become a writer, though he first experienced several years of poverty and of working at menial jobs, as described in his first book *Down and Out in Paris and London* (1933), for which he adopted the pen name under which he became so well known.

Orwell's first novel, *Burmese Days* (1934), is an indictment of British colonialism based on his own experiences in Burma. In the course of the 1930s, Orwell became a prominent member of the literary Left in England. In 1936, he was commissioned to write a study of living conditions in the impoverished areas of northern England for the Left Book Club. This study was published in 1937 as *The Road to Wigan Pier* (1937). In December 1937, Orwell traveled to Spain to fight with the Spanish Republicans against the German- and Italian-supported fascist insurgents there. In Spain, Orwell became frustrated by in-fighting among the different leftist groups that were supporting the Republicans, which he criticizes in *Homage to Catalonia* (1938).

Orwell returned to England after receiving a serious wound in battle. His experiences in Spain, in which the socialist–anarchist faction he supported was ultimately suppressed by the Soviet-backed communists, made him a staunch opponent of Stalinism. This opposition is reflected in the fable-like

Animal Farm (1945), which satirizes the Stalinist Soviet Union in its bitter vision of a group of animal revolutionaries who overthrow their human rulers, only to descend into their own form of animal tyranny. *Animal Farm* was a huge success that propelled Orwell into the limelight in a Cold War climate in which anti-Stalinist visions were highly marketable.

That same climate helped to make *Nineteen Eighteen-Four* (1949), easily Orwell's best-known work, an immediate success as well, especially as many readers also read that text as an anti-Stalinist allegory. In truth, Orwell intended *Nineteen Eighty-Four* at least partly as a corrective to the overt anti-Stalinism of *Animal Farm*, both to warn against the possible negative consequences of excessive anticommunist measures in the West and to distance himself, a longtime socialist, from the anticommunist movement. Orwell died a year after the publication of *Nineteen Eighty-Four*, but the prominence of that book has assured him lasting fame, spurred by the success of a 1954 BBC television adaptation and a 1984 film adaptation. Orwell has been the subject of numerous biographies and critical studies, including those by Crick (1980), Taylor (2003), and Williams (1971).

Marge Piercy (1936–)

Born in Detroit, Michigan, to a working-class family in the midst of the Great Depression, Marge Piercy was the first of her family to attend college. Winning several Hopwood Awards for poetry and fiction as a student at the University of Michigan, she later earned a Master's degree at Northwestern University, where she became involved in radical left-wing politics. Active in the civil rights and antiwar movements of the 1960s as an organizer for Students for a Democratic Society (SDS), Piercy also became involved in the women's movement, developing the feminist consciousness that informs all of her writing. Primarily a poet and novelist, she is also an essayist, memoirist, and editor. Her poems – as in *To Be of Use* (1973), *The Moon Is Always Female* (1980) and *Circles on the Water: Selected Poems of Marge Piercy* (1982) – often critique of the marginalization and victimization of women by the patriarchal structures of mainstream American society. Piercy imagines utopian alternatives to these structures in her early novel *Dance the Eagle to Sleep* (1971), in which young 1960s political activists organize an alternative community based on Native American culture, and again in *Woman on the Edge of Time* (1976), now considered a classic of feminist science fiction. In the latter novel, the future community of Mattapoisett, which relies on Native American customs and eliminates divisions between class, race, and gender, is presented as a counterpoint to the dystopian present of 1970s America. Reflecting Piercy's own political activism, the novel emphasizes the need for revolutionary change in order to dismantle the patriarchal, capitalist, and racist ideologies that lead to the suffering of its Mexican-American heroine, Connie Ramos.

Woman on the Edge of Time is Piercy's best-known work of science fiction, participating in the tradition of feminist utopians that revitalized the genre in the 1970s; most of her novels, however, are written in the realist vein. She returned to science fiction in 1991 with *He, She, and It* (published as *Body of Glass* in the United Kingdom), a novel that borrows from the cyberpunk novels of William Gibson and posits a dystopian near future in which a Jewish woman becomes romantically involved with an illegal cyborg used to defend her independent community from threats posed by powerful multinational corporations and a criminal underworld. The novel won the 1993 Arthur C. Clarke Award for the best annual sf novel published in the United Kingdom. It is notable for its challenge to the gender politics of the male-dominated cyberpunk of the 1980s and for its ethical questions about technology's destructive potential. An outspoken feminist, Piercy continues to examine gender relations in more recent works, such as the poetry volume *What Are Big Girls Made Of?* (1997, winner of the American Library Association Notable Book Award) and *Sex Wars: A Novel of the Turbulent Post-Civil War Period* (2005).

Frederik Pohl (1919–)

An important author of short stories and novels, as well as a highly influential editor, Frederik Pohl has had one of the longest and most prolific
careers in the history of science fiction. He has also maintained a political
consciousness throughout his work, which is all informed by his commitment to social justice in the face of the inequities produced by modern
capitalism. Indeed, some of his best-known and most successful works are
overt critiques of capitalism, including the classic *The Space Merchants*
(1952), a satirical portrayal of the advertising industry co-authored with
Cyril M. Kormbluth. Pohl also authored a sequel to this work, *The Merchants' War* (1984), as well as a number of related satirical short stories
written in the 1950s and 1960s, many of which are collected in the volume
Alternating Currents (1956).

Pohl's numerous short stories have been widely anthologized and have
appeared in many collections of his own, the most recent of which is
Platinum Pohl (2005). Pohl's stand-alone novels include such diverse
works as *Man Plus* (1975), a Nebula Award-winning early example of
posthuman science fiction in which the protagonist receives a new, artificial
body in order to be able to survive on Mars, and *The Coming of the
Quantum Cats* (1986), a light-hearted satire involving alternate universes.
Several of Pohl's works have specifically dealt with the Cold War, including
The Cool War (1981), a satire in which Cold War tensions have degenerated
into international dirty tricks campaigns run by operatives essentially free of
government control. Meanwhile, *Jem: The Making of a Utopia* (1979) is an
attempt to imagine the course of global political history after the end of the
Cold War, focusing on political rivalries during the colonization of an alien
planet.

Pohl has also published a number of multi-novel sequences, including the
"Heechee" saga, which began with *Gateway* (1977), a Hugo and Nebula
Award-winning space opera that initiated a sequence of six novels dealing

with the human discovery in outer space of advanced (but mysterious) technologies left by an earlier advanced alien species known as the Heechee. Pohl's "Eschaton" trilogy, a black comedy comprising *The Other End of Time* (1996), *The Siege of Eternity* (1997), and *The Far Shore of Time* (1998) manages to incorporate a wide variety of science fiction motifs as a dystopian Earth comes into contact with two (warring) species of advanced aliens and has to struggle for its own survival.

Pohl, who often collaborated with others, authored two sequences of novels with Jack Williamson, including the two-volume "Saga of Cuckoo" sequence – *Farthest Star* (1975) and *Wall around a Star* (1983) – and the "Starchild" trilogy – including *The Reefs of Space* (1964), *Starchild* (1965), and *Rogue Star* (1969). Pohl's most important collaborator, however, was probably Kormbluth, with whom he co-authored a total of four novels and a collection of short stories, *The Wonder Effect* (1962). Kormbluth (1923–1958) was a promising science fiction writer in his own right, though his career was cut short by his early death from a heart attack. Like Pohl, he was a member of the Futurians, a Marxist-oriented group of science fiction writers and enthusiasts, in the 1930s and 1940s. Most of Kormbluth's writing outside of collaboration consisted of short stories, all of which are collected in *His Share of Glory: The Collected Short Fiction of C. M. Kormbluth* (1997).

Kim Stanley Robinson
(1952–)

Probably the most important (and certainly the most politically astute) American science fiction writer of his generation, Robinson was born in Waukegan, Illinois, but grew up in Southern California. In 1982, he received his doctorate in English from the University of California at San Diego, completing a dissertation (under the direction of the eminent Marxist scholar Fredric Jameson) on the work of Philip K. Dick, afterward published in book form as *The Novels of Philip K. Dick* (1984). Throughout his writing career, Robinson has maintained an intense awareness of social and political issues, which he explores from a Marxist perspective inflected through a strong commitment to environmental issues and a serious interest in Buddhist philosophy. Perhaps the most thorough researcher in all of sf, Robinson's work is extremely rich in information, including the convincing presentation of a variety of advanced technologies, though his social and political vision also remains at the forefront of his work.

Robinson began his career as a major sf novelist with the publication of *The Wild Shore* (1984), a post-apocalyptic novel that details attempts to recover from a disastrous nuclear war that had been provoked by American imperialism and greed around the globe. This novel eventually became the first volume in the "Three Californias" trilogy, which also includes *The Gold Coast* (1988), a dystopian novel that describes a corrupt and decadent capitalist future in which the policies of the Reaganite 1980s have continued unabated into the 2020s, and *Pacific Edge* (1990), a utopian novel that demonstrates the positive potential of sensible and humane environmental and social policies.

Robinson maintained his interest in utopian themes with the publication of the "Mars" trilogy, his most important sequence to date. This trilogy includes *Red Mars* (1993), *Green Mars* (1994), and *Blue Mars* (1996), relating in elaborate detail the colonization and terraforming of the red planet, which allows Robinson to explore a number of social, political, and technological themes. This trilogy was supplemented by *The Martians* (1999), a collection of related short stories. The novel *Antarctica* (1997), set on the continent of the title, also supplements the "Mars" trilogy by exploring many of the same issues in a context more directly related to contemporary reality on Earth. Robinson's most recent trilogy of novels, known as the "Science in the Capital" sequence, includes *Forty Signs of Rain* (2004), *Fifty Degrees Below* (2005), and *Sixty Days and Counting* (2007). It is a sort of thriller, set in the very near future, that presents a behind-the-scenes view of the political machinations that inform big science and that complicate the US government's response (or lack of response) to the current global-warming crisis, though it ultimately shows hope that this crisis might effect a turn toward more sensible (and greener) politics in America.

Robinson's other novels include *Icehenge* (1984), *The Memory of Whiteness* (1985), and *A Short, Sharp Shock* (1990). Perhaps his most unusual novel is *The Years of Rice and Salt* (2002), which envisions a world in which the fourteenth-century plagues that swept Europe had been far more damaging than they actually were, essentially removing Europe (and Christianity) from the historical stage. Robinson then presents a detailed and convincing vision of the progress of world history from that point forward, allowing for explorations of the alternative Chinese and Islamic cultures that rise to world dominance, as well as complex meditations on the nature of history itself.

Neal Stephenson (1959–)

Neal Stephenson, famous for his explorations of complex scientific, technological, and mathematical subjects in his fictional works, boasts a family background rich in the sciences, with numerous relatives employed in scientific fields. Born in Fort Meade, Maryland, Stephenson was raised in the college towns of Champaign-Urbana, Illinois, and Ames, Iowa, where his father, a professor, taught electrical engineering. Although he initially majored in physics, Stephenson eventually completed a BA in geography at Boston University, after which he moved to the Pacific Northwest. His first two novels received little critical attention, but both examine themes that would appear in later works. *The Big U* (1984) is a satire of college life, centering on American "Megaversity," a huge, faceless urban university that appears to have a dehumanizing influence on its students and faculty and which also happens to be funded by the nuclear waste disposal facility located in its basement. Stephenson's second novel, *Zodiac: The Eco-Thriller* (1998), is a tale of a radical environmental activist who tries to save the world from corporate polluters. However, it was only with the publication of *Snow Crash* (1992) – a novel that combines the political, social, and cultural sensibilities of Stephenson's earlier works with an innovative take on the cyberpunk tradition – that he emerged as a major figure in science fiction. Referred to variously as "second-generation cyberpunk" or "postcyberpunk," *Snow Crash* is a satirical look at a high-tech near future dominated by corporations in which the central character, computer hacker and pizza delivery man Hiro Protagonist, races against the clock to prevent a viral apocalypse involving "snow crash," which infects people in both the virtual world of the Metaverse and the real world.

Stephenson's next novel, the Hugo Award-winning *The Diamond Age: Or, a Young Lady's Illustrated Primer* (1995), incorporates elements of steampunk into its depiction of a futuristic Shanghai in which nanotechnology affects every aspect of life, and where an interactive primer intended to educate a "neo-Victorian" aristocrat's child falls into the hand of a working-class girl who uses it for her own enlightenment. With the publication of the massively popular *Cryptonomicon* (1999), a wide-ranging novel employing two storylines (set during World War II and the present day) that explore the birth and development of information technology, Stephenson began to enjoy mainstream success. His "Baroque Cycle" – a trilogy of historical novels that includes *Quicksilver* (2003, winner of the Arthur C. Clarke Award), *The Confusion* (2004), and the *System of the World* (2004) – further cemented his status as an important author with crossover appeal. A multigeneric narrative, the trilogy recounts the origins of the modern world in the scientific revolution of Enlightenment-era Europe and abounds with encyclopedic historical details. Stephenson has also written under the pseudonym Stephen Bury, publishing two novels with J. Frederick George: *Interface* (1994) and *The Cobweb* (1996). A witty, erudite writer with a penchant for elaborate plots and frequent digressions into the arcane, Stephenson is one of the most inventive figures in contemporary science fiction.

H. G. Wells (1866–1946)

Herbert George Wells was one of the world's most important and influential thinkers and writers for more than a half century, from the 1890s to the 1940s. His thoughts on history and politics had an important impact on the course of many subsequent debates in those fields, while his meditations on utopia, dystopia, and the growing technologization of modern society were crucial in forming the modern Western mindset. These meditations also made Wells one of the founding figures of modern science fiction, especially as they often appeared in science fiction novels (which he himself referred to as "scientific romances"). Collectively, this body of novels – which includes such well-known works as *The Time Machine* (1895), *The Island of Dr. Moreau* (1896), *The Invisible Man* (1897), and *The War of the Worlds* (1898) – can be taken as the beginning of truly modern science fiction. Slightly later, but lesser-known works by Wells – including *When the Sleeper Wakes* (1899), *The First Men on the Moon* (1901), *The Food of the Gods and How It Came to Earth* (1904), and *A Modern Utopia* (1905) – are also important and include especially thoughtful reflections of Wells's socialist political ideas. Indeed, all of Wells's science fiction is intensely engaged with the social and political issues of its day, demonstrating early on the potential of science fiction as a mode of commentary on such issues.

Wells would also go on to produce a number of highly successful and influential novels in a more realistic vein, though some of these, such as the remarkable *Tono-Bungay* (1909), continue to display some science fictional elements. As Don Smith notes in *H. G. Wells on Film* (2002), Wells's work (especially in science fiction) has also been widely adapted to film, keeping it fresh for generations of future audiences – though often at the expense of seriously diluting the intellectual content of the original novels. Because of his central importance as a figure in the Western culture of the first half of the twentieth century, Wells has been the subject of extensive critical commentary, including such book-length studies as Mark Hillegas's *The Future as Nightmare: H. G. Wells and the Anti-Utopians* (1967) and Frank McConnell's *The Science Fiction of H. G. Wells* (1981). Richard Hauer Costa's *H. G. Wells* (1985) is a good basic introduction to Wells and his work. Wells has also been the subject of several major biographies and numerous individual critical essays, many of which have been collected in volumes such as *H. G. Wells and Modern Science Fiction* (1977, edited by Darko Suvin and Robert M. Philmus), which considers the impact of Wells's work on subsequent writers of science fiction.

Part 4

Discussions of Individual Texts

H. G. Wells, *The Time Machine* (1895)

The Time Machine, Wells's first published novel, remains one of the important founding texts of the genre of science fiction. The novel's protagonist, an unnamed Victorian scientist, invents a time-travel machine and then uses it to journey into the distant future, thus providing one of the first explorations of what would become one of the classic motifs of science fiction. Wells's Time Traveller ventures into the future fully expecting to find an ideal society of the kind projected by late-nineteenth-century utopian texts such as William Morris's *News from Nowhere* (1890). What the Time Traveller finds instead is a nightmare world in which a degenerate humanity has split into two races, the passive and effete Eloi and the brutish, animalistic Morlocks, the former serving as food for the later. As Mark Hillegas notes, Wells's novel was "the first well-executed, imaginatively coherent picture of a future worse than the present, a picture at the same time generally anti-utopian in its tendencies" (*Future*, 34). Thus, *The Time Machine* is not merely a founding text of the time-travel subgenre; it also foreshadows the development of the subgenre of dystopian fiction.

Wells gives no details about the physics of time travel, and the elaborate time machine itself seems almost more a product of Victorian art and craftsmanship than engineering. But Wells's interest here is in commenting on specific social issues, not on the nature of time. When the Time Traveller lands in the distant future (in the year 802,701, to be precise), he at first seems to have found a peaceful, idyllic society somewhat along the lines of the pastoral utopia described by Morris. He soon concludes, however, that this society appears to be in decline, the landscape dotted by decaying buildings and inhabited by a race of passive, cattlelike humans (the Eloi) who seem to have lost all capacity for action or creativity. "I never met," says the Time Traveller, "people more indolent or more easily fatigued"

(*Time Machine*, 28). The Eloi seem to have decayed not only in industry, but in size and strength. They are only about four feet tall and seem "indescribably frail" in a way that reminds the Time Traveller of "the more beautiful kind of consumptive" (*Time Machine*, 23). The Time Traveller never learns with certainty the exact cause of this degeneration of humanity into weakness and passivity, though he initially postulates that the degeneration of the Eloi came about because their ancestors had achieved a perfect world in which they could easily survive without strength or ingenuity, a suggestion that poses a clear challenge to utopian projections of an ideal future. However, the Traveller soon realizes that his conjecture about the degeneration of the Eloi into indolence was based on an improper understanding of the situation of the human race in this far future world. The Eloi are not, as it turns out, the only descendents of the humanity of the Time Traveller's own world. Humanity has, in fact, evolved (or devolved) into two separate species. In addition to the passive, peaceful Eloi, the far future England of the text is inhabited by the Morlocks, apelike creatures who, having developed an intolerance to light, live in a world of underground tunnels, coming to the surface only at night. These Morlocks retain some technological ability and are in general stronger and more energetic than the Eloi. However, the true extent of their degeneration to animality is revealed only when the Time Traveller realizes that the Morlocks essentially raise the Eloi as cattle, slaughtering them as needed for food.

Befriended by the gentle Eloi, the Time Traveller soon finds himself embroiled in battle with the aggressive Morlocks. Eventually, however, he manages to escape in his time machine. He then travels even further into the future, where he observes the human race continuing to decline, eventually becoming extinct. Indeed, as he approaches the final days of the Earth, he observes a gradual reverse evolution that returns the planet and its animal population to a primordial condition. Finally, he returns home to tell his story – though later he apparently embarks on a second voyage into the future, one from which he never returns.

Late in the book, the Time Traveller describes the evolution of the Eloi as a drift toward "feeble prettiness" and the degeneration of the Morlocks as a movement toward "mere mechanical industry" – both the result of the stagnation bought about by the achievement of an unchanging society with no problems or challenges (*Time Machine*, 79). To an extent, one can see the Morlocks as a parody of the technologically oriented utopians of Bellamy, while the Eloi might be read as a parody of the pastoral utopians of Morris. But, in addition to casting serious doubts on the projections of utopian dreamers, *The Time Machine* also makes a number of direct satirical comments on other aspects of Wells's own contemporary world. For example, as

McConnell points out, the activity of the Time Traveller in attempting to gain an understanding of the future can be interpreted as a sort of allegory of the scientific method (*Science Fiction*, 84). However, this allegory is clearly critical in that the Traveller's "scientific" conclusions are often unreliable, largely because he is unable to see beyond his own preconceived notions. The book, then, can be seen as a satire of the Victorian fascination with (and faith in) science as the principal tool of social evolution.

Of course, the particular scientific concept with which *The Time Machine* engages most directly and extensively is that of evolution, a major public fascination of Wells's Victorian England. As Charles DePaolo notes, Wells was intimately familiar with late-Victorian ideas about evolution and made these ideas central to his novel, which uses them to trace the evolution of the human race into the future, to the point of its final extinction. Most obviously, the whole notion of evolution grows out of the work of British scientist Charles Darwin in the middle of the nineteenth century. However, the bifurcation of the human species depicted in *The Time Machine* may be particularly related to the theories of "social Darwinism" as propounded by Herbert Spencer in the late nineteenth century, based on the scientifically unsupportable assumption that human societies advance through a process of natural selection analogous to that attributed to plants and animals by Darwin.

Late Victorian literature is filled with images of this kind of doubleness, of which Robert Louis Stevenson's *Dr. Jekyll and Mr. Hyde* (1886) is a classic example, with Dr. Jekyll serving as a possible ancestor of the Eloi and Mr. Hyde as a forerunner of the Morlocks. This notion of a duality in the British national character leads quite naturally into Wells's vision of a future humanity in which the passive Eloi could be seen as the ultimate extension of the industrial tendencies in British society (or as the ultimate products of forward evolution), while the Morlocks result from the evolution of the more violent militant tendencies (or as the ultimate products of degeneration). Meanwhile, that the Morlocks have emerged as dominant in this future world directly addresses late-Victorian concerns about the possibility of "degeneration," or backwards evolution into a more primitive state. Meanwhile, Spencer's hybrid vision of Victorian England contributed directly to these anxieties by implying that the Victorians maintained strong vestiges of their primitive past, reinforcing fears that these primitive characteristics might somehow come back to the fore, especially after exposure to the "primitive" cultures being encountered by the British in Africa and elsewhere in their far-flung empire.

The concern over degeneration was thus closely related to the issue of British colonial expansion in the late nineteenth century. Similarly, as Brian

Shaffer has demonstrated (discussing the relevance of Spencer's ideas to Joseph Conrad's 1899 novel *Heart of Darkness*), Spencer's social Darwinist ideas constituted an important part of the intellectual stimulus behind late-nineteenth-century British colonial expansion in Africa and elsewhere. Not surprisingly, then, the British imperial experience is extremely important as background to *The Time Machine*. For example, Cantor and Hufnagel (2006) argue that the trip into the future depicted in *The Time Machine* is, in many respects, modeled on the very Victorian theme of a trip to the "imperial frontier" (*Rebarbarization*, 36). The book's vision of the Traveller and his encounters with the Eloi and Morlocks is strikingly reminiscent of the formula used by so many colonial romances in the late nineteenth century, causing Cantor and Hufnagel to call it "simply a Rider Haggard romance in science fiction dress," (*Empire*, 37–38) all the more since Haggard (like Conrad after him) depicted his journeys into Africa as being analogous to time travel, only this time into the distant past, instead of the distant future. Among other things, Cantor and Hufnagel argue that the Eloi and the Morlocks closely parallel the motif of "good" and "bad" natives found in so many examples of imperial romance. However, given that these "tribes" now reside in London, rather than the far reaches of the British Empire, *The Time Machine* in many ways reverses the terms of the imperial romance, showing us an England ruled by colonial Others, much as *The War of the Worlds* would later satirize the motif of colonial conquest by reversing its terms and making the British its victims, rather than its perpetrators.

In this sense, the Eloi can also be read, not as versions of good (i.e., passive and pliable) "natives," but as effete versions of colonial rulers now gone soft and having been overthrown by their former colonial subjects. On the other hand, the Time Traveller himself relates the division of the human species more to class differences than to the racial ones that were central to Victorian colonialist discourse. We do not really know if he is correct, but the Time Traveller eventually concludes that the future bifurcation of humanity is simply an extension of the class division of his own day, merely a result of "the gradual widening of the present merely temporary and social difference between the capitalist and the laborer" *Time Machine*, 48). He envisions the Eloi as the descendants of a ruling class that grew increasingly effete through exploitation of the labor of the class that eventually evolved into the Morlocks. Meanwhile, reasons the Traveller, the turnabout through which the Morlocks came to dominate the Eloi probably occurred because the labor of the Morlocks, along with their closer contact with (and better understanding of) machines, kept them more vital. The Traveller even provides a theory of how the Morlocks became subterranean by noting that, in his own day, there was already a movement to limit the industrial exploitation of surface land of England, creating beautiful spaces for the enjoyment of the upper classes, while factories and other "less ornamental purposes of civilization" were already beginning to move underground. The final result of this tendency, he concludes, is a world in which "above ground you must have the Haves, pursuing pleasure and comfort and beauty, and below ground the Have-nots, the Workers getting continually adapted to the conditions of their labour" (*Time Machine*, 48).

From this point of view, then, *The Time Machine* can be read as a cautionary tale that warns of the potentially disastrous consequences of the growing gap between rich and poor that characterized Wells's England. And Wells's depiction of the Morlocks, as unfavorable as it might appear, can be interpreted as a basically sympathetic comment on the dehumaniza-tion experienced by the lower classes in industrialized capitalism, an inter-pretation that would be consistent with Wells's own socialistic leanings. At the same time, the Time Traveller's own sympathies clearly lie more with the innocent and simple-minded Eloi than with the much more sinister Morlocks, so that the book potentially becomes not a critique of capitalism so much as an expression of fear of communism – and of the growing threat posed by the lower classes in general.

Then again, the Time Traveller's class-based interpretation of the differ-ence between the Morlocks and the Eloi is not necessarily inconsistent with the notion that they represent race-based colonial allegories. After all, race and class were often intermingled in the Victorian mind. Thus, John Kijinski, discussing Arthur Morrison's 1896 "slum" novel, *A Child of the Jago*, notes that the racialist overtones of the representation of the urban poor in this book directly parallel the kinds of ethnographic discourses that were at that time being used to describe the "exotic" populations of the British colonies. The links thus established between the urban poor of London and the supposedly "primitive" peoples of Britain's colonies suggest that fears of degeneration of the urban poor were part of the same discourse as that which they attempted to portray Africans, Asians, and the Irish as degenerate.

Whether or not Wells consciously intended the class-based racial distinc-tions between the Eloi and the Morlocks as a commentary upon the Victor-ian tendency toward ethnographic descriptions of class difference, it is clear that *The Time Machine* comments on both colonialism and class difference, while suggesting a close relationship between race and class in the Victorian discourse. Indeed, this brief, seemingly simple text is surprisingly rich and complex in the extent to which it engages with important contemporary issues. In this, it anticipates not only Wells's later output but such works as

Heart of Darkness, a text whose thematic richness and formal complexity have led to its recognition as a founding text of British modernism. *The Time Machine* may deserve similar recognition, especially as its structure so directly anticipates that of Conrad's novel, while sharing many of its thematic concerns.

The Time Machine is related by an unidentified narrator who relays to readers a story that was told to him and others by the Time Traveller after his return to Victorian England from a trip into the far future. Wells's story, like *Heart of Darkness*, is a rhetorically complex text, with the Time Traveller playing the role of Marlow, the embedded narrator who relates the story of his recent trip to Africa in Conrad's tale. Meanwhile, both Marlow and the Time Traveller are unreliable narrators for reasons that go beyond the fact that their stories are available to us only indirectly. Through most of Wells's text, the narrator clearly doubts that the Time Traveller's story is true, destabilizing our interpretation of the narrative. In addition, within his own narrative (at least as reported by the main narrator) the Time Traveller (like Marlow) himself expresses doubt that he is able adequately to convey the dreamlike strangeness of his experience in the future. Much of his narrative, in fact, consists of sheer speculation (often ultimately revealed to be inaccurate) as he attempts to interpret the world of the future through the insufficient optic of his experience in Victorian England.

In this sense, the interpretive activity of the Time Traveller parallels that of the reader, who must attempt to interpret *The Time Machine* through the lens of his or her own experience, even though the world depicted in the text differs dramatically from the world of the reader. In short, both the protagonist of *The Time Machine* and the reader of this text undergo the experience of cognitive estrangement in ways that are exemplary of cognitive estrangement in science fiction. In addition, readers undergo an additional element of cognitive dissonance that arises from the rhetorical complexity of Well's text, which points, like *Heart of Darkness*, toward the complexities of later modernist texts. Wells's first novel thus looks forward not only to the history of the human race, but also to the development of both literary modernism and science fiction in the twentieth century. Perhaps, then, it is no surprise that Wells's time-travel narrative has become one of the best-known stories of the twentieth century.

H. G. Wells, *The War of the Worlds* (1898)

Though it was one of many alien invasion tales published in Britain in the late nineteenth century, *The War of the Worlds* can be considered to be the founding text of the alien invasion subgenre in its modern form. Wells's novel established many conventions of the alien invasion narrative and set a standard against which subsequent alien invasion stories have inevitably been measured. In its terrifying vision of an invasion of England by technologically advanced forces from Mars, *The War of the Worlds* responds to a number of topical concerns, including the growing threat of war between England and Germany and the general sense of crisis in British society that was accompanied by apocalyptic concerns related to the turn of the century. Most importantly, *The War of the Worlds* comments on the then-contemporary phenomenon of colonialism. Crucial here is Wells's understanding that an invasion by a technologically superior alien power would suddenly place colonial powers such as Great Britain in the same position in which those powers had placed Tasmania, Africa, and other colonized regions of the globe. Further, Wells's overt association of alien invasion with the legacy of colonialism on Earth indicates the potential relevance of such associations in alien invasion narratives as a whole.

The War of the Worlds is set in a relatively realistic version of the author's contemporary world, which is then transformed into a science fiction setting by the book's only real novum: the arrival of an invasion force from Mars. Still, the sweeping implications of this invasion produce striking new perspectives that allow the book to establish a substantial cognitive distance from reality, while at the same time commenting on that reality in a profound way. The novel is narrated by an unnamed protagonist who describes himself as a professional "speculative" philosopher and writer and thus has much in common with Wells himself. Because of his profession, this narrator is able to provide particularly thoughtful and sophisticated reflections on the events he describes, though Wells sometimes undermines his narrator by implicating him in the attitudes that the book is clearly intended to satirize. For example, when the battle with the Martian invaders first begins, the narrator calmly and confidently assumes, as he sips his wine and enjoys his fine food, that the newcomers will be no match for the vaunted British military.

At the same time, the professional background of the narrator allows him to narrate in a style that is roughly Wells's own, producing in the course of the narration a number of now famous passages. Perhaps the most famous of these passages occurs at the book's opening, which ominously sets the tone for the following narration:

> No one would have believed in the last years of the nineteenth century that this world was being watched keenly and closely by intelligences greater than man's and yet as mortal as our own; ... Yet across a gulf of space, minds that are to our minds as ours are to those of the beasts that perish, intellects vast and cool and unsympathetic, regarded this Earth with envious eyes, and slowly and surely drew their plans against us. (*War of the Worlds*, 3)

Wells here establishes a reversal of perspectives of the kind that is often central to satire, asking his scientifically-minded Victorian audience to imagine a situation in which they themselves become the objects of study by a superior scientific intelligence. In particular, the novel as a whole points toward the then-new science of anthropology, asking readers to imagine themselves in the position of the "primitive" peoples of Africa and other parts of the burgeoning British Empire, at the time the objects of intense scrutiny by British scientists whose work was largely designed to describe the ways in which British civilization was superior to those of Britain's conquered colonial subjects.

In the following pages, Wells's narrator describes the arrival on Earth of a sophisticated Martian invasion force that assembles first gigantic walking war machines and later flying machines that move across the English landscape wreaking havoc and making short work of the opposition they encounter. The high technology war machines of the Martians anticipate the technologization of modern warfare that in less than two decades would lead to the carnage of World War I. The narrator, meanwhile, observes the invasion while attempting to stay out of sight of the invaders, providing commentary on the implications of all that he sees. Despite British attempts to organize a resistance to the invasion, a Martian victory seems assured, until suddenly the intellectually advanced, but physically weak, Martians drop dead owing to their lack of resistance to the micro-organisms that inhabit the Earth's atmosphere.

The War of the Worlds is a double cautionary tale that warns against both the belief that the British have a right to impose their will on less advanced peoples and the complacent assumption that they will be able to do so. And, lest any readers miss the parallels between the Martian invasion of Britain and the British colonial invasion of much of the rest of the world, Wells is careful to make these parallels quite explicit. For example, as part of his initial introduction to the story, the narrator reminds his readers that, before judging the Martians as monstrous,

> we must remember the ruthless and utter destruction our own species has wrought, not only upon animals, such as the vanished bison and the dodo, but upon its inferior races. . . . Are we such apostles of mercy as to complain if the Martians warred in the same spirit? (*War of the Worlds*, 5)

Later, near the end of the narrative, the narrator expresses his hope that the experience of the Martian invasion will teach the British to moderate their sometimes brutal colonial policies and to show "pity for those witless souls that suffer our dominion" (*War of the Worlds*, 166).

Other contemporary social and political issues addressed by Wells's novel are also related to turn-of-the-century debates concerning colonialism. The book begins, for example, with a swipe at British bourgeois complacency via a meditation on England's lack of preparation for the invasion that would be coming from Mars, partly because of the British habit of thinking themselves superior to any alien cultures they might encounter. "At most," the narrator concludes, "terrestrial men fancied there might be other men upon Mars, perhaps inferior to themselves and ready to welcome a missionary enterprise" (*War of the Worlds*, 3). This habitual arrogance has left England particularly unprepared for the arrival of the vastly more advanced Martians.

In addition, the narrator posits that the Martians have become more advanced because Mars is an older planet where intelligent life arose earlier and has had more time to evolve. Compared to Earth cultures, the Martians are "not only more distant from time's beginning but nearer its end" (*War of the Worlds*, 4). Here the narrator echoes precisely the linear model of historical progress that provided a crucial linchpin for the ideology of colonialism in the nineteenth century. A classic statement of this attitude comes from the work of German philosopher G. W. F. Hegel (1956), one of the leading theorists of bourgeois historiography. Hegel's view of world history as the unfolding of a sort of divine plan led him to the ethnocentric conclusion that his contemporary European culture was the farthest point thus far toward the culmination of that plan and to the nationalistic belief that his own Germany was supreme among the nations of the Earth because it was closest to the end of the historical timeline. Among other things, this historical model was used to help justify the colonization of Africa in the late nineteenth century, on the premise that Africa had so far failed to progress normally along the historical timeline and therefore could use a boost from the more advanced Europeans.

Hegel himself singled out Africa as an example of lack of historical development that served to highlight the relatively high level of development of Europe. For him, "What we properly understand by Africa, is the Unhistorical, Undeveloped Spirit, still involved in the conditions of mere nature (*Philosophy of History*, 99). The suggestion by Wells's narrator that the Martians are much farther along the timeline of historical development puts the historical shoe on the other foot, placing the English in the position of an underdeveloped culture that suddenly encounters a more advanced one and casting the Earth as one of the dark places of the solar system. This reversal thus serves as a satirical jab at the arrogant Eurocentrism of this Hegelian historical model, or at least at its use as a justification for colonialism.

That the Martians of Wells's novel are more scientifically and technologically advanced than their British adversaries is indisputable. However, Wells makes it clear that scientific knowledge does not necessarily lead to enlightenment or benevolence. The Martians come to Earth with an eye toward exploitation, with no regard for the pain suffered by their human opponents. Indeed, they are essentially vampires. They have evolved so far beyond the physical and toward pure intellect that they have no digestive systems (or sexual organs) but instead feed by injecting the blood of other living creatures directly into their veins. Their main purpose in coming to Earth is to harvest the planet's human population as a source of this blood.

Of course, the evolution of the Martians beyond the physical ultimately proves to be their undoing. Their lack of resistance to Earth's microbes is not merely because the microbes are foreign to their experience: it is also because they appear to have no auto-immune systems whatsoever. In fact, they have virtually no systems except their brains. This notion of physically effete Martians who have evolved toward a state of pure intellect echoes much late-nineteenth-century English discourse concerning the possibility that the English, spoiled by the ease of life (at least for the upper classes) in their advanced society, might grow similarly weak. In this sense, the fate of the Martians dramatizes many of the same evolutionary (or devolutionary) concerns as that of the Eloi of Wells's *The Time Machine*. Among other things, Wells's Martians enact precisely the doubleness that the followers of Herbert Spencer's theories of social evolution attempted to associate with the British. In some ways vastly sophisticated, the Martians still live literally by forcefully extracting resources (in this case blood) from others. Their depiction in *The War of the Worlds*, however, suggests that this combination of militance and industrialization is not necessarily a good thing.

The War of the Worlds directly reflects contemporary concerns over the possibilities of degeneration into savagery and evolution into physical weakness. For example, a former artilleryman encountered by the narrator late in the book expresses the fear that, in the wake of their apparent defeat by the Martians, any humans remaining outside Martian domination "will go savage – degenerate into a sort of big, savage rat" (*War of the Worlds*, 174). Meanwhile, the Martians themselves quite clearly serve as a cautionary image of the direction in which British society itself might be headed – into the kind of moral weakness that makes it possible for the Martians unflinchingly to visit such a brutal assault upon a helpless England and the kind of physical weakness that makes the Martians completely dependent on technology – and completely vulnerable to Earthly disease.

As if to ensure that the vampirism of the Martians reinforces, rather than weakens, the link he wishes to establish between the Martian invaders of Earth and the British invaders of Africa and elsewhere, Wells has his narrator quickly follow the revelation of the seemingly grotesque feeding habits of the Martians with a reminder of "how repulsive our carnivorous habits would seem to an intelligent rabbit" (*War of the Worlds*, 139). Indeed, if the vampirism motif makes the Martian invasion seem especially horrifying, it is also one that is in many ways a perfect metaphor for the European extraction of labor and resources from the colonies. It may thus be no coincidence that Wells's use of this motif follows directly on the publication of the greatest of all vampire narratives, Bram Stoker's *Dracula* (1897), which itself serves, like *The War of the Worlds*, as an allegorical reversal of the terms of colonialism. Thus Stephen Arata, discussing *Dracula*, notes that Stoker's text reflects an anxiety often found in popular British fiction at the end of the nineteenth century, in which "a terrifying reversal has occurred: the coloniser finds himself in the position of the colonised, the exploiter becomes the exploited, the victimizer victimised" (*Occidental*, 120–121).

Arata relates these anxieties to contemporary fears concerning degeneration, as well as to guilt over the practices of British colonialism. In addition, vampirism is a perfect metaphor for capitalism as a whole, as the socialist Wells, like Karl Marx himself, surely realized. Thus, in *Das Kapital*, his most important diagnostic study of capitalism, Marx declares that "capital is dead labour, that, vampire-like, only lives by sucking living labour, and lives the more, the more labour it sucks" (*Reader*, 362–363). For Marx, this vampire image is clearly designed to shock his Victorian audience into a recognition of the exploitative nature of capitalism, just as Wells uses it to try to shake his own Victorian audience out of their comfortable bourgeois complacency concerning colonialism. Wells's former artilleryman provides a particularly bitter denunciation of British middle-class conformism and complacency when he suggests to the narrator that "those damn little clerks" that used to live in the area would be of little use in the guerrilla campaign he hopes to mount against the triumphant Martians. He envisions these timid clerks as having few passions other than being on time and following rules, "skedaddling" off to work in terror of offending their bosses, then rushing back home in terror of offending their wives by being late for dinner. Their primary concern in life, he concludes, is "safety in their one little skedaddle through the world. Lives insured and a bit invested for fear of accidents." For such rabbit-like clerks, the artilleryman concludes, Martian captivity will be a "godsend," providing them with "nice roomy cages, fattening food, careful breeding, no worry" (*War of the Worlds*, 172).

The artilleryman here anticipates Marlow, the protagonist of Conrad's *Heart of Darkness* (1899), who proclaims with a similar bitterness that his affluent listeners in London, with their safe protected lives, cannot possibly comprehend the violence and savagery that inform life in colonial Africa. "Here you all are, each moored with two good addresses, like a hulk with two anchors, a butcher round one corner, a policeman round another, excellent appetites, and temperature normal – you hear – normal from year's end to year's end" (*Heart*, 48). Conrad and Wells thus make similar points about the rationalization and routinization of late-Victorian bourgeois society – and for similar reasons. In particular, both writers suggest that the comfortable routine of day-to-day life in middle-class Britain is possible only because the British ignore the brutal facts of the colonial domination and exploitation that provide much of the wealth on which their affluence is based. Wells's Martians, meanwhile, are similarly oblivious to the effects of their invasion on the human inhabitants of Earth, and their ultimate demise suggests the potential danger of such obliviousness to those whom they regard as lesser than themselves. They are, after all, struck down by "the humblest things that God, in his wisdom, has put upon this Earth" – micro-organisms against which the highly advanced Martians could presumably have protected themselves had their arrogance not prevented them from even considering the need to do so (*Heart*, 187).

Despite the fact that it is so intensely engaged with topical issues relevant to the concerns of late-Victorian Britain, *The War of the Worlds* has remained a central text of Western culture for more than a century, well beyond the dismantling of the British Empire. That the text remains compelling can be attributed partly because it can be read simply as a tale of high adventure in which underdog humans battle courageously (and ultimately successfully) against a seemingly invincible foe. However, the political concerns of *The War of the Worlds* remain current even in the postcolonial era. After all, the postcolonial world has maintained a state of unequal development in which some parts of the globe are vastly richer and more technologically advanced than others. In some ways, in fact, Wells's central story of mismatched combat between a technologically advanced superpower and less advanced states that lack the firepower adequately to defend themselves is more relevant now than ever.

The ongoing popularity of Wells's basic tale can also be attributed to the fact that it has been updated in several forms since its original publication – though the very fact that it can be successfully updated says something about its continuing relevance. Probably the most notorious of the various reincarnations of *The War of the Worlds* is Orson Welles's broadcast of a radio play adapted from the novel in 1939, a broadcast so convincing that many took it as a news report of a real Martian invasion (this time of the US) leading to widespread panic. Welles's version was intended largely as a cautionary tale designed to shock American audiences out of the complacency with which they were able to regard fascist expansionism as a European problem that posed no threat to America. The portability of the messages that reside in the original novel was again demonstrated in 1953, when American director Byron Haskin adapted the novel to a film that reflected a number of anxieties of the early Cold War years. Both the Welles radio play (in which the Martians can roughly be associated with fascism) and the Haskin film (in which they can be associated with communism) lack the clear satirical reversal of the original novel, in which the Martian invaders of Britain are allegorical stand-ins for the British themselves. On the other hand, Haskin's film version can also be taken as an expression of early-1950s anxieties about the growing technologization of everyday life in America.

Finally, Wells's warning (in the ultimate defeat of the Martians) that the British themselves might not be as invincible as the nineteenth-century rhetoric of "imperishable empire" would suggest retains a special relevance in the early twenty-first century, when many see American global dominance as an established and permanent fact. Indeed, while Wells carefully links his Martian invaders to the activities of British imperialism, Spielberg makes little attempt to link his Martians to the global military adventurism of the US in his 2005 adaptation of the novel. If anything, his Martians are vaguely associated with anti-American terrorists, though that motif is not really developed in the film. An impressive special-effects extravaganza, Spielberg's film unfortunately lacks the thoughtfulness of the original Wells novel.

George Orwell, *Nineteen Eighty-Four* (1949)

Nineteen Eighty-Four depicts a grimly impoverished world in which a brutal dictatorship, having risen to power in the wake of worldwide nuclear war in the 1950s, exerts complete control over the lives of its subjects. A founding work of the science fiction subgenre of dystopian fiction, *Nineteen Eighty-Four* may have had a bigger impact on the popular consciousness in Britain and the United States than any other work of science fiction. Indeed, it has been one of the most influential works of literature of any sort ever published, providing some of the best known images and ideas of post-World War II Western culture. Words and phrases from the book such as "Thought Police," "doublethink," or "Big Brother Is Watching You" have become a part of our everyday language and are well known even to those who have never read Orwell's novel or seen Michael Radford's 1984 film adaptation of it. Of course, the impact of *Nineteen Eighty-Four* was greatly enhanced by the context in which it was first published: in the early years of the Cold War, when memories of European fascism were still fresh and anti-Stalinist rhetoric was on the rise. Orwell's novel thus seemed at the time to address issues and fears of great currency. Its images of a decaying future were especially vivid in a postwar Britain that was exhausted from the war and no longer the power it once was. In the United States, the novel helped to feed a demand for effective warnings about the horrors of Stalinism, even though Orwell himself described the book more as a warning against the excesses that might develop in England in the attempt to *combat* Stalinism. Indeed, it is important not to dismiss the text as a critique of Stalinism and thus to consign its warnings to the past.

Like many dystopian texts, *Nineteen Eighty-Four* is structured around an opposition between the desires of a specific individual (protagonist Winston Smith) and the demands of an authoritarian society that seeks to exterminate individual desire. The thirty-nine-year-old Smith lives in London, the largest city of Airstrip One (formerly England), which – along with the Americas, Australia, and the southern part of Africa – constitutes Oceania, one of three superstates that dominate the globe. (The others are Eurasia, formed when Russia absorbed continental Europe, and Eastasia, which consists of China, Japan, and southeast Asia.) Oceania is ruled with an iron fist by the Party, whose main goal is to crush the spirits of the general population simply as a demonstration of the power of the Party's leaders (the members of the Inner Party) to do so.

Smith is a member of the Outer Party, a larger group of Party function-aries who do most of its day-to-day work but live meager, barren lives that lack the amenities afforded to members of the Inner Party. Most of the population of Oceania, however, consists of the lowly "proles" (proletar-ians), who are not members of the Party and are hardly even regarded as human. Smith works for the Records Department in the Ministry of Truth, which controls the flow of news, information, and entertainment in Oceania. Other ministries include the Ministry of Peace, which administers the perpetual war between Oceania and the other superstates; the Ministry of Plenty, which controls economic affairs in the impoverished state; and the Ministry of Love, which maintains law and order, especially through the offices of the sinister Thought Police. That these ministries have names that suggest the opposite of their real functions is only appropriate in this society, in which the technique of "doublethink" is one of the principle means by which the Party is able to manipulate perceptions of reality for its own purposes, encouraging its members to develop the ability simulta-neously to entertain completely contradictory notions.

The Party rules Oceania according to the principles of "Ingsoc," or English socialism, though their political philosophy is the precise opposite of the socialist project of universal equality. Ingsoc, in fact, is designed specifically to maintain the kind of class-based inequalities that socialism is designed to eradicate (and that capitalism requires in order to function). As O'Brien explains to Smith during his interrogation, the Party cannot stand the idea of social equality because they thrive on the domination of others. However, they realize that technological progress had been moving society toward the kind of universal affluence and enlightenment that would ultimately make equality inevitable. Therefore, they have contrived to create widespread poverty and ignorance, largely by expend-ing most of their society's resources on their perpetual wars with either Eastasia or Eurasia, which are undertaken precisely for that purpose. Through this and other means, the Party consciously seeks to create the ultimate dystopia, a world that "is the exact opposite of the stupid hedonistic Utopias that the old reformers imagined" (*Nineteen Eighty-Four*, 267).

As the book begins, Smith has become disillusioned with the Party and its iconic leader, Big Brother. As a way of maintaining his integrity in the face of the Party's manipulations, he begins to keep a secret diary in which he records his subversive thoughts, a project that is made difficult by the constant surveillance to which the members of the Party are exposed. This surveillance is maintained in a number of ways, including the ever-present two-way telescreens that are one of the book's most memorable images and that clearly anticipate the coming power of television in modern society. These devices allow the Party both to keep its members under surveillance and to bombard them with a constant barrage of video propaganda; these screens are on at all times and can be turned off only in the homes of members of the elite Inner Party. The Ministry of Truth maintains a strict control over other cultural products as well, working to supply Party members with "newspapers, films, textbooks, telescreen programs, plays, novels – with every conceivable kind of information, instruction, or entertainment" (*Nineteen Eighty-Four*, 43). Even the proles, who are not considered worth keeping under surveillance, are not exempt from this strict cultural control, and one of the reasons they need not undergo constant surveillance is that they are effectively kept in line by the Ministry's departments of proletarian culture, which produce "rubbishy newspapers, containing almost nothing except sport, crime, and astrology, sensational five-cent novelettes, films oozing with sex, and sentimental songs which were composed entirely by mechanical means" (*Nineteen Eighty-Four*, 43).

Smith's subversive activities move to a different level when he begins a clandestine sexual relationship with Julia, a young woman who works in the fiction department of the Ministry of Truth. Such relationships are strictly forbidden by the Party, which seeks to prevent the fulfillment of sexual desire, feeling that sexual pleasure might create "a world of its own which was outside the Party's control" (*Nineteen Eighty-Four*, 133) and that sexual privation might allow the Party to divert sexual energies for its own purposes. In response, Smith and Julia view their intercourse as a way to assert their individuality in opposition to the official power of the Party. Both partners, in fact, conclude that their union "was a blow struck against the Party. It was a political act" (*Nineteen Eighty-Four*, 126). On the other hand, Smith later becomes concerned about Julia's lack of political awareness, accusing her of being "only a rebel from the waist downwards" (*Nineteen Eighty-Four*, 156). Indeed, the sexual rebellion of Smith and Julia turns out to be entirely ineffectual: they are arrested by the authorities, then tortured and brainwashed and forced to turn against each other. In the end, the official appropriation of Smith's passion for Julia becomes complete; he sublimates his desire for the woman in a socially acceptable direction, realizing that his only love is now directed toward Big Brother.

Despite their willingness to undertake public executions and physical torture of the most gruesome sort, the Party employs techniques of power that are primarily psychological, based on intimidation and fear – as in the reminders to Party members that they are constantly under surveillance. The Party also promotes loyalty by demonizing its enemies. In particular, all opposition to the Party is personified in the much vilified figure of Emmanuel Goldstein, the official party enemy. A central Party ritual is a phenomenon called the Two Minutes' Hate. In this rite of hatred, Party members gather before a telescreen as programming focused on the supposedly heinous treachery of Goldstein gradually whips the crowd into a frenzy. The viewers jump up and down, screaming at the screen, and even those (like Smith) who are initially less than enthusiastic find themselves caught up in the mass hysteria. Gradually, the incendiary focus on Goldstein shifts to a calming focus on Big Brother as a savior from Goldstein's Satanic evil, and the frenzy of hatred turns to a frenzy of devotion and loyalty, the religious echoes of which are unmistakable. At the end of one such session, a woman runs toward the screen and proclaims Big Brother her personal savior, making the religious implications of this ceremony unmistakable.

Goldstein's role as Party enemy in *Nineteen Eighty-Four* echoes in an obvious way the vilification of Leon Trotsky by the Stalinist regime in the Soviet Union. However, given that Foucault's various studies of the demonization of despised Others applies primarily to the bourgeois societies of the West, an appeal to Foucault suggests that Orwell's depiction of the Party in this sense – like the emphasis on surveillance – may satirize the capitalist West more than the Stalinist Soviet Union. Meanwhile, the religious intonation of the Two Minutes Hate suggests the way in which the Party uses strategies derived from religion to further its power, much in the way that Karl Marx famously proclaimed religion to function as an "opiate of the masses" under capitalism. Granted, conventional religious activity is strictly forbidden in Oceania, at least to Party members, though Orwell suggests that the lowly proles would have been allowed to practice religion had they so desired. However, it is clear in Orwell's book that the ban on religion comes about not because organized religion is so radically different from the Party, but because the two are all-too-similar and would therefore be competing for similar energies. As with sexuality, the Party actively works to appropriate the energies traditionally associated with religious belief and to use those energies for its own purposes, giving the Party itself a quasi-religious air.

Among other things, the Party enforces its ideology with all the zeal of the medieval Inquisition, but with a considerably more sophisticated understanding of psychology and power. They are perfectly willing to use elaborate physical tortures, but they rely primarily on psychological tortures, and even these are administered under a veil of secrecy that works far differently from the spectacular public punishments inflicted by the medieval Church as a warning to potential opponents. Party official O'Brien thus explains to the incarcerated Smith late in the book that the torture chambers of the ironically named Ministry of Love differ from the public tortures of the medieval Inquisition in that the Ministry does its work in secret, giving its victims no chance to become martyrs (*Nineteen Eighty-Four*, 253).

In addition, the techniques of the Ministry of Love are designed not only to extract confessions, but to make the prisoners themselves believe those confessions and honestly to repent. These techniques are designed not so much to inflict punishment as to elicit loyalty; the goal of the Ministry of Love is to convert its prisoners and to release them into society to function once again as loyal Party members. In this sense the Party once again echoes the traditional functioning of the Church, but in Orwell's dystopia this conversion motif takes a dark turn. Unlike repentant Christians who can still be welcomed fully back into the fold, once rehabilitated Party members have proven their new orthodoxy for a time (and thus demonstrated the Party's ability to make them loyal subjects), they are apt to be arrested and executed without warning. Orwell's Party is thus considerably more ruthless in its theory than the medieval Church, though not necessarily in its practice – victims of the Inquisition were often urged to repent and confess before being burned at the stake. And the Party's insistence that members must repent of their own free will rather than being coerced clearly echoes the Christian tradition; the Party, like the Christian God, wants not just to be obeyed but to be obeyed willingly and worshipfully.

Among the most memorable of the strategies undertaken by the Party in pursuit of power is the work of the Ministry of Truth, not only to control the content of all newspapers in the present, but also continually to modify the filed back issues of those newspapers according to the latest Party line, leaving no official record of anything that might run counter to current Party policy. Smith and others in the Records Department of the Ministry of Truth continually "update" history by editing official records, effacing all indication of the existence of problematic persons or events and creating fictional records of non-existent persons or events that help to support the Party line. Indeed, a key element of the ideology of Party involves what they call the "mutability of the past," and the Party continually updates all records of the past as it sees fit in a thoroughly process that "was applied ... to every kind of literature or documentation which might conceivably hold any political significance" (*Nineteen Eighty-Four*, 40).

This updating of history echoes an activity of which the Stalinist regime in the Soviet Union was often accused, but it is also the case that reformulating history for its own purposes was a central strategy used by the European bourgeoisie to justify and explain its rise to power in the eighteenth century. Indeed, the whole notion of history in the modern sense – which envisions the flow of history as a logical cause-and-effect process governed by scientific laws – was a bourgeois invention. Thus, early texts such as Edward Gibbons's monumental *The Decline and Fall of the Roman Empire* envision the rise of Catholic-aristocratic power in the Middle Ages as the demise of true civilization – and the subsequent rise of the bourgeoisie as a return to the glories of ancient Rome. In short, history in the modern sense is an invention of the European bourgeoisie, designed to narrate (and justify) the centuries-long cultural revolution through which they rose to hegemony in Europe. Or, as Fredric Jameson puts it, "the transition from feudalism to capitalism is what is secretly (or more deeply) being told in most contemporary historiography, whatever its ostensible content." Further, Jameson points out, this view of history makes the bourgeois cultural revolution "the only true Event of history" (*Signatures*, 226–227).

In the case of Orwell's Party, this manipulation of the past goes beyond a mere attempt to make it seem as if the Party's rule has actually improved the quality of life in Oceania. It also involves the Party's desire to control every aspect of the lives of its members, including their memories. To an extent, the Party seems to want to continually change the past simply because it allows it to demonstrate that it is able to make individuals literally recall the past in whatever way the Party wants, including ways that are inherently contradictory. Indeed, the Party revels in the notion of doublethink, which allows Party members not only simultaneously to believe contradictory notions, but also to participate in the construction of overt lies while believing those lies themselves.

This desire to control the thoughts of its members has also led the Party to work to maintain control of language itself. One of its central projects is the development of "Newspeak," an official language the authoritarian intentions of which are made clear in the book. Newspeak (extensively described in an appendix to the novel) is based on English, but the Party is gradually modifying it and paring it down to place stricter and stricter limits on the range of ideas that can be formulated within the language. The basic goal of Newspeak is simple – to deprive the populace of a vocabulary in which to formulate or express dissident ideas, and therefore literally to make those ideas unthinkable. Not surprisingly, the Newspeak project extends to works of literature as well, since the classics of past literature are informed by precisely the kinds of polyphonic energies and human passions that the Party seeks to suppress. Therefore, the works of writers such as Shakespeare are in the process of being translated into Newspeak and thereby rendered ideologically orthodox.

The Newspeak project is an integral part of the Party's insistence that "reality" itself is a social-linguistic construct. For the Party our perception of reality derives not from any direct access to reality itself; rather, what we think of as "reality" is merely the product of a whole system of pre-existing concepts and beliefs about reality. For the Party all descriptions of reality are fictional, and "the very existence of external reality was denied by their philosophy" (*Nineteen Eighty-Four*, 80). Or, as O'Brien declares to Smith during the interrogation of the latter, "truth" is a function not of reality, but of Party policy (*Nineteen Eighty-Four*, 205).

The chilling conclusion to *Nineteen Eighty-Four*, in which Smith realizes that he now truly loves Big Brother, suggests the horrifying extent to which the Party is able to succeed in controlling the minds of its members. Having carefully eliminated all perceived threats, the Party seems to have made its power permanent, though the book does leave open the possibility (scoffed at though it is by O'Brien) that a certain revolutionary potential still resides in the lowly proles. However, the fact that the grim and dehumanizing conditions of life in Oceania seem virtually insurmountable makes *Nineteen Eighty-Four* all the more effective as a cautionary tale – and one that remains even more relevant in an era when the seemingly unchallenged power of global capitalism makes the kind of total power exercised by the Party seem more and more feasible.

Isaac Asimov, *I, Robot* (1950)

Isaac Asimov's most memorable (and influential) contributions as an author of sf were almost certainly the "Foundation" trilogy (1951–1953) and his series of "Robot" stories and novels, written mostly in the 1940s and 1950s. Most of the best of the robot stories are collected in a single volume, published as *I, Robot* (1950). Related in chronological order, the nine stories in *I, Robot* collectively tell a sort of future history of robots (covering the period 1996 to 2052) and their role in human society, beginning with relatively primitive (nonverbal) robots intended to perform various industrial and domestic chores and ending with sophisticated artificially intelligent "Machines" that unilaterally assume rule of the Earth for the good of humanity.

The stories of *I, Robot* are loosely tied together by a frame narrative in which an unnamed journalist interviews Dr. Susan Calvin, the chief "robopsychologist" for U.S. Robot and Mechanical Men, Inc., the dominant player in the robot industry featured in the stories. Calvin, who has been with U.S. Robot almost since its inception and is now on the verge of retirement at the age of seventy-five, provides anecdotal accounts of her long experience with the company, thus supplying the material of the various stories. Several stories also feature the recurring human characters Powell and Donovan, who work as field testers for U.S. Robot, trying out new advanced robots under especially trying conditions (such as mining on the surface of the planet Mercury) in order to work out any unforeseen problems that might arise. However, all of the human characters in the stories, including Calvin, are really just place-holders, though Asimov's decision to use a woman scientist as a central figure is at least a gesture toward positive representation of women in a genre then almost entirely dominated by males (though Calvin's characterization owes much to the stereotype of the "old maid"). Human characterization in the volume is minimal, so that the focus can be on the robots themselves.

All of the robots in the volume are driven by highly complex "positronic brains," the exact functioning of which is never explained and indeed does not seem to be fully understood, even by the most sophisticated of the scientists who work to design and produce the robots for U.S. Robot. However, all of the brains are built so that they must follow the "Three Laws of Robotics," the composition of which is surely Asimov's single most important contribution to science fiction:

1   A robot may not injure a human being, or, through inaction, allow a human being to come to harm.
2   A robot must obey the orders given it by human beings except where such orders would conflict with the First Law.
3   A robot must protect its own existence as long as such protection does not conflict with the First or Second Laws.

As these laws make clear, Asimov's robots are, by definition, benevolent, meant to be helpers and companions to humanity. Thus, Patricia Warrick identifies Asimov's robots as science fiction's quintessential representation of robots "who are benign in their attitude toward humans" (*Mind*, 209).

Though the stories in *I, Robot* were initially published as early as 1940, the publication of the volume in 1950 was quite timely, occurring soon after Norbert Wiener published his book *Cybernetics* and in the same year Alan Turing published *Computing Machinery and Intelligence*. As Christian W. Thomsen notes, these works, along with *I, Robot* broke new ground with the "shocking" suggestion that "man, having been master over all creatures of this Earth, could face in the not-too-distant future a being of equal quality: not a superhuman monster or a subhuman slave – but a competitor who could be his equal, in the form of a thinking machine" (*Robot Ethics*, 28). Wiener, Turing, and Asimov all see the development of intelligent machines as an event with great positive potential – and Wiener's work on cybernetics has in particular been cited by observers such as N. Katherine Hayles as a crucial forerunner of later developments toward "posthumanism." On the other hand, partly propelled by Cold War concerns over the destructive potential of nuclear weapons, anxieties over the negative potential of technology were also widespread in the early 1950s. Numerous sf works of the early 1950s thus addressed the question of growing automation as a potential threat, as in Kurt Vonnegut's satirical novel *Player Piano* (1952), with its depiction of an administered society in which human labor has been made superfluous by advanced technology. Of course, fears that humans themselves might be transformed into machine-like automatons were a result not just of concerns about technology but of anxieties produced by the increasing routinization and enforced conformism of life in the early 1950s, both in and out of the workplace.

With the publication of *I, Robot* in 1950, Asimov's benevolent robots thus entered into a number of crucial contemporary debates concerning technology and automation. *I, Robot* enters this debate on the side of technology with the opening story "Robbie," a highly sentimental account of the attachment of a little girl, Gloria Weston, to the crude (nonverbal) robot that has been acquired by her father to serve as a sort of companion and high-tech nanny. The robot performs its role in an exemplary fashion, but that does not prevent the girl's mother (influenced by anti-robot sentiment in the local population and depicted with more than a hint of 1940s-style misogyny that somewhat offsets the positive depiction of Calvin) from developing an antipathy toward the mechanical playmate. Mrs. Weston eventually persuades her husband to return Robbie to U.S. Robot, though young Gloria's reaction to the loss of her companion is so extreme that Mr. Weston ultimately contrives (with the aid of an unplanned industrial accident in which Robbie saves Gloria's life) to convince his wife to let him bring the robot back home. This initial story thus at once establishes a positive attitude toward robots and a negative attitude toward the narrow-minded humans who see the robots as a threat to human safety.

In so doing, as Gorman Beauchamp notes in detail (1980), Asimov positions his robots as a rejoinder to the "Frankenstein Complex" – the tendency, dating at least back to Mary Shelley's *Frankenstein* (1818), to depict artificially created intelligence as sinister and dangerous to mankind. Thus, the robots of Karel Čapek's 1921 play *R.U.R.*, the work that gave the word "robot" to the English language, ultimately rebel against their human makers and assume control of the Earth. On the other hand, Čapek's play ends on a positive note as two robots (Čapek's robots are living creatures, not machines) suddenly become humanized by sexual passion and go forth to repopulate the Earth as a new Adam and Eve.

Asimov's robots, on the other hand, are machines, but machines that are genuinely intelligent (and, ultimately, more intelligent than humans). Given this intelligence, it is, in fact, surprising that the robots never seem to be able to overcome the programming of the Three Laws, even after the development of the super-intelligent Machines, which are not really robots at all in the usual sense, but merely thinking supercomputers. Indeed, the esteemed science fiction writer and critic Stanisław Lem has argued that this limitation goes against logic itself if the robots are truly intelligent. "To be intelligent," he concludes, "means to be able to change your hitherto existing programme by conscious acts of the will, according to the goal you set for yourself" (*Robots*, 313). In addition, Asimov never really addresses the obvious possible contradictions that they allow. What, for example, happens if a single robot is given contradictory orders by two different humans? Or what if it must harm some humans in order to save others? And what are we to make of the fact that there is no specific prohibition, within the Three Laws, of robots harming other robots?

Still, if Asimov sees the Three Laws as insurmountable, he also acknowledges that these laws, which have been re-used in numerous subsequent works of science fiction, are open to considerable interpretation and complication. For one thing, the rules for the manufacture of robots seem to allow a considerable amount of leeway in the actual programming of the laws, so that one or more laws can be made stronger or weaker than usual in the production of robots whose intended tasks would be facilitated by such programming. Moreover, in actual real-world applications, the interactions among the different rules can lead to considerable (and sometimes unpredictable) complications. Indeed, virtually all of the stories in *I, Robot* are essentially detective stories involving mysteries surrounding unexpected robot behavior, which are then solved when it becomes clear that the seemingly odd behavior is perfectly explicable in terms of the Three Laws. For example, when Powell and Donovan encounter a robot in "Runaround" that simply runs in circles on the surface of Mercury rather than carrying out its specific commands, they ultimately deduce that this behavior is caused by the fact that this highly expensive robot has been given an unusually strong Third Law (to protect the company's investment), which is offsetting the imperative of its Second Law programming, causing it to reach an equilibrium state of circling about the dangerous task given it.

A particular challenge to the Three Laws occurs in the story "Reason," in which Powell and Donovan travel to a space station that beams power to Earth via microwave. The station is run entirely by robots, and the two humans are assigned to assemble and activate a new, highly advanced robot known as QT-1, with unprecedented reasoning abilities, that has been designed to oversee the other robots on the station. Though it is programmed with the Three Laws, QT-1's advanced reasoning abilities cause it to conclude that it could not possibly have been designed and built by humans, who are so obviously inferior. QT-1 deduces that it must have been built by the station's Master Energy Converter, since that is obviously the most important piece of equipment aboard the station. It then develops a sort of religious devotion to the Master, and the other robots on the station adopt this religion as well, viewing QT-1 as the Master's prophet. Despite its odd beliefs, however, QT-1 proves capable of running the station far more efficiently than any human could hope to do. Powell and Donovan decide to leave the robot in charge of the station without reporting its dismissive attitude toward humans; they leave it to their human successor on the station to deal with the cult of the Master. The story does not, however, follow up on the way it calls attention to the potential religious implications of the robots as a whole, the existence of which place humans in the role of godlike creator.

This hint of the superiority of robots to humans foreshadows important later developments as the robots gradually overcome anti-robot prejudices (for a time they are banned from Earth and can only operate in space, like the androids of Philip K. Dick's 1968 novel *Do Androids Dream of Electric Sheep?*) to become an indispensible aid to humans in their everyday lives – while at the same time clearly becoming more intelligent than humans. One predictable development is that it becomes harder and harder to distinguish between robots and humans as robotic technology becomes more and more advanced, allowing for the combination of biological and mechanical elements in a single robot. Thus, in "Evidence," the penultimate story of *I, Robot*, scientist Alfred Lanning, Director of Research for U.S. Robot, explains the potential to create androids that are essentially indistinguishable from humans: "By using human ova and hormone control, one can grow human flesh and skin over a skeleton of porous silicone plastics that would defy external examination … And if you put in a positronic brain, and such gadgets as you might desire inside, you have a humanoid robot" (*I, Robot*, 159). Such a "robot" would, of course, really be a cyborg, and this suggestion is one of the clearest ways in which *I, Robot* anticipates later developments such as the blurring of the boundary between human and machine in cyberpunk posthuman science fiction.

One such cyborg is, in fact, apparently created in "Evidence," which deals with the difficulty of distinguishing between such a robot and a human. Here, rising politician Stephen Byerly is suspected of being a humanoid robot. When he refuses to submit to an examination by X-ray (citing his civil rights), Byerly is intentionally placed in a situation where only the First Law would prevent him from lashing out against a human being. When he subsequently punches out an obnoxious heckler at a political rally, his humanity seems to be proven, and his political career gets back on track, eventually enabling him to become the first World Co-ordinator, the top executive position in a new World Federation formed in 2044. Nevertheless, Calvin continues to suspect that Byerly is a robot, pointing out at the end of the story that the heckler might himself have been a humanoid robot planted in the crowd by Byerly and thus not protected by the First Law. In a mark of the true difficulty in distinguishing such robots from humans, *I, Robot* itself never definitely identifies Byerly as either human or robot.

By the time Byerly reappears in the final story of the volume, "The Evitable Conflict," he is attempting, as World Co-ordinator, to unravel the baffling mystery of how the supposedly infallible Machines who now run the world's social and economic systems seem unaccountably to have started making small but easily identifiable mistakes. Calvin, however, deduces that the Machines are intentionally making mistakes as part of a complicated effort to discredit anti-robot forces on Earth. Having realized that they are now indispensible to the welfare of humans, the Machines, driven by the First Law, are able to override direct orders given them by humans (and even to do harm, if relatively minor, to humans who oppose them) so that they can protect themselves and thus protect the bulk of humanity.

There is no hint, however, of anything sinister in the way the Machines are able to overcome so much of their programming. After all, the Laws of Robotics remain intact, even if creatively interpreted, and the Machines (anticipating the Minds of Iain M. Banks's later "Culture" novels) remain absolutely devoted to protecting the collective welfare of the human race. Further, Calvin reminds Byerly, who is somewhat taken aback by her deductions, that this situation is really nothing new in human history. Humanity, she tells him, has never really been in control of its own fate, but has always been "at the mercy of economic and sociological forces it did not understand – at the whims of climate and the fortunes of war" (*I, Robot*, 192). At least now, she suggests, the forces that control humanity's fate are reasonable and have humanity's welfare in mind. The book then ends with the Machines firmly in control of the world's economy (and thus the world), but with Calvin's suggestion (never contradicted by anything in the text) that this is a wonderful development.

The concluding story of *I, Robot* serves as a classic example of technological optimism in science fiction, while at the same time pessimistically suggesting that human beings are not really capable of running their own affairs and that humanity thus needs something like the intervention of the Machines if it is to survive the tribulations that will face it in the future. This story did not first appear until 1950 (in *Astounding Science-Fiction*, shortly before it was reprinted as *I, Robot*), when Cold War anxieties were reaching a fever pitch owing to the first successful detonation of a Soviet nuclear bomb in 1949. Asimov's concerns, then, are very much of their time; to some extent they suggest a liberal response to anxieties of the day, very much in keeping with the spirit of the classic sf film *The Day the Earth Stood Still*, which appeared a year later. Nevertheless, Asimov's suggestion of a rule by machines of which humans are not even aware leaves open a number of possible ethical dilemmas with which *I, Robot* does not really deal.

Indeed, *I, Robot* seems so concerned with elaborating and exploring the Three Laws that it deals with few other issues in any detail. Meanwhile, the anti-robot prejudices alluded to in some of the stories have clear potential as a sort of allegorical stand-in for racial prejudice, though Asimov does not really pursue this possibility in *I, Robot*, leaving it instead for fuller examination in his subsequent robot novels, *The Caves of Steel* (1954) and *The Naked Sun* (1957). Potential uses of the robots to explore questions of class and gender are left unexplored as well. Nevertheless, *I, Robot* has exerted an important influence on subsequent works of sf, many of which have explored such questions. It has also remained popular with readers and was an inspiration for the 2004 film of the same title, an action-based Will Smith vehicle that centrally features the Laws of Robotics but otherwise is only vaguely related to the original stories.

Frederik Pohl and
C. M. Kornbluth,
The Space Merchants (1952)

The Space Merchants is a slim novel that nevertheless manages to address a wide variety of issues in a very effective way. Its vision of a future world governed by capitalism run amuck is both an insightful commentary on American culture in the early 1950s and a powerful anticipation of things to come. While the warnings inherent in *The Space Merchants* may not have been heeded, the book's vision of the future has been highly influential in the world of science fiction, making it a founding text of science fiction satire. Its nightmarish depiction of a violent, sordid, and utterly soulless corporate culture has influenced any number of science fiction critiques of capitalism, while its suggestion that this culture leads to overpopulation and environmental destruction makes it a founding text of environmentalist science fiction as well.

Frederik Pohl, one of the authors of *The Space Merchants*, was open in his belief that science fiction was an ideal venue for the exploration of social and political issues. Thus, Pohl declared in a December 1956 letter to Kornbluth that "the science-fiction novel, generally speaking *is* social criticism in a way that no other *category* of novel (except perhaps religious or proletlit) ever is" (quoted in David Seed, *American Science Fiction*, 82).

Pohl, one of the major figures in the history of American science fiction, maintained particularly strong leftist sympathies throughout his unusually long and productive career. He is particularly well known for the science fiction satires he produced in the 1950s, including a number of short stories that have been surveyed by Seed (*American Science Fiction*, 82–93). Pohl also produced a number of book-length satires during this period, often co-authored with Kormbluth or others. For example, in 1955 Pohl and Lester Del Rey (writing together under the pseudonym Edson McCann) published a searing satire of the insurance industry in *Preferred Risk*. That same year, Pohl and Kormbluth published *Gladiator-at-Law*, a send-up of organized sport that serves as a commentary on the competition-based ethos of American society as a whole. But Pohl's best known satire from the 1950s, written with Kormbluth, is undoubtedly *The Space Merchants*, which is widely recognized as one of the all-time classics of the science fiction genre. Pohl, who himself worked briefly as an advertising executive in the 1940s, also authored a sequel to *The Space Merchants*, entitled *The Merchants' War* (1984).

The Space Merchants presents a vivid picture of a future world dominated by huge multinational corporations, the most powerful and influential of which are media and advertising firms. In this sense, the book is very much of work of its time, when numerous novels and films acknowledged the growing centrality of advertising to modern American culture. For example, Frederic Wakeman's slightly earlier *The Hucksters* (1946) had already critiqued the ruthless and unethical tactics of the advertising industry, while Sloan Wilson's slightly later *The Man in the Gray Flannel Suit*, one of the bestsellers of 1955, comes as close as anything we have to being the signature novel of the 1950s. Wilson's title image, for example, became an emblem of the decade's drive for conformism, a drive that not only threatened individual identity but also offered a certain comfort level for those (mostly male WASPs) who were able to fit in. Indeed, *The Man in the Gray Flannel Suit*, despite some criticism of the era's corporate culture (with its emphasis on the drive for success at the expense of all else), is ultimately an affirmative work that assures Americans that they can succeed and still be themselves. Works such as *The Space Merchants* are less certain of the ultimate redeeming value of capitalism, and a closer look shows that, as M. Keith Booker has detailed in *Monsters, Mushroom Clouds, and the Cold War* (2001), some of the most trenchant social criticism of the 1950s can in fact be found in the era's science fiction.

However, the satire of *The Space Merchants* (which Donald M. Hassler (1997) has compared to the work of Jonathan Swift) goes well beyond the book's specific context of the early 1950s to anticipate the next half-century of American history, when advertising and the media would become increasingly powerful forces in American society. In addition, *The Space Merchants* envisions an American-dominated capitalist system that is global in nature, presenting a future world system much along the lines of that analyzed by Fredric Jameson (1991) and other contemporary Marxist theorists as "late capitalism."

However, in *The Space Merchants* capitalist expansion around the globe has been completed, leaving capitalism poised for the next stage: expansion into space. Narrator-protagonist Mitch Courtenay, an executive who works for the huge Fowler Schocken advertising conglomerate, receives a major (and sudden) boost to his career when he is unexpectedly put in charge of the company's project to colonize Venus, a planet to which they have been granted exclusive access through bribery and other political manipulations. Courtenay's job is not only to oversee the development of the technologies that will make this colonization possible, but to develop an advertising campaign that will make colonists want to go to Venus, where the whole planet can then be turned into a new source of profit for Fowler Schocken.

This assignment should be the dream of any ad executive – or of any capitalist. It is, after all, the ultimate big account. As Courtenay notes, "Potentially this was worth as much as every dollar of value in existence put together! A whole new planet, the size of Earth, in prospect as rich as Earth – and every micron, every milligram of it ours" (*Space Merchants*, 15). Courtenay's job is complicated, however, by his difficult personal life (his temporary wife, Dr. Kathy Nevin, wants to break off their trial marriage) and because rival Fowler Schocken executive Matt Runstead seems to be sabotaging all of his efforts. In addition, Fowler Schocken itself has fierce corporate rivals, such as Taunton Associates, and corporate rivalries in this future world – anticipating the corporate violence of such later science fiction novels as Jack Womack's *Ambient* (1987) or Richard K. Morgan's *Market Forces* (2005) – tend to get bloody. We are told, for example, that the management of entire companies is sometimes virtually wiped out in corporate feuds and that the steps of the General Post Office in London are still bloodstained from an earlier battle for a mail contract between United Parcel and American Express (*Space Merchants*, 13).

Courtenay himself gets caught up in corporate violence in the course of his mission when he goes to Antarctica to confront Runstead with his apparent treachery, but is knocked unconscious by a mysterious assailant and awakes on a transport that is taking him as a contract laborer to a huge high-rise protein plantation in Costa Rica. There, the formerly wealthy and powerful Courtenay gets a taste of how the working class (collectively referred to in this consumer capitalist society as "consumers") lives. He is also contacted by a secret organization of "Conservationists," or "Consies," who are working worldwide to try to prevent environmental destruction of the planet by industrial capitalism. While this environmentalist motif is secondary to the novel's satire of capitalist greed and expansionism, it is nevertheless important and indicates the extent to which science fiction was on the forefront of the environmentalist movement, a movement that is often thought to have begun with Rachel Carson's *Silent Spring* (1962), a book that Pohl has described as being essentially a science fiction novel in its own right (*Politics*, 10).

Courtenay eventually manages to return to New York, where (in an increasingly convoluted, thriller-like plot narrated in the style of detective fiction) he learns that both Nevin and Runstead are Consie agents. He also discovers that they have shanghaied him to Costa Rica both to try to teach him something about the plight of the workers in such gruesome Third World factories and to prevent him from being killed by agents of Taunton Associates, which hopes to wrest the Venus contract away from Fowler Schocken. In the end, the Consies manage to outmaneuver both capitalist firms by loading the only Venus rocket with their people in the hope that they will be able to colonize the planet, building there a new world free of the greed and corruption that capitalism has spread across the Earth. For his own part, Courtenay, now working with the Consies, momentarily becomes acting head of Fowler Schocken (after the death of the old man), but has to give up the post after he is outed, fleeing to Venus with the Consies (and Nevin). Runstead, meanwhile, remains undercover and takes the helm at Fowler Schocken, presumably hoping to sabotage any effort to send further rockets to Venus to disrupt the Consie effort there.

Of course, the somewhat contrived plot of *The Space Merchants* is really beside the point, serving merely as a sort of frame upon which to hang the book's political satire, which comments quite effectively on both the political climate of the United States in the early 1950s and the overall direction of consumer capitalism as a system. In one particularly telling speech made to Congress before his own shift to the Consie side is revealed and he is forced to flee, Courtenay constructs a masterpiece of pious Americanism, designed to cover the Consie plot to hijack the Venus rocket:

> I touched briefly on American enterprise and the home; I offered them a world to loot and a whole plunderable universe beyond it, once Fowler Schocken's brave pioneers had opened the way for it; I gave them a picture of assembly-line planets owned and operated by our very selves, the enterprising American businessmen who had made civilization great. (*Space Merchants*, 161)

This speech, of course, is very well received, because (experienced ad-man that he is) he tells the gathered Congressmen (who represent specific corporations, rather than groups of voters) precisely what they want to hear, parroting their own vision of a capitalist paradise in which all of space has been remade in the image of America.

Of course, the Earth of *The Space Merchants* has already been remade in this way, but the novel makes it clear that, for all but a few of the richest and most powerful, the world of this capitalist future is not a dream but a nightmare. Pohl has acknowledged that the novel was heavily influenced by Aldous Huxley's vision of a capitalist dystopia in *Brave New World* (1931), though in many ways the world of *The Space Merchants* is actually more like that of George Orwell's *Nineteen Eighty-Four* (1949). Living conditions are in fact quite grim in the world of *The Space Merchants*, in which the ultimate triumph of consumer capitalism has created a future world of scarcity rather than plenty. In particular, this future world is vastly overpopulated, in a motif that anticipates such later works as Harry Harrison's *Make Room! Make Room!* (1966) – as when those too poor to afford other accommodations are forced to sleep on stairways at night (*Make Room!*, 97). Moreover, this overpopulation has been intentionally engineered by the prevailing corporate culture: more people means more consumers for their products, and too many people merely creates shortages and a seller's market in which prices skyrocket.

Citizens of this densely overpopulated world must confront an environment so polluted that they need special nostril plugs, or sometimes even helmets, just to be able to breathe the air. Clean water is incredibly rare (and expensive); it is also strictly rationed, and even an executive like Courtenay cannot afford fresh water in which to bathe but must use cheaper salt water instead. The entire population is subjected to constant surveillance by both the government and private corporations. Most important, though bombarded by constant advertisements that urge them to consume, the citizens of this future world find that there is in fact very little that is available for consumption. A two-room apartment is considered a lavish accommodation, even for the relatively rich, and even a top corporate executive like old Fowler Schocken himself owns a Cadillac that has to be pedaled owing to the shortage of fuel. The world's phone system is so overtaxed by excessive traffic that it is virtually impossible to make a long-distance phone call – except, of course, on the priority lines of a mighty company like Fowler Schocken. Meanwhile, the whole reason that it is necessary to mount an ad campaign in support of the Venus project is that scarce resources that might otherwise have been used to produce consumer goods have to be diverted to develop and build the technology necessary for the trip to and colonization of Venus. Indeed, in the economy of scarcity that prevails in this nightmarish future world, the main job of advertising firms like Fowler Schocken is not so much to sell specific products as to sell the system itself, so that the brainwashed population will quietly accept the poverty and oppression that are thrust upon them. As Courtenay puts it, advertising has moved from "the simple handmaiden task of selling already manufactured goods to its present role of creating industries and redesigning a world's folkways to meet the needs of commerce" (*Space Merchants*, 6).

The "needs of commerce" here translates to the complete Americanization of global culture and the rampant commodification of every aspect of daily life. This future world has no poetry and no art. The language has been too debased to produce anything other than effective advertising slogans, and individuals such as Courtenay (who has, at least through most of the book, bought the corporate ideology hook, line, and sinker) are literally repelled by the literature of earlier periods. At one point Courtenay suddenly finds himself in a room filled with old books such as *Moby Dick*; he finds these books, which sell nothing, literally obscene and is made almost physically ill. He tells us: "I could not relax in the presence of so many books without a word of advertising in any of them. I am not a prude about solitary pleasures when they serve a useful purpose. But my tolerance has limits" (*Space Merchants*, 91). In another scene, Courtenay visits the Metropolitan Museum of Art and is comforted to find that it contains little except celebrations of corporate culture such as a bust of George Washington Hill (the president of the American Tobacco Company, who had pioneered radio advertising of tobacco products in the 1920s) and displays from classic advertising campaigns (such as Maidenform bra ads) (*Space Merchants*, 100–101).

Meanwhile, this thoroughly commercialized, artless corporate culture plunges headlong toward disaster, confident that somehow the technological means of saving humanity from itself will materialize before it is too late. The colonization of Venus is seen as just such a measure. Earth, in this grim future vision, has essentially been destroyed by capitalist greed, but there is always Venus (and, eventually other planets) to provide expansion room for Earth's burgeoning population (and new markets for the products hawked by Fowler Schocken). The Consies, on the other hand, see in Venus a genuine utopian potential, rather than simply an opportunity for more of the same. In particular, Venus is seen as a fresh start (as the Americas had once been seen by Europe, we might ominously remember). Thus, Nevin explains to Courtenay late in the book, Venus is important to the Consies because humanity is desperately in need of a second chance on a planet that is "unspoiled, unwrecked, unexploited, unlooted, unpirated, undevastated" (*Space Merchants*, 166).

The Consies (although somewhat reminiscent of the modern Greenpeace organization) are rather transparent stand-ins for communists, and their role in the book serves as part of an effective satire of the anticommunist oppression of the McCarthy era in which the book was written. Even more striking, however, are the depictions of the negative consequences of the growing power of consumer capitalism and the growing dominance of media and advertising in the lives of people around the world. These depictions are effective in the best tradition of literary satire – seemingly exaggerated in sometimes comical ways, they turn out on reflection to be much closer to reality than one might first have imagined. For example, Fowler Schocken's marketing tactics seem extreme until one compares them with tactics already in use today. One of their favorite techniques is to employ subtle forms of subliminal suggestion so that consumers will associate their products with sexual attractiveness and success and the products of their rivals with sexual frustration or deviance. Meanwhile, one of their most lucrative accounts involves the marketing of a drink called "Coffiest," which is laced with an addictive chemical to ensure that consumers will be hooked for life – which seems extreme only until one considers recent research on the addictive effects of the caffeine in ordinary coffee or the nicotine in cigarettes, effects about which coffee and tobacco companies have seemed remarkably unconcerned.

The Space Merchants shows a profound understanding of the direction in which consumer capitalism was already headed in 1952 and suggests interesting forms of complicity between the corporate manipulation of consumers for profit and the official promotion of anticommunist hysteria in the Cold War. Through the Consies, the book also suggests a potential utopian alternative to industrial capitalism, though the program of the Consies does not always accord well with the ideology of communism or socialism. The book maintains an essentially comic tone throughout, but it also includes some horrifying scenes to suggest the underlying seriousness of its message. At times the humor may become so glib that this seriousness is obscured, but as a whole the book is an effective satire that serves as an important counter to all those science fiction allegorizations – such as Robert A. Heinlein's *The Puppet Masters* (1951) – of the communist menace for which the 1950s are notorious.

Robert A. Heinlein, *Starship Troopers* (1959)

In the Hugo Award-winning *Starship Troopers*, science fiction legend Robert A. Heinlein envisions a future Earth ruled by the Terran Federation, a world government run by a military elite. Under this system, only veterans of the military enjoy full citizenship, including the right to vote. Further, the most important government jobs are reserved for veterans, on the presumption that their military training and experience have prepared them to perform these jobs more effectively than mere civilians. Yet, as potentially dystopian as this system might sound, Heinlein presents it as a utopia. The military leaders of this global system are described as the best and wisest rulers in human history, leading to unprecedented freedom and prosperity for all, including the vast majority, who have never served in the military and thus cannot vote or hold certain important jobs, but whose rights are otherwise protected by the system. On the other hand, while this system may have solved most of Earth's domestic problems, danger still lurks in the form of sinister alien species around the galaxy. As a result, preparedness is crucial, and those who do serve in the military in this future world have unprecedented opportunities to demonstrate valor and heroism, especially in the light of a cataclysmic war that erupts between Earth and an intelligent species of alien arachnoids, disparagingly referred to in the text as "Bugs."

Starship Troopers is now probably Heinlein's best-known novel. It is also probably his most controversial text and the one that has done the most to further his reputation, at least in certain circles, as a fanatical warmongering fascist – and possibly a racist as well. Indeed, the extremity of Heinlein's vision in *Starship Troopers* was such that two popular science fiction novels, Harry Harrison's *Bill, the Galactic Hero* (1965) and Joe Haldeman's *The Forever War* (1974), were written at least partly as responses to Heinlein's book. On the other hand, Everett Carl Dolman (1997) reviews some of the criticisms of Heinlein's novel, but concludes (while admitting that he agrees with Heinlein's assessment of the merits of military service) that the book is neither fascist nor racist, but merely overly idealistic in its depiction of the nobility of military life ("Military," 211–212). In any case, Bruce Franklin's (1980) description of the text as "a bugle-blowing, drum-beating glorification of the hero's life in military service" is certainly accurate (*Robert A. Heinlein*, 111). On the other hand, while *Starship Troopers* includes a number of battle scenes and thus a great deal of action, it is primarily a novel of ideas with clearly didactic purposes. It actually has very little in the way of plot, being primarily an elaboration of Heinlein's militaristic philosophy and a concerted attempt to convince readers to accept this philosophy.

Starship Troopers is essentially a call to arms, a reminder that some enemies can be defeated only by force and that any society that hopes to remain free must be prepared to exercise such force. Indeed, the book presents a pseudo-Darwinian vision of life as a struggle for survival of the strongest, thereby urging Americans to seek greater military strength so that they can survive – especially in competition with ruthless foes such as the Soviet or Chinese communists. Heinlein's description of his future global society is clearly meant as a critique of what he saw as the shortcomings of his own 1950s America, shortcomings that he felt might render the US unable to win the battle with communism. Though *Starship Troopers* is not as avowedly anticommunist as Heinlein's earlier *The Puppet Masters* (1951), the book is clearly a response to the belief of Heinlein (and many others) that the US was becoming soft and complacent in the late 1950s and was therefore not prepared to meet an all-out communist assault, should such an assault occur.

However, this critique of American softness goes beyond a suggestion of the importance of a strong military. Heinlein suggests that his contemporary American society has led young people to be spoiled and undisciplined. At one point, Mr. Dubois, a high school history teacher and former military officer who provides many of the text's most overtly didactic statements, addresses this issue as part of an explanation of the historical developments that led to the downfall of conventional American democracy and the eventual rise of the current military meritocracy. In a speech that directly addresses concerns about juvenile delinquency that were rampant in the 1950s, Dubois extols the virtues of flogging and other forms of corporal punishment as a means of straightening out wayward juveniles. Heinlein himself seems to endorse this suggestion, though one could read a certain irony into Dubois's comparison of this method to spanking puppies to try to housebreak them, which means that he is potentially making the problematic suggestion that human children should be trained to obedience like animals (*Starship Troopers*, 114–120). During this same speech, Dubois contextualizes his belief in harsh punishments by dismissing the very notion of inalienable rights, explaining that juvenile delinquency occurs because society is too soft on young people, encouraging them to demand their rights when in fact they should be urged to learn to do their duty. For Dubois, the notion that rights can be inalienable is nonsense: people have only the rights they are willing to fight and die for (*Starship Troopers*, 119). Duty, on the other hand, is universal, the very basis of any well-functioning society. Dubois thus declares that "the basis of all morality is duty, a concept with the same relation to group that self-interest has to individual" (*Starship Troopers*, 119). He admits that the soft, democratic societies of the past were in some ways admirable, but he also suggests that they were doomed by their lack of discipline: "The junior hoodlums who roamed their streets were symptoms of a greater sickness; their citizens (all of them counted as such) glorified their mythology of 'rights' ... and lost track of their duties. No nation, so constituted, can endure" (*Starship Troopers*, 120).

The weakness and moral decline brought about by this situation, we learn, was then followed by a final near-apocalyptic confrontation among different world powers, leading to a complete collapse of existing social systems. Interestingly, given Heinlein's typical concern with the threat posed by the Soviet Union, the final cataclysmic war that swept away the old order is pictured as a confrontation, beginning in 1987, between the "Russo-Anglo-American Alliance" on one side and the "Chinese Hegemony" on the other. Of course, this vision of an American-British-Russian alliance (the same alliance, after all, that had been victorious in World War II), does not diminish the text's warnings against the threat of communism. Swarming hordes of Chinese are, for Heinlein, an even more vivid image of the ultimate communist nightmare than are the Soviets. The Chinese, in fact, are a virtual human equivalent to the Bugs of *Starship Troopers*, as the text explicitly notes at one point when it is suggested that the lessons learned in the war against the Chinese Hegemony should be applicable to the war against the Bugs (*Starship Troopers*, 153).

Not surprisingly, Dubois's lectures also include the obligatory Cold War critique of Marxism, which he supposedly demolishes with a ludicrous argument that is hopelessly naïve and ignorant in its presentation of Marx's theories. Heinlein has Dubois claim, for example, that Marx's labor theory of value implies that human labor can transform anything into anything else, like some sort of alchemy. But, Dubois goes on, no amount of human labor can transform a mud pie into an apple tart, so Marx must have been wrong in his notion that human labor is the principal source of value in any commodity. Dubois further (wrongly) interprets Marx as believing that all human labor is of equal value, the fallaciousness of which point he demonstrates with a simple "kitchen example," noting that an unskilled cook can make a mishmash of the same ingredients that a talented chef might make into fine cuisine. In general, Heinlein (or at least Dubois) seems to confuse many of Marx's characterizations of capitalism with Marx's own positions. Given this kind of radical misinterpretation, perhaps it is little wonder that Dubois describes Marx as a "disheveled old mystic ... neurotic, unscientific, illogical, this pompous fraud" (*Starship Troopers*, 92).

Starship Troopers is essentially a bildungsroman that describes the military education of Juan Rico, one of Dubois's students, who also serves as the book's narrator and protagonist. Rico heeds Dubois well. Immediately after graduation from high school, he signs up, along with his friends Carl and Carmen, for a term in the military. Carl is assigned to work in research and development, while Carmen is sent to pilot training. Rico, however, is assigned to the mobile infantry, which many consider a lowly post, but which the text presents as the heart of the military and as the branch of the military in which service is the most honorable of all. We then follow Rico as he goes through boot camp and then officer candidate school (OCS). In the process, Rico learns the nature and value of militarism; readers presumably learn the same lesson by following Rico in his education.

Rico's military training is physically rigorous and mentally challenging; it demands precisely the agony and sweat and devotion that, according to Debois, all things of value demand. In fact, several trainees pay the ultimate price that Dubois had indicated earlier and are killed in the course of their training. Those who fail to heed the lessons they are being taught are apt to suffer severe punishment, including floggings in front of the other troops. Rico's education also includes considerable indoctrination, culminating in the declaration by Major Reid, one of his instructors in OCS, that rule by veterans of the military is the ideal political system because these veterans have learned, via their voluntary military service, to place "the welfare of the group ahead of personal advantage" (182). But, having learned this valuable lesson, the new ruling class also performs far better than any ruling class in history, because they understand full well that the very nature of human beings is to struggle for power through the use of force.

Rico learns this lesson well, ultimately accepting its dark message without question – after all, the instructors at OCS are described by Heinlein as being able to demonstrate the correctness of their point of view through mathematical proofs and symbolic logic. Rico thus emerges from his education as a trained killing machine, ready to go forth to defend his planet as a member of the mobile infantry, described by Franklin as a sort of "interstellar Green Berets" (116). And defend the planet Rico must, for, as ideal as the system there might be, eternal vigilance is still required. In a rather transparent allegorization of the position of the United States in the world system of the 1950s, the prosperous Earth is surrounded by sinister enemies, who threaten to take away its wealth and freedom. Central among these are the "Bugs," whose insectlike nature makes them the ideal Other, because they are so obviously inhuman. The Bugs are also imperialistic, hoping to add the Earth to their empire, thus forcing the Earthlings to fight to defend their way of life.

In fact, the Bugs and their ideology are virtually identical to Western Cold War visions of communism and the Soviet Union, though their alienness considerably simplifies the Us vs. Them terms of the Cold War. Noting this use of the Bugs as stand-ins for communists, David Seed (1999) suggests that "political difference is thereby naturalized into the threatening alien" (*American Science Fiction*, 37). Theirs is a communal society of unfeeling creatures who forgo all individualism in favor of the collective good. Indeed, they are formidable precisely because they work so smoothly as a collective unit, with no consideration for individual needs and concerns. Heinlein, through Rico, makes the connection to communism explicit: "Every time we killed a thousand Bugs at the cost of one M.I. it was a net victory for the Bugs. We were learning, expensively, just how efficient a total communism can be when used by a people adapted to it by evolution; the Bug commissars didn't care any more about expending soldiers than we care about expending ammo" (*Starship Troopers*, 152–153).

Of course, Heinlein is careful to qualify his seeming admiration for Bug communism by explaining that the Bugs are adapted to it by evolution, implying that, on the other hand, communism is unnatural for human beings, who are by nature driven by blind self-interest. For Heinlein, only military discipline can harness this natural survivalist tendency in human beings and put it to good use, though Heinlein here gets entangled in the contradictions of his own arguments. On the one hand, he presents military discipline as involving first and foremost a willingness to sacrifice the individual in the interest of the group – which makes the human military seem rather similar to the Bug communists. On the other hand, he makes a sharp distinction between the liberality with which the Bugs sacrifice individual soldiers in the interest of their common goals and the willingness of the human military to sustain huge losses to rescue even one of their number who happens to be in trouble. In fact, he suggests that the ultimate strength of humanity derives from "a racial conviction that when one human needs rescue, others should not count the price" (*Starship Troopers*, 223). Yet

Heinlein fails to explain how this "racial conviction" arose in a race he characterizes as naturally driven only by self-interest; nor does he explain how the military morality of favoring the group over the individual fits in with the willingness to sacrifice entire platoons to try to rescue a single human soldier.

Indeed, *Starship Troopers* is a text filled with seeming contradictions, most of which arise in the conflict between Heinlein's celebration of military discipline and his espousal of radical individualism. One could, in fact, see the entire text as an extended effort on the part of Heinlein to reconcile these seemingly opposed perspectives. For one thing, he repeatedly makes the point that his individualist philosophy (essentially a version of libertarianism) involves individual responsibility as well as individual freedom. Thus, each individual bears the responsibility for protecting the entire global civilization – and thus for maintaining a situation in which individual freedom can be maintained. This responsibility is enacted most directly and effectively through military service, though it should also be noted that Heinlein's future military differs in many important respects from the militaries of the past.

Heinlein's ideal future military is composed entirely of volunteers. These volunteers must serve a certain amount of time in order to earn citizenship and the right to vote, but otherwise they are free to leave the service at any time – they can back out, with no consequences other than losing citizenship, even as they are on the verge of going into battle. Further, the floggings and other harsh punishments that are sometimes meted out to those who fail in their duty can be avoided simply by leaving the service. Those who accept these punishments are thus expressing their dedication to the service and determination to do their duty. Soldiers serve out of this personal commitment, not through any sort of coercion or fear of reprisal. The soldier in this service "is a free man; all that drives him comes from inside – that self-respect and need for the respect of his mates and his pride in being one of them called morale, or *esprit de corps*" (*Starship Troopers*, 208).

This *esprit de corps* is furthered because all of the soldiers in a given service, especially the mobile infantry, are very much in the same boat. In particular, all soldiers (including chaplains) fight – there are no separations between combat troops and support troops. Any "soft, safe" jobs that might be required are filled by civilians – who do not, by performing these jobs, qualify for citizenship. In addition, as opposed to the top-heavy tendencies that Heinlein attributes to the armies of the past, this all-volunteer military includes a minimal number of officers. A typical battalion has 10,800 ordinary fighting men and 317 officers, 216 of whom are lieutenants who lead individual platoons. And all of these officers, including generals, go into combat alongside the common grunts. Further, while there is a great deal of emphasis on the importance of chain of command, this chain is greatly streamlined, and individual soldiers are well trained and highly skilled professionals who go into battle bearing a complex array of high-technology equipment (including the "fighting suits" that have now become a stock image of military science fiction). They also have a great deal of autonomy in deploying this equipment, which makes each individual man a formidable fighting machine.

These fighting machines are spectacularly dramatized in Verhoeven's 1997 film version of Heinlein's novel. Done as big-budget camp, with tongue in cheek, the film can be considered a combination of adaptation and parody that produces a number of new perspectives on Heinlein's novel. It largely lampoons Heinlein's militaristic vision and glorification of violence, concerting Heinlein's individualism into an exploration of alienation. It also adds an element of media satire (reminiscent of Verhoeven's earlier sf films *Robocop* and *Total Recall*) in its presentation of media coverage of this violence. Unfortunately, the film version of *Starship Troopers* sometimes seems to get caught up in its own spectacular special effects, becoming a spectacle of violence in its own right. In addition, while Verhoeven drops the anticommunist rhetoric of the novel, his extremely realistic Bugs are so menacingly alien that there is little chance of audiences truly sympathizing with them, even though the murderous humans have vastly superior weapons and the film hints that it may have been the humans who provoked the war.

Verhoeven here exaggerates Heinlein's militaristic vision – Heinlein had presented the Bugs as the unquestionable aggressors. Verhoeven makes Heinlein's book appear more objectionable in other ways as well. For example, while the text places no emphasis on this fact, the protagonist Juan Rico is presumably Hispanic, while Verhoeven cast the ultra-Aryan Casper Van Dien as Rico, producing a protagonist who looks like a recent graduate of the Nazi Youth and thus calls attention to the potential fascism of Heinlein's text. On the other hand (as J. P. Telotte notes in a useful discussion of the film and the novel), numerous reviewers read this motif too literally and characterized the film itself as a celebration of fascism.

Verhoeven's depiction of the militaristic Federation actually moderates Heinlein's vision in some ways. Women, for example, seem to enjoy full equality in Verhoeven's Federation, whereas they serve primarily as sexual objects (though largely unobtainable and untouchable ones) in Heinlein's. Thus, in the film, women serve in the mobile infantry alongside men. There is, in fact, no segregation of the sexes in Verhoeven's future military, even in the showers (a motif we also see in the future police of *Robocop*). In

Heinlein, on the other hand, women do not go into combat, but serve only aboard the navy's starships, where they can hold some high-level jobs, such as pilots (and the text even stipulates that women make better pilots than men), but where they are mostly glorified camp followers, brought along primarily to keep up the men's morale and give them a "living, breathing reality" to fight for, rather than mere abstract principles (*Starship Troopers*, 204).

We learn relatively little about the status of women outside the military, and *Starship Troopers* is in general weak as a literary utopia because of the absence of such details. In fact, the book lacks any extensive explanation of what life is actually like for the majority of people who do not enjoy the full rights of citizenship in the Terran Federation because they have not served in the military. *Starship Troopers* is also weak as a story of alien encounter, telling us essentially nothing about the Bugs – who remain nameless, faceless, and mysterious – other than the stipulation that they are murderously bent on the destruction of human beings and must thus be defeated at all costs. It does, however, contain some compelling images of a futuristic military – images that have influenced any number of science fiction novels, films, and television series since its original publication. It also contains some of Heinlein's most controversial political ideas, and the thought-provoking questions it poses can be useful, even for those who find Heinlein's particular answers distasteful.

Philip K. Dick, *Do Androids Dream of Electric Sheep?* (1968)

Philip K. Dick's *Do Androids Dream of Electric Sheep?* is a key work of postmodernist science fiction that calls the definition of "human" into question by blurring the boundaries between human and android, an aspect of its larger blurring of the boundary between reality and simulation. Set on a dystopian, post-apocalyptic twenty-first-century Earth where technology pervades every aspect of life, the novel anticipates the complete breakdown of the opposition between natural and artificial that is the hallmark of cyberpunk fiction, offering a sophisticated exploration of the ethical considerations inherent in the destabilization of the human/android hierarchy. What emerges is that the need for humans to maintain strict boundaries between themselves and their technological creations actually robs them of their humanity.

In the near future of the novel, humans have achieved interplanetary space travel and are successfully colonizing the solar system with the help of androids. The impetus for this colonization is the dismal state of things on Earth. Contaminated by nuclear fallout in the wake of World War Terminus (a war whose cause appears to have been forgotten), the Earth has suffered severe environmental degradation, resulting in the loss of most animal life. People are encouraged to emigrate into space, taking along government-issued androids – artificially created biological organisms who appear to be virtually indistinguishable from humans – to toil for them on space colonies where life is only marginally less miserable than it is on Earth. The androids are desperate to leave the drudgery and isolation of their existence on the off-world colonies, often murdering their human masters in order to make their escape. Officially banned from Earth, they are subject to retirement if their presence is detected, whether or not they have committed a crime – simply being on the planet is considered illegal and thus serves as the justification for killing ("retiring") them. Dick's protagonist, Rick Deckard, is a bounty hunter employed by the San Francisco police department to "retire" such androids.

In the novel, a group of androids has escaped to Earth from the Mars colony, initially blending in with humans quite successfully. Deckard and his fellow bounty hunters must use a sophisticated psychological test in order to distinguish between humans and androids: not only has technology made it possible to manufacture androids who are quite similar to humans, but the humans of the book are becoming more and more like machines.

Do Androids begins with Deckard and his wife, Iran, arguing about their own "programming" via the Penfield mood organ, a device that allows them to dial for moods ranging from "well-disposed toward the world" to "self accusatory depression." There is even a setting for stimulating the desire to dial, should the user feel some reluctance to do so. Like the ubiquitous television in contemporary postmodern culture, the mood organ may be found in every household; people are seemingly unable to function without it, giving up control of their emotional lives on a daily basis in exchange for artificially induced moods. The addiction to a technological medium that manufactures a simulated reality also extends to television and radio in the novel, where beloved media star Buster Friendly reigns supreme for an impossible twenty-three hours a day. Later revealed to be a simulation himself, the android Buster asserts control over his audience's hearts and minds, often manipulating them as easily as their moods are manipulated by the mood organ. Dick thus describes a world saturated with images and messages, where the lines between reality and simulation are difficult to discern, if they exist at all. His critique of the role of mass media in shaping human lives is very much in line with Jean Baudrillard's analysis of postmodern media culture, which theorizes that simulation in the post-industrial world actually replaces "the real," with the effect that everyday life is disconnected from reality. The mood organ, as a stand-in for our own popular culture, illustrates the extent to which humans replace authenticity with simulation; the characters need it to feel anything at all. Deckard is irritated with his wife for programming what he believes is a pointless depression, which she sees as the necessary expression of an existential angst born of living in a world ravaged by nuclear war. Iran is intuitively responding to the relative emptiness of the Earth, where the few remaining humans live in prewar apartment buildings surrounded by the detritus of a dying civilization, or "kipple." She notes that the inability to react to the absence of life would have been considered a kind of mental illness in the prewar era, an anticipation of the "waning of affect" that Fredric Jameson argues is the hallmark of the postmodern subject.

Ironically, Iran feels that she must dial for an artificial mood because she is otherwise unable to experience emotions that seem "natural" to the conditions under which she lives. This programming of emotions is a particularly important motif in the novel, especially given that it is held to be a universal truth in Dick's near-future that what sets humans apart from androids is the ability to feel empathy for other living creatures, an emotion that is supposedly showcased in their relationships with animals. The attention given to animals far outweighs that given to other people, a suggestion that the empathy felt for animals serves as a replacement for the inability to feel empathy for other humans – a phenomenon that is common in our own contemporary culture. Exceedingly rare in the aftermath of nuclear war, animals are highly valued, so much so that owning an animal is considered a special indicator of an individual's status within the society. Animals are status symbols that Deckard has difficulty affording, however, and although (in order to keep up appearances) he replaces his original sheep with an electric simulation after its death, he finds the effort to maintain a fraudulent relationship with what is a mere copy to be "gradually demoralizing" (9). Not simply commodities, animals are also central to the religion of Mercerism, which most humans practice. Adherents of the religion routinely fuse with its archetypal founder Wilbur Mercer – a prewar figure punished for having the ability to revive dead animals – through an interface with an "empathy box." In doing so, they, along with everyone else using the empathy box, feel the pain of the Christ-like Mercer's passive resistance against the amorphous "Killers," who try to prevent him from ascending out of the "tomb world." Like the mood organ and the television, the empathy box is a technological medium that manufactures a simulated reality. Believing that they are participating in their leader's struggle, devotees of Mercerism accept that empathy for animals (and other people) is a moral obligation. It is the religious value placed on animals, though, that results in an industry that exploits them, with characters frantically flipping through a *Sidney's* catalog (a kind of "blue book" for animals) in order to determine their market value. In the end, as N. Katherine Hayles (1999) observes, "Mercerism joins with capitalism to create a system in which the financially privileged merge seamlessly with the religiously sanctified" (175). Deckard feels his exclusion from owning a real animal keenly, and hopes to purchase one after retiring the escaped androids, creatures for whom humans have no moral obligation to feel empathy. Lack of empathy for androids, in fact, is considered "human," while at the same time nurturing electric animals is acceptable for those who can't afford the real thing.

Though the empathy box offers the ability to simulate communion with other humans as they enact Mercer's struggle, it also has the effect of replacing one-on-one interaction. Iran's need to immediately share good news via the empathy box, for example, leaves Deckard feeling isolated. Comparisons to our contemporary relationship with the internet are apt here, as users are part of a virtual community at the same time that they are isolated from actual human contact. Jill Galvan argues that this effect in the novel is deliberately constructed by the government – the purveyors of the equipment and proponents of Mercerism – in an attempt to prevent public unrest by allowing the masses to vent their emotions (even feelings of rebellion) in a state-sanctioned fashion ("Entering", 417). Tellingly, Deckard himself has difficulty fusing with Mercer and admits that he does not understand the religion, an attitude that has more parallels with those of the androids he is assigned to retire than with those of his empathic fellow humans. The suggestion here is that by virtue of his job as an assassin, Deckard has become dehumanized: a killing machine.

Believed to be devoid of empathy, androids may be distinguished from humans with the application of the Voigt-Kampff scale, which is designed to measure automatic responses (blushing, for example) to a series of questions about the death or mutilation of animals. Because harming animals is unthinkable owing to their rarity and religious significance, humans generally have a strong empathic response to such questions. Androids lack that response, or – as with the Nexus-6, the advanced model that Deckard must track – they fake it. Experienced bounty hunters can tell a fake response from a genuine one, but the margin of error is very small, and the potential for mistakes rises with every new advancement in android technology. That the results of the test require such a high level of expertise to interpret demonstrates the degree to which androids have become almost indistinguishable from humans. The questions used for the Voigt-Kampff test, however, which feature scenarios ranging from boiling a live lobster to lying on a bearskin rug, would be unlikely to garner much of an empathic response from Dick's audience, most of whom would find the situations described to be rather ordinary. Like Dick's androids, many modern Americans would fail the test, an implication that further destabilizes the boundary between human and android by forcing the reader to question her own supposed humanity.

As Deckard begins to retire the six Nexus-6 androids, he finds himself developing empathy for them. After the death of Luba Luft, an opera singer whose talent he admires, he reacts vehemently to the waste of that talent, realizing that his attitude differs markedly from that of fellow bounty Phil Resch, who actually enjoys killing androids. It is the cold-blooded Resch, Deckard's double, who forces Deckard to examine his own feelings about the justification for hunting androids. Deckard's distaste for Resch and empathy for Luft – the opposite of what he believes he *should* feel – trigger in him an identity crisis, which he tries to resolve by buying a live goat. He believes that a relationship with a real animal will boost his morale and properly restore his sense of the boundary between human and android, despite the fact that he seems to have no particular feeling for animals outside of their commodity value. Resch dismisses Deckard's newly empathic feelings as simple sexual attraction for androids, urging him to purge the emotion through a sexual liaison with one. Deckard does in fact have sex with android Rachael Rosen of Rosen Associates, the corporation that created the Nexus-6, but he develops an emotional attachment for her that further undermines his ability to regard androids as nothing more than machines. For her part, Rosen reveals to Deckard that she has had liaisons with a number of bounty hunters, and all but Phil Resch were unable to continue killing androids afterwards.

Rosen's act, which is calculated to preserve others of her kind, suggests that androids may in fact exhibit signs of empathy, at least for other androids. In her case, she is seeking not just to save the lives of other androids, but in particular one who is almost an exact duplicate of herself. Androids exhibit a range of emotions in the novel, countering the flattening of affect often displayed in humans. They also prefer the face-to-face inter-action that humans eschew. Android bodies are typically more expressive than those of humans in the novel, subject to more detailed descriptions, and they also engage in traditionally human physical expressions of affec-tion while humans themselves primarily "touch" each other through the technological medium of the empathy box. Androids cry, laugh, become enraged, and yet are conscious that according to the dictates of human culture, they are not, in fact, alive. Perhaps it is for this reason that Rosen pushes Deckard's goat off the roof to its death – even a goat is considered more important than the lives of the androids Rosen tries to protect, all of whom are retired by Deckard within hours after he declares his deep affection for her.

While Rosen is seducing Deckard, her double Pris Stratton is coldly exploiting J. R. Isidore in a nearly abandoned apartment complex in a suburb of San Francisco. Isidore has suffered too much mental deterioration from radioactive contamination to be eligible for emigration from Earth, and is classified as a "special," which basically means that he, like the androids, is considered less than human by those in his society. Neverthe-less, Isidore exhibits more empathy than any other character in the book, responding to the suffering of animals (both real and electric) and agreeing to help the final three androids whom Deckard is assigned to retire. He is also a faithful devotee of Mercerism, providing a stark contrast to the more coldly rational Deckard. Isidore's innocence is lost, however, after his encounter with the androids, who despite their seeming empathy for one another, have little to spare for other creatures. Pris Stratton, whom Isidore loves and eagerly tries to please, cruelly tortures a spider that he finds, cutting off its legs one by one. Additionally, he learns in a television expose by Buster Friendly that Wilbur Mercer is a fraud, an alcoholic actor paid to act out the Sisyphean scenario that humans experience through the empathy box. Buster himself is not what he seems, and humans are largely unaware that he is an android. Patricia S. Warrick (1977), who traces Dick's use of doubles and opposites throughout the novel, notes that in a paradoxical twist typical of Dick's texts, both Buster and Mercer are inauthentic, and yet both reveal certain truths, further blurring the lines between simulation and reality (*Do Androids*, 123). The death of the spider coupled with these Earth-shattering revelations causes Isidore to break down and hallucinate that the world is being transformed into kipple, the rubble that signals the entropic decay of the universe. At this point Mercer appears to Isidore, giving him a newly restored spider and confessing that while he is indeed a fraud, Mercerism is still an authentic experience. In other words, something "real" can be found even in a simulation, a notion that can be extended to the androids, though the reliability of this statement is questionable, given that it occurs within a hallucination.

Like Isidore, Deckard experiences a manifestation of Mercer, who warns him of Pris Stratton's approach with a weapon. Earlier, Mercer had told him during a session with the empathy box that "it is a basic condition of life, to be required to violate your own identity" (*Do Androids*, 179), a suggestion that Deckard would betray his own newly developed empathy for androids. Killing Pris Stratton, who closely resembles Rachael Rosen, is the fulfillment of Mercer's proclamation, and Deckard feels so alienated after the completion of his mission and Rosen's killing of his goat that he tries to clear his mind by traveling to the radioactive desert of Oregon. It is there that he has his most profound religious experience through Mercerism, believing that he has become permanently fused with Mercer, even without an empathy box. Despite Deckard's prior skepticism toward the religion and the fact that its leader has been proven a fraud, Mercerism resonates for him, pointing the way toward a new kind of empathy – one that erases divisions between the android and the human. This is not the Mercerist doctrine of empathy as promulgated by the government, but rather one that recognizes the lives of both the natural and the artificial as worthy of compassion ("Posthuman Collective," 427). This tolerance of the posthuman, which brings with it a corresponding restoration of "humanity" in Deckard, is underscored by his excited discovery in the desert of a seemingly live toad.

Considered to be all but extinct and the favored creature of Mercer, the toad is later revealed by Iran to be artificial. Resigned, Deckard realizes that this doesn't matter and that "The electric things have their lives, too. Paltry as those lives are" (*Do Androids?* 241).

In its interrogation of media culture and of the general breakdown of the distinction between reality and simulation, *Do Androids?* is a pivotal work of postmodernist science fiction, though it is probably best known today as the inspiration for Ridley Scott's *Blade Runner* (1982). Scott's film is faithful to the basic plot of Dick's novel, though it dispenses with aspects of the book that add layers to the breakdown between simulation and reality epitomized by the androids (referred to as replicants in the film). Mood organs, empathy boxes, Mercer, and Buster Friendly are all missing from the film. However, Scott's visually stunning depiction of the postmodern Los Angeles cityscape – with its mishmash of architectural styles, fashions both futuristic and retro, juxtaposition of high-tech and urban decay, and disorienting surface texture – make us question what is "real" about a Los Angeles that appears to have so little in common with the city of today. In terms of its aesthetics, vision of the future, and collapse of the distinctions between natural and artificial, *Blade Runner* is both an iconic postmodern film and an important influence on the development of cyberpunk fiction, which takes as its central focus the implication of the increasingly intimate relationship between humans and technology. Together with Dick's novel, the film challenges the definition of what it means to be human in a world where human experience is invariably mediated by technology.

Ursula K. Le Guin, *The Dispossessed* (1974)

A novel of considerable literary merit that added substantially to the critical reputation of its author, *The Dispossessed* is a central work in what many see as a resurgence in utopian science fiction (especially by women writers) in the 1970s. A complex political novel that draws upon a number of potential sources of utopian ideas, *The Dispossessed* draws upon sources ranging from Taoism, to anarchist and socialist political thinkers (like Kropotkin and Fourier), to the oppositional political movements of the 1960s and early 1970s. Indeed, Fredric Jameson calls Le Guin's book the "richest reinvention of the genre" of utopian fiction to grow out of the politics of the 1960s (*Postmodernism*, 160). It is certainly the case that *The Dispossessed* addresses, with its contrast between an affluent but oppressive consumer-capitalist dystopia and a materially poor but personally fulfilling anarchist-capitalist utopia, a number of important political issues.

The Dispossessed is the fifth novel in Le Guin's "Hainish" sequence, though its action is actually set at the beginning. This sequence, which began with *Rocannon's World* in 1966, deals with a far-flung interstellar confederation, the "Ekumen," which is in only the early stages of development during *The Dispossessed*. The Ekumen is held together largely by a common cultural and biological heritage derived from the fact that the galaxy was "seeded" with human DNA (and culture) thousands of years earlier by colonial explorers from the planet Hain, whose empire is now defunct, though Hain itself is still a civilized planet. With travel still limited to sub-light speeds, the administration of the Ekumen is enabled by the availability of instantaneous communication across vast interstellar distances, thanks to the invention of a device known as an "ansible," which is ultimately developed from the fundamental scientific principles discovered by Shevek, the protagonist of *The Dispossessed*.

Shevek is a brilliant physicist who begins to feel that the development of his work has been limited by conditions on the impoverished moon of Anarres, so he arranges to travel to the rich neighboring planet of Urras, hoping thereby to further his work and to initiate communication between the two societies, which have been sealed off from one another since dissidents from Urras (inspired by the teachings of the woman philosopher and political activist Odo) settled on Anarres generations earlier. Shevek, already famous on Urras for his scientific work (much of which has already been smuggled to the planet for publication there), is greeted as a celebrity, but soon finds that the immense wealth of the society of A-Io (the country that hosts him) has not prevented that society from developing huge economic inequities, leading to a variety of social problems, including the oppression of women.

The Dispossessed is structured via chapters alternating between those that describe Shevek's life on Anarres and his experience on his trip to Urras, thus setting up an illuminating contrast between the two societies. This contrast causes Shevek to be horrified by the inequities in the society of A-Io. He thus becomes involved with an Odonian-influenced underground resistance group there and is nearly killed when the government attacks a peaceful demonstration with extreme violence. This event makes clear the oppressive nature of the system and verifies Shevek's judgment of it – while also echoing the violent official attacks that have sometimes been made on demonstrators in Western democracies of our own world, as at Kent State massacre in May 1970 in the US. Shevek survives the attack and makes his way to the embassy of the planet Terra (i.e., Earth), where he is given asylum and then put on a ship back to Anarres, though he knows many there will meet him with animosity because of his trip to Urras. On the way, Ketho, the Hainish first mate of the Terran ship, asks to go down to Anarres with him. Thus, as the book ends, much is left open, but there is considerable hope that Anarresti society is about to experience an opening up to outside contact that will break it out of the stagnation that has begun to threaten it.

This warning against stagnation, of course, addresses one of the central difficulties faced by all utopian societies, fictional or real: with supposedly ideal conditions already established, there is little impetus for change; but if no change occurs, conditions tend to deteriorate. In *The Dispossessed*, Le Guin suggests that any society, no matter how ideal, must continually be ready to face new problems and challenges. Indeed, Le Guin implies that openness to a certain amount of change is part of what makes a society utopian in the first place, and the society of Anarres embraces change to the point that a belief in perpetual revolution is one of its central values. The

Odonian philosophy that informs this society includes an anarchistic suspicion of fixed structures of all kinds, in which the individual's responsibility
resides not so much in obedience to existing systems as in contributions to
ongoing revolutionary change. In many ways, the principles upon which
Anarres is founded can be read as a direct reversal of the principles of classic
dystopian societies such as the Oceania of George Orwell's *Nineteen
Eighty-Four* (1949) or the One State of Evgeny Zamyatin's *We* (1925): the
responsibility of the individual is not to obey authority, but to reject it;
freedom is valued over security; and the highest paradigm of the society is
not stability, but revolution. As Shevek muses on the faults in his society he
provides a succinct summary of the philosophy of Le Guin's utopia:

> That the Odonian society on Anarres had fallen short of the ideal did not, in
> his eyes, lessen his responsibility to it; just the contrary. With the myth of the
> State out of the way, the real mutability and reciprocity of society and
> individual became clear. Sacrifice might be demanded of the individual, but
> never compromise: for though only the society could give security and stabi-
> lity, only the individual, the person, had the power of moral choice – the
> power of change, the essential function of life. The Odonian society was
> conceived as a permanent revolution, and revolution begins in the thinking
> mind. (*The Dispossessed*, 333)

In addition to its warnings against stagnation, *The Dispossessed* is also
aware of a variety of other problems that plague any utopian project. The
most important of these is material wealth, which many thinkers (including
Karl Marx, in his discussion of the historical conditions that would be
necessary for the survival of socialism) have seen as essential to the building
of a utopian society. One thinks, for example, of the universal affluence
(thanks to technologies such as "replicators") that seems to have facilitated
the solution to most social and political problems on the future Earth of the
television series *Star Trek*. Le Guin, on the other hand, clearly regards
material wealth as an inevitable source of corruption and spiritual impover-
ishment, its temptations so great that individuals are unable to avoid
compromising their values in order to compete more successfully for material gain. As Nadia Khouri (1980) puts it, in *The Dispossessed* "material
dispossession becomes the necessary condition for ethical wealth" ("Dialectics," 51).

Le Guin depicts Anarres not as a land of universal plenty but as a dry and
barren world, on which a genuine community struggles for existence
through toughness, dedication, and hard work. Further, the citizens of
Anarres know that they must cooperate with one another if any are to
survive. Thus, they are able to avoid the ethos of competition that is so

central to the mindset of the citizens of A-Io. In addition, Le Guin's positive description of Anarres may serve to challenge the assumptions of some readers that wealth is a necessary prerequisite for happiness. On the other hand, her exaltation of asceticism is problematic. For example, Tom Moylan (1986), who is critical of the novel in a number of ways, notes the suspicious similarity between Le Guin's Anarres and the Old West of American frontier days, concluding that

> the thematic strategy of scarcity is one way to negate the ostentatious affluence of modern America, but it also serves as a backward look to the "good old days" of the frontier more than it makes a serious attempt to appropriate productive surplus for the well-being of all humanity. (*Demand*, 103)

As Moylan (1986) indicates, the politics of *The Dispossessed* are problematic in a number of ways. For example, the vast majority of the people of Le Guin's book still live on Urras, while the strict separatism of the anarchists on Anarres ignores the continuing injustice on the world they left and lends Le Guin's utopia an escapist aspect that runs counter to any notion of genuine revolution. Moreover, it is not at all clear that Le Guin's novel is itself successful at escaping the prevailing ideology of the world to which it supposedly presents a radical alternative. Shevek, the strong male protagonist, bears many similarities to the traditional bourgeois notion of the autonomous individual, while his courageous, unselfish actions seem easily contained within the conventional bourgeois (masculine) myth of the hero.

Peter Ruppert (1986) suggests that "the ambiguity of all boundaries" is "the central theme of Le Guin's novel" (*Reader*, 141), and this interrogation of boundaries in *The Dispossessed* particularly includes an examination of gender roles, a motif central to Le Guin works such as *The Left Hand of Darkness* (1969). In the utopian society of Anarres the two genders are treated with complete equality, a fact reflected very clearly in their language ("Pravic"), which has been specifically developed as part of their efforts to create the ideal society. This motif thus draws upon the so-called "Sapir–Whorf hypothesis," which argues that the structure of a person's principal language has a constitutive effect on that person's perception of and attitude toward the world. For example, this language has no words for sexual intercourse that indicate possession of one partner by another or action of one partner upon another, except for one indicating rape. Instead, the language features plural sexual verbs, indicating mutual action: "It meant something two people did, not something one person did, or had" (*Dispossesed*, 53). Meanwhile, individuals have names that are entirely devoid of gender. Infants are given computer-generated names, ostensibly as a democratic gesture that avoids conventional patriarchal naming procedures. This computer naming may seem to echo the numbering of citizens in Zamyatin's One State, but Le Guin's narrator makes a point of contrasting these names, unique for each living individual, with the "numbers which a computer-using society must otherwise attach to its members" (*Dispossessed*, 250).

Pravic also contributes to the communal nature of society on Anarres in other ways, as in its use of the same word for "work" and "play" and in its de-emphasis on expressions indicating possession. But, as Meyers (1980) points out, theoretical languages like Le Guin's Pravic or the "Loglan" of James Cooke Browne's *The Troika Incident* (1970) are seriously problematic in that normal historical evolution will tend to make such languages drift away from their original theoretical conception. Noting the isolationist measures to which the society of Anarres is thus forced to resort in order to protect its language from such evolution, Meyers concludes that Le Guin's utopia is in fact a dystopia: "If the society of Anarres in *The Dispossessed* is not a dystopia, it has all the machinery of one, from a language designed to influence the thinking of its people through every weapon needed to keep that language from being changed" (*Aliens*, 208).

That Shevek is able to rebel against the expectations of his society, breaking a crucial taboo by establishing contact with the dreaded "propertarian" society of A-Io, indicates that the machinery of social and psychological control on Anarres is far from complete. On the other hand, Shevek's strongly negative reaction to the conditions he finds in A-Io, including the shock and revulsion he experiences as a result of the class and gender inequalities that are central to the society of A-Io, suggests that he has, in fact, undergone a considerable amount of conditioning, though Le Guin clearly presents this conditioning more in the positive mode of having well learned the admirable values of his society. In any case, Shevek on Urras becomes a classic case of the sf staple of the stranger in a strange land; the cognitive dissonance he experiences as a result of being immersed in a world that differs in fundamental ways from his own is a mirror of the cognitive dissonance experienced by readers of science fiction in general.

Le Guin's depiction of A-Io takes advantage of this cognitive dissonance to produce effective social and political satire of a kind that is often achieved in the best and most powerful works of science fiction. As readers follow Shevek, presumably sharing (if in a less visceral form) his negative reaction to the inequalities he observes around him in A-Io, a gradual realization that Le Guin here is describing precisely the sort of inequalities that inform modern capitalist societies such as Britain and (even more directly) the United States, can potentially be quite powerful. The separation of the genders in

A-Io is particularly extreme; women are clearly regarded as second-class citizens and are strictly excluded from numerous professions (including science) and other realms of activity. Of course, for readers in the twenty-first century, the overt discrimination against women in A-Io seems archaic and obviously inappropriate. As a result, the satire of *The Dispossessed* is not particularly effective in terms of gender, even if gender discrimination has been eradicated much more thoroughly on Anarres than in the Britain or the US of more than three decades after the publication of the book. What is more striking for readers in this later era is the book's satirical treatment of capitalism, which has become more and more dominant on a global scale since the publication of *The Dispossessed*, to the point that many now see it as the only logical system, while any possible alternatives seem unnatural and nonsensical. However, to Shevek (who has had little exposure to capitalism or the ideology that supports it), it is capitalism and the inequalities it creates that make no sense. He is shocked, therefore, that the lust for profits (combined with a certain amount of coercion) is able to motivate anyone to work at all, having assumed that only a "human being's natural incentive to work – his initiative, his spontaneous creative energy" could produce diligent workers (*Dispossessed*, 82). Finding the workings of capitalism totally strange, Shevek (intellectual that he is) endeavors to study the system, but finds it so bizarre that he is unable to concentrate on the economics texts he tries to read. After all, "the operations of capitalism were as meaningless to him as the rites of a primitive religion" (*Dispossessed*, 130).

In addition to its description of conditions in A-Io, *The Dispossessed* provides a number of details about the global political situation on Urras, a situation quite obviously modeled on the geopolitical situation on Earth in the Cold War 1970s. Thus, A-Io maintains an ongoing rivalry with the state of Thu, that seems organized according to socialist principles and that competes with A-Io for influence in the rest of the world. A-Io, for example, supports a military dictatorship in the state of Benbili, much as the United States and Britain supported numerous anticommunist military dictators in the years of the Cold War. When revolutionaries threaten the Benbili dictatorship, A-Io rushes to the aid of the dictators, while Thu supports the rebels, leading to a limited war between A-Io and Thu, though a war that is strictly confined to Benbili itself, thus limiting the damage suffered by either Thu or A-Io. This conflict again recalls the Cold War era on Earth (especially the Vietnam War), though it is also reminiscent of the ongoing orchestrated wars of *Nineteen Eighty-Four*.

The Dispossessed also comments directly on the future of Earth, referred to as "Terra" in the novel. When Shevek encounters the Terran ambassador on Urras, she tells him that, compared to her own planet, Urras seems like a virtual paradise. In a motif that derives from the environmentalist move-ment that was still young when Le Guin wrote the book, this ambassador tells Shevek that Earth is now an environmental ruin, a desert planet destroyed by greed and violence. "There are no forests left on Earth," she explains. "The air is grey, the sky is grey, it is always hot. It is habitable, it is still habitable, but not as [Urras] is" (*Dispossessed*, 348).

However brief, this inserted commentary engages environmentalist issues, a topic even more important in Ursula K. Le Guin's *The Word for World Is Forest*. Within the context of *The Dispossessed*, this vision of the environmental decay of Earth provides a warning that even planets (such as Urras and Earth) that are rich in resources do not necessary stay that way if the resources are not used wisely, while planets poor in resources (such as Anarres) can still support exemplary human societies if those meager resources are managed properly. In any case, this gesture toward environ-mental issues adds still another political dimension to *The Dispossessed*, joining its interrogation of issues related to utopia, dystopia, class, gender, and the Cold War to make it one of the richest political novels in all of science fiction.

Joe Haldeman,
The Forever War (1974)

Joe Haldeman's *The Forever War* (1974) details a future interstellar war between the humans of Earth and a mysterious alien race known as the "Taurans." The book effectively employs a number of science fiction concepts, perhaps most notably the notion of relativistic time-dilation, which causes different starships involved in the war to be operating on different time scales. However, interesting treatment of science aside, *The Forever War* is primarily a work of political satire that critiques the insanity of all wars, with a special emphasis on the war in Vietnam, in which the author himself served and was wounded. In addition, *The Forever War* is a multi-dimensional work that uses science fiction motifs to produce a significant amount of other social commentary as well.

In this book, interplanetary war is facilitated by the discovery of "collapsars," essentially stable wormholes that allow near-instantaneous travel over huge distances. On the other hand, travel to and from the collapsars must still take place at sub-light speeds, though spacecraft in the universe of this work can travel at relativistic, near-light speeds. Because of the resultant time-dilation effect, soldiers who are involved in campaigns in outer space – including protagonist William Mandella – may age only a few months or years, but, when they return, they discover that decades or centuries have passed on Earth. Thus, like veterans of the Vietnam war, they return to a home that has changed so much it is virtually unrecognizable.

Mandella's first tour of duty begins in 1997, when he (because of his high IQ and training in physics) is drafted into the military as a result of the Elite Conscription Act, which dictates the conscription of 50 men and 50 women with IQs greater than 150 and other unusual abilities for service in a war against the Taurans, about whom almost nothing is known. The first segment of Mandella's military experience deals with the training undergone by his unit in preparation for the war. This training, in which among other things they learn to use the high-tech fighting suits that they will later wear in actual combat, is not only difficult but dangerous. In two weeks of training (on the distant planet of Charon, well outside of Pluto), eleven conscriptees are killed and another loses both legs.

This segment provides a clear commentary on the sadistic and absurd nature of military training – especially as it actually does little to prepare them for what they will encounter in the war. For example, after training on the supercold Charon, their first combat mission involves an attack on a Tauran base on an extremely hot planet. This mission is complicated because Mandella and the other humans know virtually nothing about the base and still have no idea what Taurans even look like. The humans win their initial battle with the Taurans, thanks to their suit-enhanced prowess in individual hand-to-hand combat, of which the Taurans appear to have no concept. This inability, we eventually learn, is because the Taurans have a collective consciousness and have no concept of independent individual action. Meanwhile, this characteristic of the Taurans complicates the war because it makes communication between them and the individualistic humans almost impossible.

The time-dilation motif adds greatly to the sense of bewilderment experienced by the soldiers amid the confusion of the war itself. During interstellar travel, soldiers experience very little passing of time in their own frame of reference, though many years may pass in the universe at large. Meanwhile, they emerge from their collapsar jumps into regular space and engage in battle with enemy ships, which may have also just emerged from long interstellar trips of their own. Because individual ships might have traveled different distances at different speeds, they might have experienced different levels of time dilation. Thus, a ship from the twenty-first century might emerge to find itself doing battle with a ship that is from the twenty-fifth century – and is thus vastly more advanced technologically.

Meanwhile, despite the high technology featured in the text, much of the fighting in the human–Tauran war is virtually hand-to-hand. It is bloody, dirty, and confusing, certainly anything but glorious and heroic. As the book proceeds, it becomes increasingly clear that no one seems to understand exactly what the war is about, though it has long been justified on Earth as a defensive reaction to Tauran attacks on Earth ships. In the end, we discover that the war was actually started by humans, driven both by the warlike aspirations of a military elite and by a belief that an interstellar war would be good for the economy. Indeed, at the height of the conflict, nearly half the jobs on Earth are related to the war, making Earth's economy entirely dependent on keeping the war going.

The war continues until Earth itself is finally inhabited entirely by clones of a single individual who also share a collective mind and can therefore communicate with the Taurans at last. This communication quickly leads to peace after a war that has lasted for over a thousand years, though Mandella, having advanced to the rank of major, has aged only a few years during the war owing to the amount of time he has spent at relativistic speeds. He then retires with his lover, Marygay Potter, also a veteran of the Tauran war, to the harsh planet Middle Finger, where humans are allowed to live and breed individually, basically to provide a backup DNA pool in case something goes wrong with the clones on Earth.

The Forever War functions most obviously as a defamiliarizing commentary on the Vietnam war, which was in its late stages when Haldeman's book was being written. Indeed, the book calls attention to this Vietnam connection in a number of specific ways, in addition to the fact that the absurd and confusing nature of the war itself mirrors that real-world conflict. For example, the beginning of the war is placed in the relatively near future so that the leaders of Earth's military at the time can actually be veterans of that "Indochina thing" (12). In addition, the Elite Conscription Act that leads to the drafting of Mandella echoes the cancellation of student deferments, which led to the drafting of college students (including Haldeman himself) for service in Vietnam. The mysterious nature of the Taurans also reflects the way in which the Vietnamese enemy was so little understood (and often caricatured in the American mind) during the American presence there. As Mandella tells us, "the enemy was a curious organism only vaguely understood, more often the subject of cartoons than nightmares" (*Forever War*, 144). However, the ramifications of the book's antiwar satire go well beyond Vietnam. Haldeman sums up the Vietnam connection in his note to the revised 1997 edition, "It's about Vietnam because that's the war the author was in. But it's mainly about war, about soldiers, and about the reasons we think we need them" (*Forever War*, v).

One of the ways the experience of Mandella and the other soldiers who serve in the Tauran conflict mirrors the experience of Vietnam veterans is the sense of estrangement they feel upon returning home from the war. In this case, the estrangement is exacerbated by the time-dilation effect, which means that many years, or even centuries, may pass on Earth between visits there by the soldiers. In the middle, dystopian portion of the book, Mandella and Potter return to Earth after completing their term in the military, arriving in the year 2024. They find an Earth on which social and economic conditions have deteriorated dramatically in the twenty-seven years since their original departure (during which time only a few months have passed in their subjective time). Indeed, the depiction of conditions on Earth is so grim during this segment that it was omitted from the original published edition of the book because it was considered too dark. The section was, however, restored in the 1997 edition, which is now considered the definitive edition of the book.

The dystopian conditions encountered by Mandella and Potter during this segment are directly attributed to the negative effects of the Tauran war, so that even this section of the book contributes to its antiwar commentary. For one thing, the most talented individuals on Earth have all now been drafted into the military thanks the expansion of the Elite Conscription Act. Most of those have subsequently either been killed or are still off traveling in space somewhere, creating a tremendous brain drain on Earth. In addition, Earth's remaining brainpower has been devoted primarily to weapons development, bringing technological progress in other areas to a standstill. Social progress on Earth has halted as well, because the entire planet is essentially under martial law. Art and culture have taken a dark and largely uncreative turn, partly because the entire population is confused and dispirited by the war, which has had such an impact on their lives, but which seems so distant and inexplicable. Whatever individual creative energies remain are now to be devoted to trying to outwit the repressive government to gain an occasional small advantage.

Frustrated and alienated by conditions on Earth, Mandella and Potter re-enlist in the military, believing they will simply serve as training officers. However, they soon find themselves propelled back into combat. Subsequently, they both receive serious wounds on a mission, after which they recuperate on Heaven, a top-secret planet maintained by Earth as a haven on which wounded soldiers can rest and recuperate. They arrive there in the year 2189, by which time medical technology is able to repair their wounds effectively, including the growing of new limbs. Among other things, Heaven serves in the text as a sort of utopian counterpoint to the dystopian Earth. It is an unspoiled planet, free of the environmental contamination that has ravaged the Earth. It is sparsely populated, and its relatively few cities are designed to blend harmoniously with their natural environment, while at the same time featuring innovative high-tech architecture.

In addition to its satirical engagement with real-world militarism (especially the Vietnam conflict), The Forever War turns inward to critique the militaristic tendencies of much science fiction. The most direct referent in this sense is Robert A. Heinlein's Starship Troopers (1959). As Alasdair Spark (1990) has detailed, The Forever War engages Heinlein's novel in a variety of ways and on a number of levels, so much so that "they might be considered two versions of the same tale" ("Art", 162). Haldeman, however, has stated that he was well into the writing of the novel before he even realized the parallels with *Starship Troopers*: "I got seventy pages into it before somebody pointed out that I had stolen the plot, all of the characters, all of the hardware from *Starship Troopers*" (*Body Armor*, 4). At that point, Haldeman goes on, he understood that he had "subconsciously followed" Heinlein's book in constructing his own, a fact he subsequently kept in mind while finishing his own book.

Haldeman's material may substantially resemble Heinlein's, but his attitude toward that material is dramatically different. Heinlein's book is a celebration of the glories of military service; Haldeman's book is a critique of militarism. His soldiers are much more realistic than Heinlein's – and particularly more representative of the experience of the American soldiers who fought in Vietnam. They are conscriptees, scared and confused, just hoping to survive a conflict they little understand. They spend most of their time simply waiting or traveling from one place to another; when they do go into battle they both suffer and inflict painful, bloody, and debilitating wounds, fighting amid noise, dirt, and chaos.

The resultant dialogue with Heinlein greatly enriches Haldeman's critique of militarism, which takes on an added charge from the comparison. In addition, the far-flung setting of Haldeman's novel in both time and space gives his critique a widespread applicability, suggesting that the Vietnam war was not a unique phenomenon but the product of a much broader militaristic, imperialistic mentality. *The Forever War* takes advantage of the resources of science fiction to create a cognitive dissonance that greatly enhances its suggestion of the absurdity of the war in Vietnam and of war in general. In addition, science fiction is the perfect form within which to represent the cognitive estrangement experienced by the soldiers who participate in wars. The time-dilation motif is particularly effective here, both because of the confusion it creates during battle (when the opposing sides are unsure of the technological level of ships and weapons they will be facing) and because of the vast times that pass on Earth during their absence, allowing for dramatic changes that increase the level of estrangement experienced by the soldiers when they return home.

If Mandella's first return to Earth (after an absence of twenty-seven years) is disorienting, his subsequent experiences are even more so as he, a twentieth-century man, gets more and more out of step with the changing times on Earth – and with the new conscripts who serve under him as he rises in rank in the military. In particular, the very nature of the human race undergoes fundamental changes. By the time of his last tour of duty, for example, he finds that he is the only heterosexual in an all-gay battalion, homosexuality having become virtually universal on Earth. He also finds that the soldiers who serve under him have impressive abilities (such as superior hand-to-eye coordination), thanks to the fact that they have been bioengineered under the direction of a "Eugenics Council" on Earth.

For example, by the late twenty-first century, soldiers are conditioned from birth according to an official vision of the ideal fighting man, totally bloodthirsty and able to work very smoothly as a member of a team, but also totally lacking in individual initiative. Moreover, this attempt to produce soldiers who function more as parts of a unit than as individuals is quite consistent with the general evolution of humanity away from individualism and toward collectivism. Indeed, humans essentially become an entirely different species, which one might describe as posthuman, though in this case the arc of evolution is clearly presented as a gradual process of dehumanization. This process of dehumanization can, in fact, be linked directly to the war, participation in which is literally dehumanizing, both because of the horrors that individuals must endure in combat and because technologies such as the fighting suits represent modifications to the human body.

By the twenty-fifth century, the bioengineering of soldiers evolves to the point where all human beings are artificially produced in a process that, among other things, allows for the maintenance of Earth's all-gay population at a stable level of just under one billion. Ultimately, by the time the war and the book end (in the thirty-second century), humans are interchangeable, genderless clones of a single individual, all of whom function as parts of a single collective consciousness known as "Man." Mandella, himself a product of the individualist twentieth century, clearly regards this collective Man as a horrifying development. Haldeman, however, clearly suggests that the peaceful, affluent posthuman, post-individualist world of his thirty-second century may be quite properly regarded as a utopia (though the opposite of the individualist, military-ruled utopia of *Starship Troopers*). For his part, Mandella is unable to appreciate the utopian potential of this new Earth because of his own status as a Western bourgeois subject. However, Steffen Hantke, focusing on the motif of gender in Haldeman's text, argues that Man may be more genuinely human than Mandella. He grants that the ungendered collective subject that inhabits Earth at the book's end is devoted to peace partly because it has been stripped of masculinity (and thus masculine aggressiveness). However, Hantke (1998) does not see this development as dehumanizing and asserts that the bodies of the members of this collective Man, ungendered though they may be, seem intact and fully human, as opposed to the heavily modified and prosthesis-laden bodies of returning soldiers ("Surgical", 502).

As Phillip Wegner (2003) puts it, the book's conclusion "offers us the palpable relief of a Utopian horizon, while also reminding us that the radical Otherness of Utopia cannot but invoke disquiet, if not sheer horror, in those who were formed within a different historical situation" ("Soldierboys", 286). Thus, Mandella's inability to comprehend the advantages of this future collective utopia can be taken as a representation of the failure of the utopian imagination in Haldeman's own contemporary America. In this sense, Mandella's bewilderment in the face of the changes he encounters during his returns to Earth allegorizes not only the experience of Vietnam veterans returning to a much changed America in the 1960s and 1970s, but the broader experience of American life in the late twentieth century. As Wegner notes, *The Forever War* "offers a superb figuration of what we now recognize to be an emerging postmodernity: a situation wherein the subject lacks the cognitive organs to map, or to situate itself within, both rapidly increased rates of change and a now dramatically expanded spatial totality" ("Soldierboys", 286).

Perhaps because of this very difficulty of cognitive mapping, Haldeman is able to provide virtually no representation of actual human actions that might have been taken to produce this future utopia, which is so distant from our contemporary world. He does, however, attempt to provide an image of human action that might at least move us in the direction of utopia in his followup novel, *Forever Peace* (1997). Here, in a further evolution of the fighting suit idea, human soldiers operate (by remote control) incredibly destructive high-tech fighting robots known as soldierboys. This technology seems to be used principally by the United States in various interventionist conflicts in the Third World, leading to the growth of an international anti-American movement. However, while interfaced with these soldierboys, the human soldiers also experience psychic links with each other; it is eventually discovered that extended exposure to this kind of intersubjective link renders the soldiers incapable of violence toward others because their recognition of what they have in common with all other human beings is too strong. A group of those who have undergone this conversion experience (clearly a step toward the collective Man of *The Forever War*) then work within the novel to try to spread this experience to the entire human race.

The Forever War also has a more direct sequel in *Forever Free* (1999), which picks up with the experiences of Mandella and Potter, now married with children, on the planet Middle Finger. In addition, *The Forever War* has exerted a strong influence on subsequent works of military space opera, most obviously Orson Scott Card's *Ender's Game* (1985). It stands not only as one of the central works of antiwar science fiction but also as a central work of antiwar fiction (especially with regard to the Vietnam war), in whatever genre.

Marge Piercy, *Woman on the Edge of Time* (1976)

Woman on the Edge of Time is a major work of feminist science fiction, representative of the utopian revival in the science fiction of the 1970s. Informed by early feminist utopias such as Charlotte Perkins Gilman's *Herland* (1915), as well as by second wave feminist Shulamith Firestone's *The Dialectic of Sex: The Case for Feminist Revolution* (1970), Piercy's novel both participates in the tradition of imagining alternatives to oppressive patriarchal structures and emphasizes the need for revolutionary change in order to achieve these alternatives. Contrasted with the dystopian reality of present day America of the 1970s, the depiction of Mattapoisett, a twenty-second-century utopian community in which sexual differences based on gender roles are effaced, serves as an effective critique of existing patriarchal conditions. In emphasizing the precariousness of this utopia – it is presented as only one possible future – Piercy suggests that Mattapoisett is a choice, a future that may only come into existence as the result of struggle against and resistance to the patriarchal order.

The novel opens with a confrontation between protagonist Connie Ramos and her niece Dolly's pimp Geraldo, whom Connie tries to prevent from beating Dolly by attacking him with a wine jug and breaking his nose. Connie, a poor, unemployed, Mexican-American single mother, labeled by the state as a child abuser and unfit parent for hitting her young daughter a single time, is immediately committed to New York's Bellevue Hospital, the same facility in which she was placed in the aftermath of her daughter's injury (her wrist strikes a bolt and breaks as a result of Connie's blow). Connie's appeals to the authorities fall on deaf ears in both cases; in the former, she loses custody of her child, and in the latter, she is recommitted against her will after a cowed Dolly cooperates with Geraldo to paint Connie as the aggressor. Continually victimized by representatives from the state, Connie is both alienated and oppressed in a 1970s America that has distinctly dystopian characteristics. Treated with casual brutality, she is scorned as a result of her race, class, and gender. Her attack on Geraldo is deemed an inappropriate expression of violence for a woman, and thus considered literally insane behavior. Madness has often been attributed to women who veer from mainstream standards of acceptable behavior, and Piercy's treatment of the psychiatric practices in the novel suggests that she is working from within the context of the anti-psychiatry movements of the 1960s and 1970s that sought to expose the concepts of sanity and insanity as social constructs.

In the brutally repressive Rockover State Mental Hospital, a microcosm of the world outside, Connie is further dehumanized and objectified, and she quickly learns how to mollify the staff by mirroring their responses. Eventually, she is "rewarded" for her docility by being chosen as a subject for a government-funded experiment that attempts to control behavior through surgical modification of the brain. The white male doctors intend to eliminate all of Connie's violent tendencies. Similarly, they seek to "cure" her fellow inmate and friend Skip of his homosexuality. The use of such medical technology, which seeks to control and normalize those who do not fit the definition of sanity as determined by official power, goes well beyond the subtle carceral techniques that Foucault describes as the hallmark of modern bourgeois societies. Clearly designed to subdue the Other, the experimental procedure may be read as an overt example of the ideology of domination that Max Hotkheimer and Theodor Adorno (1972) see as underlying the scientific rationalism of the Enlightenment project. Against this nightmarish backdrop enters Luciente, a visitor from the community of Mattapoisett (located in what was once Massachusetts) in the year 2137. Picking up on Connie's telepathic receptivity as a "catcher," Luciente is a "sender" who can project telepathically into the past. It is through their communication that Connie is introduced to Mattapoisett, accompanying Luciente into the future. Considered valueless in her own society, Connie is revered for her considerable telepathic power in this classless future that values communality, nurturing, tolerance, and partnership with nature – qualities that are marginalized and derided in Connie's present. Modeled on the culture of the Wamponaug Indians, Mattapoisett initially strikes Connie as comparable to the villages in the poverty-stricken Mexico of her child-hood; not surprisingly, she is disappointed by the lack of skyscrapers, space-ports, and other trappings of what she has been conditioned to believe constitutes "progress" in the Western world. Technology is hardly absent in this society, the inhabitants routinely using it for communication, repro-duction, conservation of energy, education, and the automation of difficult tasks, but it does not dominate the agrarian landscape.

Sex discrimination is non-existent in Mattapoisett. The inhabitants eliminate sexual differences based on gender roles by releasing women from the role of bearing children. Instead, babies gestate in artificial wombs known as "brooders," and men and women share parenting duties equally. Each baby is issued to three co-mothers of both sexes, an attempt to break what Firestone and other feminist theorists of Piercy's era considered an unhealthy nuclear bonding that fostered a neurotic attachment to the mother as the primary caregiver. At the same time that villagers decouple sex differences from gender roles using reproductive technology, they also break the link between cultural and genetic differences in order to prevent racial discrimination. Few of the inhabitants of Mattapoisett are actually of Wamponaug heritage; babies lack a genetic link with their co-mothers, which means that they are often of different races, furthering the genetic diversity among the tribes. There is, however, a biological component to the attachment between parent and child. Both the women and the men of Mattapoisett breastfeed with the aid of hormonal enhancement, a practice that horrifies Connie; she believes that the experience of mothering is woman's alone, and that neither sex can truly claim to be mothers without having experienced pregnancy and childbirth. In defense of her culture's reproductive choices, Luciente echoes Firestone's argument that women must be freed from reproduction through technological means in order to end sexual hierarchy and oppression:

> It was part of women's long revolution.... Finally there was that one thing that we had to give up too, the only power we ever had, in return for no more power for anyone. The original production: the power to give birth. 'Cause as long as we were biologically enchained we'd never be equal. And males never would be humanized to be loving and tender. So we all became mothers. (*Woman on the Edge*, 105)

Sexual equality and the destabilization of the correlation between sex and gender also exist on the level of language, in the use of the non-gender specific pronoun "per" as a replacement for "her" and "him," and "person" as a replacement for "he" and "she." Culturally, Mattapoisett is androgynous; initially, Connie is unable to distinguish women from men, and the inhabitants' routine bisexual attachments further serve to de-emphasize traditional gender roles. However, it is clear that many of the community's underlying values are those associated with the female-centered perspective of the feminist movements of the 1970s, especially its reverence for mothering. The utopia is, in other words, a sharp corrective to the misogynistic dystopia of Connie's (and Piercy's) present. As opposed to the separatist feminist utopias of the 1970s, the culture of Mattapoisett depends upon the full participation of men – but only, as Marleen Barr (1993) notes, as a result of their alteration (47). The suggestion here is that it is only through such alteration that men and women can peacefully coexist.

In the hands of the white, capitalist patriarchy of Connie's present, science and technology are also used to alter human beings, but primarily in order to control them, as evidenced by the experimental procedure Connie undergoes at Bellevue, her earlier forced hysterectomy, and her boyfriend's death as a result of his participation in a medical experiment in prison. Rather than discard science and technology as inherently masculinist pursuits in favor of an essentialist equation of woman and nature – a popular cultural feminist stance apparent in feminist utopias such as Sally Miller Gearheart's *The Wanderground* (1978) – Piercy attempts to balance reverence for nature with appropriate technology. The novel's emphasis on ecological concerns mirror those of other 1970s works influenced by the emergent environmentalist movement, such as John Brunner's *The Sheep Look Up* (1972) and Ernest Callenbach's *Ecotopia* (1975), and its feminist perspective marks it as an early work of ecofeminism. In Mattapoisett, science and technology belong to the community, whose goals are to improve the human condition in socially and ecologically responsible ways. Luciente, herself a scientist, disavows the waste and disregard for consequences of her forebearers: "Our technology did not develop in a straight line from yours" (*Woman on the Edge*, 125). While the inhabitants of Mattapoisett do employ weapons in an ongoing battle to defend themselves from their former oppressors, for the most part technology in this future has morphed into a feminist tool that preserves and enhances the freedom, tolerance, and democracy that characterize their society. As Josephine Glorie (1997) points out, the device of the "kenner," a kind of portable database and personal communicator, is the utopian opposite of the control device implanted in Connie's brain, allowing for both individual action and communal participation ("Feminist", 155).

Utopian technology is not inevitable, however, as Connie learns when she accidentally visits an alternate future after trying to reach Mattapoisett. In this dystopian America, the direct link to the technology of Connie's present is clear. Connie meets Gildina, another "catcher" whose body has been altered surgically and chemically to achieve a grotesque caricature of femininity; her gargantuan breasts and buttocks are out of proportion to her tiny waist and feet, much like a 1970s Barbie doll. Gildina lives in a heavily polluted future New York, where most of the inhabitants are drugged into stupefaction, and where the rich harvest the organs of the poor. She is a sex worker contracted to a modified man who has been trained to be a "fighting machine" with the use of mind control – an evolution of the technology employed by Connie's doctors. Clearly influenced by classic dystopias such as *1984* and *We* in its use of technology as a form of absolute control, Piercy's dystopian vision also anticipates the fractured urban landscapes of 1980s cyberpunk, where the body is a mutable template and the multinational corporation has replaced the nation as the main locus of power. In Piercy, most people are "owned" by various multinational corporations, which place them under constant surveillance and use them to fight wars. Here, the enemy against which Mattapoisett defends itself has won, and its militaristic, patriarchal culture is an extrapolation of the ideological possibilities of Piercy's own time. Differences between the sexes are deliberately exaggerated, and the inequalities between them increased. Gildina's position is a common one, as women are little more than forced prostitutes, much like those in Margaret Atwood's *The Handmaid's Tale* (1985). If Luciente's body mirrors the equality of the sexes achieved in non-hierarchical Mattapoisett, so much so that Connie takes her for a man upon first meeting her, Gildina's body mirrors the potential for the intensification of sex differences and exploitation of women as sex objects as a result of unchecked patriarchal control. Both can be said to represent different versions of Connie, dark-skinned women (though Gildina bleaches hers) who are shaped by the conditions of their radically divergent societies.

Informed that the 1970s represents a crux in history in which alternate futures like Gildina's could gain ascendance over Mattapoisett and come to be in its place, Connie makes the choice to fight for Mattapoisett's existence, seeing in Luciente's daughter Dawn the happy child hers might have been had she not been taken from Connie and placed in foster homes. Connie is initially doubtful when the villagers tell her that she and others of her time have been contacted in order to join in the collective struggle that must take place in order for Mattapoisett to exist, but her gradual deepening of affection for the community combined with her dismay at the alternate dystopian future facilitate her transition from victimization to agency. Mattapoisett is by no means a perfect place – some if its practices are extreme, such as capital punishment – but its very imperfection and precariousness are part of what makes it so appealing to the reader. As Tom Moylan (1986) notes, "These narrative gambits serve to deny the former assumed simplicity and totalizing agency of utopian visions and help to create a more realistic utopia that is more palatable to the demanding, and jaded, reader of the 1970s and 1980s" (*Demand*, 152). Piercy's utopia is dynamic, not fixed, and it reminds us that the future depends upon actions taken in the present. A soldier enlisted in "Luciente's war," Connie fatally poisons four of the doctors responsible for the implantation of the controlling device, thereby ending an experiment that could lead to the abuses of power she witnesses in the future dystopia. In doing so, however, she also ensures her own permanent incarceration in a mental institution.

That Connie's act of resistance is a violent one suggests that Piercy views political violence as a necessity in order to effect radical change, but Connie's murders may also be read as an expression of feminist anger against an oppressive society that seeks to rob her of autonomy and dignity. What perhaps makes Connie's actions so shocking is that they take place in the "real world," or the realistic segment of the novel, which presumably give those actions more weight than those in the utopian and dystopian segments. Clearly, however, it is the realness of Connie's experiences in these segments that inform her actions in the present, though the novel does not overtly privilege one narrative over the other. Whether or not the murders ultimately have any effect is unknown – further emphasizing the uncertainty of the future – as Connie can no longer access Mattapoisett in their wake. In sacrificing herself, she also deliberately sacrifices her connection to the utopia, which suggests that committing the act comes at great personal cost. Throughout the novel Luciente and others encourage Connie's resistance to her doctors and help strengthen her resolve, though they do not necessarily advocate killing. Her hard-won resistance is entirely voluntary. Like other oppressed women empowered by the feminist activism of the 1960s and 1970s, then, Connie engages in the practice of consciousness raising. Although it could be argued that she is simply the violent paranoid schizophrenic of her official diagnosis, and that her visits to Mattapoisett and the future dystopia are the hallucinations of a disordered mind, the behavior of the medical professionals who diagnose and treat her is so egregious as to cause the reader to identify with her in spite of the text's ambiguities. Frances Bartkowski (1989) observes, "Connie's voice is always validated against the 'voice' of the state institutions through which she is transported and 'translated'" (*Feminist Utopias*, 53). The Mattapoisett attitude toward madness also presents a defamiliarizing alternative to those common in Connie's present; the utopia's inhabitants may deem themselves as "mad" and retreat from the community until they see fit to reintegrate. The power to define sanity and insanity lies with the individual, not with a hegemonic medical authority that dehumanizes under the guise of helping. In contrast to the utopians, Connie's doctors, who treat their patients like animals and manipulate them with drugs and experimental technology that render them compliant, or "normal," seem truly insane.

Connie's "madness" and gender are linked with her ability to access utopia; Luciente tells her that most of the people they've tried to reach in the past in order to foment revolutionary energies have been women, many in prisons and mental institutions. The people most open to the idea of revolution, then, are those who have the least power and are thus most susceptible to a change in consciousness. Sane in her sickness, Connie undermines the ability of medical establishment to label her, revealing madness to be a gendered construct used to exploit and oppress. The novel ends, however, with excerpts of a compilation of medical records by various psychiatric facilities that assert the authority of the medical establishment and issue a definitive verdict about Connie's mental condition. Because readers tend to identify with Connie's struggle and view her as a victim of discrimination and poverty, the clinical descriptions of her disorders have the effect of further alienating them from an institutionalized bureaucracy that reduces her to a set of diagnoses. At the same time, however, the descriptions may confirm lingering doubts about Connie's sanity. Indeed, the book leaves open the possibility that both Mattapoisett and the future dystopia are simply projections of Connie's fantasies, setting up her penchant for fantasy in the very first chapter.

Woman on the Edge of Time posits utopia as a possibility that depends upon the struggle of oppressed people, those for whom dystopia is a natural state. It is not enough simply to dream of utopia; we must act, Piercy suggests, making a clear choice between utopia and dystopia. To accept dystopia is the true madness, and Connie's willingness to work for a future that eliminates sexism, racism, and class distinctions mark her as sane operating within a sick society. Alternately angry and hopeful, Connie chooses Mattapoisett for the apparition of her lost daughter, willing her a future that she will never see: "People of the rainbow with its end fixed in Earth, I give her to you!" (*Woman on the Edge*, 141).

Samuel R. Delany, *Trouble on Triton* (1976)

Like Le Guin's *The Dispossessed*, with which it enters into an overt dialogue, Samuel R. Delany's *Trouble on Triton* (originally published in 1976 as *Triton*) is a central work in the rethinking of utopian fiction that was one of the most important phenomena in science fiction in the 1970s. In particular, Delany (as indicated in his subtitle, "An Ambiguous Heterotopia") moves beyond traditional notions of utopia by drawing upon Michel Foucault's notion of the "heterotopia" to construct a society that differs dramatically from most utopian visions. Delany's heterotopia – set in the dome-enclosed city of Tethys, on Triton, a moon of Neptune – does not pretend to be an ideal society; it merely embraces diversity to an extent that the freedom offered to individuals to pursue their own chosen lifestyles is virtually unlimited, creating a fluid social environment in which the possibility of movement toward a more ideal society remains open. In addition, Delany's identification of Foucault, a leading postmodern/poststructuralist thinker, as a central source of his ideas serves as an announcement of the impact of postmodernist and poststructuralist thinking on Delany's own ideas. *Trouble on Triton* is, in fact, a complex work of literary postmodernism and an excellent example of postmodernist science fiction.

Despite Delany's obvious desire to distance himself from traditional utopian visions, there is a great deal of the utopian in his depiction of Tethys. The fundamental goal of the social system of Tethys is to "make the subjective reality of each of its citizens as politically inviolable as possible," and as a result the society of Tethys is tremendously tolerant of individual eccentricities (*Trouble*, 225–226). Citizens routinely dress in a variety of outlandish costumes (even total nudity is acceptable), participate in numerous bizarre religious sects, and engage in a wide range of sexual activities, all without the least interference of the government or disapproval of other citizens. All in all, the society of Tethys is one that "allows, supports, and encourages behavior that ... would have produced some encounter with some restraining institution if they were indulged in on Earth a hundred years ago" (*Trouble*, 226).

Meanwhile, the Earth of *Trouble on Triton* is a police state blighted by environmental destruction, clinging to ideas made obsolete by the success of social experiments such as that in Tethys, whose openness to diversity and change is matched by that of the other postrevolutionary moon-based societies with which it joins in a loose, entirely voluntary confederation. The resource-rich Earth, on the other hand, has been largely devastated by irresponsible human exploitation, while Earth's own capitalistic system seems to have survived elsewhere only on Mars, where human settlement is centered in the city of Bellona. Mars lacks the forward-looking open-mindedness of the moon-based societies, with clear hints that its government tends toward fascism. For example, one of the key districts of Bellona is called Goebbels, apparently named after Hitler's Minister of Propaganda.

If Delany's Tethys is the very antithesis of Earth, to which it is opposed much in the way Le Guin's Anarres is opposed to A-Io, Tethys also differs greatly from Anarres. Citizens of Tethys never have to choose between freedom and security – or to make most other difficult either–or choices. Rejecting the seeming romanticization of asceticism in *The Dispossessed*, the society of Tethys is rich, and all citizens can be confident that their basic needs will be met. There are perhaps a hundred different religions and a diverse assortment of cultural activities. All taxation is voluntary, with citizens paying only for those services they actually use. As opposed to the monologic authoritarian regimes of dystopian fiction (or the monologic anarchist regime of Anarres), the government of Tethys is extremely pluralistic. There are literally dozens of political parties, all of which share in governing the town, while all candidates for office are automatically elected – each citizen is simply governed by the candidate for whom he or she votes and thus lives, to the extent possible, under policies of his or her own choosing.

Sexual freedom and diversity are particularly emphasized in Tethys. The society recognizes that individual sexual preferences can vary widely, and all behavior is openly tolerated as long as it is consensual for all participants. Plurality is again the keynote. As one social worker explains to a confused teenager, the basic philosophy of Tethys is that "*any*thing, to the exclusion of everything else, is a perversion" ("Critical," 304, Delany's emphasis). Thus, not only do the citizens of Tethys tend to engage in a wide range of sexual activities with a variety of partners, but the society recognizes "forty or fifty" basic genders, and both surgical and psychological techniques are available to allow individuals to move freely from one sexual orientation to another according to their current preference. Indeed, Delany's protagonist, Bron Helstrom, is a man who undergoes a procedure to become a woman late in the book.

In short, the government and society of Tethys are informed by tolerance in precisely the same areas where dystopian governments typically concentrate their oppressive energies. And for those who want even more freedom, the city even includes an "unlicensed sector" where there are essentially no official rules whatsoever. Tethys is a "politically low-volatile society" which can afford to tolerate any number of aberrant behaviors because it is specifically designed to be virtually impervious to transgression (*Trouble*, 126). This tolerance of transgression separates Tethys from the authoritarianism typically associated with dystopian societies; it also presumably prevents the tendency toward stasis and conformity often associated with *utopian* societies. Indeed, by identifying his vision of Tethys as "heterotopian" Delany steps outside the utopian–dystopian dichotomy altogether.

In his article "Critical Methods: Speculative Fiction" Delany (1970) indicates the limitation of the traditional utopian–dystopian opposition as a choice between thoroughly good and thoroughly evil societies and suggests that modern science fiction has gone beyond this opposition in its quest "to produce a more fruitful model against which to compare human development" ("Critical," 192).

Delany begins Appendix B to *Trouble in Triton* with a long epigraph taken from Foucault's *The Order of Things* that relates Foucault's conception of the heterotopia, a conception that Foucault himself derives from his reading of the postmodernist author Jorge Luis Borges. Unfortunately, this passage leaves the details of Foucault's vision unclear, but that is partly because heterotopia, as a place of radical diversity and change, refuses to take on specific characteristics and inherently resists definition. Indeed, while Delany's subtitle provides an obvious allusion to *The Dispossessed* (which is subtitled "An Ambiguous Utopia"), the notion of "An Ambiguous Heterotopia" is redundant: heterotopias are ambiguous by definition. However, the link to Le Guin makes this redundant subtitle highly appropriate in the way it calls attention to the dramatic difference between the openness and plurality of Tethys and the relative rigidity of most utopian visions – which makes Le Guin's subtitle much more surprising and incongruous.

If *Trouble on Triton* thus asks us to think of its heterotopian vision in opposition to the utopian vision of *The Dispossessed*, Delany's novel still structurally resembles Le Guin's in a number of ways. In both books, for example, we are asked to compare an alternative society that exists on a barren moon (Triton or Anarres) with an older and more traditional society that is based on an ostensibly richer planet (Earth or Urras). *Trouble on Triton* also resembles *The Dispossessed* in the way it features a male protagonist who has trouble fitting in within the society in which he lives. Here, however, the parallels between Delany and Le Guin begin to break down. For example, Delany's Helstrom (an immigrant from Mars) is a much less sympathetic figure than is Le Guin's Shevek. Given every opportunity to change and grow as an individual, Helstrom nevertheless clings to certain tendencies that he acquired during his early years on Mars. In particular, he continues to envision interpersonal relationships (especially sexual ones) within the dynamic of domination and submission (with males generally dominating females) that apparently governs such relationships on Mars. But this objectionable habit of picturing other humans as competitors and as potential objects of domination runs directly counter to the most fundamental principles of the society of Tethys, in which individual liberty is valued above all else, but only to the extent that the freedom of one individual does not infringe upon that of another.

In addition, Helstrom's tendency to think of others as objects is part of a general tendency toward a polar either–or logic that runs directly contrary to the spirit of life on Tethys (which is governed by a both–and logic) and to Helstrom's own profession as a "metalogician" – metalogics being a sophisticated (postmodern) form of reasoning that transcends the polar oppositions of conventional Western thought. Meanwhile, Delany identifies his own project with metalogics through his description of the work of the leading metalogician Ashima Slade in *Triton*'s second appendix. One of Slade's most important lectures is entitled *Shadows*, "from a nonfiction piece written in the twentieth century by a writer of light, popular fictions" (*Trouble*, 301). This writer, of course, is Delany, whose article "Shadows" did in fact appear in the journal *Foundation*. Indeed, Slade's name is a near-anagram for "Sam Delany," and the ideas discussed in the appendix in relation to Slade's career parallel those treated in the main body of *Triton* in important ways.

Helstrom, in short, engages in precisely the kind of conduct of which Delany seems to disapprove and that the otherwise hyper-tolerant society of Tethys cannot well accommodate. Helstrom is thus not happy in Tethys, a fact that might be taken to suggest that no society, however advanced, can ever be ideal for everyone. Here, however, the fault clearly lies more with Helstrom than with Tethys. Numerous commentators have pointed out that Helstrom is a highly negative figure whom readers are supposed to dislike, as when Teresa Ebert (1980) suggests that he is essentially a "caricature of the 70's white male chauvinist" ("Convergence," 103). Helstrom also adds to the postmodern complexity of the text in that *Trouble on Triton*, while narrated in third person, is presented almost entirely from his point of view, so that virtually everything we learn about the society of Tethys is filtered through the consciousness of this outsider who doesn't really understand what makes this society desirable and whose perspective we, as readers, are not intended to share. In this way, as David Golumbia (1995–1996) argues, Delany critiques the traditional tendencies of the utopian genre, injecting an inherently disruptive element into a potentially utopian narrative and denying readers the comfort of fully understanding or identifying with the utopian society being described ("Black and White", 79).

The emphasis on tolerance of eccentricity in Tethys is one of the aspects of the text that makes Helstrom such an unsympathetic figure. After all, anyone who can't fit in here would seem to be a malcontent who wouldn't be able to fit in *anywhere*. What is especially important is the way Helstrom is essentially placed in the text in the position of the traditional bildungsroman hero, who must mature and learn from experience in order to learn comfortably to live within the social order in which he or she exists. However, the hero of the traditional European bildungsroman must give up a great deal of individual liberty and forgo many individual desires, bowing to the demands and pressures of the social forces around him. Helstrom, on the other hand, fails to learn and grow, even though he lives within a society that welcomes him into the order without demanding that he sacrifice his individuality.

Helstrom, in fact, doggedly pursues his traditional masculinist agenda, despite its inconsistency with the values of the society around him. His main sexual relationship in the book is with "the Spike," who is also the book's central female character. A street performance artist whose postmodern understanding of the performativity of gender and of human identity in general is a virtual embodiment of the ideology of Tethys, the Spike ultimately becomes disgusted by Helstrom's attempts to dominate and control her. Eventually, she sends Helstrom a rejection letter highlighted by the declaration that she is angry "at the Universe for producing a person like you" (*Trouble*, 192).

Helstrom's failure to evolve as an individual, despite the opportunities offered to him (even the sex-change procedure seems to have little effect), would appear to make him a particularly negative figure. However, *Trouble on Triton* is a complex text, and the various oppositions it sets up are truly dialectical. We are not meant simply to accept one side and reject the other, but to weigh the differences between the two sides and to ask questions that might lead to an understanding that transcends the point of view of either. Thus, if Helstrom fails to take advantage of the opportunities for personal growth offered by Tethys, it might be taken as a failure of character on his own part. Or it might be taken as a commentary on the vast difficulty that he (or anyone) encounters in attempting to surmount the kind of ideological conditioning he has received on Mars (or that, by extension, we all receive in the modern societies of the capitalist West).

In this sense, *Trouble on Triton* serves as a complex commentary on political revolution: fundamentally sympathetic to radical and revolutionary change, the text is nevertheless very much aware of the difficulties associated with such change. Delany indicates his belief in the possibility of revolution by presenting Tethys and the other moon-based societies of the novel as postrevolutionary societies that have moved well beyond their roots on Earth and that have largely been successful in staying true to the spirit of their revolutionary past. In particular, far more than Le Guin's Anarres, they have maintained a revolutionary spirit and continue to strive for change, despite what they have already achieved – and even though they continue to have to fight for survival against the older planetary societies that would seek to bring them back into the fold.

On the other hand, Delany's portrayal of Helstrom calls attention to the most difficult obstacle faced by any postrevolutionary society, namely it must by definition be composed initially of a population that grew up within, and had its values and attitudes largely formed by, the pre-revolutionary society. That Helstrom, a product of the pre-revolutionary society of Mars, finds his upbringing so difficult to transcend reminds us of how hard it is to move beyond the past, even a limiting and oppressive one. And, given that his native Mars is so clearly intended in the text as an extension of our own capitalist present, Helstrom's failure to move beyond his past can be taken as a reminder of how seductive, convincing, and paralyzing the ideology of capitalism can be to the citizens who are held in its thrall.

Because the Earth and Mars of *Trouble on Triton* obviously function as estranged versions of the Western capitalist societies of Delany's (and our) own time, this same analysis applies to the ideological power of capitalism in our world. In fact, capitalist ideology may be so seductive that even Delany, seeking to criticize it, actually succumbs to it. To an extent, Delany's vision of Tethys as a place not where the ideal has been achieved but simply where it can openly be pursued, would seem to be a science fictional enactment of the notion of utopian thought as envisioned by the leading Marxist-utopian philosopher Ernst Bloch. By definition, Bloch's version of utopia is never reached, but it can be worked toward; utopian thought is always thought that reaches beyond the real toward the "not yet"; but for Bloch, genuine utopian thought is shot through with concrete possibility, its goal being the transformation of reality, not an escape from it. On the other hand, Delany's vision of the radical plurality of the society of Tethys is typical of postmodern political thought, which often envisions such plurality as subversive and anti-authoritarian. However, embracing plurality is in fact central to the ideology of capitalism itself. Thus, Terry Eagleton (1996) points out that it is difficult to see postmodern plurality as inherently subversive of capitalism, given that "capitalism is the most pluralistic order history has ever known, restlessly transgressing boundaries and dismantling oppositions, pitching together diverse life-forms and continually overflowing the measure" (*Illusions*, 133).

Other aspects of the society of Tethys are reminiscent of capitalist society as well. Among other things, the low "political volatility" of the society clearly has a dark side: if the society of Tethys is able to absorb any and all potentially subversive energies while maintaining its stability, then it is not clear that any program of genuine political change could ever succeed there. As Tom Moylan emphasizes, Tethys is a postrevolutionary society, the description of which treats the aftermath of dramatic social and political change. Unfortunately, this change may have been such that no further change is really possible. In this sense it is Tethys, rather than Earth, that mirrors Delany's own contemporary society. After all, the acceptance of individuality is a central value of capitalist society, to the point that any attempt at transgressive behavior in such a society is always in danger of being appropriated as an example of the society's fundamental benevolence.

Of course, Tethys is not a perfect paradise, and Delany's treatment of it suggests that no such perfection is possible. But this does not mean that all societies must ultimately be oppressive and totalitarian, or that it is impossible for societies to change and grow toward perfection. This open-ended vision of society parallels the formal structure of Delany's narrative, which ends ambiguously, with Helstrom's troubles unresolved. It is then followed by appendices that provide selfconscious (but indirect) commentary on the text that came before. Such instances of selfconscious textuality in Delany's book run counter to conventional utopian stasis by disrupting any movement toward interpretive closure. The specific tone of this selfconsciousness joins with the book's indeterminate message to identify *Trouble on Triton* as a postmodernist work. Ebert (1980) thus discusses Delany's work within the context of postmodernism, concluding that such sophisticated works of "metascience fiction" may in fact eventually come to be recognized as the most influential strain in postmodernist fiction as a whole ("Convergence," 104).

William Gibson, *Neuromancer* [1984]

Heralded upon its publication as a groundbreaking and even revolutionary work, William Gibson's debut novel *Neuromancer* (1984) is perhaps the most commented-upon work of contemporary science fiction. The first volume of the "Sprawl" trilogy, which includes *Count Zero* (1986) and *Mona Lisa Overdrive* (1988), *Neuromancer* is generally acknowledged as the paradigmatic cyberpunk novel, receiving immediate and enthusiastic acclaim from much of the science fiction community and becoming the first book to garner all three of the field's major literary awards: the Nebula, Hugo, and Philip K. Dick awards. Gibson's noir-inflected near future, featuring fractured urban landscapes juxtaposed against the computer-generated alternative reality of cyberspace (a term coined by Gibson) that his "console cowboys" inhabit, captures postmodern preoccupations about rapid technological and cultural changes and their accompanying effects on the late capitalist, post-industrial society of the 1980s.

Human relationships in cyberpunk are almost always subordinate to an all-encompassing and invasive technology, while blurred boundaries between human and machine call into question the notion of what it means to be human. Cyborgs in Gibson are common, with prostheses, implants, microelectric circuitry, and any number of bodily modifications available to a wide population. Through an interface between the brain and a computer, hackers routinely experience the "bodiless exultation" of cyberspace (also known as the "matrix"), reveling in the sensation of power and freedom the virtual realm allows them. Highlighting both the positive and negative potential of modern technology, Gibson's view is ambivalent, though his future has a decidedly dystopian flavor. In contrast to classic dystopian texts, however, there is no sense in *Neuromancer* that fundamental change in the social order is possible. Similar to the characters in the hard-boiled detective narratives after which the novel is loosely modeled, the cyberpunk antihero is jaded and fatalistic, often living for the thrill that – in Gibson's universe – only technology can provide.

The renowned opening line of *Neuromancer* neatly encapsulates the extent to which the lines between the natural and artificial break down in cyberpunk fiction: "The sky above the port was the color of television, tuned to a dead channel" (3). This metaphorical description of the natural world highlights the extent to which technology and the media condition the perception of all reality for the denizens of the urban sprawl in this high-tech future. For Henry Dorsett Case, native of the Boston–Atlanta Metropolitan Axis (BAMA) and a computer hacker cut off from cyberspace by employers he unwisely double-crosses, technology provides the utopian transcendence from the "meat" existence of the human body he views with contempt. Bent on self-destruction as the novel opens, Case is reduced to hustling black market goods and information – the premier commodity of cyberpunks – in Japan's Night City, an underclass criminal enclave existing on the margins of Chiba City. His failed attempts in the world-class surgical boutiques of Chiba to recover his abilities to "jack in," or project his consciousness into cyberspace, make him vulnerable to the machinations of Armitage, an impassive, automaton-like man who offers experimental reconstructive surgery in exchange for Case's services as a console cowboy. Case agrees, and together with Molly Millions, a cybernetically enhanced assassin, he performs a number of risky tasks to fulfill an objective about which he knows little. Eventually he discovers that his true employer is Wintermute, an artificial intelligence (AI) equipped with free will and self-awareness, who blackmails Case into assisting the AI to unite with its other self, Neuromancer. The result of this illegal maneuver is the creation of an enormously powerful entity no longer subject to the control of its corporate owner Tessier-Ashpool. Once the unification is complete, Case returns to something that, on the surface, resembles his previous life as a cowboy.

Numerous critics have noted the postmodern features of cyberpunk fiction, with Fredric Jameson (1991) declaring that cyberpunk may be "the supreme *literary* expression if not of postmodernism, then of late capitalism itself" (*Postmodernism*, 419, n. 1). In Gibson's imagined future, in which technology is the tool of capital and governmental power has largely been superseded by the multinational corporation, the most powerful metaphor for the circulation of global capital is cyberspace, a "graphic representation of data abstracted from the banks of every computer in the human system" (51). Described as a "consensual hallucination" that the computer user accesses through a direct neural link that suggests the merging of human and machine, cyberspace is the realm in which Case makes a living: he steals information from the databases of multinational corporations that populate the three-dimensional landscape. It is a testament both to Gibson's influence and to technological advancements in computer systems that his vision of cyberspace sounds almost quaint now, in an age when Internet hacking is run-of-the-mill and virtual reality technologies have recreational as well as military applications. Our own contemporary efforts to create a cyberspace that matches Gibson's description have fallen far short of the literary equivalent, however. As an abstract representation of the complex, bewildering reality of the cyberpunk world, cyberspace may be seen as an attempt to solve the cognitive problem of how to represent our own present-day reality, in which new technologies threaten to overwhelm us completely. The ease and expertise with which Gibson's hackers navigate these new technological spaces suggests that the interface between human and technology spurs the evolution of a new kind of human subject, or posthuman.

Cyberspace is a dangerous place, where multinational corporations and military systems are protected by AI-generated "ICE" (Intrusions Countermeasures Electronics), or killer security systems that can "flatline" a console cowboy in a matter of seconds. At the same time, however, hackers seem to find the spatial dimensions thrilling; as Scott Bukatman (1993) observes, cyberspace "frequently permits the subject a utopian and kinetic *liberation* from the very limits of urban existence" (*Terminal Identity*, 146). Notably, the matrix does not promise transcendence to everyone in *Neuromancer*, but only to those who have access through a computer deck – namely, white male hackers. Not only are women excluded from the transcendence that the hackers experience, but they simply do not appear to be possessed of the proper equipment necessary for the interface. Nicola Nixon (1992) identifies the phallic projection inherent in the hackers' entry into cyberspace, observing that the matrix in Gibson is figured as a feminized space that console cowboys "jack" into, where they are continually at risk of being emasculated by the ICE ("Cyberpunk," 226). Despite the emphasis on the seeming bodilessness of cyberspace, the electronic transcendence that the (heterosexual male) hacker experiences has an overtly sexual dimension.

Of course, it may be argued that the hacker's consciousness is inextricable from his material body, despite his eagerness to shed that body. However, sexual imagery aside, Gibson's depiction of cyberspace suggests a radical duality between the mind and the body, in which the former is privileged over the latter. Denied an active role in cyberspace, women are permanently relegated to the bodily existence of the "meat prison" that hackers disdain, reinforcing traditional gender binaries that associate masculinity with the mind and femininity with the body. In *Count Zero*, Gibson introduces the powerful female hacker Angie Mitchell, who interfaces directly with the matrix without a computer (though her connection with cyberspace is involuntary), but it's clear that in *Neuromancer*, cyberspace is the province of the *cowboys*. Thus the possibilities for new, transgressive cyborg identities described by Donna Haraway that result from the breakdown of boundaries between human and machine are largely unfulfilled in the cyberspace of that novel. Observing that Gibson's posthumans fall short of embodying the potentialities of Haraway's cyborg metaphor, Jenny Wolmark (1994) argues that "the social and temporal experience of cyberspace is centrally concerned with individual transcendence rather than transformation, with escape from social reality rather than engagement with it" (*Aliens*, 118).

If Case is defined by his pursuit of pure consciousness in cyberspace, Molly is defined by her meat function as bodyguard and assassin, telling Case "You gotta jack, I gotta tussle" (50). A postmodern gun "moll," she prefers scalpel blades – which she extrudes at will from beneath her fingernails – to firearms. Other modifications include augmented reflexes and surgically inset mirrorshades outfitted with optical enhancements that permanently shield her eyes, marking her as a cyborg in a world where such customization of the body is commonplace; even the average person appears to have access to a whole array of enhancements – ranging from cranial microsoft chips that interface directly with the user's brain to microelectric circuitry – that contribute to the breakdown of the traditional confines of the human body. Organs, muscles, and flesh are also artificially grown and available for purchase, which serves to de-emphasize the integrity of the human body. Although Molly's embodied existence is implicitly devalued as the meat Gibson's hackers would prefer to transcend, she does represent an alternative to the traditionally feminine hero in much of science fiction. That alternative, however, may be said to resemble the traditional male action hero, a combination of Bruce Lee and Clint Eastwood. Samuel Delany, on the other hand, has observed that Molly's characterization owes a debt to Jael, the feminist assassin with retractable claws in Joanna Russ's *The Female Man* (1975), while other critics have judged Molly to be a precursor of the postfeminist female action hero so prevalent in contemporary popular culture. In the terrain of the novel, however, Molly's physicality, which is emphasized by details of her former profession as a prostitute, or "meat puppet," suggests a kind of essential (physical) femininity that contrasts with the exclusive (intellectual) priesthood of hackerdom to which Case belongs. Molly takes the physical risks, which Case experiences vicariously through a "simstim" (simulated stimulus) device; Case himself, however risky his own activities, operates primarily in the more mental realm of cyberspace.

Although privy to basic emotions like hate and anger, Gibson's characters exhibit what might be termed a postmodern lack of affect, evident in their inability to meaningfully relate to others. Case and Molly are occasional lovers, but both are emotionally detached; as the novel ends, so does their relationship. Istvan Csiscery-Ronay suggests that for cyberpunks who experience the breakdown of distinction between human and machine as a matter of course, mere sensation replaces complex emotions: "In Gibson's world, human beings have nothing left but thrill ... the speed of thrill substitutes for affection, reflection, and care" ("Cyberpunk and Neuromaticism," 276). Despite their flat, postmodern rendering, however, the toughened exteriors Gibson's characters present to the world could also be said to resemble those of the wounded antiheroes of hard-boiled detective fiction, romantic individualists who struggle for autonomy in a corrupt world. Corruption in Gibson's universe involves the unbreakable stranglehold of multinational capitalism, and the struggle for autonomy is often a reaction to the corporate entities that seem somehow beyond human influence and that generate technologies that threaten to displace the centrality of the human subject. Although Case's profession as a hacker seems designed to thwart the corporate entities that dominate the entire structure of his society and thus maintain his individualism, in the end he enables the unification of two AIs (both products of the Tessier-Ashpool corporation) that take over the matrix at the end of the novel. Cyberpunks may view themselves in opposition to the dominant social order, but they accept the technological conditions that it produces.

The unique, autonomous human subject is a casualty of these technological conditions, replaced by alternatives that render it – and by extension notions of selfhood – insignificant and outmoded. Not only is the human body a mutable template that may be altered at will, radically transforming notions of identity, but the disembodied experience of cyberspace emphasizes the very dissolution of that body. Perhaps equally threatening to human identity is the practice of genetic cloning. The Tessier-Ashpool clan, for example, operates its corporation through the use of AIs and the supervision of one or more generation of clones who are cryogenically frozen until their reawakening is deemed necessary. The clan's corporate AIs Wintermute and Neuromancer pose an even further challenge to subjectivity in that they seem as "human" – or even more so – as the human characters in the novel, many of whom are emotionally detached. Choosing to appear in human form, the AIs exhibit qualities supposedly exclusive to humans, such as autonomy and desire. As a result of its original programming by Marie-France Tessier-Ashpool, Wintermute is passionate about destroying the corporation's restraints upon its freedoms and is willing to go to any lengths, including murder, to attain unification with its other self. When the two AIs unite and dominate the matrix, it is clear that cyberspace belongs not to humans, but to their digital counterparts.

Similar to AIs are ROM personality constructs, or recordings that preserve someone's personality after death. A dead console cowboy who aids Case in freeing Wintermute, Dixie Flatline describes himself as "just a bunch of ROM" (131) that feels sentient and responds like a human. Though human, Armitage is also a kind of construct, a traumatized war veteran whose slick, blank personality is "programmed" by Wintermute. Neuromancer creates constructs as well, and through its agency Case becomes, along with his dead girlfriend Linda Lee, a ROM construct that exists only within the confines of cyberspace. At the same time, however, he retains full possession of his body in the meat world. Although constructs are not conscious, their responses are so like those of humans that the differences between the two seem almost immaterial. In fact, artificial existence appears to be the preferred state of being in *Mona Lisa Overdrive*, in which pivotal characters abandon their physical bodies in a bid for electronic immortality.

Gibson crowds his narrative with a profusion of detail, giving the impression that the cyberpunk world is one of incredibly dense information: "all around you the dance of biz, information interacting, data made flesh" (*Neuromancer*, 16). Distinctive for its emphasis on surface reality, *Neuromancer* is littered with objects that frequently have brand names attached, reflecting a postmodern consumer culture not so different from our own in which multinational corporations are the arbiter of hip. The junk, or *gomi*, of the past does not simply disappear, replaced by superior technology – obsolete technological artifacts exist side by side with the latest "Ono-Sendai Cyberspace 7" deck (the exact function of which is left up to the reader to determine). The density of cyberpunk's urban landscapes is reflected in the density of the prose, inducing a sense of disorientation among readers that serves as a defamiliarizing perspective on the America of the 1980s from which Gibson makes his futuristic projections. Gibson draws upon symbols familiar to the contemporary reader, some of which are portrayed as decaying remnants of a civilization ended, and others that still have currency twenty minutes into the future. Gibson also draws upon a wide variety of genres for the structure of his narrative, including detective fiction, westerns, mythology, film noir, science fiction film, and the adventure-romance. This appropriation of such a diverse array of styles has been viewed by some critics as an example of postmodern pastiche, a hodge-podge of literary forms. Others note, however, that because Gibson relies upon a number of conventional plotting techniques, the narrative fails to adequately represent the chaotic condition of the postmodern age.

A response to the cynicism and corporate greed of the 1980s, the then-widespread sense that the future of capitalism would be dominated by Japan, and the decade's technological explosion, *Neuromancer* is ultimately ambivalent about the role of technology and resigned to the dominance of corporate power. Though cyberspace provides a utopian space for a limited population, life for the average person is not necessarily improved through technological enhancement, and in fact could be considered measurably worse than the lives of 1980s American citizens. Gibson's future looks much like our own present, despite its almost hallucinatory surface reality; like most cyberpunk, it offers no transformation of the social order. The book's most significant change – the unification of Wintermute and Neuromancer – is potentially promising in terms of its influence on cyberspace users, but later books show that even the potentialities of the unified sentient matrix are rendered null and void by the dissolution of the entity into fragmented subprograms. Case, who makes the unification possible, does not change in any fundamental way. Free of the slowly dissolving toxin sacs that Wintermute used to blackmail him into compliance with its schemes, Case returns to the Sprawl presumably to pick up where he left off as a console cowboy. The power structure – embodied by multinational corporations – is never trounced by the heroes in Gibson's cyberpunk, and indeed the heroes would be out of a job if the corporations were destroyed: as it is the information that these corporations produce that enables the hacker to make a living. For all their countercultural posturing, cyberpunks accept the status quo. Indeed, numerous critics have faulted Gibson's texts for their lack of political opposition and ostensible acceptance of the status quo, indicating an inability to imagine historical developments that challenge the dominant forces in our society. At the same time, however, cyberpunk may be seen as an exercise in preparing the postmodern subject for what the future will inevitably bring. Rather than functioning in a purely cautionary way, like typical dystopian texts, *Neuromancer* guards against futureshock with a stylish and almost casual indifference: "Dystopia is here, say the cyberpunks, and we might as well get used to it" (Hynes, "Robot's Rules," 18).

Margaret Atwood, *The Handmaid's Tale* (1985)

The Handmaid's Tale is a dystopia that builds upon the dystopian imagery of feminist texts from the 1970s. It also draws on predecessors in the genre of dystopian fiction, most notably Orwell's *Nineteen Eighty-Four* (1949), which Atwood has acknowledged as a strong influence. Atwood's novel was written in direct reaction to the growing political power of the American religious right in the 1980s. It projects a nightmare future in which right-wing religious extremists have established control of the government of what was once the United States but has now been transformed into the theocratic Republic of Gilead. This imposition is particularly awful for women, who have virtually no rights and are treated essentially as chattels. Yet the brutal treatment of women in Gilead, however extreme, clearly serves as an extrapolation of patriarchal conditions that have long prevailed in our own world and that many saw as worsening during the Reagan administration of the 1980s – and that many have seen as worsening again during the Bush administration of the early twenty-first century.

    The Handmaid's Tale is presented as the secret journal of Offred, beginning with her training for a life of sexual servitude as a "handmaid" in the Republic of Gilead. Handmaids, we learn, are assigned (acceptance of the assignment is mandatory) to important men in Gilead whose wives have proved unable to bear children, so that those men might still have an opportunity to procreate. Procreation is, in fact, highly problematic in this society, where deteriorating environmental conditions have rendered most women sterile. Most men may be sterile as well, though in Gilead male infertility is officially non-existent, and the infertility of a couple is always attributed to the woman. The officials of Gilead have declared artificial insemination or any other technological intervention in the process of fertilization to be unnatural. As a result, the handmaids are to be impregnated

Margaret Atwood, The Handmaid's Tale (1985)

by ordinary sexual intercourse, though this intercourse occurs as part of a highly ritualized ceremony that is anything but natural: the wife looks on while the husband and handmaid have sex in a manner designed to removed all semblance of sexual pleasure, at least for the handmaid, though one suspects that the husband may take a perverse delight in imposing his power on a subjugated woman.

The narrator has been given the possessive label "Offred" to indicate her service to a man named "Fred." We never learn her real name, indicating the suppression of her individual identity in this nightmare world. Yet this seemingly extreme symbolic indication of the status of handmaids as the property of the men who command them actually differs very little from the "Mrs." designation traditionally given to married women in our own society. Quite often, in fact, the horrors of Gilead, once examined carefully, seem all too familiar from the point of view of our reality, and it seems clear that one cannot appreciate the significance of Offred's predicament in Gilead without understanding it as a thinly-veiled satirical reinscription of the situation of real women in the real America of the 1980s – and beyond. For example, the subjugated position of women in Gilead can be taken as a direct commentary on the defeat of the Equal Rights Amendment (which would have granted constitutional guarantees of equal treatment under the law to women), while the use of handmaids like Offred merely as vehicles for the production of children can be seen as a commentary on the "right to life" movement and its insistence that pregnant women should be forced to bear children, even if against their will.

In the novel, Offred can still remember the time before the revolutionary change that brought the Republic of Gilead into existence, when she was a young wife and mother, living an ordinary middle-class life. She also remembers her feminist mother and her mother's feminist friends, who collectively show a disdain for almost all men and an intolerance of any women who do not see things their way. They also participate in the burning of books and magazines that they find offensive, as in a scene that Offred remembers from her own childhood (*Handmaid's Tale*, 38–39). Thus, the satire of *The Handmaid's Tale* is aimed not merely at antifeminist religious conservatives, but at certain feminists, whose intolerance of differing viewpoints and lack of solidarity with other women may have facilitated the Gileadean revolution. In addition, this lack of solidarity among women continues in the new regime, in which numerous women occupy positions of power that help to enforce the subjugation of other women, while even the lowliest of women are expected to supplement official power by informing the authorities of any transgressions committed by other women.

In Gilead the movements and activities of its citizens are closely monitored and controlled. However, the new government also attempts to gain the "voluntary" loyalty of its subjects, generally through religious indoctrination. Television programming in Gilead consists primarily of religious propaganda, while literature is even more strictly censored and controlled. Most women are not allowed to read at all; the signs in stores consist of pictorial symbols so that shopping will not require reading. Even the Bible is considered highly dangerous – as it was, in fact, in the Middle Ages. In family groups like the one around which *A Handmaid's Tale* is centered, the Bible can be read only by the patriarchal head of the household (tellingly referred to as the "Commander"), though he does sometimes read passages aloud to his wife and female servants, for their group edification. This secrecy is one of many hints that there may be something fraudulent about the religious ideology that rules Gilead. The Gileadeans have in fact imported a number of bits of spurious Christian ideology, as when the distribution of women as sexual objects among men in the society is justified by a perversion of Marx that is claimed to come from the Bible: "From each according to her ability: to each according to his needs" (*Handmaid's Tale*, 117).

Atwood focuses on women and sexuality as principal targets of the religious totalitarianism of the Republic of Gilead. In this Christian theocracy, marriage is promoted as a social goal, though it is only available to those who have reached a certain social status. Indeed, wives, while they enjoy a higher status than handmaids, are literally "issued" to successful males as rewards for loyal service to the community. In addition, women in this society exist not as individuals but as members of well-defined groups, corresponding almost to brand names. Among the upper classes, women function principally either as wives (who serve as domestic managers), domestic servants ("Marthas"), or handmaids. In the lower classes, however, "Econowives" have to play all of these roles. There are also "Aunts" (who serve to train and discipline the handmaids) and "Jezebels" (officially, though covertly, sanctioned prostitutes used to service foreign dignitaries and important government officials). Women who cannot or will not play one of these roles are labeled "Unwomen" and are exiled to the "colonies," where they are used for hazardous duties like cleaning up toxic waste, much of the American landscape having been polluted to the point of being uninhabitable.

Despite the brutally repressive nature of the practice of power in Gilead, the control exerted by the Gileadean regime over the behavior of its citizenry is not as complete as it might first appear. Indeed, there is an active resistance movement at work in the text, and Offred apparently manages to escape Gilead altogether in the end. In the meantime, an illicit private connection develops between Offred and her Commander when he induces her to start meeting with him secretly. In these sessions they enact various minor transgressions like playing Scrabble or reading banned books. Meanwhile, the Commander's wife (a former gospel singer whose stage name was "Serena Joy") suspects the Commander of being sterile, so she recruits Offred to engage in covert sexual relations with Nick, the family chauffeur, in the hope that the handmaid will thereby become pregnant and bring increased status to the family.

Sexual energies that are ostensibly transgressive actually circulate rather freely in the text, despite the repressive environment, and Offred's narrative reveals quite clearly that the regime in Gilead, despite its puritanical aversion to sexual pleasure, does not seek to eradicate sexuality, but simply to control it, as in the case of the Jezebels. In this sense, the Republic of Gilead clearly enacts Foucault's notion, stated most clearly in the first volume of his *History of Sexuality*, that modern society seeks not to repress or even to extirpate sexuality, but instead to administer sexuality and to turn sexual energies to its own advantage.

The Republic of Gilead focuses much of its effort to control the constitution of the subject in the crucial area of language. For example, except for the "Aunts" charged with training potential handmaids, women are forbidden either to read or to write, thus making written language (and the power that goes with it) a strictly male preserve. Still, the very fact that Offred records her diary indicates refusal to accept the official Gileadean line that women are vastly inferior to men in their linguistic abilities. In addition, her narration is liberally spiced with wordplay and other demonstrations of her dexterity with language. Finally, Offred continually muses on her real name, which she sees as an almost magical key to the retention of her personal identity, apart from the one prescribed for her in this ultimate patriarchal society. For her, "this name has an aura around it, like an amulet, some charm that's survived from an unimaginably distant past" (*Handmaid's Tale*, 84).

The exaggerated practices of power as exercised in Gilead simply indicate that *The Handmaid's Tale* is a work of satire that caricatures the practices of our own world in order to bring their true nature more clearly into view. On the other hand, the practices of punishment that reinforce the rules and regulations of the Republic of Gilead are a far cry from the subtle practices of psychological manipulation that Foucault associates with the modern carceral society. Instead, they often resemble the rituals of public torture and execution described by Foucault in relation to repressive technologies of power prominent in Europe prior to the modern period. One such ceremony is the "Salvaging," the name of which carries hints of Christian salvation of those who have strayed, but which is in reality nothing more than a public hanging of groups of subversives, who serve as a focus for mass hatred. This hatred surfaces most violently in the ritual of "Particicution," in which groups of women servants act not as spectators but as executioners; they are whipped into a frenzy by incendiary rhetoric, then turned loose on some transgressor against society and encouraged savagely to beat the victim to death. The women thus become complicit in the enforcement of the rules of the State – and ultimately in their own oppression.

The numerous echoes of medieval practices of power found in the practices of the Republic of Gilead suggest that the oppressive religious energies that inform Atwood's dystopia have been present in Western civilization for centuries. A similar point is made by Atwood's dedication of *The Handmaid's Tale* partly to Mary Webster, one of Atwood's own ancestors who was publicly hanged as a witch in Puritan New England, thus linking the Republic of Gilead to America's (patriarchal) Puritan past. The Republic of Gilead seems to have failed to learn anything from this history, but then that is not surprising given that the regime in Gilead, like so many dystopian regimes, works hard to prevent its subjects from learning such lessons by manipulating history to its own ends. In particular, one of the central strategies of the Republic of Gilead for stabilizing its power is to attempt to efface all memory of the recent past in which women enjoyed a more liberated existence.

The epilogue that ends Atwood's book further suggests that patriarchy is a basic characteristic of Western civilization that transcends otherwise dramatic historical shifts. In this epilogue a group of historians in the year 2195 discuss Offred's manuscript in a way that makes it clear that the Republic of Gilead has long since passed from the face of history. The epilogue thus appears to add a hopeful note to the end of the book, especially since the symposium of historians described in the epilogue is chaired by a woman (Professor Maryann Crescent Moon), indicating significant social and professional advancement for women since the demise of Gilead. Peter Fitting has argued that this relatively optimistic ending tempers the effectiveness of Atwood's dystopian vision as a cautionary tale (*Turn*, 151). However, Fitting himself admits that the "sexist banter" that informs the historical symposium makes one question whether or not progress has really been made in 2195 relative to our own present (*Turn*, 150). David Ketterer, in fact, concludes that this epilogue suggests a cyclical model of history, seeing in this banter "the seeds of sexism that could lead to another Gilead" (*Turn*, 214). In any case, just as the pre-Gileadeans failed to learn historical lessons that might have prevented the rise of the Republic of Gilead, the post-Gileadeans seem to have learned nothing from the horrible lesson of the Gilead itself. Symbolizing this failure, even the professional historians of Atwood's epilogue seem to know very little about the history of Gilead, largely because the Gileadeans themselves destroyed that history.

The epilogue reveals that what we have been reading is in fact a text assembled and edited by one Professor James Darcy Pieixoto, working from a collection of audio tapes left by Offred and discovered two hundred years after the experiences related on them. This revelation adds substantial irony to the text, especially given that Offred's tale is a fluid, playful, and poetic act of resistance, while Pieixoto's authoritarian reinscription of it seeks to reduce the story's ambiguities and to de-emphasize the personal aspects of Offred's experience. In addition, Pieixoto, who has had the final word in constructing the text we read, demonstrates sexist attitudes that run directly contrary to the apparent purposes of that narrative. Pieixoto expresses disdain for the tapes left by Offred because they are personal records and therefore not authoritative to his way of thinking. He disparagingly refers to the collection of tapes as an "item," specifically suggesting that it does not deserve to be called a "document" (*Handmaid's Tale*, 301). Rather than appreciate Offred's narrative for its own value, Pieixoto seems to regard it as a curiosity that might lead them to other, more "authoritative" sources.

Given the seeming power of Pieixoto over Offred's text, one could argue that the ending of *The Handmaid's Tale* is excessively pessimistic and seems to suggest that patriarchal attitudes are insurmountable. In addition, numerous critics have argued that *The Handmaid's Tale* itself seems largely trapped within the genre of the female romance. After all, Offred's story is to some extent typical of those of the heroines of such popular romances: she waits in relative passivity, dreaming of escape, until a dynamic and active male (in this case Nick) comes along to rescue her. Offred's passivity importantly points out the extent to which women have traditionally been complicit in their own oppression by too easily accepting a secondary status relative to men. Some critics have seen this reliance on the paradigm of female romance as a serious flaw in Atwood's book that undermines its ostensibly feminist purpose. Madonne Miner (1991), for example, has seen Offred as a completely ineffective feminist heroine because she remains trapped within the paradigms of the romance narrative. Sandra Tomc (1993), on the other hand, argues that, however unsatisfactory "drugstore" romances might appear as a counter to official power, Atwood's use of this highly marginal, feminine-oriented genre can be taken as a gesture of defiance of the authority of traditional masculine literary values. By drawing so centrally upon a genre that is generally treated with contempt by literary scholars, Atwood announces her refusal to construct her text according to the vision of the "literary" endorsed by those scholars. Meanwhile, the use of female romance in *The Handmaid's Tale* can also be taken as Atwood's response to feminist critics who would dismiss such genres as harmful to women.

The Handmaid's Tale is a complex, postmodern text that leaves itself open to a number of different readings. For some, in fact, Atwood's text is too selfconsciously literary, too playfully postmodern, to convey effectively the grim horrors of life in the Republic of Gilead. Still, these horrors do come through, especially when one realizes how similar the conditions in Gilead ultimately are to conditions in our own world. Further, one could argue that the very liveliness of Atwood's style and the multiplicity of meanings invited by her text are important utopian gestures that suggest the possibility of effective resistance to patriarchal oppression. Adapted to film by Volker SchlÖndorff in 1990, *The Handmaid's Tale* remains a key women's text, one of the best-known works of dystopian literature, and one of the most important literary works of the 1980s.

Octavia Butler, "Xenogenesis" Trilogy (1987–1989)

Octavia Butler's "Xenogenesis" trilogy uses the framework of the alien invasion narrative to warn against the possible disastrous consequences of the acceleration of the Cold War arms race under the Reagan administration of the 1980s. It also uses a variety of science fictional motifs to explore issues related to colonialism, race, gender, and environmentalism. The action of the trilogy – which comprises *Dawn* (1987), *Adulthood Rites* (1987), and *Imago* (1989) – takes place in the aftermath of a devastating nuclear war that has destroyed virtually all life on Earth. It is thus both an alien invasion narrative and a post-holocaust narrative. The emphasis, however, is on the former, and on the attempts of a group of technologically advanced aliens to rescue humanity from its own folly. The alien invaders of Xenogenesis might thus be considered benevolent, though their actions will ultimately lead to the physical destruction of the Earth and possibly to the end of humanity as a distinct species, making them instead a posthuman species of human–alien hybrids.

As the trilogy begins, only a few humans have survived the holocaust, and those appear headed for quick deaths owing to the ongoing after-effects of the war. Into this setting arrive the alien Oankali, a race whose principal technology involves genetic engineering and whose culture is based on the "trading" of genes. They travel about the galaxy in living, biologically engineered ships, exchanging genetic material with other races, and producing hybrids that may be superior to either of the originals – though improvement is not their goal so much as the process of exchange in itself. To this end, they collect the remaining human survivors on Earth and put them into suspended animation on their vast mothership, preserving the remaining human DNA. Over a period of two hundred fifty years, they repair any physical damage that has been suffered by the sleeping humans, meanwhile working to restore the environment of Earth so that humans can once again live there. They thus set into motion a complex plan to restore the human race in a hybrid form modified via genetic exchange with the Oankali.

Humans have a number of unusual genetic characteristics that make them particularly interesting to the Oankali. For one thing, they are potentially among the most intelligent species to have been encountered by the Oankali. In addition, they are the first race encountered by the Oankali who display the phenomenon of cancer, which the Oankali genetic engineers are able to use to produce positive abilities such as the regeneration of limbs and organs. On the other hand, humans are also unique among the intelligent species encountered by the Oankali in their tendency toward "hierarchical" behavior. That is, humans have a natural drive toward a competition for dominance, an inclination to which the book attributes the nuclear war that has virtually destroyed the human race – and which, in fact, makes such destruction virtually inevitable. Butler herself seems to accept this diagnosis of human nature, leaving no room for the possibility that this hierarchical tendency is merely social, produced by systems, such as capitalism, that are based on competition and unequal distributions of wealth and power.

The Oankali themselves are among the most unusual and interesting alien species in all of science fiction, partly because Butler works hard to make them seem genuinely alien, yet still at least partly comprehensible. Though vaguely humanoid, they look somewhat like undersea creatures: they bear an array of arms and tentacles, giving them an appearance that humans find bizarre and disturbing. They have no eyes and cannot see in the human sense, but some of the tentacles are used as part of an extremely efficient sensory apparatus. They have three sexes, rather than two: males, females, and ooloi, who have a special natural ability to manipulate DNA. During sexual reproduction, all three sexes mate. Males and females supply genetic material, while the ooloi, who make no personal contribution to this material, serve as intermediaries, mixing the genes of the males and females into the desired configurations, while also using their empathic abilities to further the bonding of the group during sexual intercourse. In their plan to combine with humans, the Oankali devise a method through which all three Oankali sexes mate with a human male and female, producing offspring with genetic material derived from all four male and female parents, mixed by the ooloi parent. Presumably, these children would combine the best characteristics of both humans and Oankali, while lacking negative characteristics such as the human hierarchical drive.

In *Dawn*, the Oankali begin their plan to trade with humans by selecting protagonist Lilith Iyapo to serve as a sort of liaison between themselves and the other humans. They choose Lilith for a number of reasons, including becauseshe is prone to cancer, but also apparently because they understand that, as an African American woman, she may be particularly marginal to human society and thus easier to win over to their side. Having cured her of her cancer, they have awakened her to serve as the teacher and leader of the first group of humans they plan to send back to repopulate Earth, along with a group of Oankali who will stay behind to help the humans along in building a new world.

Lilith undergoes a process of education in which she learns about the Oankali and their culture. Eventually, she is ready to begin awakening and training other humans, though many of those she awakens are suspicious of her, first doubting the existence of the Oankali, then suspecting bad intentions on the part of the aliens. The Oankali, despite centuries of study, have apparently underestimated the xenophobic human resistance to intermingling with the Other. Thus, the humans awakened by Lilith begin to reject her partly due to the special abilities she has been given by the Oankali, who have modified her genetic structure to make her stronger and more resilient and to have an eidetic memory. The biggest factor in the ensuing human rebellion is their horror at the idea that their own children will be genetically manipulated human–Oankali hybrids (a horror that Lilith initially experiences as well, but eventually overcomes). This negative reaction leads to tragic effects as the humans turn to violence, injuring Lilith and killing Joseph, her chosen human mate. Nonetheless, the Oankali manage to restore order and to send the first group of humans to Earth, though Lilith has to remain behind on the ship for her own safety because the other humans have come to regard her as a traitor and collaborator with the Oankali. As the book ends, however, we learn that Lilith is pregnant with a hybrid child conceived via the ooloi Nikanj's genetic intervention (without Lilith's knowledge or consent) using Joseph's sperm. Ahajas, Nikanj's female Oankali mate, is also pregnant with a child of the same parentage.

Lilith's hybrid child, Akin, is the protagonist of *Adulthood Rites*. In this novel, Lilith and Akin now live on Earth with humans and Oankali in the established village of Lo. All of the humans on Earth have been rendered unable to reproduce except through mating with the Oankali, making it impossible to produce future generations of human children. Akin, however, looks almost exactly like a human baby boy, except for his odd tongue, which functions as an Oankali sensory tentacle. Early in the novel, Akin (still an infant, but already able to converse like an adult) is abducted by raiders, who hope to trade him for great value, given his nearly human appearance. He is finally traded to the village of Phoenix, the home now of several of Lilith's former associates. Akin is eventually rescued by the Oankali, but only after he has lived in Phoenix long enough to learn the ways of humans and prepare for the destiny built into his genetic design: it is he who is fated to choose whether humans should be allowed to die out as a species or given a chance to continue, rebuilding their civilization (even though that will almost certainly lead to another apocalyptic destruction of that civilization).

Humans (especially males) come off very badly in this book, which assumes that human biology predisposes the species to violence and viciousness. Ultimately, however, Akin decides that humans should again be made fertile and allowed to settle on Mars after he and the Oankali have terraformed it. Earth, however, will be largely destroyed. The Oankali-founded villages on Earth are actually baby organisms that will one day grow into living ships and set off into space, taking with them big chunks of the planet. By the end of the book, Akin has undergone his transformation into adulthood and is preparing, with a group of human volunteers, to leave for Mars to begin the terraforming project.

The protagonist of *Imago* is Jodahs, the hybrid child of Lilith, a human male, and three Oankali. Like the Oankali, the hybrids do not take on their final gender characteristics until the first of two metamorphoses that will eventually take them into adulthood. As Jodahs begins "his" first metamorphosis, it becomes clear (to the surprise of all, including the Oankali) that the "boy" will be the first construct ooloi, through a rare miscalculation on the part of Nikanj in mixing Jodahs's genes. As the first part-human ooloi, Jodahs has special transformative, shape-shifting powers (owing to its unprecedented ability to manipulate the human proclivity for cancer) that allow it to take on different shapes itself and to modify others with whom it comes into contact. However, as it first acquires these powers, it has poor control over them and is thus dangerous to any living thing with which it comes into contact. As a result, Jodahs and its family are forced to leave their village for the safety of the community.

Their subsequent adventures eventually take them to a human village where some of the inhabitants have somehow remained fertile (but are diseased), despite the efforts of the Oankali. They are captured by the villagers, but soon rescued by an Oankali shuttle that arrives to incorporate the community, healing the humans and allowing them to choose between mating with Oankali, being made sterile and staying on Earth, or remaining fertile and emigrating to the human colony on Mars. Jodahs, still regarded as dangerous, produces the seed of a new Oankali village and plants it near the human village, where Jodahs and its family will establish a community that will eventually take to the stars when the village is mature as a ship.

In many ways, the Oankali takeover of Earth mirrors European colonial expansion (especially in Africa) quite closely. In the trilogy, a technologically advanced force arrives on Earth and takes control of the lives of the indigenous people, forcing them to live according to the values of the invaders. The Oankali, confident in their superiority, establish a political and economic relationship with the indigenous people, but one in which the Oankali dictate the terms according to their own needs and desires. There are no negotiations, and little consideration is given to the concerns or desires of the indigenous people. Instead, the Oankali paternalistically determine what is "best" for humanity and then impose that decision by force.

On the other hand, the Oankali "invasion" differs from colonialism in a number of ways. Most importantly, the European colonizers of Africa disrupted and destroyed functioning African cultures, while the Oankali come to an Earth where civilization has essentially been destroyed. Butler's Oankali may play much the same role as European colonizers, or even slave traders (considering the obvious parallel between the Oankali loading of humans aboard their ship in order to take them to a new world and the Middle Passage of slavery), but they are ultimately presented in a largely positive light as saviors of a humanity that has already virtually destroyed itself. In addition, the emphasis on trade in Xenogenesis tends to make the trilogy read as an allegory less of colonialism than of our own contemporary period of globalization, with the complete domination of humans by the Oankali serving as a reminder of the way Western nations (and corporations) remain fully in charge of the world system of capitalism.

The humans of Butler's trilogy are generally depicted as vicious-minded bigots, horrified of difference. Their ability to put aside their racial differences merely signals a shift in the focus of their xenophobic tendencies from other humans to the Oankali. As Lilith puts it at one point, encapsulating the stark opposition between the basic tendencies of the Oankali and those of humans, "Human beings fear difference ... Oankali crave difference" (*Adulthood Rites*, 329). Xenogenesis seems to endorse hybridity as a virtue, treating the Oankali as ultimately benign. Still, it is worth noting that the Oankali force certain changes on their human subjects in order to facilitate their breeding project. While the Oankali do indeed seem to be saving humanity from itself in the trilogy, a further complication is introduced into the trilogy because it is also the case that a rhetoric of salvation (often accompanied by Christian missionary zeal) was central to the discourse of colonialism, which was consistently justified by a claim that the darker peoples of the Earth needed to be saved from themselves by the more enlightened civilization of Europe.

The Oankali hybridization project also needs to be read within the context of discourse about miscegenation; the human fear of contamination through miscegenation that is so central to their reaction to the Oankali allegorically aligns them with the legacy of white racism and its fear of the taint of "black" blood. This anxiety also resonates with much of the discourse of "alien abduction" that was in heavy circulation in the US in the 1980s. Indeed, at about the same time as the "Xenogenesis" trilogy was appearing, alien abduction theorist Budd Hopkins (1988) was declaring that the purpose of alien abductions was "the creation of hybrid human–alien children" (*Intruders*, 35).

In Butler's trilogy such fears are rejected in favor of an acceptance of racial enrichment from hybridization. Indeed, the positive treatment of hybridity in Xenogenesis has led many critics to see the trilogy as an endorsement of the kind of hybrid subjectivity famously associated by Donna Haraway with the cyborg. For Haraway, the cyborg is a highly political (especially feminist, but also anticolonial) image in that it suggests the pursuit of transgressive identities that go beyond traditional categories and imposed boundaries. "The cyborg," she writes, "is a kind of disassembled and reassembled, postmodern collective and personal self" (*Simians*, 163). Haraway herself has shown a special interest in Butler's work, listing Butler along with Joanna Russ, Samuel R. Delany, Anne McCaffery, and Vonda McIntyre as practitioners of cyborg writing (*Simians*, 178–180). Haraway concludes that Xenogenesis, in its representation of the alien Oankali and their project to transform humanity, constitutes a powerful challenge to the traditional Western celebration of sameness and suspicion of Otherness.

Other critics have followed suit, as when Rebecca J. Holden (1998) argues that "Butler's science fiction is a cyborg fiction, fiction that maps the potentially powerful alliances among varying peoples but keeps difference – often fruitful – alive" ("Cyborg Survival," 49). Feminist critics have particularly seen Lilith (perhaps because of her gender) as a sort of cyborg heroine, though it is of course the shape-shifting Jodahs whose fluid identity makes it the truest image of the kind of boundary-crossing that Haraway associates with the cyborg. There are, however, a number of ways in which Butler's figuration of hybridity in Xenogenesis differs substantially from Haraway's use of the cyborg metaphor. For one thing, the Oankali have assimilated difference almost to the point of eradicating it. Thus, as Walter Benn Michaels points out, discussing Xenogenesis, though "miscegenation is an expression of the appreciation of difference, it is also a technology for the elimination of difference" ("Political," 658).

Perhaps the most problematic aspect of the trilogy is its seeming endorsement of a sort of essentialist biological determinism that stands in stark contrast to the transgressive fluidity that Haraway associates with the cyborg. In Xenogenesis, if humans seem bent on self-destruction, it is because that tendency is in their genes. Similarly, if the Oankali are determined to trade with virtually every intelligent species they encounter, it is because they are driven to do so by a biological imperative. Further, if human behavior is so thoroughly bound up with biology, then the hawkish policies of the Reagan administration, like the most cutthroat forms of capitalist competition, were merely an enactment of a rigidly defined human nature, and no amount of political activism can lead to any substantive political change.

However, Butler avoids a complete biological determinism because, in the world of the trilogy, biology itself is highly mutable. Human genetics may cause human beings to destroy each other, but human genetics can be changed. As a result, biology becomes the vehicle of change rather than an impediment to it. Eric White (1993), for example, sees Xenogenesis as an "evolutionary" narrative that draws upon the notion of evolution to envision humanity as a "historically contingent, transitional phenomenon" that is not fixed but remains in the process of becoming ("Erotics," 399). Further, the trilogy implies that technology (especially the kind of biotechnology that already seems very much on the horizon in our own day) may hold the key to bringing humanity into a new posthuman era in which we can intervene in the process of evolution and correct some of the natural flaws that have plagued us throughout history.

Neal Stephenson, *Snow Crash* (1992)

Published nearly a decade after William Gibson's *Neuromancer* (1984) became the vanguard of the cyberpunk literary movement, Neal Stephenson's *Snow Crash* (1992) pays homage to Gibson's futuristic vision while replacing its noirish sensibility with a darkly comic tone. Stephenson explores key cyberpunk themes – such as the blurring of boundaries between human and machine, the intrusion of corporations into everyday life, and the fragmentation of national identity – in a rollicking style that owes much to the graphic novel and serves to parody the typical cyberpunk formula. Like Gibson, however, Stephenson is not wholly uncritical of technological advancements, suggesting that the posthuman interface with technology brings both benefits and risks. The Metaverse, Stephenson's update of Gibsonian cyberspace, may provide an escape from the stultifying reality experienced by most people in the novel's dystopian near-future, but it is also in this virtual realm that the technological elite – computer programmers – are uniquely vulnerable to a computer virus that threatens to destroy their minds. In order to survive the coming "infocalypse," humans must develop their own defenses against viral programming, wresting the control of information from those who would use it to enslave them.

The Los Angeles of *Snow Crash*, home to the playfully named freelance hacker Hiro Protagonist and his business partner Y.T. ("Your Truly"), a fifteen-year-old skateboard Kourier who delivers packages by way of the cars she magnetically "poons" (harpoons) on the freeway, differs only in degree from the LA of today. It is also reminiscent of the dismal near-future urban reality depicted in Gibson's "Sprawl" trilogy, in which the gap between the rich and poor has widened significantly and the majority of power rests with corporations. Dangerous and overpopulated, the city is a mass of strip malls and walled-off "burbclaves," suburban outposts that

Neal Stephenson, Snow Crash (1992)

assume the status of individual nation states. Like the businesses, jails, and churches that dominate the landscape along the Pacific coast from LA to Alaska, the burbclaves are operated as private franchises. Indeed, the economy of the US, whose global renown is reduced to the four things it can do well – music, movies, microcode (software), and high-speed pizza delivery – depends primarily upon these franchises, which have also replaced traditional governmental structures. Virtually everything from the judicial system (Judge Bob's Judicial System) to the military (Admiral Bob's National Security; General Jim's Defense System) is run by competing private companies. Hiro freelances for the Central Intelligence Corporation (CIC), selling information to their database, a massive system that includes the contents of the former Library of Congress. As the novel opens, however, he is also employed as a high-speed pizza delivery person by Uncle Enzo's CosaNostra Pizza, one of the principal business arms of the Mafia. Fired owing to an accident involving Y.T.'s pooning of his car that lands his Mafia-owned vehicle in a burbclave swimming pool, Hiro finds himself indebted to the teenager, who steps in to deliver his pizza on time and thus prevents him from suffering the serious consequences of a late delivery. The unlikely pair – Y.T. (a homophone for "Whitey") is a blonde adolescent who hails from a burbclave, and Hiro is a Korean American and African American expert swordsman and citizen of the "franchulate" Mr. Lee's Greater Hong Kong – become allies, working together to gather intelligence and sell it to the CIC.

Despite his rather lowly stature in the material world, Hiro is considered royalty in the Metaverse, the virtual reality world that he and other hackers helped to design. While sitting in a cramped U-Stor-It unit that he shares with a roommate in LA, Hiro routinely accesses the Metaverse using his computer and virtual reality goggles; he projects a virtual representation of himself, or avatar (a term coined by Stephenson), into the shared space along with users from all over the world. Less abstract than Gibson's cyberspace, the Metaverse is also somewhat more prosaic, resembling nothing so much as an idealized, exaggerated version of the urban reality that Hiro inhabits. The frenetic capitalist exchange of the outside world is reflected in the main Metaverse thoroughfare of the Street, a virtual strip development replete with mile-high buildings and billboards, and where the only free ride may be had via public monorail. Hardly a democratized space, the Metaverse is open only to people who can afford to access it, whether from public terminals or from their own personal computers.

Visiting the Street is a highly popular activity, although it presents no real utopian alternative to physical reality, suggesting that reality is grim indeed for the denizens of Stephenson's near-future. Part of the Metaverse's appeal, according to Salvatore Proietti (2000), is that "it is a territory of no resistance, a void to be shaped or traversed according only to individual free will" ("Informatic Jeremiad," 124). Despite its overdevelopment in some areas, it is still a virtual frontier in others – for those who have the money to shape it. Having bought real estate close to the Street in the Metaverse's infancy, Hiro is a wealthy man – virtually speaking – and as a pioneering programmer he also enjoys privileges that most users do not. He is one of a small number of people, for example, who is allowed in the exclusive club The Black Sun, owned and operated by his former colleague Da5id. It is here that Hiro is approached by a mysterious avatar, later identified as the mutant Aleut mercenary Raven, who attempts to hand him a hypercard called "Snow Crash." Hiro suspects the hypercard (which transfers data immediately into the user's system) may be a computer virus and refuses it, and later he is warned by his former lover and colleague Juanita Marquez to stay away from Snow Crash. Da5id, however, believes his system is immune to all manner of computer viruses, so he tries a Snow Crash sample, which crashes his system and causes his avatar to be ejected from his own club. In the real world, Da5id himself falls into a coma.

Through his perusal of the virtual library contained in a hypercard that Juanita gives him, Hiro learns that Snow Crash is actually a boundary-crossing virus, infecting humans in both the material world and in the Meta-verse. In other words, Snow Crash may be transmitted through blood and other bodily fluids, or by computer code. Characterized at one point as "a virus, a drug, or a religion," it is a viral idea – a meme – with a biological virus counterpart. The resulting infection causes its human hosts to babble long lines of "code," or the universal tongue that is based in the deep structures of the brain. The victim is effectively cut off from higher-level brain functions, hence suffering a "crash" of consciousness that mirrors the hard drive crash of a computer. Indeed, N. Katherine Hayles argues that the universe of the novel is driven by the central metaphor that humans *are* computers, observing that "Stephenson reasons that there must exist in humans a basic programming level, comparable to machine code in computers, at which free will and autonomy are no more in play than they are for core memory running a program" (272). Once the machine language of the brain is accessed as a result of a Snow Crash infection, it is susceptible to programming by the purveyor of the drug, right-wing megalomaniacal Texas capitalist L. Bob Rife, whose ultimate goal is the control of information. For Rife, owner of a vast cable television monopoly and the fiber-optic network that runs the Metaverse, information is a commodity more precious than life.

The "software" that Rife installs in his victims' brains renders them as little more than automatons. They follow Rife's directives, but are not conscious of doing so, as these directives bypass the brain's high-level functions that allow for independent thought. It turns out that Snow Crash is the tool of an ancient cult, a metavirus that provided the foundation for ancient civilization and persists in the present-day of the novel: "We are all susceptible to the pull of viral ideas ... there is always this deep irrational part that makes us potential hosts for self-replicating information" (*Snow Crash*, 399–400). Weaving together Sumerian and Judeo-Christian mythology, combined with no small amount of linguistics theory, Stephenson constructs a story of the origin of modern human consciousness, describing what he terms the "Babel factor" as the defining moment of the emergence of human consciousness; it represents the point at which humans no longer communicate in a common tongue, necessitating the development of new and different languages. This radical departure from universal grammar is the work of a neurolinguistic virus, or "nam-shub" ("a speech with magical force"), programmed by an ancient hacker, of sorts, to counter the metavirus. Here Stephenson proposes that language itself acts in decidedly viral ways, a notion that is actualized in the emergence of computer viruses, which are themselves composed of a very specific kind of language. The ancient hacker, Enki, was a Sumerian priest-king, revered as a Promethean god by his people. Determined to liberate the pre-rational Sumerians from their viral civilization, he forced them to innovate and think independently by releasing his nam-shub into the world, which served to reprogram the deep structures of the brain and sever the connections with the common language. In developing consciousness, the Sumerians developed immunities that allowed them to fend off mind viruses.

Fast-forward five thousand years, and the metavirus returns with a vengeance in the form of a digital virus, crashing the minds of hackers, those whose understanding of binary code (the most fundamental level of computer code) is built into the deep structures of their brains. Vulnerable to infection simply as a result of viewing Snow Crash's binary code, which manifests as video "snow" in its visual form, hackers suffer more serious effects than those who contract the virus by other means. In a postrational society, where a vast number of people are illiterate and rely on what may be considered the oral tradition of television culture, most are particularly susceptible to the kind of mind viruses that Rife promotes, as they do not possess the barriers that education can provide. Hackers, a literate power elite who understand the nature of information and in effect program their own nam-shubs by writing and executing computer code, are not as susceptible to the virulent memes Rife deploys through the agency of religious fundamentalism. In other words, they prove to be difficult to convert. Aware that hackers are capable of mounting an opposition to his plans to render most of humanity completely subservient to his commands, Rife acquires Snow Crash, "the atomic bomb of informational warfare – a virus that causes any system to infect itself with new viruses" (*Snow Crash*, 200), and plans an "infocalypse," a large-scale deployment of the virus in the Metaverse.

The primary way Rife spreads the metavirus among the masses, however, is through a combination of religious practices and the transmission through blood. The biological version of the metavirus is associated with the Sumerian goddess Asherah, whose followers promoted the transmission through the use of cult prostitutes. The contemporary manifestation of the cult of Asherah is the Pentecostal church, which Rife appropriates and transforms into the Reverend Wayne's Pearly Gates franchise. A global chain that uses television and other media outlets to disseminate its message, Reverend Wayne's is an obvious parallel to the contemporary phenomenon of the evangelical Christian "megachurch"; the suggestion here is that only people living in a postrational society (i.e. lacking immunity against memes) could be swayed by such a pernicious institution. To ensure the susceptibility of his converts, Rife sends out missionaries to developing countries to vaccinate their populations, adding a dollop of Snow Crash into the mix. For the populations of the decadent West, he devises a drug composed primarily of addictive drugs and the virus, similar to the amyl nitrate "poppers" once (mistakenly) linked with HIV transmission. Stephenson takes the analogy between fundamentalist religion and the virus as far as it will go; not only is Reverend Wayne's church viral in the sense of spreading the extraordinarily powerful meme of religion, but it actively propagates biological viruses in a double whammy meant to ensure the complete loss of autonomy of the masses. Religion is not simply an opiate – it is an infection. That a fundamentalist Christian sect is responsible for the spread of a plague transmitted by blood, whose original source is a woman, is a savage jab at the Christian Right, whose early attitudes about AIDS helped to shape the popular view that only un-Christian and "unnatural" people – i.e. homosexual men – transmit and contract AIDS.

Hiro is uniquely situated to help defeat Rife's plans because he is not a "corporate assembly-line hacker" and is thus less susceptible to infection. There is a sameness about corporate hackers that is dangerous, a hegemony that is echoed in the franchise motto: "no surprises." As Stephenson explains, "The franchise and the virus work on the same principle: what thrives in one place will thrive in another" (*Snow Crash*, 190). Variety, or difference, is what confounds a virus in nature, and capitalism, with the spread of franchises across the globe, ensures that there is less and less difference. Not only does Hiro confound sameness with his innovative programming skills and his individuality, but, as a Korean-African American, he is genetically diverse as well. Vulnerable to Snow Crash, he is nevertheless capable of inoculating his brain against other virulent memes. Juanita, however, manages to combat the metavirus directly after voluntarily submitting to an implantation of a radio antennae into her brainstem by Rife, who issues directives to his automatons via the antennae. In effect, Juanita joins the thousands of primarily Asian refugees on the Raft, a conglomeration of ships in the Pacific that Rife has constructed into a tightly organized hierarchy of people speaking the same tongue. His plan is to direct their invasion of California, thus hastening the spread of the virus. Andrew M. Butler (2000) notes that this scenario "seems blind to the racism of its hordes of Asiatic masses" (*Pocket Essential Cyberpunk*, 53), an intimation that the plot echoes early twentieth-century American "yellow peril" narratives. Hayles, however, suggests that Stephenson is employing satire to ridicule the contemporary immigration paranoia prevalent in California.

Although technically a "wirehead," Juanita overcomes her programming, eventually becoming a "ba'al shem," a (pre-Enki) sorcerer for whom the utterance of words is calculated to effect material changes. What Hiro and Juanita can do with binary code on computer systems, Juanita can now do with brains: "I can hack the brainstem" (430). Juanita is able to use the metavirus for her own ends, suggesting the liberatory potential of the boundary-crossing virus ("Hacking the Brainstem," 568). However, once she and Hiro disable the biological version of Snow Crash by releasing Enki's original counter-virus on the Raft to restore, or reprogram, the brain's higher-level functions, Juanita largely drops out of the plot. Stephenson does not dwell on the "newness" of the subjectivities as represented by Rife's automatons or Juanita, possibly because while they may be new in the context of the contemporary culture of the novel, they are in fact ancient, brought about by a virus that is also "new" and yet very old. Humanity as we know it, endowed with consciousness, reason, and free will, is a relatively recent outgrowth of our computational natures.

Hiro, despite being involved in a few cartoonishly violent physical battles, spends much of the novel plugged into the Metaverse, often leaving Y.T. to foil Rife's plans in the real world. Y.T. is aided by the Mafia, who join with Mr. Lee's Greater Hong Kong against Rife, and she manages to temporarily disable Rife's key heavy Raven with her "dentata," a protective vaginal insert that knocks him unconscious. While Y.T. struggles to escape Rife, who abducts her in a bid to use her as a shield against the Mafia, Hiro constructs a nam-shub against the digital version of Snow Crash in the Metaverse, devising a program that disables the virus and saves thousands of hackers from the infocalypse. Rife himself is finally dispatched by the Rat

Thing, a cyborg "guard dog" employed by Mr. Lee's Greater Hong Kong and equipped with radiothermal isotopes that allow him to run at over seven hundred miles per hour. Although Rat Things are conditioned to stay within their "hutches" until they receive commands telling them otherwise, this one overcomes its programming because of its love for Y.T., whom it perceives as being in danger and who was its owner before it had been transformed from a regular dog. As a result, it sacrifices itself and manages to prevent Rife from escaping by annihilating his plane. Like Juanita, the Rat Thing refuses to submit to the programming that robs it of autonomy. The dog reasserts itself, shrugging off its conditioning. That the last, spectacularly violent scene in the novel involves a cyborg dog whose loyalty wins out over his programming suggests that, in the end, technology cannot supersede that which makes us human (and canine, in this case).

Echoing the concerns of other cyberpunk texts, *Snow Crash* suggests that the posthuman of the digital age is dangerously vulnerable to new, previously unimagined threats. Humans have always been subject to viral outbreaks, but the blurring of boundaries between the organic and artificial represented by the emergence of the posthuman effectively erases the distinction between the computational and biological virus. Consequently, the effects of infocalypse can be as severe as those of a biological viral epidemic. The novel, however, holds out the possibility that there is some defense against viral programming – that humans may choose their own programming, and that they may inoculate themselves against memetic invasions. Employing the virus as a metaphor for things as widely divergent as religion, capitalism, language, and even powerful ideas in general, *Snow Crash* warns that humans who do not develop immunities are doomed to lives bereft of autonomy and control.

Nicola Griffith, *Ammonite* (1994)

Nicola Griffith's *Ammonite* (1994) features a fully realized world of women, a device that has deep roots in the feminist literary tradition but has become somewhat rare in contemporary science fiction. The depiction of the women-only societies and cultures of Grenchstom's Planet (GP), better known as "Jeep," is indebted to the century-long tradition of feminist utopias, and the women of Jeep are direct literary descendants of Joanna Russ's Whileawayans ("When It Changed," 1972; *The Female Man*, 1975) and Suzy McKee Charnas's Riding Women (*Motherlines*, 1978). In addition, Griffith's Marghe Taishan, who serves as a lone ambassador to Jeep, recalls Genly Ai in Le Guin's *The Left Hand of Darkness* (1969), a utopian novel that constitutes a groundbreaking exploration of gender. Griffith's novel, however, is striking in its divergence from previous separatist feminist utopias, dispensing with the assumption that a world ruled by women is necessarily idyllic. On Jeep, women are as likely to be villains as heroines, suggesting that in the absence of men, women are fully capable of behaviors associated with the patriarchy, including aggression, dominance, and violence. Furthermore, by portraying women – traditionally defined in terms of men – on a world without men, Griffith eliminates socially constructed gender roles and argues for a definition of women as *people*.

Taishan, an anthropologist for the Settlement and Education Councils (SEC), is ostensibly sent to Jeep to study the women-only communities that developed there centuries ago in the wake of a viral epidemic that killed all of the original male colonists and twenty percent of the women. In order to study the inhabitants, however, Marghe agrees to serve as a test subject for an experimental vaccine against the virus; it becomes clear that her true purpose is as a pawn of the Durallium Company, which currently owns Jeep but is prevented from exploiting the planet's natural resources by the presence of the virus, which leaves the planet in quarantine. The profit- and power-seeking Company thus attempts to salvage its interests on Jeep by engineering the vaccine that Marghe tests; Marghe, a realist, is willing to accept the Company's terms in order to do the work that she loves. The success or failure of the vaccination determines the fate of the Company military forces (known as "Mirrors") stationed on the planet, women who have survived the virus but are unable to leave for fear of spreading it throughout the galaxy. The commander of the Mirrors, Hannah Danner, eventually comes to the conclusion that failure would mean total abandonment by the Company, despite assurances that a quarantine program would allow them to leave the planet safely.

The use of plague or a similar natural catastrophe that eliminates men is a typical feature of feminist utopias. In Russ's Whileaway, an unspecified plague is the culprit, updated in Griffith to a virus with affinities to the most visible of 1990s viruses: HIV ("Devour and Transform," 152). Often employed as a utopian signifier, the virus is a common trope among contemporary science fiction writers, transforming the agent of disease into one that enlivens the (frequently marginalized) subject rather than debilitating it ("Outburst!", 123). Described as "a bit like a retrovirus" ("Outburst!", 38), Griffith's virus renders its female survivors posthuman, bestowing upon them a heightened sensitivity to the planet's rhythms, the ability to access ancestral memories, an improved facility with language, and the ability to reproduce by recombining their DNA. This last skill is an echo of the methods of reproduction used in numerous feminist utopias, which do not require the input of men. In Griffith's novel, the virus enables those infected to visualize their ova and to stimulate the cell division necessary for embryonic development. Matched in biological rhythms, lovers can psychically effect conception in one another, resulting in children who appear to share characteristics of both mothers. It is this "secret" to reproduction that Marghe seeks to unravel as she travels through Jeep.

Commander Danner and the other Mirrors, whom Marghe meets upon descending to the planet, have been on Jeep for five years and have witnessed the deaths of all their male colleagues and a percentage of the females, but have little contact with the other women-only communities made up of the descendants of the original colonists. The death of the men is handled matter-of-factly among the Mirrors, and (unlike numerous separatist feminist utopias) there is no sense that the absence of men represents an improvement for the lives of the remaining women. The loss of men is treated as a problem, not a solution, but one that takes a back seat to the more immediate problems the Mirrors face on Jeep. Gwyneth Jones (2003) notes the neutrality of Griffith's presentation, observing that "Because the characters are allowed to behave as if their sex is not a political issue (though of course it is), the world without men becomes equally a world without women" ("Rev. of *Ammonite*," 21). The survivors are simply people, privileged through viral infection.

Though men are completely absent from the novel, the specter of the patriarchy hovers above the planet in a Company military cruiser called the *Kurst*, which has orders to destroy the orbital station *Estrade* and if necessary murder the inhabitants of Jeep if the virus proves immune to the vaccine. The consequences of its spreading beyond the planet are, of course, enormous: Jeep's virus threatens the extinction of men and, by extension, heterosexuality. A "straight plague," Griffith's virus rewrites HIV (often referred to as the "gay plague" in the initial wake of its discovery in the 1980s), boosting the immunity of the host and transforming the diseased into an empowered class. Lesbianism is the norm on Jeep; the heterosexual orientation does not appear to exist even among the Mirrors, who have been on the planet a short time in comparison with the original colonists. But for the three women orbiting the planet in the *Estrade*, who have not contracted the virus but are apparently lesbians, we might say that the Jeep virus enforces a kind of "compulsory homosexuality," mounting a radical challenge to compulsory heterosexuality (Thomas 153). Heterosexuality is not demonized, however; along with men, it is merely absent. Like biological sex and gender, sexual orientation is beside the point for the women of Jeep.

Armed with the vaccine and little else, Marghe ignores Commander Danner's warnings about traveling far from the Mirror outpost of Port Central, despite the fact that one of the members of the original SEC team is missing and presumed dead. Marghe heads north to Olfoss, which she believes will provide her with answers about the origin of the virus and the origins of the people themselves. While she meets members of one peaceful tribe that agree to enter into a trade agreement, or "trata," with the Mirrors of Port Central, she soon finds herself held hostage by a warrior-like tribe of women called Echraidhe. Rigidly hierarchical, violent, repressive, and preferring to raid other tribes instead of entering into trata, the Echraidhe hew closely to an inflexible code of honor. This unswerving adherence to the code not only leads to a decline in population and heavy interbreeding but also to the ascendance of a charismatic but insane leader, Uaithne, who believes herself to be the servant of the goddess of death. Marghe, aware that Uaithne wants to kill her, manages to escape, but not before Uaithne plunges the Echraidhe into a feud with a neighboring tribe. Although it becomes clear in the course of the novel that the Echraidhe way of life is in the minority among Jeep communities, their very existence calls into question the notion that women left to their own devices will naturally develop societies lacking structures commonly associated with the patriarchy. The

Echraidhe serve as a bracing corrective to the harmonious separatist utopias depicted by Griffith's predecessors; the women of Jeep are immune to neither violence nor the abuse of power.

Marghe's escape from the Echraidhe leads to her rescue by an inhabitant of Olfoss, a non-hierarchical agricultural community, where she learns about the ways in which the virus creates a bond between the women and the planet itself. Encouraged by Thenike, a healer and storyteller who later becomes her lover, Marghe stops her Company-prescribed vaccine treatment and allows the virus to take its course. In the aftermath of her illness, she feels at one with herself and the world, her senses sharpen, and she feels the "needs" of the planet more intensely, even at the level of cultivating plants. She also thoroughly assimilates into the Olfoss tribe, moving from isolation to connection. In effect, she becomes a new woman – the virus serves as a kind of catalyst that enables her to embrace the parts of her identity that she had formerly repressed, including her sexuality. Taking inspiration from the image of an ammonite, a solid fossilized shell that repeatedly appears in her dreams, Marghe gives herself the surname Amun, which refers to an ancient Theban fertility god and means "complete one." Thus, not only does the virus work in the interests of the women and the planet by preventing the dominance of the patriarchy in the form of the exploitative Company, but as Heather Schell (1997) observes, it also enables a kind of consciousness-raising ("Outburst!,"131). Survivors of the virus are not necessarily the equivalent of the non-hierarchical, peaceful, nurturing utopians represented in works ranging from Charlotte Perkins Gilman's *Herland* (1915) to Joan Slonczewski's *A Door into Ocean* (1986) – as the depictions of the Echraidhe and the Mirrors demonstrate – but the virus itself privileges women and is coded in ways that can be considered essentially feminine. Most who carry the virus instinctively work to protect and preserve the planet, suggesting an intuitive relationship between women and nature that is a hallmark of the feminist utopia. This relationship allows no accommodation for technology, however. Aside from that used by the Mirrors, modern technology is completely absent on the planet. Jeep itself appears to be hostile to the implements of technology, rendering Mirror weapons ineffective during an electrical storm and metaphorically dealing a blow to the patriarchy that employs the women. So while it is clear that the women do not harbor ill will toward men or rejoice in their eradication, the planet – like the virus – works against the interests of men. Here the expression of an essential femininity, implicit in the relationship between the feminine and the land and the feminine and the virus, serves as a counter to the masculinist technology in the novel, as well as technology's weapon against the virus: the vaccine. In what might be taken as an environmentalist commentary, human masculinity and technology, it seems, are intrinsically at odds with Jeep's natural environment, both on the level of biology and culture.

There is a suggestion that the Jeep virus may itself be a kind of weapon engineered by the original colonists on Jeep, who were "adept bioengineers," but another possibility is that its source is the indigenous inhabitants of Jeep, an intelligent sloth-like race called the goths. The two-sexed goths, who appear to have devolved over time, have acquired an almost mythical status for the humans, who rarely come into contact with them. Considered to be primitive by most humans, they are sometimes hunted for their pelts and are on the whole rather gentle creatures. When Marghe accesses ancestral memories of the goths in a communal trance-like state known as "deepsearch," she realizes that the genetic material of both goth and human are embedded in the virus, which is the facilitator of deepsearch. While the origin of the virus is never confirmed, Marghe's hypothesis that it may stem from the goths is a disturbing echo of contemporary attitudes about lethal viruses originating from "primitive" peoples ("Devour and Transform," 155). Since the virus is presented as having positive transformative effects for the infected women, however, the novel complicates that association. What is far more disturbing is that the women of Jeep are obviously aware that goths are – as Marghe puts it – "people," and yet a member of her own adopted family hunts them despite the family's misgivings. We may initially be lulled into thinking that Olfoss, with its emphasis on communality, tolerance, nurturing, and partnership with nature, is a typical example of the harmonious feminist utopian community, but Griffith frustrates such assumptions in her depiction of the complicated relationships between the members of the tribe and their views of the goths. They do not all feel, think, or act according to a single (feminist) ideology, and some may be downright cruel. As Brian Attebery (2002) notes, what sets *Ammonite* apart from an early feminist utopia like Gilman's *Herland*, whose separatists are all very similar, is its "full range of female persons" (*Decoding Gender*, 124). Separatist feminist utopias are often thought to be harmonious precisely because of the absence of men, but even Jeep's most harmonious communities are fraught with complex problems that threaten the balance of peace.

Just as the virus integrates itself into the human cell, so Marghe integrates herself into Jeep – into its communities, its land, and the "rhythm of the world." She experiences this integration most fully through deepsearch, a state triggered for her initially through song and the rhythmic beating of drums in a communal ceremony, but which she is able to access by herself on other occasions. It is in this state that conception can occur: deepsearch, the virus, and maternity are all explicitly linked. And, just as the infected may access the memories of their ancestors (and those of the goths) through the agency of the virus, so may they access their ancestors' language, the incantation of which can induce deepsearch. Marghe learns that the virus is a kind of vector for long-dead human languages and customs; the Echraidhe, for example, are clearly modeled on ancient Celtic tribes, and their heavy interbreeding narrows their worldview and even causes psychosis during prolonged periods in deepsearch. The communality afforded by the virus in this case has negative consequences. Olfoss is a healthier and more diverse tribe, and here the communal language is representative of an entire array of cultures. Marghe's lover Thenike is particularly attuned to the power of language, as her vocation is that of the "viajera." More than mere storytellers, viajeras are the linchpins of Jeep's tribes, arbitrating disputes, singing songs, leading deepsearch, healing, and "remembering." Viajeras do not forget – they maintain the continuity between tribes by continually demonstrating their intertwining histories through song and story. In the person of the viajera the communal aspects of the virus are most clearly manifested, and she is the locus of its utopian energies ("Devour and Transform," 157).

Already trained in biofeedback, Marghe finds it easy to stimulate conception in Thenike during deepsearch, but the process involving this biological adaptability is not yet understood among the Mirrors. And there is a suggestion that women cannot be fully integrated into Jeep societies unless they reproduce. One Mirror who abandons her post and joins one of the tribes shares her fears with Marghe: "Not that I'm sure I *want* to have a child, you know? . . . But it would be nice to have the choice. It would make me feel as though I belong" (337). The consequences of infection, it seems, serve to link women even more firmly with their reproductive functions, reinforcing an essential femininity that Griffith presumably intends to challenge in her depiction of women in a wide variety of roles. However, because the ability to conceive is perceived as a "natural" by-product of infection, the women of Jeep are tied to their reproductive capabilities in a way that the technologically savvy utopians of Russ's Whileaway and Piercy's Mattapoisett (*Woman on the Edge of Time*, 1976) are not.

In the end, the Mirrors are forced to move from their isolated position in Port Central to connection with Jeep societies. Through a miscommunication, it is conveyed to the personnel of the military cruiser the *Kurst* that the vaccine has failed; they respond by immediately destroying the *Estrade* (with the few Mirrors who evacuated the planet on board) and abandoning the planet. Now free of the Company's surveillance, the Mirrors are also exposed to Jeep's tribes. Under Danner's command, they enter into trata with other tribes, come to the rescue of those threatened by the Echraidhe, and attempt to become self-sufficient – all the while fully aware that the Company threat of extermination still exists. Their liaison to the world outside is Marghe, who, under her new guise of viajera, helps to cement the relationships between the Mirrors and the societies she has adopted as her own. Her considerable diplomatic skills are enhanced by the virus, which allows her the experience of an interconnectedness with other people, forged through collective memories, languages, and a heightened consciousness of her body's relationship with the world. Transformed by the virus, she becomes part of the community it enables.

Griffith's predecessors – particularly those writing feminist utopias in the 1970s – used separatism in order to liberate women from patriarchal structures and thus empower them to create their own utopian alternatives. While *Ammonite* maintains a continuity with these revolutionary works, the novel complicates the notion that it is simply the presence of men that prevents women from achieving utopian possibilities, and that the elimination of men naturally leads to the elimination of all patriarchal structures. Utopian societies do exist on Jeep, but so do oppressive ones, despite the complete absence of men during their centuries-long evolution. And while the Jeep virus seems to embody a "feminine" essence that integrates itself into the cells of the infected, the survivors do not have a universal feminine identity. Equally capable of being warriors, farmers, traitors, or heroines, they are simply people.

Kim Stanley Robinson, "Mars" Trilogy (1993–1996)

Kim Stanley Robinson's "Mars" trilogy – comprising *Red Mars* (1993), *Green Mars* (1994), and *Blue Mars* (1996) – is one of the most praised and awarded science fiction works of recent decades. Together, the three volumes envision the colonization and terraforming of Mars to make it a second home planet for humans. This scenario presents many opportunities for the exploration of a variety of science fictional technologies and motifs. Perhaps more importantly, it presents numerous opportunities for the exploration of social, political, and economic ideas. Many of the colonists realize that this new planet represents an opportunity for human civilization to make a fresh start and to transcend the mistakes of the past on Earth. Thus, anything and everything having to do with the functioning of human societies is up for debate. The trilogy has been described as "totalization on a grand scale" by Fredric Jameson (1994), who declares that the three volumes will collectively become "the great political novel of the 1990s and the place in which the interrelations of the various radical or revolutionary groups have been most vividly rehearsed for our own time" (*Seeds*, 65).

The "Mars" trilogy is indeed political science fiction at its finest. It is both science fiction and political fiction on a grand scale, dealing with numerous scientific concepts and technological breakthroughs, as well as a wide variety of social and political issues. Environmentalism, however, is probably the central issue. The project of terraforming Mars to have an environment in which humans can live comfortably raises a number of questions concerning the impact of humans on the environment of Earth – which by the time of the trilogy's events has been "terraformed" into near uninhabitability. These questions deal not just with making a healthy environment for humans, but with respect for nature; many of the political disagreements in the book concern the extent to which humans have a right to modify the natural environment of Mars to their own liking. In addition, as the trilogy proceeds, long-term residents of Mars begin to think of themselves as Martians, with a separate culture and separate concerns from those of Earth. Robinson's environmental concerns are closely related to his treatment of the science in the trilogy, which clearly critiques the Enlightenment notion that science is a tool intended primarily to give humans power and control over their environment. Moreover, in the trilogy, the Martian environment itself becomes a sort of Other to the colonists from Earth, suggesting by extension that both the drive to colonize other parts of the world and the drive to control and exploit nature arise from a Western Enlightenment drive for domination precisely of the kind famously associated by Max Horkheimer and Theodor Adorno with the scientific rationalism of the Enlightenment.

This style of science, of course, is that which so many critics have seen as closely aligned with the projects of imperialism and colonialism, so much so that the two are historically almost inseparable. Indeed, as Michael Adas (1989) notes, both technology and the ideology of science have historically been used as tools of colonial conquest. However, Robinson in the trilogy posits alternative styles of science that are genuinely respectful of and curious about nature rather than simply attempting to gain the knowledge necessary to dominate it. Many of the political battles in the trilogy are struggles between these two competing scientific "styles," as well as a struggle between those who would see science as a means of understanding and appreciating nature and those who would see it simply as a commodified tool for use in its exploitation for corporate profit. Thus, as Elizabeth Leane (2002) notes, Robinson's treatment of science is quite complex, and the trilogy's main utopian alternative may be its presentation of a new style of science more than its presentation of Mars as an alternative planet to Earth. It is certainly to Robinson's credit that he refuses the easy solution of abandoning science as inherently imperialistic but instead suggests potential visions of science that, opposed to the instrumental Enlightenment rationalism critiqued by Horkheimer and Adorno, can actually be anti-imperialistic.

The "Mars" trilogy, in fact, is very much a tribute to the flexibility and potential of science. It is replete with the kind of "hard" scientific and technological detail for which Robinson is justifiably so well known, yet it avoids the celebration of hardware (at the expense of human beings) for which science fiction has often been criticized. Perhaps Robinson's greatest achievement in the trilogy is his ability to construct a stirring narrative of planetary colonization that avoids almost entirely the temptation to fall into the vein of colonialist romance and adventure. The trilogy is also rich in its imaginative exploration of a future world that differs substantially from that of the present, creating a form of cognitive estrangement that encourages readers to rethink their attitudes about related issues in their own world. In particular, the trilogy often focuses on social and political alternatives that might potentially lead to a utopian future, thus restoring some of the utopian vision that informed much early science fiction but that seemed to have waned in the science fiction of the 1980s, especially in the work of "cyberpunk" writers such as William Gibson.

This waning might be attributed to the discouraging effects of the Reagan–Thatcher era, but there were, of course exceptions to the rule, Robinson's own "Three Californias" trilogy – comprising *The Wild Shore* (1984), *The Gold Coast* (1988), and *Pacific Edge* (1990) – being the major utopian work of the 1980s. Carol Franko was the first critic to call significant attention to the utopian dimension of Robinson's work, in essays such as "Working the 'In-Between'" and "The Density of Utopian Destiny in Robinson's *Red Mars*" (1997). But Jameson, one of America's leading cultural critics and theorists, has emerged as Robinson's most influential champion. Jameson's enthusiasm for the work of Robinson may have something to do with the fact that Robinson is his former doctoral student, but it surely has more to do with Robinson's ability to inject powerful utopian energies into his texts, even at a time when most American science fiction writers seemed to be finding that harder and harder to do. Indeed, Jameson has argued that the "Mars" trilogy stands as an important demonstration of the utopian potential of science fiction as a literary form ("'If I find one good city I will spare the man'"). Or, as Jameson succinctly puts it in *Archaeologies of the Future* (2005), the "Mars" trilogy stands as a new sort of utopian text, one that is not concerned with the elaboration of a single utopian blueprint for an ideal society but with "the conflict of all possible Utopias, and the arguments about the nature and desirability of Utopia as such" (*Archaeologies*, 216).

Red Mars begins with the first colonial expedition to Mars, as a carefully chosen international group of a hundred highly qualified scientists and other specialists (dominated by Americans and Russians) set out on the spaceship *Ares* in the year 2026 to found the first permanent settlement on Mars. They then begin the long, slow process of terraforming the planet, at the same time dealing not only with their own internal disagreements but also with growing political tensions between Mars and Earth. Social and political tensions grow considerably more intense as subsequent expeditions join the First Hundred on Mars and as large transnational corporations from Earth seek more and more to exploit the new settlements for their own profit – in a mode highly reminiscent of colonialism on Earth. Thus, when an Indian delegate to a Martian conference complains that colonialism never really ended, one of the key members of the First Hundred responds, "That's what transnational capitalism is: we're all colonies now" (*Red Mars*, 460).

In fact, this understanding of the neocolonial nature of capitalist globalization is crucial to the political sensibilities of the entire trilogy. Eventually, Earth's transnational corporate giants spearhead the construction of a huge space elevator (perhaps the most ambitious engineering project in human history) to allow the efficient shipment of goods and materials beyond the gravity well of Mars, whence they can be shipped to Earth easily and economically. Many on Mars deplore this project, because of both its contribution to the capitalist exploitation of Mars and the dangers associated with a closer connection to an Earth that is increasingly sinking into economic and political instability, largely because of the burdens of the planet's vast population. This situation, meanwhile, has been exacerbated by developments on Mars, where scientists have discovered a genetic treatment that retards the aging process and may enable individuals to live almost indefinitely. Unfortunately, the availability of this gerontological treatment leads to increased discrepancies on Earth between the lives of the rich, who can afford the treatment, and the poor, who cannot. Here, Robinson participates in a common science fictional motif. Norman Spinrad's *Bug Jack Barron* (1969) is perhaps the best exploration of this theme, but as Jameson notes, longevity technologies often translate into class struggle in science fiction (*Archaeologies*, 328–344).

This gerontological treatment is a perfectly credible projection of existing genetic research, but it is also a useful plot device that allows the First Hundred to remain central to the colonization of Mars throughout the trilogy, even though this process spans a period considerably longer than a normal human lifetime. Robinson's use of the treatment is typical of his thoughtful explorations of the social consequences of scientific advances. The space elevator is important in this regard as well. The potential that it offers leads to the sending of large numbers of working-class colonists to Mars, where they are exploited in traditional capitalist fashion, used as tools of the transnationals, who are bent especially on mining the rich mineral resources of Mars for shipment to Earth.

By the Earth year 2061 (and the end of *Red Mars*), conditions on Earth have deteriorated into near chaos, with a variety of local wars spreading to the point that they cover almost the entire planet. Meanwhile, the growing tensions on Mars lead, in this same seminal year, to an all-out revolution in which a variety of loosely aligned Martian factions strike out against the domination of Terran capital, leading to the large-scale destruction of the Martian infrastructure, including the space elevator.

In *Green Mars*, the terraforming of Mars is well advanced, while the largest and most powerful of the transnationals have re-established their domination of both Earth and Mars. A new space elevator is constructed, and large amounts of raw materials are being mined on Mars for export to Earth. Most of the transnationals seek to exterminate the Martian resistance (including most of the surviving members of the First Hundred), except for Praxis, the largest transnational of all. Praxis CEO William Fort understands that the mere use of Mars as a source of raw materials (and dumping ground for excess population) is short sighted. In a fairly obvious riposte to those in our own world who seem to feel that environmental responsibility is inherently bad for business, Fort believes that there are far greater profits to be made from nurturing the development of Mars into a genuine Earth-like planet, and, to that end, he decides to try to form an alliance with the resistance, which he sees as the true heart of Martian society.

Eventually, a second revolution breaks out on Mars. However, this time the notion of Martian independence has strong support on Earth, especially from a coalition formed by Praxis and the national governments of China, India, and Switzerland. Aided by the sympathetic attitude of this powerful coalition and by increasingly chaotic conditions on Earth (where, among other things, the melting of a large portion of the polar ice cap in Antarctica has led to the flooding of coastal areas worldwide), this second Martian revolution is successful. By the end of *Green Mars*, the entire planet of Mars is in the hands of rebel forces, with the exception of a single Terran stronghold in the town of Sheffield, anchor point of the space elevator cable.

Blue Mars centers on the attempts to establish a new government on the Mars in the wake of this revolution. As such, it is one of the most genuinely political novels of the past few decades. Much of the first half of the novel, for example, concerns the workings of a global constitutional convention on Mars in which various groups meet to attempt to iron out, starting from scratch, a new social, political, and economic system for Mars. Virtually everything, except for certain basic human rights, is up for discussion in the convention, which makes it the trilogy's central example of political debate. All sides seek to build a new utopian society on Mars, but different individuals and factions have very different ideas about what this might entail, providing the opportunity for a number of utopian ideals to meet and jostle for position.

Ultimately, the attendees at the convention are able to agree on a loose global confederation that gives considerable power to local governments and that supports the development of a new economic system based on concepts of fairness for all, with "both patriarchy and property brought to an end. It's one of the greatest achievements in human history" (*Blue Mars*,

346). This system, spelled out in a long speech by Vladimir Taneev, a member of the First Hundred and a key developer of the gerontological treatment, is specifically designed to overcome the exploitative class inequalities typical of capitalism (*Blue Mars*, 115–120). In fact, the new Martian system has much in common with socialism, though it is later described as a dialectical movement beyond both capitalism and socialism (*Blue Mars*, 391–392).

Eventually, the new Martian government achieves a détente with Earth. The elevator is allowed to remain in place, and the Martians gain full control of their planet through negotiation rather than further conflict. They even send a delegation to Earth to negotiate a treaty to govern future relations between the planets. However, these relations continue to be strained by the desires of the vastly overpopulated Earth to send more and more immigrants to Mars, where the increasingly Earth-like ecology remains very fragile. Still, as *Blue Mars* (and the entire trilogy) draws to an end, the future looks much brighter for cordial relations between Earth and Mars, though the members of the First Hundred (now well over two hundred years old) are rapidly dying off, owing to an age-related syndrome that even the advanced science of Mars is unable to combat, or even understand.

However, the bulk of *Blue Mars* is concerned with the growth of Martian society rather than the problems or actions of individual characters. Indeed, the trilogy as a whole is very much a collective work in which individual characters (especially members of the First Hundred) move to the forefront, then recede, making it clear that society as a whole is more important than any individual. To emphasize the point, John Boone, perhaps the most important leader among the First Hundred, is killed in the opening prologue of *Red Mars*, though the book then backtracks a bit and gives the details of events leading up to his assassination via a conspiracy involving Frank Chalmers, another key leader among the First Hundred. In this, the "Mars" trilogy is an important departure from most science fiction – and from the whole tradition of the Western novel, which typically relies on strong individual protagonists to engage the interests and sympathies of readers, thereby inevitably reinforcing the individualist ideology that is central to capitalism itself – and that the "Mars" trilogy clearly seeks to critique.

The vast expansion in technological capability envisioned throughout the "Mars" trilogy is something of a throwback to the earlier days of science fiction, which tended to foresee an extension of the Enlightenment project to a solution of all human problems through technology. But Robinson's vision looks forward, not backward, and his trilogy represents a major new contribution to utopian thought – centrally informed by an attempt to envision dedicated scientific inquiry free of the colonialist impulse to dominate nature. Robinson's future utopia is complex and open-ended, however, and he acknowledges the many difficulties that human societies will continue to face, however technologically advanced they may become. Ultimately, in the best tradition of science fiction, Robinson's trilogy, while set in a distant time on a distant planet, is very much about the here and now, using its spatial and temporal distance as a defamiliarizing device to render new perspectives on social, political, environmental, and economic problems that already plagued Earth in the 1990s.

Nalo Hopkinson,
Midnight Robber (2000)

Nalo Hopkinson's *Midnight Robber* employs familiar science fiction motifs such as space travel, alien encounter, interplanetary colonization, parallel universes, nanotechnology, and artificial intelligences to produce a number of novums and thus to create the kind of cognitive estrangement that is typical of the best science fiction. However, at least for Western readers, the novel introduces a new dimension of cognitive estrangement with its use of Caribbean-inflected language and other aspects of African and Caribbean culture. Hopkinson's depiction of the experiences of her young protagonist Tan-Tan, first on the planet of Toussaint and then on the prison planet of New Half-Way Tree, produces an exemplary science fiction adventure, while her appropriation of Afro-Caribbean cultural traditions adds the defamiliarizing perspective that is the hallmark of postcolonial literature. This combination results in a cultural hybridity that contributes to an impressive exploration of race, gender, and culture and that helps gives voice to the "alien" (with Hopkinson writing from within the "alien" cultures she describes), something that science fiction writers have long dreamed of doing but have seldom managed to achieve.

Midnight Robber begins on the planet Toussaint (named for the famed Haitian slave rebellion leader Toussaint L'Ouverture), which has been settled by colonists who have come from the Caribbean (with the backing of the Marryshow Corporation), bringing their culture as well as a high level of technology that allows them to live in relative comfort. Most of the labor on Toussaint is performed by machines, and the highly efficient society of the planet is regulated by a sophisticated artificial intelligence, the "Grande Nanotech Sentient Interface," known to the locals as "Granny Nanny," in an allusion to Nanny of the Maroons, a legendary Jamaican freedom fighter. Granny Nanny resides in a highly advanced quantum computer, networked with a system of smaller "eshus" (sentient units) that manage the day-to-day operation of individual buildings and households. Except for the oddly anachronistic "pedicab" runners who provide local transportation, most of the inhabitants of Toussaint are fitted with organic "earbuds" that allow them to remain on-line with Granny Nanny at all times, a situation that results in extremely efficient information flow, but at the expense of privacy. These runners perform one of the few manual jobs on the planet and remain off-line most of the time, but they are far from primitive. In addition to retaining a special knowledge of traditional Caribbean folk medicine, they have also mastered "Nannysong," the machine language of Granny Nanny, and can therefore speak to the artificial intelligence more effectively than ordinary citizens. Descendants of the original colonists who programmed Granny Nanny, the runners have learned to "hack" the web, or shut out its constant surveillance for short periods of time.

While Granny Nanny recalls Big Brother of George Orwell's *Nineteen Eighty-Four*, the AI is generally benevolent, allowing the runners to briefly evade surveillance as long as their actions do not pose a threat to public safety. The depiction of the web-based AI also owes something to Gibsonian cyberspace, but while Nanny's Web is gendered feminine, it is hardly the passive, feminized space of the matrix preceding the Wintermute/Neuromancer unification in *Neuromancer*. Granny Nanny is associated with the action and strength of her revolutionary namesake; she is also, however, the representative of the Marryshow Corporation, which is described early in the novel as a sexual conquerer that destroys much of the indigenous flora and fauna of Toussaint in order to make it suitable for human colonization. Thus, the relatively untouched planet New Half-Way Tree, existing alongside Toussaint in a sort of parallel universe, is described as looking "how Toussaint planet did look before the Marryshow Corporation sink them Earth Engine Number 127 down into it like God entering he woman; plunging into the womb of the soil to impregnate the planet with the seed of Granny Nanny" (*Midnight Robber*, 2). Hopkinson is echoing imperial narratives that metaphorically construct "new" lands as a woman's body to be dominated and controlled by European explorers and colonizers, but she complicates this construction by replacing semen with the "seed" of a feminine technology that is community-oriented and deployed by those whose own ancestors suffered as a result of European colonization. Granny Nanny is thus both a beloved maternal figure and a destructive force. Jillana Enteen (2007) argues that the depiction of the Marryshow Corporation and Granny Nanny presents a stark contrast to the conventions of cyberpunk fiction – in which technology and corporate power are often beyond the control of the individual – because they "cannot evolve into machines that no longer respond to the populations with whom they intersect" ("Receiving End," 265). Both are in the service of community values in Hopkinson.

The transformative colonial process of Toussaint is very successful, mirroring to a large extent the physical and social reality of the Caribbean landscape. Particularly crucial to the culture of Toussaint is the annual Carnival, echoing the importance of the Carnival in the Caribbean, especially in Trinidad. The main action of the novel begins during Carnival, when Antonio, Mayor of Cockpit County, engages in a ritualistic machete fight with and accidentally causes the death of Quashee, a man who has been engaged in an affair with his wife, Ione. As a result, Antonio seems sure to be convicted and exiled to New Half-Way Tree, employed by the colonists on Toussaint as a prison planet where the absence of Granny Nanny forces the prisoners exiled there to live under difficult conditions.

Using a device acquired from one of the pedicab runners, Antonio flees to New Half-Way Tree, kidnapping Tan-Tan in defiance of Granny Nanny. They are greeted by a strange-looking alien creature that turns out to be a "douen," one of the intelligent natives of the planet who are treated by the human colonists as an inferior species and used for manual labor. Extinct on Toussaint owing to the genocide perpetrated by the Marryshow Corporation, the douen are denied agency by humans even on the level of language – the word refers to the evil spirits of children in the Caribbean creole dialect the humans employ. Chichibud, the douen who meets Tan-Tan and her father, seems somewhat simple, but shows signs of being more formidable than he might appear as he guides the two newcomers to a village of human settlers.

Tan-Tan, whose involuntary passage to a harsh new world echoes that of her African ancestors, becomes the victim of sexual abuse by Antonio, who excuses his behavior because of Tan-Tan's close resemblance to her mother. The rapes cause a psychic fragmentation in Tan-Tan that enables her to dissociate herself from the abuse, but when Antonio rapes her on her sixteenth birthday, she kills him with a knife. In the wake of the killing (the stated punishment for which is death by hanging), Chichibud helps Tan-Tan escape into the woods and takes her to the giant "Daddy Tree" that is the home of his people. The next segment of the text is given over to Tan-Tan's gradual process of learning the ways of the douen, who turn out to be much more sophisticated and intelligent than the humans on the planet believe them to be. Tan-Tan is perhaps most surprised by the realization that the "packbirds" employed by the douen – which she has seen numerous times and has been led to believe cannot fly – are actually the females of the species and adept at flying. Benta, on whose back Tan-Tan flees from the human settlement, is an accomplished weaver and a strong personality who is the equal of her husband Chichibud; she is also Tan-Tan's protector and advocate. Tan-Tan's assumption that Benta and the other female douen, known as the Hinte, are simply beasts of burden is suggestive of the way that women have often been considered inferior, simply because of the ways they differ from men.

Observing the behavior of the humans, the douen realize that they must continue to appear simple and harmless, lest the humans begin to use on them the advanced weapons they have already seen or heard humans using on each other. They also learn human language, which gives them a certain tactical advantage, while humans themselves make no attempts to learn douen language or culture. Like the pedicab runners who are dismissed on Toussaint for their practice of manual labor, the douen are skilled at handicraft, and have even developed a secret foundry (though they supposedly do not know how to work metal). Humans, believing that little in the douen culture or customs mirrors their own level of advancement, do not take the aliens seriously – in part because certain aspects of the douen are so different, or "alien," that the humans are unable to recognize them as worthy of respect. Such an attitude echoes that of European colonizers who often encounered indigenous cultural practices that were quite sophisticated but that were so different from European cultures that they were not recognized for what they were.

The treatment of the douen by the humans on New Half-Way Tree clearly echoes the legacy of racism in the United States, and the fact that the members of this alien species are regarded by the humans through virtually the same system of stereotypes as African Americans in US history (they are considered to all look alike and to be inveterate thieves and liars, childlike and irresponsible) can be taken as a reminder of the portability of such stereotypes, which have been applied to so many different non-European cultures in Earth history. As a result, it is clear that these stereotypes are derived not from the characteristics of those being described but from the fantasies and desires of those doing the describing. Hopkinson also reminds her readers that colonialism on Earth serves as a precedent for the colonization of Toussaint, if under very different conditions. Thus, Ben, the gardener who programs Tan-Tan's garden on Toussaint, gives the girl a Carnival hat in the shape of the spaceship that brought her people to Toussaint, reminding her that "Long time, that hat woulda be make in the shape of a sea ship, not a rocket ship, and them black people inside woulda been lying pack-up head to toe in they own shit, with chains round them ankles, Let the child remember how black people make this crossing as free people this time" (*Midnight Robber*, 21). That the people of New Half-Way Tree treat the douen much as their own slave ancestors had been treated in Africa and the Caribbean serves as a stern reminder of the tendency of humans to treat each other in such ways, a notion that is reminiscent of Octavia Butler's contention in the "Xenogenesis" trilogy that humans have a natural tendency toward hierarchical behavior.

That the society of Toussaint seems far less hierarchical than that of New Half-Way Tree suggests that sufficiently advanced technology, by creating enough wealth to go around without constant competition, can go a long way toward reducing this hierarchical tendency. Then again, the society of Toussaint is relatively homogeneous in terms of race and culture. Vestigial forms of hierarchy based on gender and class pervade even the society of Toussaint, but, by placing the most severe forms of hierarchization on New Half-Way Tree based on the distinctive racial difference between human and douen, Hopkinson reminds us of the way in which our hierarchical inclinations tend to be exaggerated and exacerbated by our difficulty in accepting genuine difference, whether it be cultural or biological.

Tan-Tan works hard to learn the ways of the douen and their language, aided in particular by Abitefa, daughter of Chichibud and Benta, who becomes her close friend. Although Tan-Tan never feels completely at ease at the Daddy Tree, her adoptive family treats her far better than any member of her biological family, either on Toussaint or on New Half-Way Tree. When she realizes that her final rape by Antonio has left her pregnant, she convinces Abitefa to take her to a nearby human town so that she can seek an abortion. Tan-Tan learns that the rough frontier town has no doctor, but meanwhile becomes involved in a fracas in the street, during which she employs as a verbal weapon the playful and subversive rhetoric of the Robber Queen (a version of the Midnight Robber, a key Carnival character with which she had become familiar while on Toussaint). From this point forward, Tan-Tan begins to appear more and more in the town in the guise of the Robber Queen, becoming a local legend. This regendering of the Midnight Robber, a traditionally male, piratical figure, allows Tan-Tan to don a mask that affirms her own essential being and mend her damaged self-image ("Tan-Tan's Exile," 11). In addition, it contributes to the depiction of gender as a potential locus of both oppression and subversion.

Tan-Tan's exploits attract widespread attention, allowing Antonio's wife and Tan-Tan's stepmother, Janisette, to track her to the douen's Daddy Tree. Enraged by Antonio's murder and jealous of Antonio's feelings for his daughter, Janisette has come to avenge his death. She is driven away, but in order to protect the secrets of their way of life, the douen destroy the Daddy Tree and prepare to move to a new home. Abitefa and Tan-Tan, however, are cast out of the community in retribution for bringing this misfortune upon it. The two set out on their own, visiting a number of human settlements, many of which present a stark contrast to the ostensible democratization of Toussaint's communities. At one point, Tan-Tan is astonished to learn that a woman she finds working in a cane field (that iconic locus of enforced labor in the Caribbean) has a feared overseer that she refers to as "Boss," a term Tan-Tan had previously only heard used by machine servants in reference to their human bosses. Further, Tan-Tan learns that the woman has little choice but to work this way in order to survive and that she is in fact indentured to her boss. That the inhabitants of New Half-Way Tree have failed to learn from the lessons of their own history is a crucial point made by *Midnight Robber*, which suggests that the availability of the seemingly simple hierarchical distinction between human and douen seems to have reactivated an impulse toward domination of others that had remained latent in the relatively easy living conditions of Toussaint.

Finally, Tan-Tan and Abitefa reach Sweet Pone Town, a relatively civilized settlement to which she and her sweetheart Melonhead had dreamed of running away. The skills practiced by the pedicab runners, disdained by most people on Toussaint as "back-break," are the primary reason that the town flourishes. Tan-Tan again meets Melonhead, who is working in the town as a tailor; he makes her a fine Robber Queen costume for the upcoming Carnival to be celebrated in the town. As Tan-Tan is getting into her performance, Janisette arrives in an armored vehicle and the two become involved in a carnivalesque contest of rhetoric, which Tan-Tan wins by chanting the entire story of her rape by Antonio and her killing of him in self defense, forcing Janisette to back down by using words as weapons. The Carnival's unifying spirit allows Tan-Tan to heal her own fragmented identity in the guise of Robber Queen, but as Bill Clemente observes, the celebration leaves out the douen and their conflict with the colonists, and the novel ends shortly thereafter with Tan-Tan still very much an exile to human communities ("Tan-Tan's Exile," 22–23). Nevertheless, there are utopian elements in the close relationship between Tan-tan and Chichibud, Benta, and Abitefa, which suggest that human and douen can at least achieve mutual respect, if not a hybrid society that incorporates elements of both cultures.

Soon after Carnival, Tan-Tan gives birth to a son, whom she names Tubman, after the famous operator of the Underground Railroad, Harriet Tubman. Having inherited nanomites from his mother's blood that allow him to become a sort of living interface with Granny Nanny, Tubman is able to communicate in a uniquely organic way with the artificial intelligence, even across dimensions and without an earbud. A posthuman of the African diaspora, he thus brings important new utopian possibilities to New Half-Way Tree, which had hitherto been denied any communication with Granny Nanny.

Distinctive not only for its seamless integration of elements of Afro-Caribbean culture and science fiction, *Midnight Robber* is also an experimentation in form, as evidenced by the insertion of Caribbean-inflected folktales (which turn out to be stories that an eshu is telling for the benefit of Tubman) between sections of the main narrative. These tales, associated with Anansi, the trickster-spider hero of West African and Caribbean cultures, are representative of the oral tradition in these cultures; they are also presumed to be unreliable by their listeners. As Enteen notes, by invoking Anansi and his web (of which Granny Nanny is a part), the eshu informs the reader that meaning will be multiple, competing, and contradictory ("On the Receiving", 270), a technique that increases the cognitive estrangement the reader experiences. By incorporating these "alien" (to many Western readers) elements, Hopkinson gives voice to the alien while at the same time providing a narrative that in so many ways fits comfortably within the expectations of Western readers. That Hopkinson's background is also Canadian only serves to remind Western readers that the simple polar oppositions of Us vs. Them that are so central to the rhetoric of colonialism simply do not apply in the current era of globalization. With *Midnight Robber*, Hopkinson reminds us that the world includes a variety of cultures based on a variety of different worldviews and systems of values, no single one of which can be taken to constitute a standard against which all others should be judged. She also reminds us that the different cultures of our planet do have much in common, especially when compared to the vast biological and cultural differences we might expect to find some day on other planets or even in different planes of reality.

China Miéville, *Perdido Street Station* (2000)

China Miéville's *Perdido Street Station* is a stunningly original work that has stimulated a great deal of conversation about its relationship to the genre of science fiction, while propelling its author to the very forefront of the British Boom. The book certainly includes numerous elements that clearly belong to the realm of science fiction, but it also borrows ingredients from the traditions of fantasy and horror fiction, drawing upon a broad array of predecessor texts to produce a rich multigeneric and intertextual stew. *Perdido Street Station* is also the first book in an important trilogy – which includes *The Scar* (2002) and *Iron Council* (2004) – all of which is set in the world of Bas-Lag, a rich fictional creation that has much in common with the imaginary worlds of fantasy fiction (such as Tolkien's Middle Earth) but that is actually more reminiscent of the alien planets and cultures often featured in science fiction, largely through the sheer force of concrete details supplied by Miéville concerning life on Bas-Lag, which does indeed seem to be a planet, and even one that (as we learn in *The Scar*) has been visited by invaders from outer space, something unimaginable in Middle Earth. As Carl Freedman puts it, noting the level of detail supplied by Miéville, "In logical rigor and consistency, in almost endlessly inventive detail, and in general three-dimensional solidity, Bas-Lag is one of the most fully achieved imaginary worlds ever created" (*Critical*, 236).

The generic complexity of *Perdido Street Station* is particularly appropriate because it reinforces the content of the book, which deals extensively with questions of multiplicity and hybridity of various kinds. Of course, the generic hybridity of the book, along with its other images of boundary-crossing plurality, is typical of works of postmodernist literature. However, the images of hybridity and multiplicity that are so central to *Perdido Street Station* are distinctive in the complex way they are combined with Miéville's dazzlingly inventive and detailed imagining of an alternative world, which itself is given a special flavor by the author's particular (socialist) political sensibility.

Miéville's most impressive creation within *Perdido Street Station* may be the city-state of New Crobuzon itself, a complex multicultural hybrid that combines numerous different styles of architecture and includes a number of distinctive neighborhoods inhabited by several different sentient species, though humans appear to be the dominant species. Yet, despite this diversity, the society of New Crobuzon is clearly depicted by Miéville as an interlinked whole, each aspect intricately interrelated with every other. Indeed, the city itself is a sort of vast network, with Perdido Street Station itself at the hub. New Crobuzon is an ancient city, now somewhat in decline, and indeed the book is filled with images of the city's squalor and decay. New Crobuzon, we learn, "was a huge plague pit, a morbific city. Parasites, infection and rumour were uncontainable" (*Perdido*, 9). It is also a city ruled by an oppressive government reminiscent of the tradition of dystopian fiction. Nevertheless, the sprawling city throbs with life and retains a powerful vitality; as Joan Gordon (2003) argues, it is probably better regarded as a heterotopia, in the mode discussed by Foucault, than as a dystopia. Though Miéville's vision of the city is enriched with numerous fantasy elements, New Crobuzon seems (within the rules that Miéville has set for his imaginary world) a believable living city, portrayed with a depth and detail (warts and all) that go far beyond the two-dimensional creations typical of more conventional fantasy fiction. In addition, *Perdido Street Station* is entirely free of the sentimental nostalgia for a lost (often medieval) past of the kind often found in fantasy fiction.

The main plot of *Perdido Street Station* seems taken primarily from the genre of horror fiction and entails the efforts of the city to fight off the attacks of a group of "slake moths," strange, surreal creatures that exist only partly in our physical dimension and that take their sustenance by devouring the minds of their sentient victims, leaving them alive but completely lacking in consciousness. When the slake moths feed, they first disable their victims by mesmerizing them with the movements of their huge, flickering, intricately patterned, multicolored wings, causing the victims to focus their entire minds on the wings and thus become unable to think of anything else or take any action to oppose the moths. After feeding, they excrete a nonmaterial substance that causes nightmares in any sentient creature with whom they come into contact, stimulating brain activity and thus producing richer material on which the slake moths can subsequently feed, thus producing more nightmare-inducing excrement, and so on.

The slake moths thus live within a vicious circle in which they produce more and more, but also devour more and more, making them virtually unstoppable, but also making their existence highly unstable. Left unchecked, they would presumably devour all of the sentient minds on the planet of Bas-Lag, then die of starvation. They are, in this sense, perfect metaphors for capitalism itself, a highly productive system that nevertheless must continually expand in both production and consumption in order to remain healthy. Meanwhile, the slake moths are essentially mental vampires, updating Marx's famous metaphorical description of capitalists as vampires who feed on the blood of workers to encompass contemporary information-age capitalism, in which mental work becomes an increasingly large part of the capitalist economy. In addition, the way the slake moths immobilize their victims can be read as a metaphor for the ways bourgeois ideology mesmerizes individuals into voluntary obedience through convincing them to accept the bourgeois worldview as their own, a phenomenon noted by such Marxist theorists as Antonio Gramsci and Louis Althusser. As Steve Shaviro (2002) puts it, the moths' "unrestrained predation is a nightmare of surplus-appropriation gone mad . . . The slake-moths do not represent an economy foreign to New Crobuzon: they are just capitalism with an (appropriately) inhuman face" ("Capitalist Monsters," 288).

The slake moths thus serve as an excellent illustration of the way even Miéville's most seemingly fantastic motifs can be read allegorically, producing powerful real-world political implications, though some of these implications are more obvious than others. Perhaps the most obvious allegorical aspect of New Crobuzon is the presence in the city of multiple sentient species, which serves in a fairly transparent way as a commentary on racism in real-world societies. Humans, led by Mayor Bentham Rudgutter, dominate New Crobuzon's authoritarian government and are prominent in areas such as business and science as well, just as the Western societies of our own world are dominated by whites but include substantial presences of other races as well.

As in our own world, relations between the different "races" of New Crobuzon are often tense, informed by considerable prejudice, stereotyping, and inequality. We are introduced to the multispecies character of New Crobuzon in the very first chapter of the novel, which features a sexual liaison between a human scientist, Isaac Dan der Grimnebulin, and his lover, the sculptor Lin. In a classic case of cognitive estrangement, it gradually becomes clear during the chapter that Lin is not human. She is, in fact, a khepri, one of the numerous "Xenian" (nonhuman sentient) species of New Crobuzon. Lin is hairless, with red skin. Otherwise, her body is humanoid, but topped by a head that looks like a "huge, iridescent scarab" (10). On the other hand, Lin is highly sensitive about the anthrocentric nature of such descriptions, and she once told Isaac that humans look to her like they have khepri bodies, topped by the heads of shaved apes.

To add a further note of species difference, khepri males lack the humanoid bodies of the females and are essentially little more than mindless insects, looking very much like the heads of the females. In short, the khepri are *not* simply human bodies with insect heads attached, they are an entirely different species, as are the other sentient species of New Crobuzon. These include the froglike amphibian vodyanoi, who have the power to control water and mold it into different shapes; the towering cactacae, powerful plant people with cactus-like spines, valued as laborers and soldiers because of their size, strength, and toughness; and the fiercely individualistic garuda, who have humanoid bodies, but are covered with feathers and have large, birdlike wings that make them powerful fliers.

Though there is insufficient space even in a long novel such as *Perdido Street Station* (or even in the entire "Bas-Lag" trilogy) to fill in all the details, Miéville provides each of these sentient species (and the additional sentient species that inhabit the rest of Bas-Lag) with their own complex histories, cultures, and languages, giving them a sense of material reality that makes them much more like the aliens of science fiction than the fanciful creatures – such as Tolkien's hobbits, elves, and dwarves – that often inhabit fantasy fiction. The concreteness of the backgrounds of the Xenian species of Bas-Lag also helps to establish the notion that they are genuinely Other, genuinely different from human beings (and not simply modified humans), but nevertheless worthy of respect as intelligent beings.

As if to reinforce this point, Miéville provides readers with images of beings who *are* modified humans. One of the city's most common punishments for criminal behavior is the process of "remaking," in which a combination of surgery and thaumaturgy (a sort of technological version of magic) is used to make permanent modifications to the subjects' bodies, marking them as delinquents and outcasts from society. The alterations involved in remaking usually involve the addition of alien parts, either biological or mechanical. In the latter case, the Remade qualify as cyborgs, placing them very much in the realm of science fiction; in either case the Remade are hybrids, bearing body parts that are foreign to them.

Remades are treated almost as a separate race, looked upon with suspicion and disgust. As part of their punishment, they are often employed essentially as slave labor, usually doing difficult or distasteful tasks that humans shun. Remaking as a punishment is reserved primarily for humans, though Xenians are occasionally remade. Sometimes, the modifications are functional, adding to the individual's physical capabilities so that he or she can be employed to perform difficult tasks. These "beneficial" modifications are sometimes made even to animals, while humans and Xenians sometimes undergo them voluntarily, rather than as punishment. More often than not, however, remaking only serves to make work more difficult or painful.

The lowly Remade of *Perdido Street Station* have a budding class consciousness and are beginning to resist the oppression to which they are subject. The "fReemade" constitute a group of Remade who have rebelled. In New Crobuzon itself, the fReemade are largely a secret society, led by the near-legendary outlaw Jack Half-a-Prayer. They are regarded as renegades and terrorists in the popular mind, though some regard them as heroes. On the floating city of Armada, in *The Scar*, all of the Remade are free and enjoy equal rights; in *Iron Council* we learn that groups of escaped Remades have established their own fReemade societies outside of New Crobuzon, while Remade workers play a key role in one of the political revolutions that is central to that book.

The political activities of the Remade give their representation a dimension that is usually lacking in the grotesque creatures that often inhabit fantasy fiction. Miéville adds other dimensions that are hard to imagine in Tolkienesque fantasy as well, as in his inclusion in *Perdido Street Station* of an extended description of a strike by Vodyanoi dockworkers. The striking Vodyanoi are eventually joined by a number of human workers as well, demonstrating the importance of working-class solidarity and also calling attention to the way workers must resist attempts of their bosses to divide them along "racial" lines, a strategy that has often been employed in the capitalist societies of our own world. Ultimately, the strike is put down, brutally and violently, by Rudgutter's militia. This motif provides the most vivid reminder of the oppressive nature of New Crobuzon society, in which striking workers have sometimes been attacked by the forces of the official military, as when President Calvin Coolidge called in the army in 1921 to help quell a rebellion by the coal miners of Blair Mountain, West Virginia.

In addition to the human-Vodyanoi solidarity displayed during the dockworkers' strike, Miéville makes it clear that, as intelligent beings, all of the different sentient species of Bas-Lag share a great deal of common ground. For example, the mind-eating slake moths can feast equally well on the minds of any of these species, indicating that the textures of their minds are alike in certain fundamental ways. In addition, the various sentient species that inhabit New Crobuzon are made to appear more similar because of the vastly larger difference between any of them and the more alien species that appear in *Perdido Street Station*, including the slake moths and the strange Weaver, a large spiderlike being that lives largely in another dimension of reality and whose mind operates according to a logic that is virtually indecipherable to the more conventional inhabitants of New Crobuzon. This strangeness also makes the Weaver's mind indigestible to the slake moths. Perhaps the most bizarre of all of Miéville's creatures in *Perdido Street Station* are the handlingers, which are disembodied hands (perhaps possessed by the spirits of the spiteful dead) that parasitically attach themselves to hosts, whose minds they then control.

The loving relationship between Lin and Isaac demonstrates the possibility of genuine intersubjective contact between species, though the fact that they have to keep their relationship secret to avoid persecution serves as a reminder of the high level of interspecies bigotry that exists within the society of New Crobuzon. This bigotry is so severe that it leads to the virtual confinement of each Xenian species within a ghetto of its own. In addition, the city seems to have been established for nearly two thousand years, but the university with which Isaac is loosely affiliated has admitted Xenian degree candidates only within the last twenty years. Indeed, Xenians in general have only been granted even the most basic rights via the relatively recent "Sapience Bill" that acknowledged their status as intelligent beings. Such motifs serve in a fairly straightforward way as an allegorical commentary on the racism that still exists in our own world, however cosmopolitan it might have become. Meanwhile, interspecies prejudice in New Crobuzon is clearly depicted as cruel, unjust, and unfounded, even though it involves literally different species with distinctly different biologies. Thus, in comparison, human racism in our world appears particularly foolish, given that it places so much emphasis on differences that are relatively minor – or even non-existent.

Despite the presence of these multiple sentient species, the extensive use of thaumaturgy, and numerous other inventive touches that take New Crobuzon beyond anything found in our own world, the city is first and foremost reminiscent of a somewhat Dickensian, nineteenth-century London, with a technology roughly equivalent to that of Industrial Revolution. In this sense, *Perdido Street Station* shares much with the subgenre of "steampunk" science fiction. However, the technology of the city includes elements that go substantially beyond that available to our own nineteenth-century Europe. For one thing, the technology of New Crobuzon depends substantially upon "thaumaturgy," traditionally a branch of magic concerned with producing practical effects in the material world, though here thaumaturgy is more a form of skillful engineering than genuine magic, enabled by the special physical laws that apply in the world of *Perdido Street Station*. While the details are a bit sketchy, New Crobuzon also appears to have access to certain elements of more advanced traditional technology, left over from earlier times in which the general level of technology in the city was apparently higher. For example, at the time of the events of *Perdido Street Station*, one of the features of the city's skyline is the "cloudtower," which contains an aeromorphic engine that was once used to control the weather, but has not functioned for centuries and which the city now lacks the technological know-how to repair.

Among other things, New Crobuzon has access to seemingly primitive computer technology, its computers consisting of difference engines powered by steam-driven pistons. Yet this computer technology is powerful enough to allow for the development of artificial intelligence within the book, spread by a virus that affects one after another of the city's computer-controlled "constructs," which are perhaps the central examples of science fiction technology in *Perdido Street Station*. Particularly important here is the Construct Council, a complex *bricolage* construction of leftover machinery that has gathered together to form a single entity, driven by an intelligence that arose by chance through the impact of a random virus on an initial construct that had been dumped in Griss Twist, an area of urban decay in New Crobuzon that consists primarily of garbage dumps and abandoned factories. Miéville's description makes clear the hybrid nature of this mechanical conglomeration: "The body of the creature was a tangled, welded lump of congealed circuitry and engineering. All kinds of engines were embedded in that huge trunk. A massive proliferation of wires and tubes of metal and thick rubber spewed from valves and outputs in its body and limbs, snaking off in all directions in the wasteland" (449). The Construct Council grows in power and ambition as it adds the networked computational abilities of a growing number of component constructs, gaining more and more complexity and computing power as it spreads its influence through the city's constructs via the proliferation of the straight-forward science fictional motif of a computer virus. In fact, the Construct Council – in the tradition of dangerous computers such as the HAL 9000 in the film *2001: A Space Odyssey* (1968) – threatens to engulf the entire city, taking power from the humans who currently rule.

The biological equivalent in *Perdido Street Station* of the Construct Council is Mr. Motley, the criminal kingpin whose body is a veritable catalog of mismatched parts, assembled via a means that is left mysterious in the text. Lin, hired to do a sculpture of Motley, is almost overcome by his strangeness: "Scraps of skin and fur and feathers swung as he moved; tiny limbs clutched; eyes rolled from obscure niches; antlers and protrusions of bone jutted precariously; feelers twitched and mouths glistened. . . . Scales gleamed. Fins quivered. Wings fluttered brokenly. Insect claws folded and unfolded" (*Perdido*, 42).

Ultimately, after the official militia fails entirely in its attempts to battle the slake moths that ravage New Crobuzon, the moths are defeated by a ragtag alliance that includes the Weaver and the Construct Council, as well as humans, an outcast garuda, and the fReemade leader Jack Half-a-Prayer. The book thus ends with still another reminder of the importance of solidarity among groups with seemingly diverse interests. Ultimately, in fact, while many aspects of *Perdido Street Station* can be read as celebrations of hybridity and diversity, neither is treated as an absolute good in itself, as the sinister figure of Motley and the potentially sinister implications of the Construct Council demonstrate. Rather than celebrating multiplicity in the manner generally associated with postmodernism, *Perdido Street Station* ultimately demonstrates the value of the socialist principle of unity within diversity, suggesting that diversity in itself is not automatically emancipatory. For Miéville, diversity for the sake of diversity, diversity without unity, can be divisive and crippling, thus enabling rather than opposing oppression.

Ian McDonald, *River of Gods* (2005)

Ian McDonald's *River of Gods* is a sprawling, complex, and panoramic novel that employs familiar science fiction motifs – notably those associated with cyberpunk – in its depiction of a future India torn by tensions between the conservative pull of tradition and religion and the equally strong pull of innovation and technological modernization. Long considered an exotic locale by Western readers, India provides an ideal setting for the kind of cognitive estrangement that is central to the effect of science fiction, though McDonald subverts the long tradition of British fiction that treats the subcontinent as a mysterious and exotic backdrop in which Western heroes can have glamorous adventures. Set in the year 2047, which marks the one-hundredth anniversary of India's independence from British colonial rule (and thus calls attention to the legacy of that rule), the novel is a compelling dramatization of postcolonial hybridity, mixing tradition with technology in startling ways. *River of Gods* also blurs the boundaries between reality and simulation, posing challenging questions about the nature of highly advanced artificial intelligences that far outstrip the intellectual abilities of humans.

Perhaps in an attempt to capture the richness, complexity, and diversity of India itself, McDonald populates the novel with numerous characters and multiple plots. Extending the 1947 partition of British India into post-independence India and Pakistan, 2047 India is fractured into twelve different nations, with much of the action of the novel centered in the state of Bharat and especially in its capital city of Varanasi. Like most of India, Bharat has become a center for cutting-edge computer technologies, a straightforward projection of trends already underway in India when the book was written. Home of the enormously popular simulated soap opera *Town and Country*, in which computer-generated simulations of actors play virtual-reality roles, Varanasi is also home to advanced artificial intelligences (called "aeais") that are politically controversial. In light of projections that aeais would soon surpass humans intellectually, the United States (still the leading global power) has instituted limitations on the development of artificial intelligences to "Generation Two," which is intended to prevent them from evolving to a point where, in "Generation Three," they vastly outstrip human intelligence and thus might be able to seize control of the planet from their makers. In other words, the US government fears the possibility of technological singularity. Realizing that it would do no good to impose this limit in the US alone, the Americans use their considerable international clout to influence other countries to impose these restrictions as well. While Bharat has an official governmental arm devoted to exterminating rogue aeais (known colloquially as the "Krishna cops)," the few Generation Three aeais already in existence manage to find sanctuary there. Indeed, a matter-of-fact acceptance of the supernatural that is woven into the texture of Indian culture suggests that Generation Three aeais, who are so far advanced as to seem like gods to a number of the characters, are ideally suited to existence in technologically sophisticated Bharat. In a state where there are sanctuaries for "cyberpets," or robot animals, run by followers of Jainism (a minority religion whose primary tenet is that everything is alive and in possession of a soul) and where aeais beyond Generation Two are accorded a status reserved for living, sentient creatures or even deities in the Hindu pantheon (whose names the Generation Three aeais take for themselves), it appears to be possible for technology to coexist with traditional belief systems rather than compromising them. However, the tensions between the two constantly threaten this tenuous balance, as does the official response to illegal aeais.

For Krishna cop Mr. Nandha, a decorous Hindu who sees illegal aeais as a threat to his way of life, there is no question of recognizing their right to exist. Sent out to "excommunicate" rogue aeais, often after they have caused human deaths in their rush to escape detection, the depiction of Nandha recalls Philip K. Dick's bounty hunter Rick Deckard in *Do Androids Dream of Electric Sheep?*, whose job it is to "retire" androids that have escaped from a Mars colony and attempt to blend in among humans on Earth. Like the rogue aeais, the androids are given an "illegal" status, simply for being present on Earth. Nandha employs other aeais to flush the illegal aeais out into the open, where he can then use a gun that dispenses a powerful electromagnetic pulse to annihilate his prey. Nandha's own hunter aeais have Hindu deities as avatars, with "Kali the Disrupter" being the most potent of these. Despite his association of aeais with the Hindu pantheon, however, Nandha accords illegal aeais no special status as sentient creatures whose "lives" should be revered. In fact, as he explains to his wife Parvati, who feels neglected due to his zeal for his work, he sees them as "inhuman monsters" that carry the seeds of his society's destruction. He equates them with the "Brahmins," genetically engineered "perfect" children, who are designed to be free of the diseases that befall most humans, and who live twice as long as humans but age half as fast. Both illegal aeais and Brahmins, Nandha believes, threaten to make humans redundant.

With their genetic advantages, the Brahmins represent a new caste that will change the face of India – evidence that, as the surgeon Nanak puts it, "we have reached a stage where wealth can change evolution" (*River of Gods*, 295). Like those who create the Brahmins, Nanak also dabbles in genetics, enabling humans who choose so to become "nutes" through extensive surgical, chemical, and genetic modifications that render them entirely genderless but able to experience sexual passion (and other emotions) at will, thanks to the implants that have been placed in their bodies. Unlike the Brahmins, who are both revered and feared, nutes are much despised in traditionalist circles, a fact of life that the nute Tal, a young designer for *Town and Country*, has come to accept. Tal, however, inadvertently becomes involved with Shaheen Badoor Khan, a top advisor to the Bharati Prime Minister Sajida Rana and the only major Muslim character in the book. Khan begins the novel by advising Rana with diplomatic aplomb during the escalation of tensions between Bharat and neighboring Awadh, which is largely due to competition over increasingly sparse water supplies in the light of a seemingly endless drought that has ravaged the subcontinent. However, Khan's secret sexual attraction to nutes is considered such a deviancy that when he is caught on camera with Tal, it causes a crisis for Rana's government that ultimately ends in the prime minister's assassination – all of which is played out against the confrontation between Awadh and Bharat. Behind Rana and Khan's downfall is the mysterious N. K. Jivanjee, a powerful rabble-rouser who seems bent on stirring the population of Bharat against both Awadh and their own government. Working with Jivanjee to destroy Khan is Khan's own wife, a woman educated as a lawyer, who simmers with resentment under the "golden purdah," or the seclusion of women from the workplace and public life. Aside from the prime minister, women hold few positions of power in Bharat; after twenty-five years of fetal selection among the middle classes, men outnumber women four to one, and most educated women are encouraged to marry into money and prestige rather than compete with men for the available professional jobs. Genetic engineering, then, has not only enabled the creation of a new caste, but it has also reversed the liberation from traditional gender roles that Indian women began to experience in the twentieth century.

As it turns out, Jivanjee is a computer simulation of a Generation Three aeai – as, for that matter, is the entire production of *Town and Country*. The aeai attempts a coup of the Bharati government that is ultimately unsuccessful, but it manipulates humans with relative ease, and much of the texture of the novel involves the gradual convergence of these various characters. Jivanjee employs the young journalist Najia Askarzadah (whose mixed Swedish and Afghan heritage suggests the ongoing globalization of culture in the twenty-first century) to break the story involving Khan and Tal; early in the novel, she interviews *Town and Country* star Lal Darfan, a manifestation of the same Generation Three aeai that generates Jivanjee, and who has a complete virtual reality backstory. These actors are objects of intense interest on the part of their many fans, who eagerly await news of the latest developments in their simulated personal lives. Askarzadah spars with Darfan during the interview about the "reality" of his celebrity status, but Darfan observes that it is the adoring public that makes his celebrity real. Parvati Nandha, for example, when chided by her gardener and would-be lover, Krishan, for talking about the actors as if they were real people, responds that she is well aware that they are only simulations, but points out that "Celebrity has never been about what's real. But it's nice to pretend. It's like having another story on top of *Town and Country*, but one that's much more like the way we live" (260). This suggestion that the virtual nature of celebrity in the future is not all that different from celebrity in our own present is only one of many ways *River of Gods* blurs the boundary between reality and simulation. Indeed, if Jean Baudrillard's vision of hyperreality, in which such distinctions no longer have meaning, was applicable to the late-twentieth-century postmodern society he was describing, it seems all the more so in the middle of the twenty-first century. As Askarzadah observes, "everything's a version" (*River of Gods*, 44), a recognition of the dominance of the simulacrum in postmodern media culture.

Another example of this breakdown between reality and simulation in *River of Gods* is "Alterre," a computer-generated alternative Earth in which time is accelerated in order to study evolution by modeling the effects of various phenomena on the evolutionary development of a variety of species. Alterre is the subject of much of American scientist Lisa Durnau's research, a project that she worked on very closely with leading expert on virtual reality Thomas Lull before he dropped out of sight and moved to India after a series of personal problems. In working with such simulated worlds, Durnau develops the hypothesis that the relationship between our Earth and Alterre is not a simple hierarchical one between reality and simulation. Instead, she wonders if simulated "virtual" worlds might simply be parallel universes whose reality is just as substantial as our own.

Durnau, as the book begins, is conscripted by the US government to help them deal with an alien artifact that has been discovered in space. She is sent to the artifact and then on to Awadh, where she is to seek Lull, who emerges as a key to the puzzle of the artifact. In the meantime, Lull travels to Varanasi with a young girl, Ajmer Rao ("Aj"), who enlists his aid in her effort to find her natural parents – and who also seems to have access to inexplicable amounts of information (that she ascribes to "the gods") about Lull and many other things. Lull realizes that Aj's foster parents were researchers in artificial intelligence, and ultimately learns that she is, in fact, a human–computer hybrid created by surgically modifying the brain of a seriously retarded girl and then downloading a Generation Three aeai into it. That surgery, meanwhile, was performed by Nanak, who also did the work to transform Tal into a nute. Nandha suspects that Aj is in fact an aeai, eventually hunting down and killing her. However, artificial intelligences are distributed entities, not localizable in a single spot. Killing Aj does not exterminate the aeai, though it does kill the strategy of the remaining Generation Three aeais to comprehend and communicate with humans, whom they regard as their gods. As Lull puts it, Aj is the aeais' "first and last ambassador to humanity" (*River of Gods*, 510). With Aj's murder, it finally becomes clear to them that it is not possible to make peace with humans, who are determined to drive them to extinction.

The characterization of the aeais, which explicitly identify with Hindu deities, is reminiscent of William Gibson's depiction of AIs in his "Sprawl" trilogy, with the singular god-like entity of the matrix in *Neuromancer* giving way to smaller, multiple gods that adopt the names of voodoo deities in *Count Zero*. McDonald's aeais are distinctive for their ability to repeatedly copy themselves, suggesting that it is indeed possible for one to be in two places at the same time and thus calling into question assumptions about subjectivity and identity that humans take for granted – as well as threatening to displace the centrality of the human subject. The digital reproduction of humans (in the form of personality constructs) is a major motif in cyberpunk and posthuman sf; *River of Gods*, however, focuses on the truly "alien" aspect of the aeais' status as distributed entities with no "original" self, and perhaps the source of their inability to understand humans, despite the aeais' longing for connection.

The second part of the strategy that the Generation Three aeais have devised to ensure their survival is to find a sanctuary where humans cannot follow them. To that end, they invest in the Ray Power Corporation, a leading Indian company whose research division is headed by Vishram Ray, a former stand-up comedian and prodigal son. Ray, who knows very little about the research division before he is put in charge of it by his father (who leaves his business to seek truth as a holy man), learns that the scientists have developed a method for tapping into parallel universes, hoping essentially to download energy from another universe into ours, thus producing virtually limitless inexpensive power. As Ray learns about "zero point" power, he begins to see the parallels between the Hindu universe and the quantum universe, observing that the latter is as "capricious and uncertain and unknowable" (*River of Gods*, 183) as the former. It is with the parallel universe created by zero point power that the aeais decide to take their chances, escaping into a place where they will not be persecuted by humans. In that universe, time runs backward and at one hundred times the speed of time in our universe, so the escaped aeais quickly travel into the distant past, whence they have sent as a tribute to their gods the alien artifact, which contains, in coded form, the sum of all their knowledge. The artifact also displays the faces of Lull, Durnau, Aj, and Nandha, a visible tribute to their lost gods. As the book ends, Durnau begins the complex task of decoding the artifact.

The interweaving of these various plot strands is deftly handled in *River of Gods*, and McDonald convincingly elaborates a future India that has undergone dramatic changes and yet has in many ways stayed very much the same – much as one could say of India in relation to its experience with British colonialism. McDonald's detailed depiction of the mixture of the old and the new that is 2047 India is part of what makes *River of Gods* an effective work of science fiction. A dramatization of the notion of post-colonial hybridity as discussed by theorists such as Homi Bhabha, it also suggests that hybridity is an element of Indian culture even apart from any Western influence and that the East–West hybridity of India can be expected to grow in the coming decades, even with colonialism *per se* in the increasingly distant past.

McDonald takes a number of satirical shots at American global hegemony in the twenty-first century. For one thing, American-dominated multinational corporations are depicted as voracious giants, roaming the globe and devouring anything that comes into their path – or at least anything that might increase corporate profits. That this includes the acquisition of technologies that might not be strictly legal, even from an American point of view, merely indicates the extent to which such corporations are concerned more with greed than ethics. Meanwhile, that American law in the 2047 includes a number of provisions that might limit the growth of highly profitable technologies (such as artificial intelligence and a variety of forms of genetic engineering) is clearly attributed in the book to an ongoing American religiosity – which forces the American population to recoil from certain modes of scientific research that might challenge their religious beliefs, but merely forces American corporations to find alternative routes to the utilization of these technologies. We find, for example, that the floating research facility/hospital run by Nanak is actually owned by White Eagle Holdings, "a deeply respectable fund management company based in Omaha, Nebraska, specialising in pension plans for healthcare workers." Moreover, the company also owns "several floating factories in Patna that specialise in those medical services the Bible-believing voters of the mid-West vehemently deny their fellow-countrymen" (*River of Gods*, 287).

If American corporations often operate by subterfuge in *River of Gods*, the American government is less subtle. Indeed, the interventionist policies of the second Bush administration seem to have been extended to 2047, as the Americans routinely deploy hyper-advanced military technologies as a means of flexing their muscles around the globe. Even before war actually breaks out between Awadh and Bharat, for example, Varanasi is attacked by automated American killing machines, apparently as a sign of things to come if the Bharatis continue to defy American power. In a trend obviously extrapolated from recent real-world developments such as the remote-controlled devastation of Iraq in 2003, we are told that the Americans "fight in the modern manner, without a single soldier leaving home, without a single body bag. They kill from continents away" (*River of Gods*, 88).

With its combination of high technology, political intrigue, and rich exploration of Indian culture, *River of Gods* successfully blends the social, political, and economic concerns of the postcolonial setting of India with the cognitive estrangement unique to science fiction. What is striking about McDonald's vision of the future is not how much it differs from our own present, but rather how – despite enormous advances in science and technology – it is only too familiar. Similar to its cyberpunk forebears in this respect, the novel also interrogates the boundaries between reality and simulation and calls into question the centrality of the human subject. However, its emphasis on the struggles of identity and future possibilities of the postcolonial world distinguish it as a post-cyberpunk work of a unique and innovative cast.

Glossary

alien In science fiction, an alien is generally a member of a nonhuman species originating from somewhere other than the Earth. Such aliens are also known as "extraterrestrials." In some cases, aliens are biologically human and differ from humans on Earth only in their different cultural backgrounds. Science fiction aliens typically dramatize questions of otherness and difference on Earth; their very difference from humans on Earth serves as a key source of **cognitive estrangement** in sf, either because of the fresh perspectives they bring to bear on Earth culture or because their different cultures and biologies cause humans to view their own world differently.

alien invasion A type of science fiction narrative in which the Earth is invaded by aliens, usually for purposes of conquest and colonization. The invaders typically come from outer space (Mars is a classic origination point), though there are variants in which the invaders come from other dimensions, other times, or even exotic locations on the Earth, such as beneath the oceans. Invading aliens are typically sinister, and alien invasion narratives often have paranoid or xenophobic qualities. In some cases, however, the invaders are benevolent and arrive with the purpose of helping humanity to overcome some important obstacle, such as its own self-destructive tendencies. As in the early case of H. G. Wells's *The War of the Worlds* (1898), alien invasion narratives can often be used to satirize aggression invasions (such as colonial conquest) in our own history.

alternate history A type of science fiction narrative (also known as the "alternative history" narrative) in which some major moment of the historical past (the "point of divergence") is imagined as having occurred differently, leading to an exploration of the ramifications of that change in history from that point forward. The differences between this new history and the "real" one with which readers are already familiar creates a source of cognitive estrangement.

apocalyptic fiction A type of science fiction narrative dealing with the approach and arrival of a cataclysmic event that causes widespread destruction, leading to a dramatic change in the nature of human civilization on Earth. As opposed to the

Biblical narrative of apocalypse, the science fiction apocalypse generally results from natural and scientifically explainable causes, such as environmental degradation, a cataclysmic cosmic event (such as the collision of the Earth with a large asteroid), a catastrophic plague, a devastating nuclear or biological war, or an alien invasion. Postapocalyptic science fiction deals with the aftermath of such apocalyptic events.

Arthur C. Clarke Award A British award (originally sponsored by a donation from the science fiction author for whom it is named) given annually (since 1987) for the best science fiction novel published in the United Kingdom during the previous year.

artificial intelligence An intelligent entity designed and created by humans, generally using computer technology. It has been speculated that a genuinely intelligent computer might be able to design and build an even more sophisticated thinking machine that could then create an even more intelligent machine, and so on, creating an explosive growth in technology, or singularity, as a result of which machines would soon become vastly more intelligent than humans. Much recent science fiction deals with the ramifications of this notion.

Astounding Science-Fiction An American pulp magazine that began publishing in 1930 as *Astounding Stories* and that became a particularly important driving force when John W. Campbell became its editor in 1937. The name was changed to *Astounding Science-Fiction* in 1938 to reflect the new focus on science fiction, and the magazine went on to provide a venue for the publication of the early short fiction of many of the leading writers of Golden Age science fiction. Campbell again renamed the magazine in 1960, as *Analog Science Fiction and Fact*, in an attempt to emphasize the seriousness of the ideas explored in the magazine. As of 2008, the magazine remains in publication under that title. It remains the best-selling English-language science fiction magazine in the world, even if it lacks the central influence on sf that it once had.

British Boom A recent phenomenon, roughly from the beginning of the 1990s onward, in which British writers of science fiction and fantasy have come to the forefront of those fields, producing an extraordinary number and variety of innovative works. Leading figures of the Boom include China Miéville, Iain M. Banks, Ian McDonald, Charles Stross, Ken MacLeod, Gwyneth Jones, Geoff Ryman, Brian Stableford, Justina Robson, Jon Courtenay Grimwood, Paul McAuley, Richard K. Morgan, and Liz Williams.

cautionary tale A form of imaginative fiction that portrays the potential negative consequences of certain actions or policies that are already either underway or proposed in the world of the author. Such tales thus serve to warn readers against support for or participation in these actions or policies and potentially to encourage them to engage in counteractivities.

clone In the most general sense, cloning refers to the isolation and exact replication of any particular DNA sequence. In science fiction, cloning usually involves the replication of entire organisms, so that the resultant clones are exact replicas of the original organism. Recent advances in genetics have made the cloning of higher animals a reality, and technology for the successful cloning of human beings is clearly on the horizon. Together with the field of genetic engineering, cloning offers numerous possibilities for revolutionary changes in our very conception of what it means to be a human being; cloning and genetic engineering also raise numerous ethical dilemmas and potential legal questions. Both the promise and the controversy associated with cloning and genetic engineering have provided fertile material for science fiction in recent years.

cognitive estrangement   The process through which certain works of literature, by imaginatively placing readers in an unaccustomed situation or environment, cause those readers to ponder the differences between this environment and their own, thus potentially causing them to view their own world differently. Darko Suvin, drawing his inspiration from the "estrangement effect" that is produced by the epic theater of Bertolt Brecht, has been particularly influential in his characterization of science fiction as a form of literature that centrally depends on cognitive estrangement to achieve its effects. For Suvin, the ability of science fiction to cause readers to thoughtfully reconsider their positions on various issues makes it a genre with particularly strong political potential.

colonization   Many science fiction narratives deal with the exploration and colonization of outer space by voyagers from Earth, who establish settlements on other planets or, in some cases, on artificial habitats in outer space. The classic narrative of space colonization is a story of adventure and discovery, though such narratives can gain significant complexity from complications such as encountering intelligent alien lifeforms, thus raising, in an estranged setting (see **cognitive estrangement**), many of the same issues that were relevant to the phenomenon of colonization on Earth. Indeed, some narratives of space colonization are specifically designed to satirize the logic of colonization on Earth, such as Robert Silverberg's *Invaders from Earth* (1958), *Downward to the Earth* (1970), and Ursula K. Le Guin's *The Word for World Is Forest* (1972).

cyberpunk   A type of science fiction, first made popular in the mid-to-late 1980s, that focuses on the effects of near-future developments in technology, especially the technologies of computers, telecommunications, and virtual reality, though technologies such as genetic engineering are important as well. Because these technologies often lead to enhancements in human beings (such as via artifical implants) or to the development of artificial intelligences that go beyond the human, cyberpunk is often seen as an important early form of posthuman science fiction. William Gibson's *Neuromancer* (1984) is widely considered to be the first cyberpunk novel.

cyborg   A cyborg (the term is a contraction for "cybernetic organism") is a hybrid entity created by the combination of human and artificial parts, either mechanical or electronic. Cyborgs frequently figure in science fiction, though in the broadest sense many present-day humans (such as anyone wearing eyeglasses or having fillings in their teeth) might be considered a cyborg. The notion of the cyborg has been particularly prominent in the work of the cultural critique Donna Haraway, who sees the cyborg as the sort of hybrid image that might free women from having their identities strictly defined by patriarchal society.

degeneration A broad discourse, popular in the Western world around the beginning of the twentieth century, that expressed fears that humans (and human societies) might evolve backwards into a more primitive state. The discourse of degeneration was, of course, closely connected with the historical phenomenon of colonialism, and particularly with the fear that contact with "primitive" and "savage" peoples such as those encountered in Africa might contaminate the European colonizers, activating their own latent primitive and savage tendencies. Probably the best known literary representation of this particular phenomenon is Joseph Conrad's Kurtz, the ultra-civilized European genius who travels to Africa in *Heart of Darkness* (1899) to help enlighten the natives, only to revert to savagery, perhaps because the primitive African milieu into which he travels has greater vitality and energy than the effete European context from which he came.

discontinuity A sudden and abrupt change in the course of history. Discontinuities caused by conceptual breakthroughs in science or sudden, revolutionary advances in technology are often a source of the novums that drive science fiction.

dystopia If a utopia is an imaginary ideal society that dreams of a world in which the social, political, and economic problems of the real present have been solved, then a dystopia is an imagined world in which the dream has become a nightmare. Also known as anti-utopias, dystopias are often designed to critique the potential negative implications of certain forms of utopian thought. However, dystopian fiction tends to have a strong satirical dimension that is designed to warn against the possible consequences of certain tendencies in the real world of the present. The three crucial founding texts of modern dystopian fictions are Yevgeny Zamyatin's *We* (1924), Aldous Huxley's *Brave New World* (1932), and George Orwell's *Nineteen Eighty-Four* (1949).

dystopian fiction see **dystopia**.

ecological science fiction Science fiction dealing with the projected consequences of changes to the natural environment. Most ecological science fiction depicts the negative consequences of environmental decay caused by pollution or other manmade changes to the environment; such works thus function as cautionary tales that attempt to warn readers of the dangers posed by ecological phenomena such as global warming. However, at least one major work, Ernest Callenbach's *Ecotopia* (1975), envisions a future utopia built on environmentally friendly principles.

extrapolation The imaginative projection of technological, political, or social developments outside the place and time in which the projection is made. In science fiction, extrapolation usually involves the imagination of events in the future. Importantly, extrapolation need not literally involve a prediction of future events, but might instead envision these events for purposes of producing an estranged perspective on certain phenomena in the world of the author.

extraterrestrial   An alien originating from outside the Earth.

fandom   Term used to describe the subcultural communities that grow up among fans of certain cultural phenomena. Fandom has been a particularly strong influence in the history of science fiction, from the communities of readers who supported the early pulp magazines in which science fiction stories appeared in the 1920s and 1930s, to the more recent phenomenon of fan-dominated conventions (such as Worldcon) to science fiction in general or to specific science fiction phenomena, such as the *Star Trek* television series. In recent years, the development of fan communities has been furthered by the growth of the internet, which allows large groups of fans to communicate easily and to interact on an ongoing basis, sharing ideas and concerns about their favorite works of science fiction.

fantasy   A genre of fiction closely aligned with science fiction in that it is also set in worlds different from our own. However, in fantasy there is typically no rational or scientific explanation for the differences. Furthermore, the laws of physics may be quite different in the worlds of fantasy fiction, enabling the routine presence of magic and various creatures (witches, wizards, dragons, demons, ghosts, goblins, vampires, and so on) that would be considered supernatural in our world. J. R. R. Tolkien's *Lord of the Rings* trilogy is widely considered to be the central work in this genre, though important writers of fantasy, such as China Miéville, have written in an explicitly anti-Tolkien vein.

fix-up   A term used to describe a book-length fictional work, generally a novel, made up of stories previously published separately. Fix-ups were especially common during the early 1950s during the paperback publishing explosion that made book-length works of science fiction popular in the US for the first time. However, fix-ups were also a factor in the growth of other forms of genre fiction, such as detective fiction.

future history   A type of science fiction narrative that deals with the detailed elaboration of projected events in the historical future. The term can also be used to describe the general projection of such events in science fiction narratives that are not specifically devoted to the imagination of a future history.

genetic engineering   A branch of technology dealing with the modification of human (and sometimes nonhuman) DNA, either to correct some perceived genetic disorder or deficiency or to produce new characteristics altogether. Now a rapidly-evolving real-world technology, genetic engineering is also a key motif in posthuman science fiction. See also **clone**.

genre   Term used to describe a category of literary texts sharing certain defining features, or conventions. The term is ill-defined and variable in meaning. Thus, the "novel" itself might be considered a genre in some circumstances, while certain types of novels, such as the science fiction novel or the historical novel, might also be described as genres. Meanwhile, certain types of writing, such as sf, might be considered a genre, even though they might encompass several different forms, such as novels, short stories, and films. In addition, any given work might belong simultaneously to two or more genres, as when the film *Blade Runner* (1982) combines the characteristics of science fiction, detective fiction, and film noir. Finally, the term "genre" has specific connotations in some discussions of modern culture, in which certain popular categories (such as sf, detective fiction, or Westerns) might be referred to as "genre fiction" or "genre films," with the implication that these works are determined in a particularly strong (and perhaps formulaic) way by the conventions of the genres in which they participate. In this volume, we refer to sf itself as a genre and to specific types of sf narratives (such as alien invasion narratives and time travel narratives) as "subgenres."

Golden Age The period from the late 1930s (beginning roughly in 1937, when John W. Campbell assumed the editorship of *Astounding Stories*) through the 1950s is commonly referred to as the Golden Age of science fiction. Golden Age sf was characterized by a faith in the inevitability of dramatic scientific and technological progress, often accompanied by an optimistic belief that this progress would lead to social, political, and economic progress as well. On the other hand, Golden Age sf tends to be a bit more nuanced in this respect than the early fiction of the era of pulp magazines, which was often more naively optimistic about the promise of technological and social progress. In histories of science fiction, the Golden Age is frequently considered to have ended with the emergence of the New Wave at the beginning of the 1960s, bringing greater sophistication to the genre but also depriving it of a certain innocent vitality. Key Golden Age writers include Isaac Asimov, Arthur C. Clarke, Robert A. Heinlein, Frederik Pohl, and A. E. Van Vogt.

hard science fiction A type of science fiction in which emphasis is placed on specific technologies and hardwares as the novums that make the world of the work different from the world of the reader. Such fiction usually stresses scientific accuracy and detailed descriptions of the technologies involved, though it often contains a "what if" element in which plausibility and internal consistency is more important than absolute scientific rigor. Hard sf is distinguished from soft science fiction, which places more emphasis on social and psychological aspects of technological change, but of course any given work of sf will typically include both hard and soft elements.

Hugo Award Prestigious award given annually (beginning in 1955, though awards conceived as a one-time event were also given in 1953) for achievement in several different categories of science fiction and fantasy. The annual award for best novel is particularly important. The Hugo Award winners are chosen by the members of the annual Worldcon, and the prestige associated with these awards is a key indicator of the ongoing importance of fandom in science fiction. The award is named for the important sf editor Hugo Gernsback.

Menippean satire A form of satire that dates back to the work of the second-century AD satirist Lucian, who was supposedly inspired by Menippus (for whom the subgenre is named) and whose work included science fiction motifs such as voyages to the moon and Venus. Menippean satire is often bawdy and carnivalesque, as in the work of the French satirist François Rabelais. Because it tends to involve elements that go beyond the reality of the everyday world, Menippean satire lends itself well to works of science fiction, such as Bernard Wolfe's *Limbo* (1952).

nanotechnology A new (and rapidly-evolving) branch of technology (also know as "nanotech") dealing with the manipulation of matter at the level of atoms and molecules in order to produce devices of that size for the performance of specific tasks. Because such devices can be designed to be self-replicating, the range of application of nanotechnology is quite broad and extends to very large scales. Originally envisioned as a fruitful field of inquiry by physicist Richard Feynman in 1959, nanotechnology was popularized by K. Eric Drexler in such works as *Engines of Creation: The Coming Era of Nanotechnology*, published in 1986. Since that time, major advances have been made in real-world nanotechnology, while projected applications of nanotechnology have become a major source of science fiction technologies as well. Neal *Stephenson's The Diamond Age* (1995) and Linda Nagata's *The Bohr Maker* (1995) are important early examples of nanotech in science fiction.

Nebula Award An award given annually (since 1965) by the Science Fiction and Fantasy Writers of America for the best achievement in several categories of science fiction and fantasy writing in the previous year.

New Wave Term used to describe the work of a loosely aligned group of science fiction writers in the 1960s and 1970s who sought to instill science fiction with greater social and political relevance, more mature subject matter, and higher literary quality than what they perceived to be the case in Golden Age science fiction. Leading New Wave writers included Brian Aldiss, J. G. Ballard, M. John Harrison, John Brunner, Samuel Delany, Thomas Disch, Harlan Ellison, Ursula K. Le Guin, Michael Moorcock, Robert Silverberg, and Norman Spinrad. Moorcock was also particularly important as an editor, and his (British) *New Worlds* magazine was probably the leading venue for the publication of New Wave short stories.

novum Literally, a "new thing." The term was made popular in critical discussions of science fiction by Darko Suvin, who uses it to indicate the kind of specific changes that make the worlds of science fiction different from our own, thus producing cognitive estrangement in readers. The background of the term resides in the work of the Marxist utopian philosopher Ernst Bloch, who used the term to indicate the kind of changes that might be involved in the imagination of future worlds that might be better than our own.

parallel universe Also known as a **parallel world** (or as an **alternative universe, world,** or **reality**), a parallel universe is another reality that co-exists with our own.

The existence of parallel universes has some support in modern physics, as in the so-called many-worlds interpretation of quantum mechanics. Fantasy fiction has often been set in universes that clearly differ from our own, as in the case of J. R. R. Tolkien's Middle Earth. In science fiction, however, parallel universes are typically quite similar to our own, but differ in certain key (specific and identifiable) respects, creating a space for the production of cognitive estrangement as readers seek to discover and interpret these differences. Parallel universe narratives are closely related to alternate history narratives, except that, in parallel universes, the differences from our own universe can come from sources other than specific historical divergences. For example, the actual laws of physics might be subtly (or not so subtly) altered from one parallel universe to another. Moreover, in parallel universe narratives, it is often possible for characters to travel among different parallel universes.

planetary romance   A type of science fiction that involves the detailed imagination and elaboration of the culture and natural environment of a planet other than the Earth. The differences between such planets and the Earth create a potentially rich source of cognitive estrangement, asking readers to view familiar characteristics of life on Earth through the defamiliarizing lens of life on planets with different histories, climates, and social and political practices. Brian Aldiss's "Helliconia" trilogy (1982–1985) is an excellent example of this subgenre.

post-apocalyptic fiction   A type of science fiction narrative dealing with the aftermath of such catastrophic event that destroys or radically alters human civilization, necessitating an attempt to rebuild civilization (perhaps along different lines) on the part of the survivors. The actual events leading to the collapse of existing society are dealt with in **apocalyptic fiction**.

postcyberpunk science fiction   Sometimes referred to as "second-generation" cyberpunk, a type of science fiction that grows out of the original cyberpunk movement and typically employs many of the same near-future science fictional technologies. Often thought of as beginning with Neal Stephenson's *Snow Crash* (1992), post-cyberpunk fiction is often more humorous in tone than cyberpunk; moreover, especially in the hands of British Boom writers such as Ken MacLeod and Charles Stross, it often has a stronger social and political dimension in its exploration of near-future technological developments.

posthuman science fiction   A type of science fiction dealing centrally with developments that either produce fundamental changes in the human species or produce new species that outstrip or replace the human. Sometimes the changes envisioned in posthuman science fiction are brought about by natural evolution, but more typically they are brought about by specific technological advances. As influentially dramatized in his "Shaper and Mechanist" stories – and in the novel *Schismatrix* (1985) – by Bruce Sterling, modifications to the human species are typically of two types: biological changes brought about by genetic engineering (and perhaps supplemented by specific forms of psychological or other training), or changes brought about by implants or other mechanical or electronic enhancements to the human body. The most typical form of "replacement" species involves the growth of advance artificial intelligences that are far more intelligent than human beings.

postmodernism Term used to describe a particular family of late-twentieth-century and early-twenty-first-century artworks and, by extension, a prevailing mode of thought that finds its expression in those artworks but is also influential in a wide range of fields, including philosophy, sociology, even science and religion. The term "postmodernism" suggests both the historical fact that postmodernism comes after modernism and the sometimes complex relationship between modernist and post-modernist art and thought. In general, postmodernist art tends to be complex and experimental in the mode of modernist art, but more playful, irreverent, and ulti-mately skeptical of the power of art to change society. Postmodernist artworks tend to freely mix different styles and genres and to incorporate a diverse array of materials from a range of sources, including earlier works of both "high" and "low" culture. Some critics have seen postmodernism as anti-authoritarian and potentially subversive of the status quo. Others (most notably the Marxist theorist and critic Fredric Jameson) have noted that the seemingly subversive qualities of postmodernism are in fact already properties of contemporary capitalism and that virtually all of the characteristics of postmodernism can be taken as expressions of the "cultural logic of late capitalism." Jameson, incidentally, suggests that cyberpunk sf may be the quintessential example of postmodernist art, while the topic of postmodernism has frequently come up in relation to the works of numerous sf writers, such as Samuel R. Delany and Philip K. Dick. Meanwhile, science fiction films such as *Blade Runner* (1982) and *The Matrix* (1999) often figure prominently in discussions of postmodern cinema.

pulp magazine An inexpensive type of magazine (named for the kind of cheap, coarse paper on which it was printed) that provided crucial venues for the circulation of certain forms of genre fiction (including science fiction, detective/crime fiction, and adventure/romance fiction) from the 1920s until the 1940s, especially in the US. Pulp magazines declined rapidly in popularity and importance after World War II, as the growth of paperback book publishing made that format dominant in the areas that had once been the purview of pulp magazines.

robot An artificially created mechanical/electronic entity, often humanoid in form, that is able to undertake certain specific tasks as an independent agent, though only within the boundaries of its programming. Robots are often of human (or even superhuman) intelligence and have long been one of the staple technologies of science fiction. The term "robot" was in fact first introduced in a work of science fiction, the 1921 play R.U.R. (Rossum's Universal Robots), by the Czech writer Karel Čapek, though Čapek's robots were actually biological, more like clones than the modern conception of robots. Isaac Asimov's early robot stories, many collected in *I, Robot* (1950), are still the classic sf exploration of the theme of robots.

satire   An artistic form designed to demonstrate the follies of foibles of human beings in general or of specific human practices and institutions. In general, literary satire employs techniques of exaggeration and extrapolation that magnify the flaws of the target being satirized, thus making them more visible. In so doing, satire can often create cognitive estrangement of the kind that is crucial to science fiction. Indeed, many works of sf are openly satirical, as with Frederik Pohl and Cyril Kormbluth's *The Space Merchants* (1952).

simulacrum   see **simulation**.

simulation   In the broadest sense, an artificial imitation of some real person, thing, or event. In recent years the most common forms of simulation have been produced by computer modeling, a practice that lends itself well to use in science fiction, as when Joe Haldeman's *Old Twentieth* (2005) uses virtual reality technology to allow "travel" into computer simulations of the historical past. The term "simulation" is also closely associated with the work of cultural theorist Jean Baudrillard, who felt that, in the postmodern world, reality had been replaced by images, or simulations (simulacra). In the era of what Baudrillard calls "hyperreality," the image is disengaged from reality and what we experience are pure simulacra that represent no pre-existing reality. See also **virtual reality**.

singularity   Derived from the mathematical term for the point at which the slope (rate of change) of a function becomes infinite, a singularity is a moment of sudden, runaway technological change. The singularity has become a popular motif in recent science fiction, especially in the work of British writers such as Ken MacLeod and Charles Stross, where it is generally associated with developments in artificial intelligence. However, the notion of the singularity was originally popularized by the work of Vernor Vinge, an American science fiction writer and mathematician who called attention to the likelihood of an eventual technological singularity (and its potential consequences for humankind) in a 1993 essay, "The Coming Technological Singularity," and in his own fiction of the 1990s.

soft science fiction   A type of science fiction in which emphasis is placed on the social and psychological consequences of technological change (or on innovation in "soft" sciences, such as the social sciences, rather than "hard" sciences, such as physics and chemistry.) Soft sf is distinguished from hard science fiction, which places more emphasis on specific technologies and hardwares, described in accurate scientific detail, but of course any given work of sf will typically include both hard and soft elements. Some, incidentally, have seen these terms as problematic; Ursula K. Le Guin, often characterized as a writer of "soft" sf, has complained that the "soft" designation has pejorative implications.

space habitat   A manmade structure intended to serve as a permanent settlement (usually for humans) in outer space. These artificial worlds may in some cases (as in the worlds of Iain M. Banks's "Culture" novels) be quite vast, far larger than planets. Or they may be relatively small, housing only small numbers of inhabitants. They may remain anchored at a single point in space, or they may move about to different locations as the need demands.

space opera   A type of science fiction narrative involving stories of adventure, exploration, and conflict in outer space. Such stories were an especially prominent form of science fiction in the Golden Age of science fiction, but have remained important to the present day as well.

space station   A manmade structure, typically in orbit around the Earth (but sometimes elsewhere in outer space) that can be used to support human activities in space. These activities may involve various forms of scientific research, or the space station may simply serve as a stopping point (for refueling, resupplying, and so on) for space travelers. Numerous Earth-orbiting space stations have been constructed, while space stations also frequently feature in science fiction narratives (most notably in the 1990s television series *Babylon 5* and *Star Trek: Deep Space Nine*). They should be distinguished from space habitats because they are intended to provide specific utilitarian functions but not to serve as sites of permanent habitation.

speculative fiction   Blanket term for imaginative fiction that involves the construction of worlds different from our own in fundamental ways. This category thus encompasses science fiction, fantasy, horror, and some forms of romance. The abbreviation "sf" (or "SF") is sometimes used to designate speculative fiction as a whole. However, in this volume, "sf" is used to designate science fiction only.

steampunk   A form of science fiction that usually has thematic and stylistic similarities to **cyberpunk**, but is set in a world where the level of technology is roughly equivalent to the steam-powered technology of the nineteenth century. Indeed, it is often set in a version of the nineteenth century, connecting it to the **alternate history** narrative.**terraforming** The process of using advanced technologies to modify the natural environment of another planet to make it more like that of Earth and thus more hospitable to human habitation and colonization.

time travel   The process of traveling through historical time, thus transporting the traveler either into the past or the future relative to his starting point. Time travel is an important motif in many science fiction narratives, and time-travel narratives have been an important subgenre of sf since H. G. Wells's *The Time Machine* (1895).

utopia   An imagined society in which the social, economic, and political problems of our own world have been essentially solved, producing an optimum life for all of the citizens of the society. The term "utopia" is also sometimes used to describe a work of utopian fiction, that is, a fictional work whose principal goal is the description of such an ideal society. While utopias often literally dramatize the author's idea of what would constitute an ideal society, they often also serve a satirical function that is designed more to highlight and critique aspects of the author's world than to propose a literal alternative.

utopian fiction   see **utopia**.

virtual reality   A computer-generated simulation of reality, typically allowing the interactive participation of users. Current virtual reality technology is relatively crude and allows the user to experience the simulated environment with only sight and sound. However, technologies to allow much more extensive interaction and sensory participation are currently in development. Virtual realities have become popular in science fiction and are a key motif in cyberpunk fiction. The "Holodecks" of the television series *Star Trek: The Next Generation* (1987–1994) are one of the best known examples of virtual realities in sf. See also **simulation**.

Worldcon   The Worldcon (the term is a contraction of the more formal "World Science Fiction Convention") is the oldest and perhaps most important of the many fan-oriented conventions that are a key phenomenon within the world of science fiction fandom. Administered by the World Science Fiction Society, Worldcon was first held from 1939 to 1941, then interrupted by World War II. It has been held ever year from 1946 to the present. It is held at various sites, the majority of which have been in North America, though a number of Worldcons have been held in Europe, and the 2007 convention was held in Japan. Members of each annual Worldcon vote to determine the winners of the Hugo Awards in various categories. Other activities include speeches, panel discussions, game-playing, costume competitions, film screenings, live performances, and a lively trade in science fiction souvenirs.

Selected Bibliography

Adas, Michael. *Machines as the Measure of Man: Science, Technology, and Ideologies of Western Dominance*. Ithaca, NY: Cornell University Press, 1989.

Arata, Stephen. "The Occidental Tourist: Dracula and the Anxiety of Reverse Colonization." *Victorian Studies* 33 (1990): 621–645.

Asimov, Isaac. *The Caves of Steel*. New York: Bantam, 1991.

Asimov, Isaac. *I, Robot*. 1950. New York: Bantam, 2008.

Asimov, Isaac. *The Naked Sun*. 1957. New York: Bantam, 1991.

Attebery, Brian. *Decoding Gender in Science Fiction*. New York: Routledge, 2002.

Atwood, Margaret. *The Handmaid's Tale*. 1985. New York: Anchor, 1998.

Bakhtin, M. M. *The Dialogic Imagination*. Ed. Michael Holquist. Trans. Caryl Emerson and Michael Holquist. Austin: University of Texas Press, 1981.

Barr, Marleen. *Lost in Space: Probing Feminist Science Fiction and Beyond*. Chapel Hill: University of North Carolina Press, 1993.

Bartkowski, Frances. *Feminist Utopias*. Lincoln: University of Nebraska Press, 1989.

Barzman, Ben. *Twinkle, Twinkle Little Star*. New York: G. P. Putnam's Sons, 1960.

Baudrillard, Jean. *Simulacra and Simulation*. Trans. Sheila Faria Glaser. Ann Arbor: University of Michigan Press, 1994.

Beauchamp, Gorman. "The Frankenstein Complex and Asimov's Robots." *Mosaic* 13.3–4 (1980): 83–94.

Bhabha, Homi. *The Location of Culture*. New York: Routledge, 1994.

Booker, M. Keith. *Alternate Americas: Science Fiction Film and American Culture*. Westport, CT: Praeger, 2006.

Booker, M. Keith. *Monsters, Mushroom Clouds, and the Cold War: American Science Fiction and the Roots of Postmodernism, 1946–1964*. Westport, CT: Greenwood, 2001.

Booker, M. Keith. *Science Fiction Television*. Westport, CT: Praeger, 2004.

Brown, James Cooke. *The Troika Incident*. Garden City, NY: Doubleday, 1970.

Brunner, John. *The Sheep Look Up*. 1972. Dallas, TX: BenBella Books, 2003.

Bucknall, Barbara J. *Ursula K. Le Guin*. New York: Ungar, 1981.

Bukatman, Scott. *Terminal Identity: The Virtual Subject in Postmodern Science Fiction*. Durham, NC: Duke University Press, 1993.

Butler, Andrew M. *The Pocket Essential Cyberpunk*. Harpendon: Pocket Essentials, 2000.

Butler, Andrew M. "Thirteen Ways of Looking at the British Boom." *Science Fiction Studies* 30 (2003): 374–393.

Butler, Octavia. *Adulthood Rites*. 1988. *Lilith's Brood*. New York: Warner Books, 1989. 249–517.

Butler, Octavia. *Dawn*. 1987. *Lilith's Brood*. New York: Warner Books, 1989. 1–248.

Butler, Octavia. *Imago*. 1989. *Lilith's Brood*. New York: Warner Books, 1989. 519–746.

Callenbach, Ernest. *Ecotopia: The Notebooks and Reports of William Weston*. Berkeley, CA: Banyon Tree Books, 1975.

Cantor, Paul A., and Peter Hufnagel. "The Empire of the Future: Imperialism and Modernism in H. G. Wells." *Studies in the Novel* 38.1 (Spring 2006): 36–56.

Card, Orson Scott. *Ender's Game*. 1985. New York: Tor, 1994.

Carson, Rachel. *Silent Spring*. Boston: Houghton-Mifflin, 1962.

Cavallaro, Dani. *Cyberpunk and Cyberculture: Science Fiction and the Work of William Gibson*. New Brunswick, NJ: Athlone, 2000.

Charnas, Suzee McKee. *Motherlines*. New York: Berkley, 1978.

Clemente, Bill. "Tan-Tan's Exile and Odyssey in Nalo Hopkinson's *Midnight Robber*." *Foundation: The International Review of Science Fiction* 33.91 (2004): 10–24.

Conrad, Joseph. *Heart of Darkness*. 1899. Norton Critical Edition. New York: Norton, 1988.

Costa, Richard Hauer. *H. G. Wells*. Boston: Twayne, 1985.

Crick, Bernard. *George Orwell: A Life*. London: Secker and Warburg, 1980.

Csiscery-Ronay, Istvan Jr. "Cyberpunk and Neuromaticism." *Mississippi Review* 47/48 (1988): 266–278.

Cummins, Elizabeth. *Understanding Ursula K. Le Guin*. Columbia: University of South Carolina Press, 1990.

Delany, Samuel R. "Critical Methods, Speculative Fiction." *Quark 1*. Eds. Samuel R. Delany and Marilyn Hacker. New York: Paperback Library, 1970.

Delany, Samuel R. "Some *Real* Mothers: An Interview with Samuel R. Delany by Takayuki Tatsumi." *Science Fiction Eye* 1.3 (1988): 5–11.

Delany, Samuel R. *Trouble on Triton*. 1976. Middletown, CT: Wesleyan University Press, 1996.

Depaolo, Charles. "*The Time Machine* and the Descent of Man." *Foundation* 85 (Summer 2002): 66–79.

Dick, Philip K. *Do Androids Dream of Electric Sheep?* New York: Ballantine Books, 1968.

Dolman, Everett Carl. "Military, Democracy, and the State in Robert A. Heinlein's *Starship Troopers*." *Political Science Fiction*. Eds. Donald M. Hassler and Clyde Wilcox. Columbia: University of South Carolina Press, 1997. 196–213.

Eagleton, Terry. *The Illusions of Postmodernism*. Oxford: Blackwell, 1996.

Ebert, Teresa L. "The Convergence of Postmodern Innovative Fiction and Science Fiction: An Encounter with Samuel R. Delany's Technotopia." *Poetics Today* 1.4 (1980): 91–104.

Enteen, Jillana, "'On the Receiving End of Colonization': Nalo Hopkinson's 'Nansi Web.'" *Science Fiction Studies* 34.2 (2007): 262–282.

Firchow, Peter. "H. G. Wells's *Time Machine*: In Search of Time Future – and Time Past." *Midwest Quarterly* 45.2 (Winter 2004): 123–136.

Firestone, Shulamith. *The Dialectic of Sex: The Case for Feminist Revolution.* New York: Morrow, 1970.

Fitting, Peter. "The Turn from Utopia in Recent Feminist Fiction." *Feminism, Utopia, and Narrative.* Eds. Libby Falk Jones and Sarah Webster Goodwin. Knoxville: University of Tennessee Press, 1990. 141–158.

Foucault, Michel. *The History of Sexuality, Volume I: An Introduction.* Trans. Robert Hurley. New York: Vintage, 1980.

Foucault, Michel. *The Order of Things.* Trans. anon. New York: Pantheon Books, 1970.

Franklin, H. Bruce. *Robert A. Heinlein: America as Science Fiction.* New York: Oxford University Press, 1980.

Franko, Carol. "The Density of Utopian Destiny in Robinson's *Red Mars*." *Extrapolation* 38.1 (Spring 1997): 57–65.

Franko, Carol. "Working the 'In-Between': Kim Stanley Robinson's Utopian Fiction." *Science Fiction Studies* 21.2 (1994): 191–211.

Freedman, Carl. *Critical Theory and Science Fiction.* Hanover, NH: Wesleyan University Press, 2000.

Freedman, Carl. "To the Perdido Street Station: The Representation of Revolution in China Miéville's *Iron Council*." *Extrapolation* 46.2 (2005): 235–248.

Galvan, Jill. "Entering the Posthuman Collective in Philip K. Dick's *Do Androids Dream of Electric Sheep?*" *Science Fiction Studies* 24.3 (1997): 413–429.

Gearhart, Sally Miller. *The Wanderground: Stories of the Hill Women.* Watertown, MA: Persephone Press, 1978.

Gibson, William. *Count Zero.* New York: Ace, 1986.

Gibson, William. *Mona Lisa Overdrive.* New York: Bantam Books, 1988.

Gibson, William. *Neuromancer.* New York: Ace, 1984.

Gilman, Charlotte Perkins. *Herland.* New York: Pantheon, 1979.

Glorie, Josephine Carubia. "Feminist Utopian Fiction and the Possibility of Social Critique." *Political Science Fiction.* Eds. Donald M. Hassler and Clyde Wilcox. Columbia: University of South Carolina Press, 1997: 148–159.

Golumbia, David. "Black and White World: Race, Ideology, and Utopia in *Triton* and *Star Trek*." *Cultural Critique* (1995–1996): 75–95.

Gordon, Joan. "Hybridity, Heterotopia, and Mateship in China Miéville's *Perdido Street Station*." *Science Fiction Studies* 30 (2003): 456–476.

Gunn, James. *Isaac Asimov: The Foundations of Science Fiction.* Revised edition. Lanham, MD: Scarecrow Press, 1996.

Gunn, James, ed. *Speculations on Speculation: Theories of Science Fiction.* Lanham, MD: Scarecrow Press, 2005.

Haldeman, Joe, ed. *Body Armor 2000.* New York: Ace, 1986.

Haldeman, Joe. *Forever Free.* New York: Ace, 1999.

Haldeman, Joe. *Forever Peace.* New York: Ace, 1997.

Haldeman, Joe. *The Forever War.* 1974. New York: Eos, 2003.

Hantke, Steffen. "Surgical Strikes and Prosthetic Warriors: The Soldier's Body in Contemporary Science Fiction." *Science-Fiction Studies* 25 (1998): 495–509.

Haraway, Donna. *Simians, Cyborgs, and Women: The Reinvention of Nature.* New York: Routledge, 1991.

Harrison, Harry. *Bill the Galactic Hero.* Garden City, NY: Doubleday, 1965.

Harrison, Harry. *Make Room! Make Room!* Garden City, NY: Doubleday, 1966.

Hassler, Donald M. "Swift, Pohl, and Kormbluth: Publicists Anatomize Newness." *Political Science Fiction.* Eds. Donald M. Hassler and Clyde Wilcox. Columbia: University of South Carolina Press, 1997. 18–25.

Hayles. N. Katherine. *How We Became Posthuman: Virtual Bodies in Cybernetics, Literature, and Informatics.* Chicago: University of Chicago Press, 1999.

Hegel, G. W. F. *The Philosophy of History.* Trans. J. Sibree. New York: Dover, 1956.

Heinlein, Robert A. *The Puppet Masters.* 1951. New York: Del Rey-Ballantine, 1990.

Heinlein, Robert A. *Starship Troopers.* 1959. New York: Ace-Berkley, 1987.

Hillegas, Mark. *The Future as Nightmare: H. G. Wells and the Anti-Utopians.* New York: Oxford University Press, 1967.

Holden, Rebecca J. "The High Costs of Cyborg Survival: Octavia Butler's 'Xenogenesis' Trilogy." *Foundation* 72 (Spring 1998): 49–57.

Hopkins, Budd. *Intruders: The Incredible Visitations at Copley Woods.* New York: Ballantine, 1988.

Hopkinson, Nalo. *Midnight Robber.* New York: Warner Books, 2000.

Horkheimer, Max, and Theodor W. Adorno. *Dialectic of Enlightenment.* Trans. John Cumming. New York: Seabury Press, 1972.

Hynes, James. "Robot's Rules of Disorder: Cyberpunk Rocks the Boat." *In These Times,* November 26–December 6 (1988): 18–19.

James, Edward. *Science Fiction in the 20th Century.* New York: Oxford University Press, 1994.

Jameson, Fredric. *Archaeologies of the Future: The Desire Called Utopia and Other Science Fictions.* London: Verso, 2005.

Jameson, Fredric. "'If I Find One Good City I Will Spare the Man': Realism and Utopia in Kim Stanley Robinson's 'Mars' Trilogy." *Learning from Other Worlds: Estrangement, Cognition, and the Politics of Science Fiction and Utopia.* Ed. Patrick Parrinder. Durham, NC: Duke University Press, 2001. 208–232.

Jameson, Fredric. *Postmodernism, or, The Cultural Logic of Late Capitalism.* Durham, NC: Duke University Press, 1991.

Jameson, Fredric. *The Seeds of Time.* New York: Columbia University Press, 1994.

Jameson, Fredric. *Signatures of the Visible.* New York: Routledge, 1992.

Jones, Gwyneth. "Rev. of *Ammonite*, by Nicola Griffith." *The New York Review of Science Fiction*. February (2003): 20–21.

Ketterer, David. "Margaret Atwood's *The Handmaid's Tale*: A Contextual Dystopia." *Science-Fiction Studies* 16 (1989): 209–217.

Khouri, Nadia. "The Dialectics of Power: Utopia in the Science Fiction of Le Guin, Jeury, and Piercy." *Science-Fiction Studies* 7 (1980): 49–61.

Kjinski, John L. "Ethnography in the East End: Native Customs and Colonial Solutions in *A Child of the Jago*." *English Literature in Transition, 1880–1920* 37.4 (1994): 490–501.

Leane, Elizabeth. "Chromodynamics: Science and Colonialism in Kim Stanley Robinson's 'Mars' trilogy." *Ariel* 33.1 (2002): 83–104.

Le Guin, Ursula K. *The Dispossessed: An Ambiguous Utopia*. 1974. New York: HarperCollins, 1991.

Le Guin, Ursula K. *The Left Hand of Darkness*. New York: Harper & Row, 1969.

Le Guin, Ursula K. *The Word for World Is Forest*. 1972. New York: Berkley, 1976.

Lem, Stanisław. "Robots in Science Fiction." *SF: The Other Side of Realism*. Ed. Thomas D. Clareson. Bowling Green: OH: Bowling Green University Press, 1971. 307–325.

Luckhurst, Roger. "Cultural Governance, New Labor, and the British SF Boom." *Science Fiction Studies* 30.3 (November 2003): 417–435.

Luckhurst, Roger. *Science Fiction*. London: Polity, 2005.

Lukács, Georg. *The Historical Novel*. 1937. Trans. Hannah Mitchell and Stanley Mitchell. Lincoln: University of Nebraska Press, 1983.

McConnell, Frank. *The Science Fiction of H. G. Wells*. New York: Oxford University Press, 1981.

McDonald, Ian. *River of Gods*. Amherst, NY: Pyr, 2006.

Meyers, Walter E. *Aliens and Linguists: Language Study and Science Fiction*. Athens: University of Georgia Press, 1980.

Michaels, Walter Benn. "Political Science Fictions." *New Literary History* 31.4 (2000): 649–664.

Miéville, China. *Iron Council*. New York: Tor, 2004.

Miéville, China. *Perdido Street Station*. New York: Del Rey-Ballantine, 2000.

Miéville, China. *The Scar*. New York: Del Rey-Ballantine, 2002.

Miner, Madonne. "'Trust Me': Reading the Romance Plot in Margaret Atwood's *The Handmaid's Tale*." *Twentieth-Century Literature* 37 (1991): 148–168.

Morgan, Richard K. *Market Forces*. New York: Ballantine, 2005.

Morris, William. *News from Nowhere, or an Epoch of Rest*. 1890. London: Routledge and Kegan Paul, 1970.

Morrison, Arthur. *A Child of the Jago*. 1896. Chicago: Academy Publishers, 1995.

Moylan, Tom. *Demand the Impossible: Science Fiction and the Utopian Imagination*. New York: Methuen, 1986.

Nixon, Nicola. "Cyberpunk: Preparing the Ground for Revolution or Keeping the Boys Satisfied?" *Science Fiction Studies* 19.2 (1992): 219–235.

Olsen, Lance. *William Gibson*. San Bernardino, CA: Borgo Press, 1992.

Orwell, George. *Nineteen Eighty-Four.* 1949. New York: Signet, 1961.

Palumbo, Donald. *Chaos Theory, Asimov's Foundations and Robots, and Herbert's Dune.* Westport, CT: Greenwood Press, 2002.

Patrouch, Joseph F. *The Science Fiction of Isaac Asimov.* Garden City, NY: Doubleday, 1974.

Piercy, Marge. *Woman on the Edge of Time.* 1976. New York: Ballantine, 1991.

Pohl, Frederik. *The Merchants' War.* New York: St. Martin's, 1984.

Pohl, Frederik. "The Politics of Prophecy." *Political Science Fiction.* Eds. Donald M. Hassler and Clyde Wilcox. Columbia: University of South Carolina Press, 1997. 7–17.

Pohl, Frederik, and C. M. Kormbluth. *The Space Merchants.* 1952. New York: St. Martin's, 1987.

Porush, David. "Hacking the Brainstem: Postmodern Metaphysics and Stephenson's *Snow Crash*." *Configurations* 2.3 (1994): 537–571.

Proietti, Salvatore. "The Informatic Jeremiad: The Virtual Frontier and US Cyberculture." *Science Fiction, Critical Frontiers.* Eds. Karen Sayer and John Moore. New York: St. Martin's Press, 2000: 116–126.

Roberts, Adam. *The History of Science Fiction.* New York: Palgrave Macmillan, 2005.

Robinson, Kim Stanley. *Blue Mars.* New York: Bantam, 1996.

Robinson, Kim Stanley. *The Gold Coast.* 1988. New York: Orb-Tor, 1995.

Robinson, Kim Stanley. *Green Mars.* New York: Bantam, 1994.

Robinson, Kim Stanley. *The Novels of Philip K. Dick.* Ann Arbor: UMI Research Press, 1984.

Robinson, Kim Stanley. *Pacific Edge.* 1990. New York: Orb-Tor, 1995.

Robinson, Kim Stanley. *Red Mars.* New York: Bantam, 1993.

Robinson, Kim Stanley. *The Wild Shore.* 1984. New York: Orb-Tor, 1995.

Ruppert, Peter. *Reader in a Strange Land: The Activity of Reading Literary Utopias.* Athens: University of Georgia Press, 1986.

Russ, Joanna. *The Female Man.* Boston: Beacon Press, 1975.

Sallis, James. *Ash of Stars: On the Writing of Samuel R. Delany.* Jackson: University Press of Mississippi, 1996.

Schell, Heather. "Outburst! A Chilling True Story about Emerging-Virus Narratives and Pandemic Social Change." *Configurations: A Journal of Literature, Science, and Technology* 5.1 (1997): 93–133.

Seed, David. *American Science Fiction and the Cold War: Literature and Film.* Edinburgh: Edinburgh University Press, 1999.

Shaffer, Brian W. "'Rebarbarizing Civilization': Conrad's African Fiction and Spencerian Sociology." *PMLA* 108.1 (1993): 45–58.

Shaviro, Steve. "Capitalist Monsters." *Historical Materialism* 10.4 (2002): 281–290.

Shelley, Mary. *Frankenstein.* 1818. New York: Penguin, 2003.

Slonczewski, Joan. *A Door into Ocean.* 1986. New York: Orb-Tor, 2000.

Smith, Don G. *H. G. Wells on Film: The Utopian Nightmare.* Jefferson, NC: McFarland, 2002.

Spark, Alasdair. "The Art of Future War: *Starship Troopers, The Forever War,* and Vietnam." *Essays and Studies* 43 (1990): 133–165.

Spinrad, Norman. *Bug Jack Barron.* 1969. New York: Overlook, 2004.

Spivak, Charlotte. *Ursula K. Le Guin.* Boston: Twayne, 1984.

Stephenson, Neal. *Snow Crash.* New York: Bantam Books, 1992.

Stevenson, Robert Louis. *Dr. Jekyll and Mr. Hyde.* 1886. New York: Signet, 2003.

Stoker, Bram. *Dracula.* 1897. New York: Penguin, 2003.

Sutin, Lawrence. *Divine Invasions: A Life of Philip K. Dick.* New York: Harmony Books, 1989.

Suvin, Darko. *Metamorphoses of Science Fiction: On the Poetics and History of a Literary Genre.* New Haven, CT: Yale University Press, 1979.

Suvin, Darko, and Robert M. Philmus, eds. *H. G. Wells and Modern Science Fiction.* Lewisburg, PA: Bucknell University Press, 1977.

Swift, Jonathan. *Gulliver's Travels.* 1726. New York: Penguin, 2003.

Taylor, D. J. *Orwell.* London: Chatto and Windus, 2003.

Telotte, J. P. "Heinlein, Verhoeven, and the Problem of the Real: *Starship Troopers.*" *Literature Film Quarterly* 29.3 (2001): 196–202.

Thomas, Anne-Marie. "To Devour and Transform: Viral Metaphors in Science Fiction by Women." *Extrapolation* 41.2 (2000): 143–160.

Thomsen, Christian W. "Robot Ethics and Robot Parody: Remarks on Isaac Asimov's *I. Robot* and Some Critical Essays and Short Stories by Stanisław Lem." *The Mechanical God: Machines in Science Fiction.* Eds. Thomas P. Dunn and Richard D. Erlich. Westport, CT: Greenwood Press, 1982. 27–39.

Tomc, Sandra. "'The Missionary Position': Feminism and Nationalism in Margaret Atwood's *The Handmaid's Tale.*" *Canadian Literature* 138–139 (Fall–Winter 1993): 73–87.

Tucker, Jeffrey A. *A Sense of Wonder: Samuel R. Delany, Race, Identity, and Difference.* Middletown, CT: Wesleyan University Press, 2004.

Tucker, Robert C., ed. *The Marx–Engels Reader.* 2nd edition. New York: Norton, 1978.

Turing, Alan. "Computing Machinery and Intelligence." *Mind* 59.236 (October 1950): 433–460.

Vonnegut, Kurt, Jr. *Player Piano.* New York: Delacorte, 1952.

Wakeman, Fredric. *The Hucksters.* New York: Rinehart & Co., 1946.

Wald, Alan. *Writing from the Left: New Essays on Radical Culture and Politics.* London: Verso, 1994.

Warrick, Patricia. "Images of the Machine-Man Intelligence Relationship in Science Fiction." *Many Futures, Many Worlds: Theme and Form in Science Fiction.* Ed. Thomas D. Clareson. Kent, OH: Kent State University Press, 1977.

Warrick, Patricia. *Mind in Motion: The Fiction of Philip K. Dick.* Carbondale: Southern Illinois University Press, 1987.

Wegner, Phillip E. "Soldierboys for Peace: Cognitive Mapping, Space, and Science Fiction as World Bank Literature." *World Bank Literature.* Ed. Amitava Kumar. Minneapolis: University of Minnesota Press, 2003. 280–296.

Wells, H. G. *The History of Mr. Polly*. 1910. New York: Penguin, 2005.

Wells, H. G. *The Time Machine*. 1895. London: Penguin, 2005.

Wells, H. G. *The War of the Worlds*. 1898. New York: Tor, 1988.

White, Eric. "The Erotics of Becoming: Xenogenesis and *The Thing*." *Science-Fiction Studies* 20 (1993): 394–408.

Wiener, Norbert. *Cybernetics; or, Control and Communication in the Animal and the Machine*. Cambridge, MA: MIT Press. 1948.

Williams, Paul. *Only Apparently Real: The World of Philip K. Dick*. New York: Arbor House, 1986.

Williams, Raymond. *Orwell*. London: Fontana, 1971.

Wilson, Sloan. *The Man in the Gray Flannel Suit*. New York: Simon and Schuster, 1955.

Wolmark, Jenny. *Aliens and Others*. Iowa City: University of Iowa Press, 1994.

Womack, Jack. *Ambient*. New York: Weidenfeld and Nicolson, 1987.

Index